THE SOCIAL AND ECONOMIC FOUNDATIONS OF ASSOCIATION AMONG THE SILK WEAVERS OF LYONS, 1852-1870

THE SOCIAL AND ECONOMIC
FOUNDATIONS OF ASSOCIATION
AMONG THE SILK WEAVERS
OF LYONS, 1852-1870

George J. Sheridan, Jr.

Vol. II

ARNO PRESS
A New York Times Company
New York • 1981

Publisher's Note: This book has been reproduced from the best available copy.

Editorial Supervision: Brian Quinn

———

First Publication in Book Form 1981 by Arno Press Inc.

Copyright © 1978 by George Joseph Sheridan, Jr. All Rights Reserved.

Reprinted by permission of George Sheridan, Jr.

DISSERTATIONS
IN
EUROPEAN ECONOMIC HISTORY 1981

ISBN for complete set: 0-405-13975-6

See last pages of this volume for titles.

Manufactured in the United States of America

———

Library of Congress Cataloging in Publication Data

Sheridan, George J
    The social and economic foundations of associa-
tion among the silk weavers of Lyons, 1852-1870.

    (Dissertations in European economic history)
    Originally presented as the author's thesis,
Yale.
    Bibliography: p.
    1. Silk manufacture and trade--France--Lyons--
Employees--History. 2. Weavers--France--Lyons--
History. 3. Lyons--Social conditions. I. Title.
II. Series.
HD8039.T42F88 1981   331.7'677391242'09445823
ISBN 0-405-14013-4   80-2829

The Social and Economic Foundations of Association

Among the Silk Weavers of Lyons, 1852 - 1870

VOLUME II

A Dissertation

Presented to the Faculty of the Graduate School

of

Yale University

in Candidacy for the Degree of

Doctor of Philosophy

by

George Joseph Sheridan, Jr.

May 1978

VOLUME II

CHAPTER IV

The Transformation of the Craft

"Whenever they speak of the fabrique, they say more than ever
before that it is [all] over for Lyons ..."[1] Often the police of Lyons
heard comments like this in the silk-weavers' quarters during the 1860's.
Such comments described the sense of deep crisis the weavers believed
they were witnessing in their urban craft, worse than any they had
experienced in the past. For the first time in the history of their industry, it seemed, unemployment in some cloth specialties and low piece-
rates in others endured for nearly a decade, with little reprieve since
1860. 'Crisis' was no longer a periodic, cyclical phenomenon, but instead
was chronic -- the 'normal' situation of their industry. For the first
time, moreover, a long and deep crisis afflicted their urban craft while
their industry as a whole prospered. Urban silk-weaving was being dis-
mantled, so it seemed, in favor of silk-weaving in the countryside and
abroad.

Such dissociation of weaving from the city was an old phenomenon
in the history of European textile industries. In the woolen industry of
Yorkshire, England, for example, country and small-town industry replaced
that of the cities of York and Beverley during the fifteenth and sixteenth
centuries, as lower labor costs and freedom from guild regulation favored

---

[1]"Rapport à Monsieur Delcourt, Commissaire spécial, sur la
situation de la fabrique des étoffes de soies," September 9, 1867, AML,
I2-47(A), Situation de l'industrie lyonnaise: ... rapports sur la
soierie et les ouvriers en soie ... (1819 à 1870), No. 305.

the country over the city in a period of rising demand for woolen cloths.
For the older weaving cities, the transition to rural industry caused a
total, or near-total, abandonment of the urban trade and with it a decline
in the urban economy.[2] The dissociation of silk weaving from the city of
Lyons, at a much later period, was a more subtle process. The dissociation did not eliminate urban weaving nor did it ruin the economy of the
city of Lyons. Instead it preserved the urban sector as the last vestige
of the quality manufacture that made the silks of Lyons famous throughout
the Western world. However, it subjugated this sector to the economic
imperatives of rural production, as the price for its continued survival.
The urban weavers, or rather some of the urban weavers, continued to
make relatively high-quality fabrics, but for lower returns, because of
more frequent unemployment, more changes of style and, in some cases,
lower piece-rates. Perhaps because silk fabrics retained a sizable
luxury market for a longer period of time and held on to this market more
tenaciously than had English woolens in earlier centuries, the silk
industry of Lyons -- somewhat like the fine woolen industries in the older
Flemish and Brabantine towns of the fourteenth century[3] -- could afford

---

[2]Herbert Heaton, The Yorkshire Woollen and Worsted Industries, Vol.
X of Oxford Historical and Literary Studies, eds. C.H. Firth and Walter
Raleigh (Oxford: The Clarendon Press, 1920), pp. 58-59.

[3]Herman Van Der Wee, "Structural Changes and Specialization in the
Industry of the Southern Netherlands, 1100 - 1600," Economic History
Review, 2nd series, XXVIII, No. 2 (May 1975), 209. In the Flemish and
Brabantine woolen industry, the shift of demand to cheaper, lighter "new
draperies" was not permanent, like the shift to cheaper étoffes unies
in the silk industry of the nineteenth century. In fact, finer woolens
were temporarily favored on export markets during the depression of the
fourteenth century, since the depression affected the lower-income
consumers of the "new draperies" more adversely than the higher-income
consumers of the finer woolens.

the 'luxury' of a sizable urban production even after world demand for

silks permanently shifted its preferences towards the cheaper cloths.

The merchant-manufacturers of the city meanwhile reaped the returns from

putting-out to the countryside, and they, or other urban industrialists,

profited from servicing rural weaving with thread preparation,. thread

dyeing and cloth finishing. Their activities, along with the growth of

newer industries in the city, insured the growing wealth and continued

prosperity of Lyons despite the migration of most of its silk weaving to

the countryside.

Although it did not eliminate the urban fabrique nor undermine the

urban economy, the dissociation of silk weaving from the city of Lyons

destroyed the traditional craft solidarity among the silk weavers and,

along with this solidarity, the economic foundations of hierarchical

status associated with it. This made the experience of such dissociation

more painful 'morally' for the weavers of the better-quality fabrics than

it would have been, had their specialties been simply eliminated. They

received some work commensurate with their skills, but their earnings

fell to the same level, or below the level, of those of weavers with

lesser skills or working on lesser-quality fabrics. They retained their

status associated with these skills, largely as the vestige of an older

order of their industry, but their earnings in the present economy of

silk weaving did not confirm that status 'objectively,' or materially,

as they had in the past. Thus the traditional 'vertical' solidarity of

craft, based on a recognition of a hierarchy of cloth categories, of

weaving and mounting skills and of earnings corresponding to these,

disintegrated as the economic situations of 'superior' and 'inferior'

weavers were equalized. This disintegration of 'vertical' solidarity

joined that of the traditional 'horizontal' craft solidarity once
identifying the weaving craft with the city of Lyons. The latter
dissolved as silk weaving migrated increasingly to the countryside, and
as urban and rural weavers competed with one another for work on the silk
fabrics no longer retained exclusively by the city -- on the inferior-
quality étoffes unies for which the market was growing.

At the same time, however, the economy of the silk industry was
laying the foundations of a new kind of craft solidarity, to replace the
old kind that was disintegrating. In the 'vertical' dimension of the
craft -- in the relations among its different cloth 'categories' and
corresponding weaving and mounting skills -- this solidarity was based
more on similarity than on hierarchy of economic situations. In terms
analogous to Durkheim's types of social solidarity, it was becoming more
'mechanical' and less 'organic.'[4] This similarity of situation
characterized not only the earnings of different categories of urban
weavers but also, as the next chapter will demonstrate, the social
structures of their households. In the 'horizontal' dimension of their
craft -- in its geographical relations between urban and rural weaving --
the solidarity became more industrial and not only commercial; that is,
based on the common pursuit of industry and not only on the exchange of
the products of rural agriculture with those of urban industry. Within
this common industry, moreover, the economic and social positions of
urban and rural domestic weavers became more alike, to the extent that
both manufactured silk cloths as domestic master-weavers, instead of one

---

[4] Emile Durkheim, The Division of Labor in Society, trans. George
Simpson (New York: The Free Press, 1933, 1964), pp. 96-132.

(the rural weaver) serving the other (the urban weaver) as a 'floating journeyman' in the household of the latter. This likeness intensified as more rural weavers specialized in silk weaving, to the exclusion of other activities, approaching the traditional model of the urban weaver, and as more urban weavers concentrated on inferior-quality étoffes unies, for which cheaper rural labor had been 'traditionally' favored.

The new kinds of craft solidarity did not emerge fully during the 1860's, for this was a decade of transition. As a result, an awareness of new solidarity of craft, and a groping for such, joined a yearning for the restoration of the traditional form of solidarity in the ideological orientations and in the patterns of organization of weavers' movements of voluntary association during the decade. In the cooperative movement, for example, the new forms of craft solidarity were reflected in the 'democratic' organization of the producers' cooperative of silk weavers, without any formal distinction among cloth categories or weaving skills, but the old sense of 'vertical' solidarity was retained in the informal predominance of fancy-cloth weavers in its leadership. The old sense of 'horizontal' solidarity also remained in the restriction of the membership to urban weavers and in its intention to prevent further migration of their industry to the countryside. In the resistance movement, the new craft solidarity explained the initiative of plain-cloth weavers in the organization of the resistance federation of nearly all weaving categories and in the extension of this organization, and of its financial support, to striking rural weavers as well. But the old craft solidarity insured a certain administrative autonomy to each of the cloth categories within this federation and probably encouraged the latter's active support for the strike of fancy-cloth weavers in June-July 1870, for restoring their traditionally higher piece-rates.

This chapter explores the nature and some of the sources of the disintegration of the old solidarity of craft and the emergence of a new solidarity during the 'crisis' decade of the 1860's. The chapter also suggests some of the effects of this concurrent disintegration and reformation on the organization and aims of some of the weavers' movements of voluntary association. It focuses largely on the urban craft, and examines rural weaving only to the extent that the latter influenced the economy of silk weaving in the city. Subsequent chapters will examine, in turn, the effects of the 'crisis' of the 1860's on the weavers' household, class, neighborhood and political relations, and some of the manifestations of these effects in their movements of association.

I. The Crisis of 'Horizontal' Craft Solidarity: From Urban to
    Regional Economy

As we saw in an earlier chapter, the dissociation of silk weaving from the city of Lyons, by means of putting-out to the countryside, was the result of changing tastes and increasing price elasticity of demand in fabric markets, at a time of rising costs of raw silk. These trends favored the manufacture of the cheaper étoffes unies, and for such manufacture rural weaving was highly competitive with urban weaving because of its lower labor cost and its ability to weave cheaper cloth specialties as well as the city. During the 1850's the competition of rural weaving was felt only by some of the urban weavers -- those manufacturing the unis specialties. Continued (although not rapidly growing) demand for fancy cloths gave the urban weavers of façonnés enough work in their specialty, and the skills and surveillance needed for mounting and weaving the façonné insulated them from rural

competition. In 1860, the loss of the American market, the largest

consumer of French fancy fabrics, suddenly plunged the fancy-cloth

weavers into a severe depression lasting for more than a decade. The

reaction of most was to shift to plain-cloth weaving, but such a shift

also ended their insulation from rural competition. As a result, rural

weaving competed with urban weaving generally, as more of its weavers

shifted to the inferior cloths. The qualitative difference between rural

and urban weaving, based on cloth specialties, diminished as a consequence.

The sudden loss of the foreign market for fancy silks was the most

notable feature of the crisis of the 1860's. Exports of fancy cloths fell

dramatically from 330,925 kilograms in 1860 to 47,905 kilograms in 1866

(- 86%). The decline continued further into the 1870's. Exports

averaged 12,377 kilograms between 1872 and 1874. Demand revived

seriously in 1876, but foreign sales did not surpass 100,000 kilograms

until 1880.[5] The major result of this loss was a shift to plain from

fancy-cloth weaving by the households. Table 11 suggests the extent of

this shift by comparing the distribution of occupied looms in the city in

1846, over the three categories of plains, fancies and velvets, with the

distribution of members of the weavers' resistance society, the Société

civile de prévoyance et de renseignements pour le travail des tisseurs

de la fabrique lyonnaise (SCPR) in 1873. The table indicates an increase

in the percentage of plain-silk weaving at the expense of fancy-silk and

(largely fancy-) velvet weaving. Unfortunately, the uncertainties

---

[5]Administration des douanes, Tableau décennal du commerce de la
France (Paris: Imprimerie nationale), 2e Partie, for the years 1857 à
1866, 1867 à 1876, 1877 à 1886.

Table 11

Distribution of Looms and
Weavers in Lyons by
Category of Silk Cloth
(1846, 1873)

Category	1846[*]		1873[**]	
	Number of Occupied Looms	% of All Occupied Looms	Number of City Persons in SCPR	% of All City Persons in SCPR
Plain Silks	14,060	59.9	7,634	75.1
Fancy Silks	7,562	32.2	2,081	20.5
Velvets	1,829	7.8	445	4.4
Total	23,451	100.0	10,160	100.0

Sources: 1846: Recensement, Lyon, 1846, AML
Recensement, Croix-Rousse, 1844-45, AML
1873: Société civile des tisseurs, List of
Members, July 5, 1873. ADR, 10M-2,
Associations ouvriers tisseurs (1870-93)

[*]Includes first, second and fifth arrondissements and
town of the Croix-Rousse (1844-45 for latter). Excludes
Guillotière and Vaise.

[**]Includes all arrondissements of Lyons (1,2,3,4,5,6). The
category "Plain Silks" includes categories 1 (taffetas),
5 (satins-armures) and 7 (foulards, grèges) of the SCPR.
The category "Fancy Silks" includes categories 2 (robes,
confections, châles soie) and 3 (meubles, ornaments). The
category "Velvets" includes SCPR categories 4 (gilets,
velours façonnés), 9 (velours frisés, peluches) and
10 (velours à 2 pièces).

concerning the comparability of the two sets of data give this indication
only the value of suggestion. (See Appendix III.)

A more precise indication of the shift to plain-cloth weaving is
provided by comparing the percentage distribution of occupied looms
(over different cloth categories) in 1833 and 1844-45 with that of unoccupied and occupied looms in 1866, in the traditionally fancy-weaving
district of the Croix-Rousse (Fourth Arrondissement). (See Table 12, A
and B.) In this case, no distortions or uncertainties in the data cloud
the comparison, as in that of looms with weavers in Table 11. The conclusion suggested by the latter table -- that a significant shift occurred
from fancy-cloth weaving to plain-cloth weaving from 1846 to 1873 -- is
nevertheless supported rather strongly for the arrondissement in which
this shift was least likely to occur and for the period up to 1866.
Despite its traditionally high concentration of fancy-cloth weaving
(the highest concentration of façonnés among all weaving districts in
Lyons), the Fourth Arrondissement, like other arrondissements in the city,
wove more plain silks than fancies after 1860, even though the total
number of looms increased by 71% from 1844-45. As Table 12-B demonstrates,
this substitution of plain cloths for fancy cloths represented a replacement of exclusively fancy-loom households by plain-loom households, not
merely an addition of plain looms and plain-loom households to the
existing stock of fancy looms and fancy-loom households. The numbers in
fact underestimate the extent of plain-cloth weaving in 1866. The number
and percentage of unoccupied looms was much greater in 1866 than in
1833 and 1844-45. (The percentages were 39% in 1866, 19% in 1844-45,
and 5% in 1833.) Because of different methods of aggregating the data,
these unoccupied looms are included in the table for 1866 but not in

Table 12

Distribution of Weaving
in the Croix-Rousse by
Loom Type (1833, 1844-45,
1847 and 1866)

A. Distribution of Looms
in the Aggregate

Category	1833		1844-45		1866	
	Number of Occupied Looms	% of All Occupied Looms	Number of Occupied Looms	% of All Occupied Looms	Number of Looms Occ and Unocc	% of Total Looms
Plains	2,254	35.8	2,819	33.9	7,648	53.7
Fancies	3,416	54.3	4,453	53.5	5,295	37.1
Velvets	534	8.5	916	11.0	704	4.9
Other	91	1.4	135	1.6	604	4.3
Total	6,295	100.0	8,323	100.0	14,251	100.0
Unoccupied	332		1,391		5,524	

B. Distribution of Households
According to Loom Type
(Based on Occupied Looms
Only)

Loom Type of Household	1847		1866	
	Number of Households	% of Total	Number of Households	% of Total
Fancy Looms Only	99	63.5	43	33.1
Fancy Looms > Plain Looms	3	1.9	1	.8
Fancy Looms = Plain Looms	2	1.3	1	.8
Plain Looms > Fancy Looms			2	1.5
Plain Looms Only	52	33.3	83	63.8
Total Households	156	100.0	130	100.0

Sources: Aggregate: Recensement, Croix-Rousse, 1833, AML.
Recensement, Croix-Rousse, 1844-45, AML.
Dénombrement, 1866, Lyon, 4ème Canton,
Tomes XVI, XVII, ADR, 6M-Dénombrement.
Household: Sample, Recensement, Croix-Rousse,
1847, AML.
Sample, Denombrement, 1866, Lyon, 4ème
Canton, ADR, 6M-Dénombrement.
(See Appendix V for Construction
of Samples)

those for the two previous dates. Since the incidence of unemployment was generally greater for fancies than for plains in 1866, the extent of actual fancy weaving (occupied fancy looms) was probably lower than the table figure of 37%. Moreover, some weavers with Jacquard looms probably also accepted orders of plain cloths to weave on these looms.[6] Such cases would raise further the level of plain-cloth weaving in the Croix-Rousse in 1866.

As more of the urban industry shifted to plain-cloth weaving in this manner, competition with the rural areas affected the economy of most of the fabrique of Lyons. Such competition had an impact on the scale or capacity of economic activity, as measured by the number of occupied and total looms respectively; it affected levels of employment and occasions of unemployment; and it influenced movements and levels of piece-rates. After 1860 this competition became more severe than before that year, as rural weaving extracted not only a rising share of the increase in production of silk cloths but also a portion of the production originally carried out in the city. During the 1850's -- that is, between 1848 and 1861-65 -- the number of urban looms increased 5.1% from 33,500 to 35,215, while the number of rural looms increased 166.7%, from 30,000 to about 80,000.[7] During this period rural weaving merely extracted a larger share of the increase of total cloth production[7a] than urban weaving, as estimated by the relative number of looms. But it did not reduce the absolute level of plain-cloth production, so the city

----

[6]As indicated in Chapter I, section I-B-1, p. 68. Jacquard looms could be used to weave plain silk cloths.

[7]Table 7, Chapter II.

[7a]More precisely, total cloth production potential. Actual production (output) of each loom depended on activity and on technology (hand or mechanical) of each loom. The same remark applies to 'production' and 'output' as used in the remainder of this paragraph.

shared somewhat in the growth of aggregate production. Between 1861-65

and 1872, however, the number of urban looms decreased by 14.8%, from

35,215 to 30,000, while the number of rural looms increased an additional

12.5%, from 80,000 to 90,000.[8] Rural weaving thus replaced a portion

of the current output of the city, besides siphoning off an increasing

percentage of the extra output of plain cloths in the industry as a whole.

Three effects of this growing competition of the countryside were

more frequent unemployment even during periods of growing demand for

plain silks and a steady decline in piece-rates for weaving these. As

noted in the last chapter, the first effect appeared initially during

the 1850's. After 1860 urban unemployment at a time of rural prosperity

became not only a more frequent phenomenon but also a 'structural'

attribute of the economy of the industry. In September 1861, for example,

three-fourths of the plain looms in the city were inactive, but police

reports on the state of the industry at this time did not suggest any

simultaneous slowdown in weaving in the countryside. In June 1866, one-

half of the urban plain-silk weavers were unemployed, but again the

rural fabrique seemed to remain active.[9] In December 1866, in fact, the

reports noted that "labor tends to emigrate to the countryside ...,"[10]

and in June 1867, the police observer remarked, more generally, that

---

[8]Ibid.

[9]'Etoffes unies,' "Situation de l'Industrie à Lyon au 13 7bre
1861" (September 13, 1861), AML, I2-47(A), No. 174; 'Etoffes unies,' "15
Juin 1866," AML, I2-47(A), No. 187.

[10]'Etoffes unies,' "Situation de l'industrie à Lyon au 15 Décembre
1866," AML, I2-47(A), No. 193.

before that year, the work of "the several looms spread throughout the
nearby countryside ... held up for a long time almost without rest."[11]
Only in June 1867 did the observer indicate that the rural looms had
"also experienced a light employment during this trimester."[12] Rural
weaving apparently required a severe decline in sales of plain silks
before sharing in the unemployment of the city, for exports of plain
cloths dropped suddenly to 2,153,536 kilograms in 1867 from 2,323,490
kilograms in 1866.[13] Even the rural unemployment rate was not as high
as that of the urban weavers, which reached two-thirds of all plain-
cloth looms.[14] As several fabricants admitted in the early 1870's,
unemployment generally afflicted "the workers of the city more directly"
than the rural weavers, since the latter were kept working as long as
possible during periods of falling sales of cloth, while the former were
dismissed at the least intimation of decline.[15] The vassalage of the
urban fabrique to rural industry had indeed become rooted in the structure
of the silk-weaving economy of Lyons.

More unusual than frequent unemployment were the occasional slowdowns in urban weaving during periods of stable or increasing foreign

---

[11]'Etoffes unies,' "Situation industrielle au Juin 1867," AML, I2-47(A), No. 197.

[12]Ibid.

[13]Ibid.; 'Etoffes unies,' "Situation industrielle au 15 7bre 1867," (September 15, 1867), AML, I2-47(A), No. 198; Administration des douanes, Tableau décennal, 1857 à 1866.

[14]Ibid.

[15]"Réponses de la Chambre Syndicale des Soieries de Lyon," Enquête Parlementaire Sur les Conditions du Travail en France (Rhône, 1872-1875), Second Questionnaire B, IX, AN, C 3021, Enquête sur les Conditions du Travail en France (1872 à 1875), Région du Sud-Est (Rhône).

demand for plain cloths and the persistence of low wages for most types
of plain cloths even during periods of high or rising employment. Between
June 15 and October 3, 1859, for example, up to one-half of the plain
looms in the city were immobilized due to insufficient orders. Average
daily wages for journeymen weavers declined from 3.50 francs to 2.00
francs for the cheapest articles and from 4.00 francs to 2.50 francs for
the better plain fabrics.[16] During the same period exports of plain
silks rose continuously from 1,260,242 kilograms in 1858 to 1,574,725 kilograms in 1860.[17] During the year 1866, plain-silk exports again rose to
2,323,490 kilograms from 2,171,341 kilograms in 1865, and yet the proportion of unemployed weavers of plain cloths in Lyons increased steadily
from one-fourth on March 15, 1866 to one-half on June 15.[18] Except for a
short, light recovery between September and December, the decline continued into the near-total unemployment of 1867. Even during the
recoveries of 1862, 1865 and 1868-69, the average annual (daily) wage for
weaving most types of plain silks remained very low -- ranging from 1.10
francs to 1.75 francs for the inferior articles (as compared with 2.00
francs to 3.50 francs in 1859), and from 1.25 francs to 3.50 francs for
the better plain silks (as compared with 2.50 francs to 4.50 francs in 1859).[19]

[16]'Etoffes unies,' "Situation industrielle au 15 Juin 1859" and
'Etoffes unies,' "Situation industrielle au 3 7bre 1859," (September
3, 1859), AML, I2-47(A), Nos. 166, 167.

[17]Administration des douanes, Tableau décennal, 1859 à 1866.

[18]Ibid.; 'Etoffes unies,' "Situation industrielle - 15 mars 1866 -
Soieries et industries qui s'y rattachent" and 'Etoffes unies,' "15
Juin 1866," AML, I2-47(A), No. 186, 187.

[19]'Etoffes unies,' "Situation industrielle," 1859, 1862, 1865, 1868,
1869, AML, I2-47(A), Nos. 166-168, 176-177, 179, 183-185, 201-205 bis,
206-208, 211-212.

Both of these phenomena -- urban unemployment during periods of industrial prosperity and low piece-rates -- were, again, effects of rural competition. Both reflected the increasing dependence of the urban silk-weaving economy on that of the region, dominated by the low-wage labor market of rural household and factory weavers.

In reaction to this dependence, the urban weavers organized a producers' cooperative and a federation of resistance societies to halt the migration of their industry to the countryside and to restore to the urban craft its traditional pre-eminence in determining piece-rates and conditions of work in the fabrique. The producers' cooperative, the Association of Weavers, sought to take over urban weaving by putting out silk thread and cloth orders directly to the weavers, its members, without the intermediation of the fabricants. These weavers were exclusively urban, and they hoped to prevent the further decline of the urban craft by controlling ever larger shares of production and by favoring urban over rural weavers in the distribution of cloth orders. In October 1866, following a threatened demonstration against the emigration of the fabrique to the countryside, the silk weavers accepted government approval of their association as a société anonyme and a loan to help it begin business, instead of restriction of putting-out to the countryside, as they had originally demanded.[20] They withdrew the latter demand so easily in part because they believed that their association would achieve the same end. As the police reported in December 1866, the weavers of

---

[20]"Les Réclamations des Tisseurs," Le Progrès (Lyon), October 20, 1866; "Lettre de M. de la Valette sur le chômage lyonnais" and letter from weavers Gargnier, Chépié et al. in response, Le Progrès, October 28, 1866.

Lyons "place[d] much hope for revival of the _fabrique_ on the establishment which is being organized under the large association of weavers."[21]

The weavers harbored the same expectations of halting the movement
to the countryside and thereby 'reviving' their industry through their
organization of resistance societies later in the decade to enforce
recently-negotiated increases in piece-rates. In December 1869, when
the resistance movement was entering the stage of 'mass' organization
under the leadership of the plain-cloth category, the police described
the movement as "a great awakening among the weavers."

> Conversations on the subject are heard everywhere, and
> everyone has this tremendous enthusiasm for preventing
> the _fabrique_ from leaving Lyons, for bringing it back
> instead. They expect to attract labor from the country-
> side to the city -- not all labor but some which left
> the city -- and they see no other way [of achieving this]
> than making all the _fabricants_ pay the same piece-rate.[22]

Thus, besides halting the emigration of the _fabrique_, the weavers
expected their resistance societies to eliminate the worst consequences
of rural competition. In particular, they expected their organization
to force all piece-rates up to a level determined by the collective
strength of the urban weavers instead of allowing urban rates to fall
to a level determined by the dispersion, lower living costs and poverty
of rural labor. In this way, the city would again dominate the labor
market of silk-weaving as a whole and no longer be subject to the labor

[21]"Rapport à Monsieur Delcourt, Commissaire Spécial, sur la
situation de la fabrique des étoffes de soies au 4e Trimestre Xbre
1866," December 8, 1866, AML, I2-47(A), No. 301.

[22]"Rapport à Monsieur Delcourt, Commissaire Spécial, sur la
situation de la fabrique de soieries," December 7, 1869, AML, I2-47(A),
No. 315.

market of the countryside.

In order to revive this domination by the city, however, the rural weavers also needed to be organized into the resistance movement. Unless their piece-rates were raised, by the collective force of resistance, to the levels of the city, they would continue to compete against urban weavers. This simple law of economics destroyed any attempt to keep the resistance movement exclusively urban and anti-rural. Economic necessity forced traditional aspirations for a city-concentrated, city-dominated craft to merge with a newer vision of the silk-weaving trade including both urban and rural elements. In this newer vision the 'horizontal' solidarity of the craft was extended from an urban to a regional framework of economic activity, and the purpose of organization, especially organization for industrial resistance, was to make solidaire what had once been competitive in the labor market defined by this regional framework. In the confrontation between its original motivation and the organizational necessity imposed by economic reality, industrial resistance thus carried the germ of a profound ambivalence of ideological purpose. Resistance aimed to restore the 'traditional' identification of craft with city, and, at the same time, to realize the newer vision of 'horizontal' solidarity identifying craft with region.

This ambivalence was reflected in the first strike support action of the newly-formed resistance federation of silk weavers, the Société civile (SCPR). This was the strike of rural weavers in the department of Isère in March-April 1870. The strike was directed against several fabricants of Lyons putting out cloth in this area, and its major demand was an increase of piece-rates. In March 1870 several embryonic séries (organizational cells) of striking weavers of the arrondissement of

La-Tour-du-Pin (Isère) appealed to the members of the SCPR for financial
assistance, at the organizational meeting of the society. One of the
members of the SCPR, Clatel, a leader of the fancy-weavers' delegation,
expressed some doubts concerning the wisdom of supporting the rural
weavers so soon.[23] He articulated, in effect, the hesitations of those
members of the new association who regarded its mission as exclusively
urban, or least primarily urban. Such a view was probably more typical
of the fancy-cloth weavers, among whom, as we will soon see, the
'traditional' view of the city-centered craft was strongest.

The assembly, dominated by the plain-cloth weavers, greeted
Clatel's hesitation with "so to speak generalized reprobation." They
responded to the rural weavers' request not only with funds but also
with the dispatch of envoys to stir up support for the strike in the
countryside of Isère.[24] The urban weavers of the SCPR, especially the
plain-cloth weavers constituting its largest single category, clearly
regarded high piece-rates for rural weaving in their own interest as
well. In fact, only by raising rural piece-rates to the level of those
in the city could the urban weavers defend their gains against threats of
further migration of the industry to the countryside. This perception of
their ties with rural labor, to the point of planning "rural séries" in
the statutes of their resistance organization, indicated a conception of
their craft and the 'proper' frontiers of its labor market much larger
than in the past. This conception included not only the urban craft

[23]Report from Police Commissioner of the Brotteaux to Prefect of
Rhône concerning meeting of weavers, March 28, 1870, AML, I2-45, Sociétés
coopératives de production et de consommation (1849 à 1870), No. 156.

[24]Ibid.; report from Police Commissioner of Canton of Morestel to
Under-Prefect of La-Tour-du-Pin, April 2, 1870, ADI, 166M-1: Grêves
(1858-1877).

but also silk weaving in the countryside. Thus, despite the hopes of
these weavers for a restoration of their urban craft -- an aspiration
articulated in extreme form by the fancy-cloth weaver Clatel as a revival
of exclusively urban 'horizontal' solidarity -- their vision extended
to a new form of 'horizontal' solidarity as well, one based on the region
rather than on the city alone.

II. The Crisis of 'Vertical' Craft Solidarity: From Hierarchy to
     Equality

     The transformation of the framework of 'horizontal' craft
solidarity from urban to regional occurred as traditional 'vertical'
solidarity of craft disintegrated and as such solidarity was reformed
on a new economic and social basis. Disintegration followed the separation of the different cloth 'categories' and of the different 'specialties'
within each category according to their differing experience of economic
conditions, especially conditions of employment and movements and levels
of piece-rates. The hierarchy of earnings corresponding to that of skills
required for weaving these different categories and specialties of silk
cloths also dissolved as this separation of conditions reduced the
earnings of the more highly-paid categories and specialties to those of
the more lowly-paid. This equalization of earnings (that is, of annual
income) created the basis for a new kind of solidarity among the
qualitatively different categories and specialties of cloth weaving.
This solidarity was built upon equality and similarity of economic
situation rather than upon hierarchy and difference of situation. Such
a dual movement consisting of disintegration of traditional 'vertical'
solidarity, on the one hand, and of the emergence of a new kind of
'vertical' solidarity, on the other hand, was evident both in conditions

of employment of silk weavers during the 1860's and in movements and
levels of average daily wages they received for their work.

Disintegration of 'vertical' craft solidarity resulted primarily
from the radical dissociation of conditions of employment and movements
of piece-rates between the 'superior' (fancy-cloth) categories of the
fabrique and the 'inferior' (plain-cloth) categories after 1860. Loss
of the American market for fancy silks plunged weavers of the latter
into severe, secular unemployment, while weavers of plain silks remained
employed more regularly, because of rising demand for their product at
home and -- after the Anglo-French Commercial Treaty of 1860 -- abroad
as well. Piece-rates of plain-cloth weavers plummeted, however, as
rural weaving competed more intensively with urban weaving. Piece-rates
of fancy-cloth weavers remained relatively high, because of their insulation by their skills from competition of rural labor. Their subjection
to very different economic forces after 1860, therefore, made weavers of
fancy silks experience their economic conditions differently than
plain-silk weavers -- more differently, in fact, than in the past.
These differences destroyed the solidarity of experience of cycles of
employment especially -- an experience which had served as an economic
basis for their craft solidarity in the past. At least one of weavers'
movements of voluntary association, the resistance movement of the late
1860's, recognized this dissociation of craft solidarity by favoring
organizational and administrative autonomy for each of the different
cloth categories.

Equalization of earnings, dissolving the hierarchy of earnings
associated with different cloth categories, was primarily the result
of more frequent or secular unemployment in the more highly-paid

'superior' categories, reducing their earnings to the level of the more
lowly-paid, but more regularly employed, 'inferior' categories. A more
subtle erosion of the hierarchy of earnings derived from the inversion
of traditionally primary relations among movements and levels of wages,
for the different cloth categories, from relations corresponding to
qualitative differences among these to relations corresponding to
quantitative differences between their maximum-wage specialties and
minimum-wage specialties considered together, irrespective of category.
In other words, differences between maximum wages and minimum wages paid
within each qualitatively-different cloth category became more significant
indicators of differences in relative movements and levels of compensation than differences among wages corresponding respectively to certain
cloth categories. The combined effect of equalization of earnings and
subordination of quality-based hierarchy of wage movements and levels to
quantity-based differences was the economic erosion of traditional
'vertical' solidarity of craft, based upon a qualitative hierarchy of the
cloth categories. Economic situations once differing among these
categories became more alike. Thus a new 'mechanical' solidarity, based
on this similarity of situations, emerged to replace the disintegrating
'organic' solidarity, based on a hierarchy of differences. As in the
case of changing 'horizontal' solidarity of craft, the weavers reacted
to this equalization of situations in an ambivalent manner, in their
movements of voluntary association. They resisted it, attempting to
revive the 'traditional' differences of earnings and piece-rates among
the cloth categories and, with these differences, those of status within
the craft associated with each category. And they embraced equalization,
recognizing in effect the strength of organization based upon equality

of situation and directing this strength either to a renaissance of
the urban craft in the cooperative movement, or to the building of
weavers' economic power in the resistance movement.

A. Conditions of Employment and Their Effects

The dual movement affecting 'vertical' craft solidarity -- dissociation of economic conditions, destroying traditional solidarity, and
equalization of economic situations, reforming craft solidarity on a
new economic basis -- was evident most directly in the conditions of
employment of weavers during the 1860's and in the effects of these conditions on earnings. The movement was observable on two levels -- that
differentiating silk cloths by 'categories', especially that differentiating 'inferior' plain-cloth categories from 'superior' fancy-cloth categories -- and that differentiating cloth 'specialties' within each category, in particular 'common' specialties from 'rich' specialties. Unemployment and rural competition (the latter affecting absolute levels
of piece-rates), separated the economic conditions of the plain-cloth
categories (étoffes unies and velours unis) from those of the fancy-cloth
categories (étoffes façonnées, velours façonnés, châles and ornements
d'église) and also the economic conditions of 'common' specialties within
each of these six categories from the 'rich' specialties. The consequences
of these differing conditions on earnings equalized, however, the economic
situations of weavers in plain and fancy categories, on the one hand,
and of weavers of 'common' and 'rich' specialties within each category,
on the other hand. This section will trace in closer detail this combined separation and equalization, using the quarterly reports of the
local police on the situation of the silk industry in Lyons as a

guide.[25] (See Appendix IV for a discussion of this source.)

The change in conditions of employment after 1860 was most striking among weavers of fancy silk cloths (étoffes façonnées) -- those most affected by the loss of the American market. Weavers who continued to accept fancy orders concentrated largely on dress ornament and haute nouveauté rather than on the rich dress fabrics which had established the reputation of Lyons in the past. "The rich fabrics with large designs have not been in style for several years," reported the police observer of the fabrique in March 1866, "which means that this article goes always from bad to worse and cannot hope to be restored except by the caprice of fashion."[26] Such dresses were made only on order, and such orders "became more and more rare."[27] Fancies for ornamenting silk and other textile dress fabrics were still in demand, however, along with passementerie, the traditional ornamenting ribbon enjoying a new prosperity in the 1860's.[28] But such petits façonnés had to be produced in greater variety than in the past, in order to satisfy the ever fickle craving for novelty. Weavers of these 'common' fancy cloths thus made many varieties of samples, to attract potential buyers with large displays. Manufacture of samples increased in 1866 and 1867 to prepare for the displays at the Exposition of Paris. The maison Schultz, for example,

[25] Reports on the industrial situation of the fabrique of Lyons from June 1859 to March 1870, AML, I2-47(A), Nos. 166-213.

[26] 'Etoffes façonnées,' "Situation industrielle - 15 mars 1866 - Soieries et industries qui s'y rattachent," AML, I2-47(A), No. 187.

[27] 'Etoffes façonnées,' "Situation industrielle au Mars 1869," AML, I2-47(A), No. 207.

[28] See for example, 'Etoffes façonnées,' "Situation industrielle - 15 mars 1866 - ...," AML, I2-47(A), No. 186.

one of the most prominent manufacturers of fancy haute nouveauté,

accelerated its annual invention of new styles between 1862 and 1869,

especially between 1865 and 1867 to prepare for the Exposition. (Table

13)

Table 13

Number of Varieties of
Haute Nouveauté Silk
Styles Displayed Annually
by the Maison Schultz of
Lyons, 1861 to 1870

Year	Number of Varieties	Year	Number of Varieties
1861	22	1866	58
1862	45	1867	56
1863	41	1868	45
1864	48	1869	61
1865	52	1870	17

Source: Archives of Samples of Maison Schultz, BMTL.

For the weavers of these petits façonnés, samples manufacture

required frequent changes of design and mountings of the loom. This made

their work more complex and less profitable, for reasons discussed in

Chapter I.[29] Such efforts did not succeed in attracting many new clients

in any case.[30] The demand for most designs was therefore short-lived.

As a result, even though such work earned more per piece than work on

plain silks, frequent mountings and delays between orders made the

---

[29]Chapter I, section I-B-2, pp. 77-82.

[30]'Etoffes façonnées,' "Situation industrielle au Xbre 1867,"
(December 1867), AML, I2-47(A), No. 200.

overall economic situation of these skilled fancy weavers little
different from that of the plain-cloth weavers. "If labor is compensated
better in this article," wrote the police observer in March 1865, "the
fluctuations and unemployment it experiences make the situation of the
major part of the workers as bad as that of workers manufacturing the
common cloths."[31] Three years later the observer reported that the
"ordinary fancies always occupied some looms; but the interruptions of
work which occur frequently, combined with many changes of design on
the looms, are forcing the worker little by little to abandon a profession whose product is insufficient to provide for his needs."[32]

Weavers of plain cloths did not face the secular decline in
employment forced upon the fancy silk weavers. They endured occasional
short periods of partial unemployment in 1859, 1861, 1866-67 and 1868-
69, but these differed little from the short-term cyclical crises to
which they had been accustomed in the past, even during the 1850's.
Only in 1861 and 1867 did such crises produce near-total work stoppage.
Even then the plains produced more orders than the fancies.[33] Instead,
the weavers of plain silk cloths were subject to a rapid and severe
decline in piece-rates and to the persistence of low piece-rates throughout the decade. As we saw earlier, these low rates were the result of

---

[31]'Etoffes façonnées,' "Situation industrielle - 15 mars 1866 -
...," AML, I2-47(A), No. 186.

[32]'Etoffes faconnées,' "Situation industrielle au Mars 1869," AML,
I2-47(A), No. 207.

[33]'Etoffes unies,' "Situation industrielle," October 3, 1859; March
13, June 13, September 13, 1861; March 15, June 15, 1866; March 15,
June, September 15, December 1867; March, June, December 12, 1868; March,
June 15, September 14, 1869, AML, I2-47(A), Nos. 168, 172-174, 186-187,
196-198, 200-201, 204, 206-208, 211.

rapidly growing competition of rural weaving. Such competition also
caused urban weavers of plain cloths to suffer unemployment even during
periods of rising demand for their product. In both respects their
economic conditions differed from those of fancy-cloth weavers, who were
more insulated by their skills and by the need for surveillance of
their work from the competition of rural weavers. Their piece-rates
remained higher than those of plain-cloth weavers,and when these declined,
they did not do so as severely or as rapidly as those of plain-cloth
weavers. Although unemployment of fancy-cloth weavers was more severe
and chronic than that of plain-cloth weavers, it did not persist when
demand for their product occasionally revived.

The invasion of the countryside had a varied record of success in
imposing its low-wage, 'perverse' employment solution on the different
specialties within the plain-cloth category. The 'rich' plains --
armures, satins, gros de Naples -- were generally more insulated from
such competition than the 'common' plains, such as the taffetas. In
June 1860, many urban weavers of plain silks recovered from their unemployment of the previous year by switching to armures. "The armure
seems to have a much larger following this year," reported the police
observer. The "workers have generally abandoned the other articles to
make the latter which requires only a few small changes in the looms."[34]
In June 1866, when the slowdown affected half of the plain-cloth weavers,

[34]'Etoffes unies,' "Situation industrielle au 15 Juin 1860,"
AML, I2-47(A), No. 170.

the armure was "the only one which procured continued work..."[35] In

September 1867, when the crisis affecting rural weaving as well left

two-thirds of the 'common' plain silk looms inactive, the "rich plains,

such as: satins, armure, Gilets, ombrelles, were a bit more favored..."[36]

Wages for weaving these better plain fabrics were also less sticky

(upwards) during favorable periods than were wages of the 'common' cloth

weavers. Between September 15, 1866, and March 15, 1867, "maximum"

wages for plain-cloth weaving (wages for 'rich' plains) remained 3.50

francs each semester, at least as high as the wages for the last two

trimesters of 1859 (3.50 francs and 2.50 francs respectively). "Minimum"

wages (for 'common' plains) during the same period 1866-67 were 1.50

francs by comparison, lower than the lowest recorded wage of the year

1859 (2.00 francs).[37] During the recovery of plain silks, from March

to June 1868, "many fabricants were forced to increase by 5 and 10

centimes per meter the wage of certain articles, such as: gros de

Naples and armures," because of a lack of workers.[38] Rural labor

could not fill such a labor shortage for the 'rich' plain silks as it

could for the 'common' plain silks. The 'rich' cloths required

greater skill and surveillance during weaving, which only urban weavers

could provide. This consideration effectively insulated the more

---

[35] 'Etoffes unies,' "15 Juin 1866," AML, I2-47(A), No. 187.

[36] 'Etoffes unies,' "Situation industrielle au 15 7bre 1867" (September 15, 1867), AML, I2-47(A), No. 198.

[37] 'Etoffes unies,' "Situation industrielle," 1859, 1866, 1867, AML, I2-47(A), Nos. 166-168, 186-187, 192-193, 196-198, 200.

[38] 'Etoffes unies,' "Situation industrielle au Juin 1868," AML, I2-47(A), No. 204.

skilled plain-cloth weavers of this specialty from rural competition.
The fashions of London and Paris also favored the weavers of 'rich'
unis to some extent. For their best dress models, fashion in the two
capitals still relied on quality fabrics, which the 'rich' weavers
were accustomed to producing.

Towards the end of the decade, however, such advantage of 'rich'
plain-silk weavers began to weaken. As early as June 1866, the police
observer noted the beginnings of a slowdown in the 'rich' cloth
specialties. In September he remarked that the "common plains article
is the only one which occupies some hands at this time; all the others
are, not in unemployment, but in a worse situation than last trimester..."[39]
In late 1867, when a light recovery favored the 'rich' cloths, the
political events of Rome "put a complete stop to this spurt and the
situation of these articles fell back down to the level of the others."[40]
By late 1868 - early 1869, the 'rich' cloth no longer had any advantage
over the 'common' cloth. "In the last trimester we noted a little bit
more activity in the manufacture of some articles than in others," wrote
the police observer in March 1869; "today they are all at the same
level."[41] Later in the year, this equalization of employment conditions
reverted back to inequality, this time in favor of the 'common' cloths.
"The manufacture of articles of inferior quality is that which provides

---

[39]'Etoffes unies' "Situation de l'Industrie au 15 7bre 1866,"
(September 15, 1866), AML I2-47(A), No. 192.

[40]'Etoffes unies,' "Situation industrielle au Xbre 1867,"
(December 1867), AML, I2-47(A), No. 200.

[41]'Etoffes unies,' "Situation industrielle au Mars 1869," AML,
I2-47(A), No. 207.

most work ... As for the manufacture of articles of superior quality,
it faces short but very frequent periods of unemployment."[42] By
September the outlook was even worse for the 'rich' unis. While
inferior plain silks provided "rather regular work," there "was not
the least activity in the manufacture of the other articles..."[43]
Though insulated from the competitive pressures of the rural labor
market, the 'rich' unis finally succumbed to the same change in taste
in the markets of fashion which had relegated fancy-cloth weaving to a
much smaller-scale activity with a very uncertain future.

The 'victory' of weavers of 'common' plain silks was Pyrrhic at
best. While their work became more regular, their wage remained so low
that they had to weave day and night merely to satisfy their very basic
needs. Even then they did not earn the full value of their piece.
The poorer quality of silk thread put out to them for their low-grade
cloth increased their thread wastes and slowed their weaving speed
through frequent thread breakages. The poor thread quality was most
often the result of 'loading' the expensive fiber with foreign material
during dyeing. As we saw earlier, this was one means used by fabricants
of black plain silks during the 1860's to add weight to the fabric.
Such 'loading' limited severely the extent to which the weaver of these
silks could increase his income, even when work was abundant and when
wages did not fall. In June 1868, for example, the police observer
reported that

[42]'Etoffes unies,' "Situation industrielle au 15 Juin 1869," AML,
I2-47(A), No. 208.

[43]'Etoffes unies,' "Situation industrielle au 15 Septembre 1869,"
AML, I2-47(A), No. 211.

> The situation of the said article in now in a more
> satisfactory condition than last trimester, in terms of
> the quantity of work; but, unfortunately, the bad quality
> of silks resulting either from their origin but more from
> their excessive loading in dyeing... makes their manufacture
> more and more difficult and causes the worker losses of
> time.[44]

High and uncertain raw silk prices, which were responsible for

such 'loading' to begin with, aggravated even further the situation of

weavers of 'common' plain cloths. Fabricants of these articles were

less willing to put out new orders before silk prices could be quoted

with some certainty. "In fact, the indecision which still exists in

commercial transactions," reported the police observer in March 1868,

"hurts the pursuit of large affairs; manufacture takes place only step

by step, and a large number of fabricants wait as much as eight days

between the receipt of a completed piece and the putting-out of a new

one."[45] Even such small delays could be disastrous for a weaver of

'common' unis forced to live on a daily wage of 1.25 to 1.75 francs.

The combined effect of cyclical unemployment, low wages and wastes and

delays caused by bad thread produced genuine destitution for the largest

number of such weavers. "To this unemployment," reported the police

observer during the crisis of 1867, " ... has been added the bad

quality of silks to be woven, so that the loss of time experienced by

the worker reduces his day to such a minimal wage that it is no longer

possible for him to provide for his needs."[46]

----

[44]'Etoffes unies,' "Situation industrielle au Juin 1868," AML,
I2-47(A), No. 204.

[45]'Etoffes unies,' "Situation industrielle au Mars 1868," AML,
I2-47(A), No. 201.

[46]'Etoffes unies,' "Situation de l'Industrie à Lyon au 15 Mars
1867," AML, I2-47(A), No. 196.

Fancy velvets and plain velvets displayed the same comparative
tendencies as étoffes façonnées and étoffes unies, with differences
between them even more exaggerated in some respects. The major
difference was the more regular employment of weavers of plain velvets,
but at a very low wage, because of rural competition, and the severe
and frequent unemployment of the very highly-paid fancy-velvet weavers,
because of the preference of fashion for cheap unis over rich brocades.
The wages of plain velvet weavers had been traditionally the lowest in
the fabrique, because of the relatively unskilled quality of the work
and the consequent availability of cheap rural labor. In 1859, a year
of good wages, velvet weavers in Lyons received at best only 1.75 to
2.00 francs per day for their work, as compared to 2.00 francs to 2.50
francs for weavers of étoffes unies during their worst trimester of
that year. Such wages did not decline much below this 1859 'subsistence'
level for velvet weavers during the 1860's. The lowest wage was 1.25
francs in the first trimester of 1862, and this was exceptional.[47] But
plain-velvet wages did not rise much either, or rather rose only
exceptionally and very briefly, despite the strong demand for this velvet
fabric. The availability of rural labor explained largely the persistence
of low wages at a time of favorable demand. Assimilation of urban
and rural labor for weaving velvets was achieved more easily than for
weaving étoffes unies. Because of this assimilation, differences
between city and country in experiencing cycles of employment were much
weaker throughout most of the decade than in the regular plain-silks

---

[47]'Velours unis,' "Situation industrielle," 1859 - 1870, AML,
I2-47(A), Nos. 166-213.

category. In December 1866, the recovery from a mild recession of the previous trimester was felt equally in both sectors. The "movement which occurred in the city in the manufacture of velvets has extended to the surrounding areas as well," declared the police observer of the fabrique.[48] Both areas also experienced together the more severe unemployment which began to set in in late 1867. "The slowdown of work which has been noted in this category towards the end of the last semester," wrote the observer in September 1867, "has increased during this one, as much in the city as in the country."[49] Even though the same police agent remarked earlier, in June 1866, that outside Lyons "work is more regular, more abundant and the looms are almost all occupied," the difference between these 'normal' conditions of the rural areas and the worst conditions of the urban fabrique of velvets was small. "Its situation [in Lyons]," reported the observer, "had changed little in several years now and never can one count more than a third of the looms in a state of inactivity."[50]

The relative homogeneity of the plain velvets category facilitated this assimilation of urban and rural labor markets. The category had few 'rich' specialties insulated from the rural market by special skills or need for surveillance. As a result of this homogeneity, velvet weaving migrated to the countryside more rapidly and in larger

[48]'Velours unis,' "Situation de l'industrie à Lyon au 15 Décembre 1866," AML, I2-47(A), No. 193.

[49]'Velours unis,' "Situation industrielle au 15 7bre 1867," (September 15, 1867), AML, I2-47(A), No. 198.

[50]'Velours unis,' "15 Juin 1866," AML, I2-47(A), No. 187.

proportions than weaving of _étoffes_ _unies_. This migration left few
weavers in Lyons to assert an urban autonomy in methods and cycles of
production. "There exist very few looms in Lyons," declared the police
observer in June 1859. "The manufacture of plain velvets tends every
day to move into the countryside."[51] The small number of weavers of
better plain velvets -- those who earned wages of 3.00 or 3.50 francs
in 1866 and 1867[52] -- were therefore more vulnerable than the weavers
of the 'rich' _étoffes_ _unies_ to elimination in unfavorable periods. In
1868, for example, these weavers could not resist with their skills
alone the total migration of plain velvet weaving to the countryside,
when demand for better styles in most categories plummeted. Nor could
they resist the subsequent reduction of all wages in the category to
the lowest rural levels. In the last months of 1868, _fabricants_ of
plain velvets launched an unconcealed campaign against urban weaving.
The police observer explained the campaign as a program for the final
equalization of urban and rural labor markets:

> The bad situation of this article on the site of Lyons
> is due in large part to the assimilation made by the
> négociant of the wages of the countryside to those of
> the city. The expense which burdens the worker living
> in Lyons does not permit him to work at the same rate as
> the worker of the country and forces him little by little
> to abandon an industry whose return is inadequate to
> provide for his needs and for those of his family.
>
> By acting in this manner, the négociants will
> succeed, as they wish, to transport the manufacture
> of velvets entirely outside of the cities.[53]

---

[51]'Velours unis,' "Situation industrielle au 15 Juin 1859," AML,
I2-47(A), No. 166.

[52]'Velours unis,' "Situation industrielle," 1866, 1867, AML,
I2-47(A), Nos. 186-187, 192-193, 196-198, 200.

[53]'Velours unis,' "Situation industrielle au 12 Xbre 1868,"
(December 12, 1868), AML, I2-47(A), No. 206.

For the first time in the decade, at least, urban velvet weavers were
forced into widespread unemployment, while the looms of the countryside continued to work at full capacity. "The unemployment which is
being felt in the city, does not weigh on the large number of looms
dispersed in the surrounding areas of Lyons, where the work is said to
be abundant and regular." It "is probable," wrote the same observer,
"that, in a few years, this article will be manufactured only in the
countryside."[54] The urban weavers did not allow this to happen, however, at least not this soon. They mobilized resistance to the forced
reduction of wages, organized rural weavers around their program and,
favored by an upswing in demand for silk goods, managed to impose a
wage increase on the fabricants towards the end of 1869. Their new
Corporation des tisseurs de velours unis, ville et campagne maintained
the increase for four years.

Weavers of fancy velvets were insulated by their skills and by
the luxury of their cloth, requiring close watch during weaving, from
the competition of rural labor. But their category was more acutely
susceptible to long periods of unemployment which fashion and political
events, such as the American Civil War, imposed on most 'rich' cloths.
The story of fancy velvet weaving during the 1860's was in fact similar
to that of the étoffes façonnées. Beginning in 1861, a decade of
secular unemployment set in for the 'rich' fancies for clothing. Only
a few brief spells of relief, in June 1864 and June 1865, for example,
interrupted this unemployment. As in the case of the étoffes façonnées

[54]'Velours unis,' "Situation industrielle au Mars 1869," AML,
I2-47(A), No. 207.

for dress fabric, fashion turned its attention to cheaper, less
elegant cloths. "The fashion of velvet clothing has been de-throned
by that of clothing of fantaisie, which has in its favor the advantage
of cheapness."[55] To resist the decline of the 'rich' cloths, fabricants
of fancy velvets began in 1865 to put out orders for velours nouveautés.
Though less finished than the dress velvets, such nouveautés favored a
much wider variation of style to attract the novelty-seeking buyer and
was less expensive besides. But as in the case of the fancies ornament
and hautes nouveautés, such variety required more frequent changes of
design on the loom, retarding the weaver's work and diminishing his
return. This problem was especially serious between 1865 and 1867, when
fabricants tried promoting their new product with sample displays.
"Half of the looms are still inactive," reported the police agent in
September 1866, "and those which are operating are employed in the manufacture of samples, work which gives the worker almost no return, because of the many changes [of design] made in the loom."[56] Because of
such changes of design, the higher wage received by the fancy-velvet
weavers, as compared with other categories, often did not compensate for
the loss of work. Consequently, the overall situation of many of these
skilled workers differed little from that of weavers of lower-paid plain
cloths. "Nothing has changed in the wages of the worker who, although
relatively better compensated, is constantly drawn back to the same

[55]'Velours façonnés,' "Situation industrielle - 15 Mars 1866 - ...,"
AML, I2-47(A), No. 186.

[56]'Velours façonnés,' "Situation de l'industrie au 15 7bre 1866,"
(September 15, 1866), AML, I2-47(A), No. 192.

situation as the worker of other categories by unemployment and by the
loss of time occasioned by the changes of looms."[57]

Even though interrupted by frequent delays, the weaving of
velours nouveautés proved a more enduring source of employment than the
fancy dress velvets. Towards the end of the decade, the comparative
situation of the superior 'rich' cloths and the inferior 'common' cloths
(nouveauté) in the fancy velvet category was similar to that of grands
façonnés and petits façonnés. In good months, such as June-September
1868 and April 1869 - March 1870, the "rich article continued to
suffer ... but the article nouveauté provided rather abundant and
regular work."[58] And in less favorable months, such as September 1868 -
March 1869,[59] the 'typical' state of affairs was very much like that
described for the first trimester of 1869:

> The manufacture of rich fancy velvets which, during the
> last trimester, was in an unsatisfactory condition, has
> remained since then in a completely stagnant state.
>
> The ordinary nouveauté article still occupies some
> looms, but the worker faces many interruptions of work
> as a result of the difficulty he encounters in the
> renewing of orders on the part of the merchant.[60]

---

[57] 'Velours façonnés,' "Situation industrielle - 15 Mars 1866 - ...,"
AML, I2-47(A), No. 186.

[58] 'Velours façonnés,' "Situation industrielle," June, September 12,
1868; March, June 15, September 14, December 1869; March 15, 1870, AML,
I2-47(A), Nos. 204, 205 bis, 207-208, 211-213. Citation taken from
'Velours façonnés,' "Situation industrielle au 12 September 1868," AML,
I2-47(A), No. 205 bis.

[59] 'Velours façonnés,' "Situation industrielle au Mars 1869," AML,
I2-47(A), No. 207.

[60] Ibid.

Weavers of shawls and church fabrics -- among the most elegant,
skillfully wrought products of the fabrique lyonnaise -- fared at
least as well as the weavers of étoffes façonnées and velours façonnés,
though frequently better because of the special kinds of markets for
their products. Although they experienced frequent periods of unemployment throughout the decade, such was not abnormal for shawls and church
cloths. Seasonal changes were traditionally stronger for them than
for most other types of silks. Favorable seasonal factors sometimes
perked up an otherwise faltering demand and obscured, for a few months
at least, the underlying reality of stagnation. Church cloth weaving
revived during the Easter and Christmas seasons, for example, and during
the season of the Fête-Dieu, between 1865 and 1868, even though the
"real situation of this category did not remain any less unfavorable
than before" the seasons of religious celebration.[61] Moreover, neither
church cloths nor shawls depended as strongly on the American market
as the étoffes façonnées. Consequently, they did not suffer long
secular decline like the latter. During the first half of the year
1866, orders for church ornaments from Mexico and the United States
supplemented the seasonal demands "occasioned by the solemnities of the
Fête-Dieu," to provide "a certain animation," even "a light improvement
in the activity of labor...."[62] Wages in both categories also remained
high throughout most of the decade. Even during the worst periods of
unemployment, the conditions of shawl and church-cloth weavers were

[61]'Ornements d'église,' "Situation industrielle au 12 Septembre
1868," AML, I2-47(A), No. 205bis.

[62]'Ornements d'église,'"Situation industrielle - 15 Mars 1866 -
Soieries et industries qui s'y rattachent," AML, I2-47(A), No. 186.

usually considered better than those of weavers of other categories
of silk cloth.

Yet some aspects of the specialized markets of these highly-
skilled weavers made them susceptible to especially severe unemployment.
"[R]elations interrupted for a long time with Mexico, Italy and Spain,"[63]
one result of Napoleon III's controversial diplomacy during the late
Second Empire, caused the worst crisis of church-cloth weavers in the
decade. This crisis extended the "dead season" of 1866 first into "an
absolute lack of orders, at a time when one observes every year, on the
contrary, a recovery of work,"[64] and then into unemployment of two-
thirds of the workers in 1867.[65] Revolution in Italy and war in Germany
in 1866 and 1867 immobilized one-half to two-thirds of the shawl looms
because of a sudden fall in orders from these two major foreign buyers.[66]
The highly-skilled shawl and church-cloth weavers did not escape, moreover, the influence of changes in fashion in favor of inferior cloths.
Such influence was especially strong in the shawls category towards the
end of the decade. In the first trimester of 1869, the police observed
a tendency to substitute a lighter, inferior-quality shawl, cheaper to
manufacture, for the high-quality shawl for which Lyons had been

---

[63]'Ornements d'église,' "Situation industrielle au 15 7bre 1867,"
(September 15, 1867), AML, I2-47(A), No. 198.

[64]'Ornements d'église,' "Situation de l'industrie à Lyon au 15
Decembre 1866," AML, I2-47(A), No. 193.

[65]'Ornements d'église,' "Situation industrielle au 15 7bre 1867."

[66]'Châles au 1/4,' "Situation de l'industrie au 15 7bre 1866,"
(September 15, 1866); 'Châles au 1/4,' "Situation industrielle au
Juin 1867," AML, I2-47(A), Nos. 192, 197.

traditionally renowned. "Except for one or two houses which are
determined to keep their specialty, the others, being little concerned
about the reputation which Lyons had acquired, have for some time put
out an excessively light article which earns them a premium of 10, 15 and
up to 20 centimes on the price of labor."[67] This tendency was in fact a
reaction to the steadily growing competition of Paris and the Nord in
the production of shawls, which was first noted at the end of 1865.[68]
This competition was so severe in 1868 that shawl weavers began leaving
Lyons for the weaving centers of northern France.[69] This migration left
the impression that the specialty tended "each day to disappear from
Lyons."[70]

As a result of these changes, the same differences in conditions
of employment between weavers of 'rich' shawls and weavers of 'common'
shawls characterized this category as other fancy-cloth categories.
In 1866, the only difference between "the rich article" and "the common
article" was the wage offered for weaving each. By June 1868, however,
some fabricants had reduced the wages of 'rich' shawl weavers to the
levels of 'common' shawl weavers in order to resist competition from
the north.[71] One year later, the major difference between the two

[67]'Châle au 1/4,' "Situation industrielle au Mars 1869," AML,
I2-47(A), No. 207.

[68]'Châle au 1/4,' "Situation industrielle," December 15, 1865;
March 15, 1866; December 1867, AML, I2-47(A), Nos. 185, 186, 200.

[69]'Châle au 1/4,' "Situation industrielle au 12 Xbre 1868,"
(December 12, 1868), AML, I2-47(A), No. 206.

[70]'Châle au 1/4,' "Situation industrielle au Mars 1869," AML,
I2-47(A), No. 207.

[71]'Châle au 1/4,' "Situation industrielle au Juin 1868," AML,
I2-47(A), No. 204.

shawl specialties was that familiar to the categories of étoffes

façonnées and velours façonnés: "The manufacture of the rich shawls

[was] in a state of inactivity and there [were] only the light articles,

less favorable to the workers, which [occupied] the largest number of

looms."[72] The same difference marked the two specialties in the

church-cloths category. In December 1867 the police observer reported

that "repairs and the manufacture of common cloths alone provide a bit

of work to the ordinary worker, but those who work only on the production

of rich cloths, and especially the embroiderers, have been unemployed

for a long time."[73] Apparently it took an exceptional ecclesiastical

event -- the convocation of the First Vatican Council -- combined with

Christmas celebrations in the year 1868 to revive work for weavers of

'rich' and 'ordinary' vestments alike.[74] Such sporadic factors in the

demand of this category softened the experience of crisis among its

weavers, and shielded them from full exposure to the market forces

which forced down wages and levels of employment without respite for

their fellow craftsmen in other categories of the silk industry of

Lyons.

The crisis of the 1860's thus separated not only the conditions

of the 'plains' categories from that of the 'fancies' categories but

also the conditions of 'common' and 'rich' specialties within each

---

[72]'Châle au 1/4,' "Situation industrielle au 15 Juin 1869," AML,
I2-47(A), No. 208.

[73]'Ornements d'église,' "Situation industrielle au Xbre 1867"
(December 1867), AML, I2-47(A), No. 200.

[74]'Ornements d'église,' "Situation industrielle au 12 Xbre
1868," (December 12, 1868), AML, I2-47(A), No. 206.

category, especially during the second half of the decade. The
criteria of separation were primarily the level and stability of
employment. These were high in the 'plains' categories and in the
'common' specialties, and low in the 'fancies' categories and in the
'rich' specialties. At the same time, however, the economic situation
of weavers in the various categories and specialties, as measured by
their annual earnings, became more alike. Because of their differences
in employment, weavers of fancy cloths and 'rich' specialties received
little more income, and sometimes less, than weavers of plain cloths
and 'common' specialties. In other words, as economic conditions
dissociated the traditionally similar employment experiences of weavers
in the different categories and specialties, these conditions also
equalized their traditionally different economic situations. The same
process that destroyed one of the economic foundations of traditional
'vertical' solidarity of craft, based on a hierarchy of economic
situations, thus created the foundations for a new kind of 'vertical'
solidarity, based on equality of situation.

B. Movements and Levels of Wages

    As for wages, the impact of the crisis of the 1860's was less
apparent. Observers commented generally that weavers of plain cloths
received very low wages, and weavers of fancies, shawls and church
cloths received much higher wages which did not, however, always
compensate for their loss of employment. The structure of wages in fact
changed more than such general comments suggested. As described
earlier, relative movements and levels of wages 'responded' more to
quantitative differences within the cloth categories than to
qualitative differences between them, associated with different cloth

types, weaving techniques and weaving skills. In other words,
differences between 'specialties,' indicating maximum and minimum wages
for each cloth category, rather than differences between the categories
themselves, determined relations among movements and levels of wages.
This change occurred generally after 1865 and affected some cloth
categories more than others. This effect was experienced as more or
less intensive dissociation of minimum from maximum specialties within
each category and as a corresponding merging of specialties in different
cloth categories according to the similar quantitative criterion
(maximum wage versus minimum wage). In this way, the changes in wage
movements and levels, just like the changes in conditions of employment,
both destroyed an economic foundation of traditional 'vertical' craft
solidarity and created an economic basis for a new 'vertical' solidarity.

Such changes in relative wage movements and levels are revealed by
a systematic analysis of the same data from which the observation of
contemporaries concerning conditions of employment were made. These
data consist of readings of end-of-trimester minimum and maximum wages
for each of six 'categories' of silk cloth: _étoffes unies_, _étoffes
façonnées_, _velours unis_, _velours façonnés_, _châles_, and _ornements d'église_.
The reading covers a twenty-nine trimester period beginning in April
1859 and ending in March 1870. Twelve of these are trimesters between
1859 and 1863 and seventeen between 1865 and 1870.[75]

---

[75]Trimesters ending June, October 1859; June, September, December
1860; March, June, September 1861; March, September, December 1862;
December 1863; June, September 1865; September, December 1866;
March, June, September, December 1867; March, June, September, December
1868; March, June, September, December 1869; March 1870. Source: AML,
I2-47(A), Nos. 166-213.

The wages represent average daily earnings of journeymen weavers gathered by agents of the local police who observed and reported in detail the conditions of the industry during each trimester. Too much credence must not be given, of course, to the absolute levels of these wages, because of large variations in piece-rates according to particular circumstances and products. Differences between category and specialty values, as well as differences between maximum and minimum values, however, reasonably indicate the prevailing situation with some accuracy, since such differences were a major concern of the trimestrial reports and were reported systematically. Such reporting, moreover, was conscientious and reliable. Few claims were made on the basis of mere speculation or hypothesis. In September 1869, for example, the police observer frankly admitted his inability to make precise determination of the wage of church-cloth weavers, rather than offering a mere guess. "The piece-rate is always the same," he reported; "but the numerous periods of unemployment which the worker experiences do not permit establishing in a precise manner the average of his wage."[76] In a few cases, I have estimated such gaps in the reports to provide a complete series for calculating correlations between wage groups of similar size, basing such estimates on prior and succeeding wage levels. Appendix IV discusses in greater detail the reliability and utility of these police reports for analyzing wage movements and levels.

Two aspects of wage structure are especially interesting for the study of relative changes in the twelve separate wage groups (six

---

[76]'Ornements d'église,' "Situation industrielle au 14 Septembre 1869," AML, I2-47(A), No. 211.

'categories', two 'specialties' -- 'rich' (maximum wage) and 'common'

(minimum wage)--per category). These are the levels of wages and the

movements of wages, or correlated changes in wage levels, among these

twelve groups. Levels and movements are analyzed here successively

for four sub-sets of these twelve groups -- the 'range' set, the

'category' set, the 'specialty' set, and the 'summary category' set of

wages. The 'range' set consists of three wage series -- averages of

all wages (of all twelve groups), labelled AVWG; averages of all

minimum wages (of six minimum-wage groups), labelled AVNWG; and

averages of all maximum wages (of six maximum-wage groups), labelled

AVXWG. The 'category' set consists of six wage series, each representing

averages of minimum and maximum wages for each cloth category --

étoffes unies (plain cloths) EU; velours unis (plain velvets) VU:

étoffes façonnées (fancy cloths) EF: velours façonnés (fancy velvets) VF;

châles (shawls) C; and ornements d'église (church cloths) OE. The

'specialty' set consists of twelve series, each representing one of the

original twelve wage groups, and the 'summary category' set (to be

explained later in more detail) averages plains categories (EU, VU)

and fancies categories (EF, VF, C, OE). In the nomenclature for each

group, N is the symbol for the minimum wage series of each cloth

category, and X is the symbol for the maximum wage series, so that EUN,

for example, represents the minimum wage series for étoffes unies and

EUX the maximum wage series for the same category. Table 14

summarizes these four groups of wage series. Changes in patterns

of related levels and movements of wages will be investigated within

each of these four sets of wage series over the decade beginning June

1859 and ending March 1870. In particular, changes will be examined

TABLE 14

Summary of Wage Series

'Category' Set (Cg)		'Specialty' Set (S)		'Summary Category' Set (SCg)		
		Max (-X) 'Rich'	Min (-N) 'Common'			
Name	Symbol			General	Max (-X)	Min (-N)
Plains (U)						
Etoffes unies	EU	EUX	EUN	AVU	AVUX	AVUN
Velours unis	VU	VUX	VUN			
Etoffes façonnées	EF	EFX	EFN	AVF	AVFX	AVFN
Velours façonnés	VF	VFX	VFN			
Fancies (F)						
Châles	C	CX	CN			
Ornements d'église	OE	OEX	OEN			
'Range' Set (R) →	AVWG	AVXWG	AVNWG			

Formulas

$$\text{'Range' (R)} = \{ \Sigma Cg/6,\ \Sigma S_X/6,\ \Sigma S_N/6 \}$$

$$\text{'Category' (Cg)} = \{ (EUX + EUN)/2, \ldots, (OEX + OEN)/2 \}$$

$$\text{'Specialty' (S)} = \{ EUX, \ldots, OEX, EUN, \ldots, OEN \}$$

$$\text{'Summary Category' (SCg)} = \begin{cases} \text{General} = \{ \Sigma U/2,\ \Sigma F/4 \} \\ \text{Max} = \{ \Sigma U_X/2,\ \Sigma F_X/4 \} \\ \text{Min} = \{ \Sigma U_N/2,\ \Sigma F_N/4 \} \end{cases}$$

between the two periods October 1859 - December 1863 and June 1865 -
September 1869.[77]

Relative wage movements will be studied first, by using correlation
analysis to identify wage groups whose serial movements were closely
related or relations among which changed most strongly from one period
to the next. In other words, those cloth categories, and those range
groups within such categories, will be sought in which wages rose and
fell from one observed trimester to the next, together in the same
direction (positive correlation), together in opposite direction
(negative correlation), or 'irregularly,' that is, with no association
between wage movements (zero or low correlation). By comparing such
levels and directions of association for the two 'halves' of the decade
(1859-63, 1865-69), some of the most prominent changes in the 'structure'
of wage movements during the decade will be identified.

Graph 6 plots the 'range' set of wage series for the entire
period for which data are available -- overall average wages AVWG,
average minimum wages AVNWG, and average maximum wages AVXWG. The
graph demonstrates the remarkable ability of the maximum wage groups
to maintain high and occasionally increasing wage levels over most of
the period, in spite of the relatively high incidence of unemployment

---

[77]Averages for June 1859 and for December 1869 are separated from
their respective year groups because of their exceptional character.
The first period (June 1859) antedated the crisis under examination and
therefore represented a pre-crisis situation. The second period
(December 1869) witnessed the beginning of the weavers' resistance
movement and the successful negotiation of wages in several cloth
categories to pre-crisis levels. This resistance movement, and
associated wage increases, continued through March 1870. The wage
data for December 1869 and March 1870 are therefore averaged together
as a single period group, representing, again, generally higher wage
levels than those prevailing in the crisis of the 1860's.

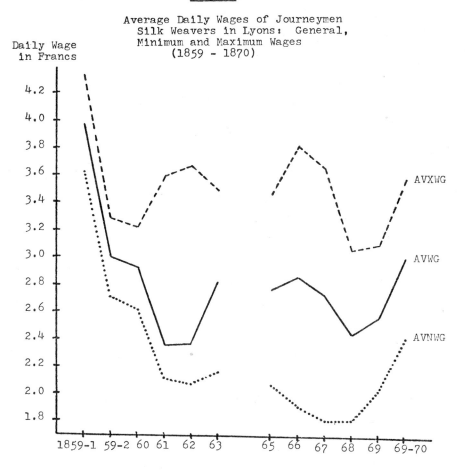

Graph 6:

Average Daily Wages of Journeymen
Silk Weavers in Lyons: General,
Minimum and Maximum Wages
(1859 - 1870)

Daily Wage
in Francs

——————— : AVWG - Average Wages

••••••••••• : AVNWG - Average Minimum Wages

—— —— —— : AVXWG - Average Maximum Wages

for the high-wage categories and specialties. The major exceptions
occurred in late 1859-1860 and in 1868. In the first case, the Italian
crisis affected demand for shawls, the American Civil War suddenly
destroyed the market for fancy cloths, and a decline of the market for
silks in general suddenly reduced the demand for skilled labor. In
the second case, orders for the quality fabrics exhibited in Paris in
1867 had terminated and with these the demand for labor to weave
samples. In both cases, piece-rates probably declined as a result of
falling labor demand. The minimum wage groups, on the other hand, were
unable to resist more general movements towards a fall in wages. They
were also incapable of benefiting very much from tendencies to raise
wages before 1869. So severe and persistent was the wage decline in
the minimum wage groups that these depressed the overall average to a
declining or only mildly rising position in years of marked rise in
maximum wage groups, such as 1861, 1862 and 1866.

Even more important, the movement in minimum wage levels became
increasingly independent of that of maximum wage levels and, to a lesser
extent, of the overall average levels, in the second half of the decade,
as compared with the first. This is evident from a comparison of the
correlation coefficients of the three average-wage series for the
period October 1859 to December 1863 (eleven trimestrial observations)
with the coefficients for the period June 1865 to September 1869
(fifteen trimestrial observations). Table 15 summarizes the coefficients
for these two periods:

Table 15

Zero-Order Correlation Coefficients
for 'Range' Set of Wage Series
(October 1859 - December 1863;
June 1865 - September 1869)

Correlated Pair	1859-63 (NC=11)		1865-69 (NC=15)	
	r	s	r	s
AVWG - AVNWG	.94	.001	.35	.208
AVWG - AVXWG	.96	.001	.92	.001
AVNWG - AVXWG	.79	.004	-.05	.851

r: Correlation coefficient

s: Two-tailed t-test of significance (Ho: $u_1=u_2$; H_1: $u_1 \neq u_2$). The higher the level of significance s, the less likely the means of the two series will be different; hence the less 'strength' there is to reject H_o. In other words, the higher the level of significance, the less likely one wage series is able to 'predict' the other wage series, hence the less correlated are the two series. The number of 'cases' (trimesters) upon which r and s are based is indicated by the abbreviation NC.

The very high correlation among wage movements of all three series in 1859-63 remained high in 1865-69 only for the overall series as compared with the maximum wage series (AVWG-AVXWG). The relationship between the movements of the overall series and the minimum and maximum wage series became much weaker in the later period, however. The relation between the maximum and minimum wage series (AVNWG-AVXWG) became clearly insignificant in this same period. Minimum wages for weaving silk cloths thus seem to have obeyed a different 'law' than maximum wages after 1865, whereas before that time they followed a trend not very different from maximum wages.

This result becomes more evident and significant when wage movements of cloth categories are compared with minimum and maximum wages as a whole. For the sake of simplicity, Table 16 analyzes the 'range' series of wages (AVNWG, AVXWG) correlated with only two silk-cloth category series, called 'summary category' series -- a plains category series (AVU) and a fancies category series (AVF). The plains series is the average of the series for étoffes unies (EU) and velours unis (VU), the fancies series the average of series for étoffes façonnées (EF), velours façonnés (VF), châles (C) and ornements d'église (OE). The average minimum wage series of the summary categories are labelled AVUN, AVFN ; the average maximum wage series of the summary categories are labelled AVUX, AVFX. (See Table 14 for summary description of these wage series.) Graph 7 shows that average plains wages (AVU) were lower than average wages in general (AVWG), and that average fancies wages (AVF) were higher than average wages (AVWG), throughout the decade. Yet, as 1-a of Table 16 demonstrates, wage movements of the two summary categories AVU and AVF did not dissociate after 1865 as did wage movements of the minimum series AVNWG as against the maximum series AVXWG. In fact, ties between AVU and AVF strengthened somewhat in 1865-69, as the increase in r and the decrease in s suggest. Correlations 2-a and 3-a show that this strengthening was largely the effect of a stronger association between the maximum wage sub-series of the two summary categories, AVUX-AVFX, after 1865, and a relatively unchanged, solid association between the minimum wage sub-series AVUN-AVFN.

Correlations 1-b show that ties between the low-wage AVU series and the minimum wage series AVNWG, and ties between the high-wage AVF series and the maximum wage series AVXWG, both weakened after 1865.

Table 16

Zero-Order Correlation Coefficients for 'Summary Category' Set of Wage Series as Compared with 'Range' Set of Wage Series. (October, 1859 - December, 1863;   June, 1865 - September, 1869)

	Correlated Pair	1859-63 (NC =11)		1865-69 (NC=15)	
		r	s	r	s
1- a)	AVU - AVF	.53	.094	.62	.013
b)	AVU - AVNWG	.66	.026	-.12	.673
	- AVXWG	.69	.018	.96	.001
	AVF - AVNWG	.91	.001	.60	.018
	- AVXWG	.93	.001	.74	.001
2- a)	AVUN- AVFN	.61	.045	.59	.020
b)	AVUN- AVNWG	.77	.005	.79	.001
	- AVXWG	.61	.046	-.34	.213
	AVFN- AVNWG	.97	.001	.96	.001
	- AVXWG	.77	.005	.08	.783
3- a)	AVUX- AVFX	.51	.106	.78	.001
b)	AVUX- AVNWG	.51	.107	-.31	.258
	- AVXWG	.70	.016	.94	.001
	AVFX- AVNWG	.79	.001	.21	.447
	- AVXWG	.97	.001	.94	.001

DF = Degrees of Freedom

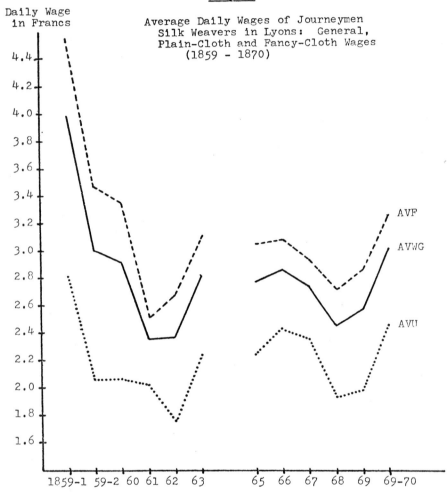

Graph 7:

Average Daily Wages of Journeymen
Silk Weavers in Lyons: General,
Plain-Cloth and Fancy-Cloth Wages
(1859 - 1870)

Daily Wage
in Francs

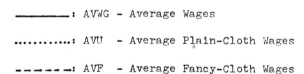

_____ : AVWG - Average Wages

.... : AVU - Average Plain-Cloth Wages

— — — — — : AVF - Average Fancy-Cloth Wages

This result, along with the strong correlation between minimum wage
series AVUN - AVFN and between maximum wage series AVUX - AVFX, suggests
that movements of wages were tightening up more strongly by range than
by category after 1865. Minimum wages of either summary category,
plains or fancies, moved in stronger association with minimum wages of
the other summary category, and of minimum wages in general, and
maximum wages of either did the same with maximum wages of the other
category, and of maximum wages in general. Minimum wages, irrespective
of category, meanwhile moved more independently of maximum wages.
Correlations 2-b and 3-b demonstrate this for each combination of
range and summary category series (AVUN, AVFN, AVUX, AVFX) with the two
range series in general (AVNWG, AVXWG). In each combination of minimum
category (AVUN, AVFN) with minimum in general (AVNWG), or of maximum
category (AVUX, AVFX) with maximum in general (AVXWG), the strength of
association r increased, or remained high, after 1865. In every
combination of a minimum series with a maximum series, however, the
strength of association decreased significantly. In no case did the
category of silk cloth have any noticeable effect on the strength of
association between wage series.

Movements of wage series after 1865 thus tended to become more
strongly associated, or at least to remain as strongly associated,
within maximum wage series as a whole and within minimum wage series as
a whole, even when such series were differentiated internally according
to their category components. Ties between maximum wage series and
minimum wage series weakened, however, even when these were differentiated
in the same manner. In short, after 1865, the difference between maximum
wages and minimum wages became a more significant indicator of different

markets affecting the movement of wages, than the difference between the
technologically-distinct, traditionally separate cloth categories,
plains and fancies. The change was largely the result of the
assimilation of the wage movements of the best-paid weavers of plain
cloths to the movements of the best-paid weavers in the fabrique as a
whole, and of the assimilation of the wage movements of the least-paid
weavers of fancy cloths to the movements of the least-paid weavers in
the fabrique.

The correlation coefficients between the two 'summary category' wage
series (AVU, AVF) and the two 'range' series (AVNWG, AVXWG), on the one
hand, and the six original 'category' series (EU, VU, EF, VF, C, OE), on
the other hand, confirm this conclusion and locate more precisely the
sources of the observed change. Table 17 summarizes these coefficients
(r) and their associated significance levels (s) for each of the two
periods within the decade, 1859-63 and 1865-69. As the table shows,
ties between each of the two original plains category series EU and VU
and the plains summary series AVU generally strengthened -- as indicated
by the reduction in the values of s -- from a rather strong association
in 1859-63. Ties between each of the original fancies category series
VF, C, and OE, however, weakened after 1865. Thus the internal
coherence of the summary category series -- the strength of association
between each summary category series (AVU, AVF) and its respective
category serial components -- increased after 1865 for the plains AVU
and decreased for the fancies AVF. The only exception to the decrease
of the latter was the association between EF and AVF, which remained
as strong after 1865 as before that date.

While the two original plains category series (EU, VU) correlated

Table 17

Zero-Order Correlation Coefficients for Six-Group 'Category' Set of Wage Series as Compared with 'Summary Category' and Minimum-Maximum 'Range' Series. (October, 1859 – December, 1863; June, 1865 – September, 1869)

Category Symbol	Category Name	Correlated with AVU				Correlated with AVF				Correlated with AVNWG				Correlated with AVXWG			
		1859-63		1865-69		1859-63		1865-69		1859-63		1865-69		1859-63		1865-69	
		r	s	r	s	r	s	r	s	r	s	r	s	r	s	r	s
EU	Plain Cloth	.75	.008	.90	.001	.84	.001	.84	.001	.80	.003	.19	.487	.90	.001	.93	.001
VU	Plain Velvet	.73	.011	.67	.006	.07	.828	.05	.818	.17	.616	.59	.021	.11	.755	.53	.043
EF	Fancy Cloth	.45	.167	.56	.031	.94	.001	.92	.001	.82	.002	.55	.035	.88	.001	.68	.006
VF	Fancy Velvet	.73	.011	.06	.833	.88	.001	.00	.940	.81	.002	.30	.277	.93	.001	.15	.589
C	Shawls	.64	.035	.40	.143	.81	.003	.51	.053	.91	.001	.18	.522	.70	.016	.47	.078
OE	Church Cloth	.14	.683	.20	.477	.87	.001	.43	.108	.68	.020	.53	.043	.78	.008	.18	.531

more strongly with their 'summary category' series (AVU), each of the former correlated less strongly with the minimum-wage 'range' series (AVNWG) after 1865, contrary to our expectations of the behavior of the wages in these relatively low-wage cloth categories. The correlation coefficient r between EU and AVNWG fell from a highly significant .80 in 1859-63 to a very insignificant .19 in 1865-69. The coefficient of correlation between VU and AVNWG changed from a weak positive value before 1865 to a strong negative value after 1865, indicating that the wages for plain-velvet weavers moved inversely to the average of minimum wages paid in all categories, again contrary to our expectations. Correlation between each of the plains categories EU, VU and the maximum-wage range series AVXWG, however, remained strong (for EU-AVXWG) or became stronger (for VU-AVXWG) after 1865. Wages of the traditionally low-paid plains categories thus moved in stronger association with wages of the highest-paid weavers in all categories after 1865. At the same time, wages of the traditionally higher-paid fancy categories (EF, VF, C, OE) moved in weaker association with the maximum-wage series AVXWG after 1865 than before and, more surprising still, less strongly than the plains category EU with AVXWG. These results enable us to identify the statistical source of the substitution of 'range' differences (minimum versus maximum wage series) for 'category' differences (plains versus fancies wage series), observed earlier as the major determinant of correlated wage movements after 1865. This substitution was apparently the result of an inversion of wage behavior on the part of plain-cloth wages and fancy-cloth wages with respect to their levels relative to one another. Lower-level plain-cloth wages moved more closely with maximum wages in the fabrique, and less closely with minimum wages, while high-level fancy cloth wages moved in reverse fashion. The strong coherence of the plains category wages, moreover, intensified statistically the 'perversity' of their movement relative to maximum wages.

Table 18 traces the origins of this substitution even further, namely, in the correlation between the maximum wage series (-X) and the minimum wage series (-N) in each original category of cloth, on the one hand, and the two 'summary category' series (AVU, AVF) and the two 'range' series (AVNWG, AVXWG), on the other hand. As 18-a shows, both the stronger internal coherence of the plains summary category series and the stronger association of plain-cloth wage movements with maximum wage movements in all categories was exclusively the result of high correlations between wages paid to the best-paid weavers of étoffes unies (EUX) and of velours unis (VUX), on the one hand, and AVU and AVXWG, on the other hand. Wages paid to the least-paid weavers in the two first categories (EUN, VUN) correlated less strongly, or negatively, with plains category wages as a whole (AVU) and with maximum wages as a whole (AVXWG), after 1865 as compared to before, and as strongly or more strongly with minimum wages as a whole (AVNWG) in 1865-69. Both étoffes unies and velours unis split apart, in short, between their minimum wage specialties and their maximum wage specialties, each under the domination of a different 'alien' law -- the law of minimum wages in general and of maximum wages in general. Table 19, which pairs EUN-EUX and VUN-VUX directly, shows this split as a radical dissociation of EUN from EUX after 1865 (r falls from .86 to .07) and as a radical negative association, or opposition, between VUN and VUX (r falls from .89 to -.56) in the same period. The maximum-wage 'law' thus cemented the

Table 18

Zero-Order Correlation Coefficients for Twelve-Group 'Specialty' Set of Wage Series as compared with 'Summary Category' and Minimum-Maximum 'Range' Series.
(October, 1859 - December, 1863; June, 1865 - September, 1869)

a)

Category Symbol	Correlated with AVU				Correlated with AVNWG				Correlated with AVXWG			
	1859-63		1865-69		1859-63		1865-69		1859-63		1865-69	
	r	s	r	s	r	s	r	s	r	s	r	s
EUN	.67	.024	.02	.950	.87	.001	.81	.001	.79	.004	0	.998
VUN	.77	.005	.59	.020	.35	.297	.43	.106	.19	.583	.70	.004
FUX	.76	.007	.95	.001	.70	.016	.03	.928	.93	.001	.98	.001
VUX	.68	.031	.74	.001	.01	.981	.63	.012	.02	.943	.65	.009

b)

Category Symbol	Correlated with AVE				Correlated with AVNWG				Correlated with AVXWG			
	1859-63		1865-69		1859-63		1865-69		1859-63		1865-69	
	r	s	r	s	r	s	r	s	r	s	r	s
EFN	.89	.001	.78	.001	.85	.001	.77	.001	.69	.018	.33	.232
CN	.62	.041	.32	.250	.86	.001	.36	.188	.47	.140	.12	.665
OEN	.90	.001	.35	.197	.82	.002	.51	.052	.71	.015	.11	.709
VFN	.90	.001	.09	.747	.93	.001	.59	.021	.85	.001	.46	.087
EFX	.88	.001	.91	.001	.71	.015	.38	.163	.94	.001	.81	.001
CX	.81	.002	.51	.053	.81	.002	.09	.741	.75	.008	.66	.008
OEX	.76	.007	.45	.089	.49	.129	.53	.043	.70	.017	.20	.479
VFX	.80	.003	.06	.843	.67	.024	.65	.009	.42	.001	.42	.119

Table 19

Selected 'Specialty' Cross Relations

(October, 1859 - December, 1863; June, 1865 - September, 1869)

Correlated Pair	1859-63		1865-69	
	r	s	r	s
EUN - EUX	.86	.001	.07	.815
VUN - VUX	.89	.001	.58	.023
EFN - EFX	.77	.006	.76	.001
CN - CX	.65	.009	.29	.295
OEN - OEX	.77	.006	.97	.001
VFN - VFX	.84	.001	.22	.436
EU - VU	.09	.795	.27	.322
EUN - VUN	.17	.618	.38	.157
EUX - VUX	.07	.829	.59	.020
EUN - VUX	.11	.745	.63	.013
VUX - VUN	.18	.604	.70	.004
EU - EF	.83	.002	.79	.001
EUN - EFN	.80	.003	.71	.003
EUX - EFX	.88	.001	.80	.001
EUN - EFX	.71	.015	.40	.137
EUX - EFN	.61	.045	.36	.192

plain-cloth identity of both categories, by strengthening the association of each with AVU, but, in the process, weaned them away from
their traditional deference to low-wage movements in the fabrique to
cleave instead to itself, their new partner, high-wage movements in the
industry. Minimum wage series in both plain-cloth categories meanwhile
lost their 'category' identity but only to remain loyal to the traditional
behavior of plain-cloth wages, following the movements of minimum rather
than maximum wages.

The fancy-cloth categories did not manifest the same internal
dissociation between their maximum and minimum specialties. Such internal splitting was severe only for shawls wages (CN, CX) and for
fancy-velvet wages (VFN, VFX). Even for these, it was not as great as
for the two plain-cloth categories. (See Table 19.) The deterioration
of a fancy-cloth identity through falling correlation with the average
wage series AVF, in those categories where such occurred (C, OE, VF),
was shared by minimum and maximum wage series alike in each of these
categories. (See Table 18-b.) Within each of the two important
fancy categories étoffes façonnées (EF) and ornements d'église (OE),
moreover, the association between minimum-wage series and maximum-wage
series (EFN-EFX, OEN-OEX) remained strong in both periods (1859-63,
1865-69). After 1865 especially, this strong intra-category cohesion
clearly distinguished these two fancies categories from the two plains
categories EU and VU.

Besides causing significant differences in intra-category behavior,
movements of minimum wages versus maximum wages not surprisingly were
the source of maintained or strengthened inter-category associations
of wage movements as well. Such inter-category correlations usually

resided on high correlations between the respective minimum and maximum
series of two different categories. For the sake of brevity, only
two of these inter-category relations pertinent to the subsequent
discussion will be mentioned. These were the associations between
étoffes unies and velours unis (EU-VU), and between étoffes unies and
étoffes façonnées (EU-EF). Table 19 lists all inter-category correlation
coefficients and levels of significance between these two categories,
differentiated by their maximum and minimum specialties as well as
by their category averages. Relationships between EU and VU clearly
strengthened after 1865, although the coefficient of correlation was
not especially high ($\underline{r}$ = .27) even in 1865-69. The tendency to stronger
positive correlation was apparently the result of increased correlation
between both the minimum wage series (EUN-VUN) and the maximum wage
series (EUX-VUX). Clearly, however, the more strongly associated pair
was the latter -- between movements of wages of the best-paid weavers
of EU and the best-paid weavers of VU. Cross relations between
specialties of the two categories (EUN-VUX, EUX-VUN) do not account in
any way for the increasing association between the more general category
series (EU-VU), and in fact negate any movement in that direction, EUN-
VUX and EUX-VUN both becoming more negatively correlated. The same
general pattern characterizes the EU wage series as compared to the EF
wage series. Overall category association (EU-EF) and associations
between minimum specialties (EUN-EFN) and maximum specialties (EUX-EFX)
remained strong and positive, while the relationships between cross-
specialties (EUN-EFX, EUX-EFN) became weaker after 1865. The only
difference between the pair EU-EF and the pair EU-VU was the strong
positive association between EU and EF even before 1865, an association

that remained strong after that date and, we might add, at a much higher
level of correlation than the association between EU and VU after 1865.
In both cases, nevertheless, the source of increasing or maintained
positive association was the same law of minimum and maximum-wage series.
This 'law' cemented together wage movements in the two different
categories on the basis of their minimum-wage specialties, on the one
hand, and their maximum-wage specialties, on the other hand. This self-
same 'law', one might note again in passing, also split apart the EU and
VU categories internally, between their minimum-wage poles and their
maximum-wage poles, whereas the cohesion of the two poles within the EF
category was not weakened by the reign of this law. Such a difference
suggests that the underlying change in relative wage movements was the
radical dissociation of the movements of the lowest wages in the lowest-
paid categories, EU and VU, from the movements of wages in general,
leaving the highest wages in EU and VU to re-define their category as
more 'deferential' to movements of maximum wages, but leaving the
relatively high-wage category EF intact and behaving 'as expected.'
Graphs 6, 7, and 8 do indeed give the impression that the fall of
minimum wages, especially in the EU category, was the major change in
wage movements after 1865.

Such a change was consistent with the indications of the police
observers from which this wage data was collected. According to these
reports, the most striking characteristic of wages during the decade
was their extremely low level for weavers of plain cloths, at least in
comparison with the recent past. This low level was primarily the
result of a decline in piece-rates paid to weavers of plain cloths.
The decline of unis piece-rates and the persistence of low piece-rates

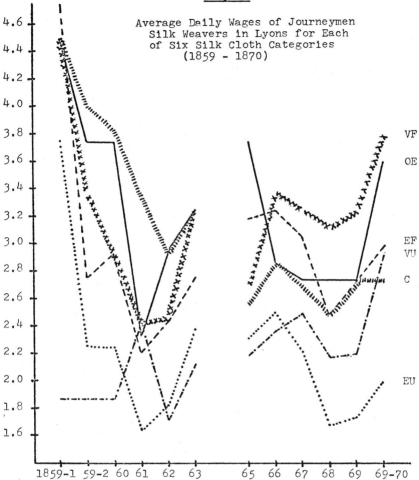

Graph 8:

Average Daily Wages of Journeymen
Silk Weavers in Lyons for Each
of Six Silk Cloth Categories
(1859 - 1870)

```
........ : EU - Etoffes Unies (Plain Cloths)
- - - - : EF - Etoffes Façonnées (Fancy Cloths)
-.-.-. : VU - Velours Unis (Plain Velvets)
xxxxx : VF - Velours Façonnés (Fancy Velvets)
//////// : C  - Châles (Shawls)
———— : OE - Ornements d'Eglise (Church Fabrics)
```

even in periods of high de' nd was the result of a premium placed by
the market on low-cost pr .ion. at a time of rising or uncertain
prices for raw silk, and the increasing competition of rural labor for
weaving the plain cloth. The first factor, deriving from the demand
for the final product, also influenced the demand for the least-paid
fancy cloth weavers (especially weavers of 'common' étoffes façonnées)
and presumably also the piece-rates paid to them. The same market
which preferred low-cost, easily-varied étoffes unies sought out petits
façonnés, as cheap ornament for unis dresses, to increase their variety
of style. Through this product-market channel affecting levels of
piece-rates,wage movements between plains and fancies categories,
including movements between the lowest wages in each, remained highly
correlated. (See Appendix IV for discussion of the relationship between
'piece-rates' and 'wages'.)

The second factor causing piece-rate declines in the plains
category, the competition of rural labor, was, on the contrary, an
autonomous supply factor (supply of labor) not influencing the piece-
rate for any of the fancy products, not even the lowest paid, because of the
specialized technology, skill and surveillance required for the latter,
possessed almost exclusively by urban weavers. This rural labor factor
thus exerted additional downward pressure on the piece-rates of unis
weavers, especially on the lowest in the category, without affecting
minimum piece-rates in the fancy category. The apparently anomalous
high correlation between EUN and EFN (Table 19) was -- assuming my
interpretation was correct -- partially the effect of the two specialties' sharing in some of the same conditions of demand for labor, through
related demand conditions in their respective product markets, but

partially also the effect of coincidence. The result of such exceptionally strong downward pressure on the piece-rates of weavers of plain
cloths -- especially the least-paid weavers of étoffes unies, who were
most easily replaced by unskilled rural labor -- was the observed
radical dissociation of the minimum wage movements of EU and VU from the
maximum wage movements of the same categories. These maximum wages were
paid, for the most part, to the most skilled weavers in each plain-cloth
category for manufacturing the better-quality unis, and these weavers
were presumably less exposed than the minimum-wage plain cloth weavers
to the competition of rural labor.[78]

The tendency of minimum wage movements to separate from maximum
wage movements after 1865, both in the fabrique as a whole and within
the separate cloth categories, was apparent in the relative levels of
wages and not only in their relative movements from one trimester to
the next. Graph 9 plots relative wage levels on a scale from 0 (lowest
annual wage) to 1 (highest annual wage) for all twelve specialties.
Except for maximum étoffes unies wages (black EU) after 1867, maximum
châles wages (black C) in 1869-70, and maximum velours unis wages
(black VU) in 1865, all maximum wages were higher than all minimum wages
after 1865, regardless of the category for which they were maxima or
minima. Before 1865, on the contrary, minimum wages of some categories
were frequently higher than maximum wages of other categories, or vice-

---

[78]This interpretation would require a certain modification for
comparison of wage movements of plain-cloth categories -- étoffes unies
and velours unis -- with wage movements of fancy-cloth categories
châles, ornements d'église and velours façonnés. Not all of these
were subject to the same product market as the étoffes façonnées and
therefore not to the same conditions of demand for labor determining
(in part) their respective wages.

versa. Thus again, as for wage movements, the more significant
difference in wage levels after 1865 was the 'range' difference --
whether they were maximum wages or minimum wages in their category --
rather than the 'category' difference, the dominant distinguishing
feature before 1865. Within the set of minimum wages or of maximum
wages, however, the cloth category remained generally significant in
determining a 'hierarchy' of wages after 1865 as well. Graphs 8 and 9
demonstrate this most effectively. Weavers of plain cloths of both
categories, étoffes unies and velours unis, received more or less con-
sistently the lowest of the minimum wages, or the lowest of the maximum
wages, for their work; and weavers of the fancy cloths -- étoffes
façonnées, velours façonnés, châles and ornements d'église -- nearly
always received the highest wages within each range set.

The changes of wage movements and levels towards greater uniformity
among the minimum wages and among the maximum wages of all categories
tended to reduce the differences in compensation between plain-cloth
weaving and fancy-cloth weaving in particular. Most of the fancy-cloth
weavers had to weave the lower-paid 'common' fancy specialties throughout
most of the decade, since these were, in general, the only fancy cloths
demanded by the market. Their compensation was therefore not very
different -- or at least not as different as in the past -- from that
of many plain-cloth weavers in the industry. As their average wages
fell to those of these plain-cloth weavers, their claim to superior
status lost its 'objective' economic foundation. Such wage-based status
strengthened, however, among the few, rarely-employed weavers of 'rich'
fancies, whose piece-rates remained high or even increased. But theirs
was not an exclusive claim, for the weavers of 'rich' plain cloths earned

Graph 9:

Average Daily Wages of Journeymen
Silk Weavers in Lyons: Maximum
and Minimum Wages in Each of
Scaled Daily   Six Silk Cloth Categories
Wages   (1859 - 1870)

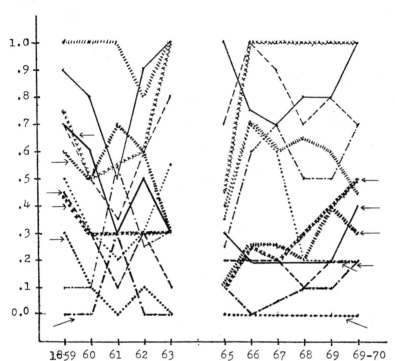

:EU - Etoffes Unies
:EF - Etoffes Façonnées
:VU - Velours Unis
:VF - Velours Façonnés
:C - Châles
:OE - Ornements d'Eglise

Red: Minimum Wages (⟶)
Black: Maximum Wages (Others)

not much less per piece than they, especially as compared with the past.
In short, as wage movements and levels for the two traditionally
different cloth categories, plains and fancies, converged, the
solidarity of plain-cloth weavers and fancy-cloth weavers in a common
craft became one based on similarity rather than on hierarchy of
compensation.

    C. The 'Vertical' Solidarity of Association: Ambivalent Themes
       and Forms

    Such assimilation of wage movements and levels between plains
and fancies weavers, and the equalization of their earnings because of
different conditions of employment, together may explain why both
experienced the crisis of the 1860's as a common trauma, despite their
differing experiences of unemployment and rural competition. The
effects of the crisis were the same, even if the causes were different.
This communuity of experience may explain why the first new movement of
association after 1860, the cooperative movement, was craft-wide rather
than category-specific. The producers' cooperative, the Association of
Weavers, especially avoided internal distinctions of weaving category.
Its purpose was the preservation of the urban craft from extinction,
an extinction threatening all categories alike, or at least so it
seemed, viewing the crisis from its effects rather than from its causes.
In this way, the cooperative movement recognized as its foundation the
newer 'mechanical' form of 'vertical' craft solidarity, built upon
similarity of economic situations.

    Cooperation and, even moreso, industrial resistance, neverthe-
less continued to affirm the 'old' form of 'vertical' solidarity, based

on the traditional hierarchy of economic situations, and the distinctions
among the cloth categories, based on the more recent separation of the
economic conditions of the latter. Such affirmation was not entirely
regressive. As the study of wage movements and levels indicated, the
fancies categories étoffes façonnées and ornements d'église did not lose
their category identity entirely. Wage movements within these categories
were similar and conditions of employment were less different than between plains and fancies. Weavers in these two categories experienced
the cycles of economic change together and in the same way, not in dis-
located fashion, as within the plain velvet and plain silk categories.
The status of the trained fancy-cloth weaver did not fall automatically,
moreover, with the reduction of his wage. The struggle of association
thus easily became a battle for the preservation of threatened status
without losing touch with real economic and social conditions, when undertaken by fancy-cloth weavers or in the name of their traditional
prestige within the craft. Not surprisingly, then, fancy-cloth weavers
were especially prominent in the leadership of the cooperative movement,
in the initiation of the resistance movement and in the major 'class
struggle' undertaken by the weavers' resistance federation in 1870.
Their prominence suggests that they regarded these movements as means
of restoring not only the urban craft as a whole, and thus traditional
'horizontal' solidarity, but also of strengthening their status and
restoring their superior compensation within the craft, reviving the
traditional 'vertical' solidarity as well. In the weavers' own words
(as reported by the police) "[n]othing but the return of the façonné
... would make the Croix-Rousse live as it should ..."[79]

[79]"Rapport à Monsieur Delcourt, Commissaire spécial, sur la situation
de la fabrique des étoffes de soies," March 8, 1868, AML, I2-47(A), No. 310.

Weavers of fancy silks, for example, were very active in the
cooperative movement and dominated its leadership. Of the founders and
first administrators of the consumers' cooperatives living in the Croix-
Rousse in 1866, 58% had more Jacquard looms than plain-cloth looms,
as compared with 34% of an unweighted sample of weavers in the eastern
portion of the same section of the city, where the residences of
cooperative and mutual-aid leaders were concentrated. The organizers
and administrators of the Association of Weavers had the largest
proportion of fancy-loom households -- 76%.[80] Clearly fancy-cloth
weaving was a strong indicator of cooperative leadership, especially of
leadership in the most 'advanced' form of cooperation -- that of
production. Weavers of fancy silks became leaders because they, more
than any other category of weavers in the fabrique, expected from
cooperation the restoration of the dignity of their craft, and of their
own distinction within the craft.

In the resistance movement, fancy-cloth weavers were prominent
both as initiators and as the focus of the longest, most heavily
financed strike. Furniture-cloth weavers, belonging to the category
ornements d'église, negotiated the first increases in piece-rates with
their employers following the economic recovery of 1869. They organized
the first resistance society in August-September of that year, and even
forced some of the recalcitrant fabricants in their category to accept
piece-rate levels agreed upon by their colleagues. The plain-cloth
weavers followed their lead, and their entry into the resistance

[80]George Sheridan, "Idéologies et structures sociales dans les
associations ouvrières à Lyon de 1848 à 1877," Bulletin du Centre
d'Histoire économique et sociale de la Région lyonnaise, 1976, No. 2,
20-25, 42, 45.

struggle made it a mass movement.[81] Once organized into a resistance

federation of several categories in the _fabrique_, the movement supported

two major strikes -- that of the rural weavers of Isère, in March-

April 1870, and that of the fancy-cloth weavers of Lyons, in June-July

1870. The latter was the most prominent, most widely-publicized action

of the federation, lasting nearly two months. In this strike, the

urban plain-cloth weavers of the resistance federation (SCPR) supported

the traditionally 'superior' category of their craft.[82] The strike was

hardly favored by the economic conditions of fancy-cloth weaving, which

remained in the languished state that had afflicted it throughout the

decade. The motivation for the fancy-weavers' defense of their _tarif_

was therefore less the desire for a share in rising prosperity, as it

had been in 1831, than the desire for the restoration of a wage consonant

with their traditional status as skilled weavers. Support for their

demand and for their action by the SCPR as a whole suggested the

recognition of their 'superior' status by plain-cloth weavers as well.

In other words, the strike recognized and affirmed implicitly the

traditional solidarity of craft based on hierarchy of economic situation.

---

[81]"Chronique locale," Le _Progrès_, October 24, 30; November 11, 17, 18; December 2, 1869; police reports concerning meetings of weavers of ornements de meubles, Levants and unis; August 28, 30; September 4, 23; November 8, 1869, AML, I2-47(B).

[82]See police reports to Special Police Commissioner and to Prefect of Rhône concerning strike and lock-out of fancy-cloth weavers, June 13 - August 2, 1870, AML, I2-47(B), Corporations: ouvriers en soie ... (1819 à 1870), Tisseurs façonnés; Ministère du Commerce, de l'Industrie, des Postes et Télégraphes, Office du Travail, Les associations professionnelles ouvrières (Paris: Imprimerie nationale, 1899 - 1904), II, 279-280.

The same recognition and affirmation of hierarchy characterized the
resistance movement as a whole, which sought to restore piece-rates to
the more hierarchical levels of 1859, before the crisis of the 1860's
submerged wage differences among cloth categories into differences
between maximum wages and minimum wages in general.[83]

A similar 'traditionalism' was evident in the emphasis placed
by cooperative and resistance movements on the restoration of quality
in cloth manufacture. Such emphasis was primarily a reaction against
the subordination of qualitative norms to quantitative standards,
rather than against the equalization of economic situations to which
such standards were applied. Equality was accepted as long as it emerged
out of an 'equal' respect for the quality of product for which Lyons
was traditionally renowned. In the cooperative movement, the concern
with quality was evident in the refusal of the Association of Weavers
to load the silk threads put out to its weavers with foreign material
during dyeing. Such loading cheapened the cloth at the expense of its
durability, luster and 'genuineness' as silk fabric. For the tradition-
minded weavers such a practice was harmful to the reputation of their
industry and 'disloyal.' "I am told," wrote the police observer of the
fabrique in June 1867, "that in the name of loyalty and in the interest
of the entire fabrique, should this example be followed, the

---

[83]Even though all negotiated piece-rates did not attain these 1859
levels, some categories managed to restore their minimum wages to levels
appropriate to the quality of the cloth category. The weavers of
ornements d'église, for example, secured raises in minimum wages for
their specialty to a level above the maximum of weavers of étoffes unies,
as one would have expected from the qualitative differences between the
products of the two cloth categories. (See Graph 9, p.351 , especially
wages for '69-'70 on the graph.)

administrators of the Society of Weavers have committed themselves to
not having this silk thread loaded in dyeing."[84] Since loading of silk
thread also made it more susceptible to breakage during weaving -- a
'scourge' most common in the weaving of black étoffes unies -- this
concern with quality defended the 'material' interests of plain-cloth
weavers in the Association while affirming a traditional value dearest
to the weavers of fancy silks who dominated the administration. In
other words, quality of manufacture was a theme that united values and
interests of plains and fancies weavers together and thus appealed at
once to notions of 'vertical' craft solidarity embodying hierarchical
and egalitarian elements. A similar concern for quality of manufacture
joined the aspiration for equality, in this case equality of compensation, in the weavers' resistance movement. By "making all the fabricants
pay the same piece-rate," the weavers hoped that "the buyer [would] thus
be forced to choose only the best-made product."[85]

Whether hierarchical or egalitarian, the craft solidarity presumed and affirmed in these ways at least accepted the notion of the
integral unity of the trade. Whether by clinging to the tradition of
'organic' solidarity or by following the new path to 'mechanical'
solidarity, the silk weavers regarded their economic situation, destiny,
and possibilities of responding to both as collective rather than
individual. Yet, as this chapter has indicated, the economy of the silk

---

[84]"Rapport à Monsieur Delcourt, Commissaire spécial, sur la
situation de la fabrique des étoffes de soie," June 8, 1867, AML, I2-
47(A), Situation de l'industrie: rapports sur la soierie, No. 304.

[85]"Rapport à Monsieur Delcourt, ...," December 7, 1869, AML, I2-
47(A), No. 315.

industry in fact separated the conditions of employment of the
different cloth categories, especially those of fancies from those of
plains; and, as Graph 2 (Chapter II, p.167) suggests, the economy
presaged a different destiny for these two weaving categories. Demand
for plain silk cloths continued to rise, while that for fancy silks
continued to languish, or declined even more. This separation of
conditions especially influenced patterns of collective organization
in the resistance movement. In contrast to its predecessor of the early
1830's, the movement of the late Second Empire emerged out of the
independent resistance and organization of the separate cloth categories
and remained highly de-centralized even after the category societies
united into a single resistance federation. In the late 1820's and
early 1830's the Society of Mutual Duty, the first weavers' resistance
organization, was formed as an association of master-weavers of all
categories of silk cloth and remained a highly centralized association
throughout its most militant period. The resistance movement of 1869 -
1870, by contrast, began with the separate efforts of furniture-cloth
weavers, weavers of Levant cloths and weavers of taffetas (unis) to
negotiate wage increases with fabricants in their specialties and to
organize chambres syndicales to enforce such wage increases as they
were able to attain. In November 1869, the weavers of confection cloths,
meeting separately for confection nouveauté and confection arumures;
the journeymen weaving grenandines unis; the popeliniers; and the
weavers of crêpes de chine, tussah, fantaisie and grège, articles
Gilet, plain velvets, and armures and fancies for dresses, each formed
separate commissions and separate projects for rate increases to
negotiate with fabricants putting out their particular brand of

cloth.[86] Several of these merged into one of the ten original

'categories' federated under the Société civile de prévoyance et de

renseignements pour le travail des tisseurs de la fabrique lyonnaise

(SCPR), organized in March 1870. Within this federation, each category

retained much of its autonomy. Strike funds collected from membership

dues remained within the séries into which the categories were divided,

until the séries were taxed by the central administration to support

a particular strike. The commission of the category retained its

independence in negotiating piece-rates and called upon the central

administration only for auxiliary support. The central committee of

course made decisions concerning financial support for partial strikes

by its members, but even in this capacity, the categories were

represented by their delegates forming the committee. These were

selected by their respective cloth categories, and each category had

the same number of delegates.[87] The Société civile (SCPR) did not

include, moreover, all cloth categories in the silk industry. The

weavers of plain velvets formed their own resistance society, the

Corporation des tisseurs de velours unis, ville et campagne. The

Corporation des tisseurs de velours à deux pièces, originally the

tenth category of the Société civile (SCPR), seceded from this

---

[86]See police reports concerning meetings of different categories
and specialties in 1869 - 1870, AML, I2-47(B), Corporations: ouvriers
en soie.

[87]Titles II - IV, Société civile de Prévoyance et de Renseignements pour le Travail des Tisseurs de la Fabrique lyonnaise (Statutes,
1870), AML, I2-47(B), No. 953; report from Prefect of Rhône to
Minister of Interior on societies and associations, April 5, 1874, ADR,
10M - 2, Associations d'ouvriers tisseurs (1870-93), Société civile de Prévoyance
et de Renseignements des Tisseurs.

federation in 1872 to form its own association.[88] The resistance
movement of the late Second Empire was clearly much more de-centralized
than its predecessors of the early July Monarchy, and much more
sensitive to specific organizational identity based on particular
'category awareness.' It reflected, in short, the separation of
economic conditions among the different cloth categories which was one
of the most prominent features of the crisis of the 1860's in the silk
industry of Lyons.

Thus, in their aspirations, policies and patterns of organization,
the cooperative and resistance movements of the 1860's reflected the
dual character of change in the 'vertical' solidarity of the silk
weavers' craft. Such change included the dissociation of cloth
categories, causing disintegration of traditional 'organic' solidarity,
and the association of categories on a new basis, permitting the
emergence of a new 'mechanical' solidarity. In their affirmation of
craft unity, these movements appealed both to traditional sentiments in
favor of hierarchy of weaving status and economic situation and to more
recent notions recognizing the equality of earnings and the convergence
of wage movements and levels. In their ideological and practical
promotion of quality of manufacture in particular, these movements
embraced hierarchical and egalitarian values together, with no apparent
conflict of party or purpose. As in their joint appeal to city-
centered and region-centered notions of 'horizontal' solidarity of
craft, the ambivalent recognition and promotion of apparently

[88]Office du Travail, Les associations professionelles
ouvrières, II, 280, 284-285.

inconsistent notions of 'vertical' craft solidarity caused no 'crisis'

of ideology in these movements.   Perhaps ambivalence was itself their

only 'correct' or 'true' ideological stance during this period of

economic and social transition.

CHAPTER V

The New Order of the Household

During the 1850's, the traditional order of the household dissolved.
Seeing only disarray and conflict among masters, journeymen, apprentices
and dévideuses, the silk weavers considered this dissolution a sign of
the 'demoralization' afflicting their trade. The economic 'crisis' of
the 1860's accelerated this destruction of the old 'internal order' of
the household, to prune away all that could not persist in an economy
of chronic unemployment, low piece-rates and standardization of cloth
quality at 'inferior' levels. This pruning reduced the size, the
employment of non-relatives and non-residents, the proportion of males
and the entrepreneurial role of the master in the household economy.
Since it affected especially the households which were traditionally
large and strong in these respects -- those weaving fancy cloths -- this
pruning made the social structure of the fancy-cloth households more
similar to that of the plain-cloth households. What remained was a new
kind of household economy and society -- small and intimate, intensely
familial, feminine, 'artisanal' (as opposed to 'entrepreneurial'), and
equal among the different categories of cloth manufacture. Associated
with this new kind of household order was the menace of a new kind of
'demoralization' -- one that threatened not social order, based on
authority and obedience, but virtue, based on the moral integrity

-362-

of the master-weaver in his relations with subordinates, especially with young female workers.

Just as the 'crisis' of the 1860's created the foundations of new forms of craft solidarity, even while it weakened or destroyed the old forms, so the 'crisis' replaced the old order of the household with a new order, while it carried even further the disintegration of the former. As in the transformation of craft solidarity, the weavers' movements of voluntary association also manifested this simultaneous destruction and creation of household solidarity, in their sense of collective purpose, in their organizational identity and in their collective action. Recognizing both the limitations and the possibilities of their new economic situation, the master weavers organized consumer cooperatives, for example, to economize by reducing household expenses rather than by maximizing household earnings. Recognizing the larger role of women in their trade, these consumers' cooperatives, some of the mutual aid societies and the resistance societies admitted female members, unlike most workers' associations in the past. Yet the same consumers' cooperatives also sought to restore to the master weaver his traditional entrepreneurial role in providing cheap food in his neighborhood, when that role was being taken away from him in the weaving of silk fabrics in his household. The moral ideology of association in the 1860's, moreover, tried to revive the traditional sense of moral integrity in household relations and thus to restore to household solidarity its traditional association with personal virtue.

This chapter will examine concretely and in detail the changes in household solidarity caused by the 'crisis' of the 1860's and the manifestation of these changes and their effects in the cooperative,

mutual aid and resistance movements of this decade. The changes themselves
will be described, both statistically and verbally, as transformations of
the economic and social structure of the household -- of its size (numbers
of looms and persons), of the kin relations of its members, of their sexes
and ages, and of the 'entrepreneurship' of its master. The statistical
description uses a static comparison of household structure in 1847 - 1851
with that in 1866, and the literary description includes impressions of
contemporaries confirming, elaborating and explaining the statistical
description. The chapter thus combines close inquiry into quantitative
sources, constructing indices and using formal analytic techniques where
necessary, with simple exposition of informal impressions. This combination seeks to capture the change in household order with closer precision
than use of either method or source alone would allow. The chapter then
examines the effects of these changes on the moral environment of the
household and the manifestation of these effects in the cooperative
and mutual-aid movements of the 1860's.

I. Change in the Economic and Social Structure of the Household

   A. The General Pattern of Change

     Change in the economic and social structure of the weavers'
households during the 1860's had two prominent features. First, these
were changes in certain economic and social characteristics of individual
households. Such characteristics were the number and type of looms, the
number of persons residing in the household, the kin relations of these
persons to the head of the household, their sexes and ages and the level
of 'entrepreneurship' of the household as indicated by the relationship
of number of occupied looms to numbers of household residents of weaving

age. Second, these were changes in the degree of difference between households weaving plain silk cloths for the most part, and those weaving primarily fancy cloths, as this difference was 'measured' by the same economic and social characteristics. In other words, these were changes in 'plain-loom households' (as the first will be called throughout this chapter) as compared with 'fancy-loom households' (as the second will be called), and not only in the numbers and 'qualities' of looms and persons in the average individual household.

The most prominent observable changes of the latter sort -- those in the average individual household as indicated by the majority of households in the statistical samples -- were the following: the substitution of plain looms for fancy looms (a change discussed at length in Chapter IV), the decrease in the average number of looms and persons per household (that is, in household size), the familialization of the co-resident and working household, a greater feminization of the co-resident household (in 1866 as compared with 1847), an increase in the proportion of young children (under 14 years of age) and adults (aged 21 and over) at the expense of adolescents (aged 14 to 20 years), and a decline in the level of 'entrepreneurship' of the household. The substitution of plain looms for fancy looms made these households economically 'simpler' in terms of the quality of cloth they wove. The reduction in size and the familialization of the households made them more intimate. Feminization combined with changes in age balance made the households more malleable economically, and the decline in entrepreneurship made them more 'artisanal' in the sense described in Chapter I.[1]

---

[1]Chapter I, section I - B - 1, pp. 62-66.

These various tendencies were more or less intense, and sometimes
even contradictory, in some types of households as opposed to others,
when such types were defined by the same traits used to describe the
structure of the average individual households. In particular, changes
in households weaving fancy cloths primarily (changes in the characteristics
noted above) were much more intensive than changes in predominantly plain-
loom households. In one instance, that of age balance, fancy-loom
households changed in a different direction than plain-loom households --
a direction favoring a reduction in the proportion of children and a
preservation of that of adolescents. The major consequence of these
differences in changing social structure was an equalization, or 'standardization,' of structure between the two loom-types of household, very
much like the 'equalizing' effect of different conditions of employment
for the two categories of weavers on their respective economic situations.

Table 20 summarizes this standardization of household structure.
The table shows how strongly the two loom-types of household were very
different in 1847, with respect to the several social and economic
characteristics discussed, and very similar in 1866. In 1847, plain-
loom households had fewer looms and persons, many more relatives and
females than fancy-loom households. The latter were largely populated,
well-endowed with looms, and employed mainly males not related to the
master-weaver, thus making these households very 'entrepreneurial.'
By 1866, however, both plain-loom households and fancy-loom households
were small, in terms of numbers of looms and persons, strongly familial
and 'artisanal,' and comprised largely of females. Their similarity was
largely the result of a major transformation of the fancy-loom households,
towards the traditional plain-loom type, since the changes in plain-loom

Table 20

Changes in the Social and Economic
Characteristics of a Typical
Silk-Weaver's Household from
1847-51 to 1866

	Traditional State (1847-51)	Direction of Change Relative to Traditional State (1847-51 to 1866)	New State (1866)
Plains Households			
Number of Looms	Few		Few (But More)
Number of Persons	Few	↑↓ (Small)	Few
Kin Relations – Residents	Familial	↗ (Small)	Familial
Kin Relations – Workers	Familial	Same	Familial
Residency of Labor	Resident	↑↓ (Small)	Resident
Sex	Feminine		Feminine (Less)
Age	?	Less Adolescent	Strong Child, Weak Adolescent, Mild Adult
Fancies Households			
Number of Looms	Many	↓	Few
Number of Persons	Many	↓	Few
Kin Relations – Residents	Non-Familial	↓	Familial
Kin Relations – Workers	Non-Familial	↓	Familial
Residency of Labor	Resident	↓ (Small)	Resident (Less)
Sex	Masculine	↓	Feminine
Age	?	Less Child, More Adult	Mild Child, Mild Adolescent, More Adult

households were practically negligible. The only difference between the
two loom-types of household in 1866 was their age balance. Plain-loom
households had very few adolescents, many children and a modest though
significant number of adults. Fancy-loom households, by contrast, had

more adolescents, many more adults and fewer children, than plain-loom
households.

The following sections analyze separately and in greater detail the
changes in household size and kin relations, in sex and age balance within
the household, and in its degree of 'entrepreneurship.' In each section,
the changes in plain-loom households are separated from changes in fancy-
loom households and compared with the latter. The statistical analysis
of these changes uses samples of silk-weavers' households for 1847, 1851
and 1866 to describe changes from the early, or 'traditional,' period
(1847 - 1851) to the later, or 'novel,' period (1866). The samples are
taken from fiscal and population censuses of the most concentrated weavers'
district of the city, the Croix-Rousse (Fourth Arrondissement after 1852).
Weavers' households of the Croix-Rousse in 1866 will be compared with
weavers' households in the same area, in 1847 and 1851. The fiscal
census of the Croix-Rousse will provide the data for the study of these
households in 1847, and the population census of the same district will
do the same for 1851 and 1866. To ease somewhat the task of data collection
and analysis, stratified systematic samples of weavers' households in the
same quarters of the Croix-Rousse were used for all three years. The
samples were stratified according to the geographical distribution of
residences of members of associations, for the examination of which this
study was intended as a prelude. (See Appendix V.) The censuses permit
an examination of the novelty of weavers' households in 1866, or the lack
thereof, in the major economic and social characteristics of interest --
the number and type of looms, the number and 'qualities' of persons living
in the household (sex, age and kin relation to head), and the extent of

possible 'entrepreneurship' on the part of the master-weaver in allocating
looms among the household labor force.

The censuses of 1847 and 1866 both provide detailed information
concerning the number and type of looms in each household (uni, façonné,
velours, passementerie, bas and tulle), and the state of activity of these
looms (occupied or unoccupied). The information is comparable, except for
the types of unoccupied looms, which is specified in 1866 but not in 1847.[2]
Both also provide comparable data on the number and sexes of persons in
each household and their kin relation to the head of the household, at
least given certain assumptions. Children of the head are clearly
identified in both cases. Non-child relatives, such as co-resident
parents or siblings of the head or his spouse, are strongly suggested
in the 1866 census by the rule of listing the original surname (that is,
surname before marriage, which would be the maiden name of the wife) of
each person in the household. This rule permits matching of surnames of
residents with those of the head and spouse to identify non-child kin.
The 1847 census does not list surnames of any member of the household
other than the head but does classify parents of head or spouse and
sometimes other non-child kin in a separate category. Non-relatives
are suggested as household members whose surnames do not match those
of the head or his wife in the 1866 census, or as members not classed
as kin in 1847. The major sources of error in following this method of
determining kin relations are, in 1866, that of missing some distant

---

[2] This is not a very serious deficiency, however. The proportion of
households in the 1847 sample with all looms unoccupied was very small
(5%), the proportion with all or most looms occupied was larger than in
the 1866 sample (72% in 1847 as compared with 56% in 1866), and a negligible
proportion of households in both samples gives evidence of combining loom-
types in a single shop (6% in 1847, 4% in 1866), so that chances of missing
significant loom-types in the unoccupied category of the 1847 sample are
rather small.

relatives with an apparently alien surname, or that of identifying a
merely coincidental surname match as a kin relation, and, in 1847,
that of missing kin relations classed under another category, such as
apprentice or journeyman. In the first case, the likelihood of error
is small, because of the care of census-takers in noting exact kin
relations when these were not immediately obvious. The likelihood of
errors in the second case (1847) is much greater, so that in making
comparisons of the two periods in matters of kinship the possibility
of such error must be accounted and, where possible, alternative sources
with more accurate kinship information (such as the census of 1851) must
be used as a check.

The censuses of 1847 and 1866 do not provide information as broadly
comparable for the ages of household members. The census of 1847 lists
only the age of the head and the age group of his or her children (less
than 10 years of age or greater than or equal to 10). The census of 1866,
however, provides the exact age of each member. Since the official
format of this census is the same as that of 1851, the sample from the
latter can be used to study the change in age structure of the household,
between the beginning of the Second Empire and 1866. The same 1851
census lists surnames of each member and therefore is, strictly speaking,
more comparable than the 1847 census to the 1866 census for the question
of kinship as well. Its utility for this more important question, as we
shall see later, is much reduced, however, by the lack of any loom data
in 1851. The 1847 census, moreover, also specifies the state of non-child
members of the household (apprentice or journeyman), which compensates
somewhat for the lack of precise age data.

The census samples of the Croix-Rousse in 1847, 1851 and 1866 thus

provide a static comparison of the loom and person characteristics of
co-resident households for two separate periods -- before and at the
beginning of the changes in demand and production patterns under the
Second Empire (1847, 1851), and at the nadir of the crisis of the 1860's
in which those changes reached a climax (1866). Because of the static
quality of my sources, short and long-term effects are almost impossible
to distinguish. The value of the statistical evidence which follows
will be therefore more illustrative than demonstrative. Because the
unit of observation is the co-resident household, moreover, most
personal characteristics of non-resident workers are beyond observation.
Comparison of the total active and inactive looms with the number of
household residents of weaving age does permit, however, a precise statement of the minimum limits of self-sufficiency of the co-resident group
for the work of the household. Such comparison provides the basis for
the construction of an index of 'entrepreneurship,' which will be used
for the study of that question.

B. The Intimate Foyer: Small and Familial

In the early 1870's, the merchant-manufacturers Faye and Thevenin
of Lyons noted, in a questionnaire concerning the weavers of the city,
that among "the household shops which they employ there are few where
there is more than one outside worker..."[3] The same fabricants remarked
that the average number of children per household was "one or two,"[4] and

---

[3]"[Réponses de] Mrs. Faye et Thevenin F[abric]ants de soieries à
Lyon (Rhône)," Enquête Parlementaire Sur les Conditions du Travil en France
(Rhône, 1872 - 1875), Troisième Questionnaire C, XXII, AN, C 3021, Enquete
sur les Conditions du Travail en France (1872 à 1875), Region du Sud-Est (Rhône).

[4]Ibid., Troisième Questionnaire C, XIX.

the Chambre Syndicale des Soieries (a professional association of merchant-manufacturers of Lyons), responding to the same question, estimated this number at "two or three" at most and "tending to decrease."[5] The impression of the silk-weaver's household given by these responses was that of a small, familial foyer of life and work.

The more precise estimates of household size and kin relations derived from the census samples give the same impression in 1866 and also suggest a significant change in these respects from 1847. In 1866, the average number of members of the household other than head and spouse was 1.95 (based on a sample of 104 households). This was about 28% less than the average 2.72 household members in 1847 (based on a sample of 148 households). In other words, between 1847 and 1866, the average personal size of the household had declined. This diminution was primarily the result of a reduction in the number of non-relatives (in relation to the head of the household) from an average of 1.81 members to 1.15 members (- 36%). The number of relatives also fell but to a smaller extent -- from 2.00 members to 1.77 members (- 11%). Although the average number of relatives had been larger than the average number of non-relatives both in 1847 and in 1866, the more severe decline in the latter widened the distance between the two on the average. In other words, the reduction in household size between 1847 and 1866 was largely the effect of a familialization of resident members of the household.

Table 21 demonstrates this familialization by classifying households according to the number of non-relatives to the head (Nonrel) as

[5]"Réponses de la Chambre Syndicale des Soieries de Lyon," Enquête Parlementaire, Troisième Questionnaire C, XIX, ibid.

compared with the number of relatives to the head, including children

and non-child kin (Rel), and then distributing all households in the

sample over the categories defined by such classification (Kin-Type

of Household). Between 1847 and 1866, the proportion of households

Table 21

Distribution of Silk-Weavers' Households by
Kin Relation of Members (Other Than
Spouse) to Head of Household, Croix-Rousse
Sample (1847, 1866)

Kin-Type of Household	1847 Number of HH's	% A		1866 Number of HH's	% A	
Nonrel only	34	23.0		15	14.4	
Nonrel > Rel	22	14.9	65.0	3	2.9	37.5
Nonrel = Rel	26	17.6		12	11.5	
Nonrel < Rel	14	9.5		9	8.7	
Rel only	52	35.1		65	62.5	
Total HH's (A)	148	100.1		104	100.0	
		% B			% B	
Nonrel=Rel=0	30	16.9		36	25.7	
Total HH's (B)	178			140		

Sources: Sample, Recensement, Croix-Rousse, 1847, AML.
Sample, Dénombrement, 1866, Lyon, 4ème Canton,
ADR, 6M-Dénombrement.

with one or more non-relatives declined from 65% to less than half (37%),

while the proportion of households with children or other kin increased

from less than half in 1847 to 62%. The number of households with no

members besides the head and spouse (Nonrel=Rel=0) also increased over

the same period. Co-resident households became more familial, in short.

Comparison of the 1866 sample with that of 1851, for which kinship

information is more certain, generally confirms this familialization of

the household. Although the percentage of households in the 1851 sample with more relatives than non-relatives (out of a total of 175 households) was nearly the same as that in 1866 (70% in 1851, as compared with 71% in 1866), the proportion of households with more non-relatives than relatives decreased (from 24% in 1851 to 17% in 1866) and the proportion of households with no members besides head and spouse, therefore entirely familial, increased (from 17% in 1851 to 26% in 1866).

Familialization and reduction in size of the weavers' households affected both plain-cloth and fancy-cloth categories alike. There were, however, some important differences between the two categories. Table 22 summarizes the changing distribution of households classed by kin relation to the head, separately for plain-loom households (here defined as those households in which the number of plain looms was greater than the number of fancy looms) and for fancy-loom households (those in which the number of fancy looms exceeded the number of plain looms). Table 23 does the same for household size.

Table 22

Distribution of Weavers' Households,
by Loom Type and by
Kin Relations of Members to Head
Croix-Rousse Samples (1847, 1866)

Kin-Type of Household	Plain-Loom Households		Fancy-Loom Households	
	1847	1866	1847	1866
a. Number of Households				
Nonrel only	10	10	21	4
Nonrel > Rel	3	2	17	–
Nonrel = Rel	2	5	20	6
Nonrel < Rel	2	6	11	1
Rel only	23	40	23	22
Total HH's	40	63	92	33
b. Percentage of Total Households				
Nonrel only	25.0 ⎫	15.9 ⎫	22.8 ⎫	12.1 ⎫
Nonrel > Rel	7.5 ⎬ 42.5	3.2 ⎬ 36.5	18.5 ⎬ 75.0	0. ⎬ 33.3
Nonrel = Rel	5.0 ⎮	7.9 ⎮	21.7 ⎮	18.2 ⎮
Nonrel < Rel	5.0 ⎭	9.5 ⎭	12.0 ⎭	3.0 ⎭
Rel only	57.5	63.5	25.0	66.7
	100.0	100.0	100.0	100.0

Sources: Ibid.

Table 23

Average Number of Members per
Weaver's Household (Other Than
Head and Spouse), According to
Loom Type of Household

	Plain-Loom Households			Fancy-Loom Households		
	1847	1866	% Change	1847	1866	% Change
Average Members	1.97	1.94	- 1.5	3.06	1.76	-42.5
Average Rel	1.83	1.79	- 2.2	2.14	1.62	-24.3
Average Nonrel	1.47	1.17	-20.4	1.88	1.00	-46.8

Sources: Ibid.

Both tables indicate a clear difference between the two loom-types
of household with regard to changes in kin relation and size. Although
familialization and reduction in household size occurred in both types,
the movement in these two directions was notably stronger and more
significant in the fancy-loom households. As Table 22 shows, plain-loom
households were largely familial both in 1847 and in 1866. The major
change between the two dates was simply the reduction in the proportion
of households with non-relatives only, or with more non-relatives than
relatives. The proportion of households with relatives only increased,
but not very much -- only by six percentiles. Fancy-loom households,
on the other hand, were relatively non-familial in 1847. In that year,
41% of the households had more non-relatives than relatives, against
37% with more relatives than non-relatives. In 1866, however, these
proportions were reversed -- 12% with more non-relatives against 70%
with more relatives. More to the point, the proportion of fancy-loom
households with relatives alone jumped from 25% in 1847 to 67% in 1866.
Because of these shifts in the fancy-loom households, the difference
between these and plain-loom households, in proportion of households
with relatives alone as against households with at least one non-relative,
was negligible in 1866, whereas such difference had been very large
indeed in 1847. Weavers of fancy cloths, on the average, took on
co-resident non-relative labor as little as weavers of plain cloths
in 1866, whereas in 1847 they tended to take on significantly more
non-relatives than the plain-cloth masters.

Table 23, describing changes in average personal size of households, tells the same story for the number of household residents. In

1847, the number of persons per household in all categories -- total persons (other than head and spouse), relatives and non-relatives-- was significantly larger in fancy-loom households than in plain-loom households. In 1866, the average household size of the former was clearly less than in the latter. The decline for fancy-loom households was largest for the non-relative category, but in all three categories, the percentage decline was greater, and the resulting average levels smaller, in 1866 for fancies households as compared with plains households. The overall effect was, again, a rapprochement between the personal sizes of fancy-loom households and plain-loom households.

The reduction in average household size and the concentration of this change in the fancy-loom households was also evident in the 'loom-size' of the household -- its economic capacity, or scale, as measured by the number of looms. As Table 24 below illustrates, the average number of looms per household declined between 1847 and 1866.

Table 24

Number of Silk Looms per Household
Croix-Rousse Samples
(1847, 1866)

Number of Looms per Household	All Households* 1847	All Households* 1866	Plain-Loom Households 1847	Plain-Loom Households 1866	Fancy-Loom Households 1847	Fancy-Loom Households 1866
a. Number of Households						
1	16	18	12	16	4	2
2	49	47	25	34	22	11
3	50	43	9	25	38	16
4	34	19	3	5	28	13
5	4	2	–	1	3	1
6	1	–	–	–	1	–
Total HH's	154	129	49	81	96	43
b. Percentage of Total Households						
1	10.4	14.0	24.5	19.7	4.2	4.7
2	31.8	36.4	51.0	42.0	22.9	25.6
3	32.5	33.3	18.4	30.9	39.6	37.2
4	22.1	14.7	6.1	6.2	29.2	30.2
5	2.6	1.6	0.	1.2	3.1	2.3
6	.6	0.	0.	0.	1.0	0.
	100.0	100.0	100.0	100.0	100.0	100.0
c. Average Number of Looms per Household						
	2.77	2.53	2.06	2.27	3.07	3.00

Sources: Sample, Recensement, Croix-Rousse, 1847, AML.
Sample, Dénombrement, 1866, Lyon, 4ème Canton,
ADR, 6M-Dénombrement.

*Includes households with 'varieties'--plain looms and
fancy looms together and/or with other type looms, such
as velvet or shawl looms

Households with 1, 2 or 3 looms represented a larger proportion of the
sample in 1866 as compared with 1847, while those with 4, 5 or 6 looms
represented a much smaller proportion. This decline reflected in
particular the smaller proportion of fancy-loom households in the total
sample in 1866, as well as a certain decline in the number of fancy looms
per household. This is seen more clearly in the respective averages for
plain-loom households and for fancy-loom households. The average number
of fancy looms per household declined only 2% (3.07 to 3.00 looms per
household), and yet remained higher than the average number of plain
looms per household. The latter increased by 10% (2.06 to 2.27 looms
per household). The overall decline in households with looms of all
types (9%, from 2.77 to 2.53 looms per household) -- composed largely
of the plain-loom households and of the fancy-loom households -- was
therefore mainly the effect of the larger proportion of plain-loom households, with fewer looms on the average than fancy-loom households, in the
1866 sample as compared with the 1847 sample. As the detailed distribution
demonstrates more clearly, the most significant change in number of looms,
on a household-by-household basis, was the rather large increase in the
number of three-loom plain-cloth households, at the expense of the smaller
two-loom and one-loom households. This reflected both the increasing
opportunities for loom 'accumulation' in the weaving of plain cloths
and probably also the greater wealth of a larger proportion of plain-
cloth weavers than in the past, many of whom were former fancy-cloth
masters who shifted to unis when the demand for their more elegant
product declined. Although the data is silent on the matter, these
plain-cloth weavers were perhaps among the more-skilled, better-paid
of their category whose wages, as we saw earlier, tended to move at a

level and in concordance with the maximum wages in the _fabrique_ as a whole. They were also less likely than the smaller households to depend on the cloth orders of a single merchant-manufacturer[6] and more likely to consider employing outside labor, as the master-weaver Weichmann had suggested in 1850.[7] Although the majority of plain-cloth households remained at the relatively dependent, familial, probably low-paid one or two-loom level -- and most fancy-cloth households remained at the opposite end of the spectrum, with three or more looms per household -- the development of an important 'transitional' three-loom category among plain-cloth households, the proportion of which was near that of fancy-cloth households in the same category, reduced some of the potential wealth and income differential between plain-cloth and fancy-cloth weaving (using number of looms as a proxy for both). In other words, in their numbers of looms as in their numbers and kin relations of household residents, fancy-loom households became more similar to plain-loom households by 1866, whereas twenty years earlier, the two types of households had been quite different.

The reasons for the _rapprochement_ of the two types were quite simple. The decline in the number of fancy looms per household was the result of great unemployment and instability in the fancy-cloth category in the 1860's. Extra looms in the household beyond three or four were likely to lie idle for years and simply forced up rents and taxes for the larger shop to house them. For the same reasons, the number of persons in fancy-loom households decreased, and these households became more familial. Less labor was needed because of the reduced demand

---

[6]Chapter I, section I - C, pp. 87-90.

[7]Chapter I, section I - B - 1, pp. 63-66.

for fancy cloth, and the costs of taking on nonrelative 'transitional-
state' labor were so high in this period of long and frequent inactivity
as to cancel the advantages of exploiting this labor in the manner described in Chapter I.[8] The weaver's family supplied his necessary labor
at lower cost, and he hired outsiders on a short-term basis to occupy
additional fancy looms when the market warranted this. Inversely, the
number of plain-cloth looms increased in the households, as noted before,
because the demand for plain cloths was more stable and because some
plain-cloth weavers had accumulated small fortunes in fancy-cloth weaving
at a previous time, with which they purchased a relatively large number
of plain-cloth looms.

The small, familial household-shop thus became typical of the
internal order of life and work for nearly all weavers of the fabrique,
regardless of their cloth category. In an economic sense, this household
type preserved for the master weaver a certain autonomy of the work
process, but at the cost of reducing the size of his enterprise. It
enabled him to economize in his household budget by reducing shop costs,
for this, as we saw in Chapter I, was the primary contribution of family
labor to net earnings;[9] but it limited his revenues to the smaller capacity
of looms and labor that the family could provide. In a social and moral
sense, this new household type restricted affective solidarity based on
lodging together, to relations among blood kin, more than in the past.
Instead of promoting an extension of the bonds of paternal and filial
attachment to non-relatives 'adopted' as resident workers, the weaver's

---

[8] Ibid, pp. 69-71.

[9] Ibid, pp. 61-62.

household strengthened the 'natural' identification of affective solidarity with blood relations and isolated the family, socially and morally, from outsiders. The household-shop became a more intimate foyer than in the past, but the bonds of intimacy were exclusive and biological rather than expansive and 'social.'

C. The Malleable Foyer: Feminine and Young

Examination of the sex and age balance of the household residents refines this image of the exclusive, intimate foyer with that of a 'malleable' foyer, that is, a foyer capable of adapting its living standards and working conditions to changing and often adverse economic circumstances. Such malleability derived largely from the feminization of household residents and, to a lesser extent, from changes in the age balance of the household, giving its younger members a more prominent position. Since females and youth were generally easier to 'exploit' than males and adults, these changes made the household more adaptable to external circumstances, favoring, as much as possible, the interests of the master weavers at the same time. Feminization affected the non-relative segment of the household as well as the relative segment and therefore made more malleable even those households that were less familial. As in the case of household size and kin relations, these changes were most notable in fancy-loom households and had the effect of making the latter more like plain-loom households in sex and age characteristics.

The feminization of the silk-weavers' households was evident in the early 1870's, as responses of contemporaries to the parliamentary enquiry on working conditions suggested. In its general observations

on the weavers of the fabrique, for example, the Chambre Syndicale des
Soieries noted that "the worker called journeyman working on the loom of
the master weaver is composed 2/3 of women and girls."[10] The census
sample for 1866 made a similar case for the change in sex balance of
households since 1847. Table 25 summarizes data concerning sex distributions for all households considered together and for plain-loom
households and fancy-loom households considered separately.

Table 25

Distribution of Weavers' Households,
by Loom Type and by Sex
of Members
Croix-Rousse Samples (1847, 1866)

Sex Balance of Household	All HH 1847	All HH 1866	Plains HH 1847	Plains HH 1866	Fancies HH 1847	Fancies HH 1866
a. Number of Households						
Males only	38	25	10	13	23	8
Males > Females	22	12	1	8	17	3
Males = Females	26	15	4	9	18	6
Males < Females	27	8	10	5	17	1
Females only	35	44	13	28	17	15
Total Households	148	104	38	63	92	33
b. Percentage of Total Households						
Males only	25.7	24.0	26.3	20.6	25.0	24.2
Males > Females	14.9	11.5	2.6	12.7	18.5	9.1
Males = Females	17.6	14.4	10.5	14.3	19.6	18.2
Males < Females	18.2	7.7	26.3	7.9	18.5	3.0
Females only	23.6	42.3	34.2	44.4	18.5	45.5
	100.0	99.9	99.9	99.9	100.1	100.0

c. Percentile Change from 1847 to 1866

Males only	- 1.7		- 5.7		- .8	
Males > Females	- 3.4	- 5.1	+10.1	+ 4.4	- 9.4	-10.2
Males = Females	- 3.2		+ 3.8		- 1.4	
Males < Females	-10.5	+ 8.2	-18.4	- 8.2	-15.5	+11.5
Females only	+18.7		+10.2		+27.0	

Sources: Ibid..

_____

[10]"Réponses de la Chambre Syndicale des Soieries de Lyon," Enquête
Parlementaire, Premier Questionnaire A, Observations, AN C 3021.

The table indicates an increase in the percentage of females residing in
the weavers' households from 1847 to 1866. As section c. of the table
illustrates best, the percentage of predominantly female households
(categories Males < Females and Females only) increased between the
two years, while the percentage of largely male households (categories
Males > Females and Males only) decreased. The first set of households
(predominantly female) therefore represented not only a greater percentage
of total households in the 1866 sample than the second set (predominantly
male households), but the proportion by which the first exceeded the
second was much greater in the 1866 sample than in the 1847 sample.

Such feminization affected fancy-weavers' households more than
those of plain-cloth weavers. Fancy-cloth weaving had been traditionally
more strongly male than female, plain-cloth weaving more strongly female
than male. In 1847, 43% of fancy-loom households were predominantly male,
as compared with 37% predominantly female and 20% Males = Females. More
than half of the predominantly male fancy-loom households (25 percentiles
of the 43%) had no females at all. In the same year, however, only 29%
of plain-loom households were predominantly male, as compared with 60%
predominantly female and 10% Males = Females. By 1866, the sex balance
of fancy-loom households reversed, on the average, in favor of the predominantly female households. Only 33% of fancy-loom households were
predominantly male in that year, as compared with 48% predominantly female.
In the plain-loom households, the traditionally strong female position
weakened somewhat, so that only 52% of the plain-loom households in the
sample were predominantly female, as compared with 33% predominantly
male. The trend in favor of a larger proportion of predominantly-female
households among weavers as a whole -- a trend here called 'feminization'--

was thus the combined effect of a significant increase in the proportion
of traditionally more feminine plain-loom households in the sample and a
significant shift of fancy-loom households to a more feminized state,
making these more like plain-loom households in their sex balance. This
latter shift consisted especially of a wholesale replacement of males by
females in nearly half of the fancy-loom households in 1866, thus increasing the percentage of all-female fancy-loom households by 27
percentiles over the 1847 proportion. Nearly half of the fancy-loom
households (45%) had only females (besides the master-weaver head), and
nearly all of these households (89%) could rely on their resident members
to occupy all active looms, as will be demonstrated in the next section.
(See Table 31, pp. 409-10) These facts together suggest that women wove
on the fancy-cloth looms more than in the past, and were not merely
confined to auxiliary tasks, just as more men were forced to work
plain-cloth looms than before 1860. This was indeed the most significant
feature of the feminization of the weavers' households during the 1860's,
for, as Chapter III demonstrated,[11] the substitution of female compagnonnes
for journeymen had occurred in many plain-loom households during the 1850's
and even earlier. The importance of this change in sex roles for fancy-
cloth weaving should not be exaggerated, however. The fancy silks demanded
by the market in the 1860's were not the richly-wrought, skillfully-executed
dresses of the past, but rather the simple fancy ornaments and nouveautés.
Some, if not all, of these female fancy-cloth weavers probably wove plain
silks on the fancy looms as well, since the demand for plain silks was
more constant and fancy looms were technically capable of weaving them.

---

[11]Chapter III, section I - C - 1, pp. 249-250.

The feminization of fancy-cloth weaving was therefore not so much an important economic or technological (skill-related) change as a change in the status of these female weavers and of the skilled male fancy weavers, who were long accustomed to consider most females in their specialty as auxiliary workers rather than as weavers.

The change in age balance in weavers' households from the earlier to the later period is somewhat more difficult to trace. Because of the lack of precise information concerning ages in the 1847 census, the census of 1851 is used instead for the earlier period. Unfortunately, the latter census does not distinguish between plain-loom households and fancy-loom households, as does the census of 1847. Plain-loom households and fancy-loom households are therefore compared respectively with the aggregate distribution of the 1851 sample rather than with their corresponding plains and fancies households of that year. This is a much less satisfactory method of examining changes in the separate loom-types of household but is the best possible given the lack of loom data in 1851. Table 26 summarizes these data.

Table 26

Distribution of Weavers' Households by Loom Type and
by Age of Members. Croix-Rousse (1851, 1866)

a) Number of Households

% of HH Members In This Age Group	Children (Ages 1-13) 1851	1866 All HH	1866 Plains HH	1866 Fancies HH	Adolescents (Ages 14-20) 1851	1866 All HH	1866 Plains HH	1866 Fancies HH	Adults (Ages 21 and Over) 1851	1866 All HH	1866 Plains HH	1866 Fancies HH
0	53	45	16	19	59	66	36	16	74	53	23	16
1-49	19	8	3	2	33	13	3	4	25	8	4	2
50	15	11	7	2	16	9	4	4	13	9	5	2
51-99	19	8	4	3	12	3	1	1	6	6	2	0
100	31	30	16	5	17	11	2	6	19	26	12	11
TOTAL	137	102	46	31	137	102	46	31	137	102	46	31

b) Percentage of Total Households

% of HH Members In This Age Group	Children (Ages 1-13) 1851	1866 All HH	1866 Plains HH	1866 Fancies HH	Adolescents (Ages 14-20) 1851	1866 All HH	1866 Plains HH	1866 Fancies HH	Adults (Ages 21 and Over) 1851	1866 All HH	1866 Plains HH	1866 Fancies HH
0	38.7	44.1	34.8	61.3	43.1	64.7	78.3	51.6	54.0	52.0	50.0	51.6
1-49	13.9	7.8	6.5	6.5	24.1	12.7	6.5	12.9	18.2	7.8	8.7	6.5
50	10.9	10.8	15.2	6.5	11.7	8.8	8.7	12.9	9.5	8.8	10.9	6.5
51-99	13.9	7.8	8.7	9.7	8.8	2.9	2.2	3.2	4.4	5.9	4.3	0
100	22.6	29.4	34.8	16.1	12.4	10.8	4.3	19.4	13.9	25.5	26.1	35.5
TOTAL	100.0	99.9	100.0	100.1	100.1	99.9	100.0	100.0	100.0	100.0	100.0	100.1

c) Percentile Change from 1851 (% 1866 - % 1851)

% of HH Members In This Age Group	Children (Ages 1-13) 1866 All HH	Plains HH	Fancies HH	Adolescents (Ages 14-20) 1866 All HH	Plains HH	Fancies HH	Adults (Ages 21 and Over) 1866 All HH	Plains HH	Fancies HH
0	+5.4	-3.9	+22.6	+21.6	+35.2	+8.5	-2.0	-4.0	-2.4
1-49	-6.1	-7.4	-7.4	-11.4	-17.6	-11.2	-10.4	-9.5	-11.7
50	-.1	+4.3	-4.4	-2.9	-3.0	+1.2	-.7	+1.4	-3.0
51-99	-6.1	-5.2	-4.2	-5.9	-6.6	-5.6	+1.5	-.1	-4.4
100	+6.8	+12.2	-6.5	-1.6	-8.1	+7.0	+11.6	+12.2	+21.6

As the table illustrates, the proportion of households with one or more members aged 14 - 20 declined between 1851 and 1866, partly in favor of an increased proportion of households with more children aged less than 14 years than any other age group, but mostly in favor of households in which there were more persons aged 21 and over than children and adolescents. This general impression requires much modification, however, when plain-loom households are considered separately from fancy-loom households. First, the loss of adolescents was much more noticeable among the plain-loom households than among the fancy-loom households. Between 1851 and 1866, the proportion of plain-loom households with no adolescents, as compared with the 1851 aggregate, was 35.2 percentiles greater, and the proportion of plain-loom households with one or more adolescents, similarly compared, was less in each proportional category (1 - 49%, 50%, 51 - 99%, All). Over the same period, the proportion of fancy-loom households with no adolescents increased only 8.5 percentiles above the 1851 aggregate, and the proportion of households with all adolescents and half adolescents increased as well (by 1.2 and 7.0 percentiles respectively). The loss of households with no adolescents was therefore nearly compensated by the addition of households with at least as many adolescents as other age groups.[12] The overall increase in predominantly adult households was, on the contrary, stronger among

---

[12]In 1847, the proportion of households in which one-half or more of the working members older than ten (including all children above ten but not including master-weaver and his wife) was an apprentice, was slightly higher for fancy-loom households (14.4%) than for plain-loom households (8.6%) -- a difference of 5.8 percentiles, or 67% of the plain-loom figure. In 1866, the proportion of households with 50% or more adolescents of all kinds was especially larger in fancy-loom households (35.5%) as compared with plain-loom households (15.2%) -- a difference of 20.3 percentiles, or 134% of the plain-loom figure. This confirms the impression of a greater

fancy-loom households than among plain-loom households, although not absent from the latter. The major difference between the two concerned the proportion of households with adults only. The increase of adults among the fancies households was exclusively the effect of a large increase in the adults-only category (21.6 percentiles over the 1851 aggregate), whereas the increase among the plains households was divided between a 12.2 percentile increase in adults-only households and a 1.4 percentile increase in households only half adult. In the child age group, fancies households lost rather than gained, relative to the 1851 aggregate, in proportion of households with children in all proportional categories, so that 22.6 percentiles more households in 1866 had no children at all. The proportion of plain-loom households with one-half children, on the other hand, increased 4.3 percentiles, and the proportion of such households with children only increased 12.2 percentiles.[13] The overall trade-off of adolescents for children and adults was therefore primarily the effect of the predominance of plain-loom households in the 1866 sample. These households 'lost' adolescents and 'gained' children, or even more likely, simply had more children than the fancy-loom households which dominated the 1851 aggregate sample. Among fancy-loom households, the trade-off consisted more precisely of that between children and adults, in favor of the latter. This trade-off left the

loss of adolescents in plain-loom households than in fancy-loom households between the two years.

[13]This apparent increase, however, is less certain than the apparent decrease in fancy-loom households, because the basis of comparison was the 1851 aggregate, dominated proportionally by fancy-loom households. The latter tended to have fewer children than plain-loom households, in general, as examination of the 1847 census demonstrates. For example, in 1847, the proportion of plain-loom households with 50% children of the master under ten years of age was 40%, as compared with only 24% of the fancy-loom households with the same proportion of children in this age group.

position of adolescents in the households of fancy-cloth weavers in 1866 not especially different from their position in the households of weavers in general in 1851.

The decline in adolescents in plain-loom households was due largely to the severe reduction in piece-rates in this sector to near subsistence levels. This reduction left the master less leverage to exploit the economic gains of apprenticeship and made apprenticeship less attractive to young men and women. The risks of taking on apprentices -- in the form of unoccupied labor which the master was obliged to support -- were fewer in plain-cloth weaving than in fancy-cloth weaving, because of the greater stability of employment in the plain-cloth sector. But the gains of occupying additional looms with such apprentices were very small at the low piece-rate for plain silks. The marginal worker earned little or no more than his bare subsistence upkeep. The supply of apprenticeship labor for weaving plain silks was low, moreover, because of the competition of rural areas from which apprentices had been recruited traditionally, for the labor of young people, especially that of young males. Instead of migrating to the city of Lyons to enter the fabrique, many now remained in their native villages to weave plain silks, for which the rural demand was in fact usually more stable than the urban.

By 1866 plain-loom households were more numerous than fancy-loom households even in the traditionally fancy district of the Croix-Rousse. The decline of adolescents in the plains households therefore created the impression of an overall decline in apprenticeship by the 1860's. The retiring president of the Conseil des Prud'hommes, Jules Bonnet, noted the great reduction in the number of apprenticeship contracts in 1863, 1864 and 1865. A total of only 146 contracts had been registered in those three years, as compared with 360 contracts in the preceding three-year period, 1860 - 1862.[14] On an annual basis, the number of contracts in the latter period was also very small, compared with the 1850's, as Table 27 demonstrates. The table probably even underestimates

Table 27

Number of Contracts of Apprenticeship
Registered at the Conseil des
Prud'hommes of Lyons

Year	Number of Contracts per Annum
1853	800
1855	412
1860, 61, 62	120 (annual average)
1863, 64, 65	49 (annual average)

Sources: Felix Bertrand, Report of President of Conseil des Prud'hommes de Lyon to Prefect of Rhône, June 29, 1854; Bertrand, Compte-rendu des travaux du Conseil des Prud'hommes de Lyon, année 1855 (Lyon: C. Bonnaviat, 1856); Jules Bonnet, Compte-rendu des Travaux du Conseil des Prud'hommes pendant la dernière periode triennale (Lyon: C. Bonnaviat, 1866), ADR, U - Prud'hommes de Lyon, Correspondance relative aux élections (1806 à 1870).

the extent of the decline since 1853, since many more contracts were made verbally in that year, hence not registered at the Council. Although no firm evidence of a decline in verbal contracts along with the decline in registered contracts is readily available for the 1860's, reports of contemporary observers suggest that such was indeed the case. In September 1868, for example, the police noted that "in many categories

---

[14]Jules Bonnet, Compte-rendu des Travaux du Conseil des Prud'hommes pendant la dernière periode triennale (Lyon: Imprimerie Typographique et Lithographique de C. Bonnaviat, 1866), ADR, U - Prud'hommes de Lyon, Correspondance relative aux élections (1806 à 1870).

[of silk weaving] no more male or female apprentices are being trained, the manufacture of silks is even abandoned in favor of other more remunerative trades."[15]

Unlike most plain-loom households, fancy-loom households remained receptive to the apprentice age group, despite the chronic unemployment in their category. These households retained or even increased the proportion of adolescents among their residents. The relative strength of adolescents, however, was not equal for all of these households. It differed, in particular, with variations in their kin relations and in their sex balance. Adolescents held a strong place in fancy-loom households that were strongly non-familial and feminized, but held a weaker place in relatively familial, masculine fancy-loom households. In other words, fancy-loom households seem to have preserved a relatively high percentage of adolescents when these youth were not related to the head of the household and when they were females -- female apprentices and journeywomen (compagnonnes), in short. Tables 28 and 29 demonstrate this by differentiating households by predominant kin-type and sex balance (respectively) before tracing the change in percentage of household members in the adolescent age group from 1851 to 1866. Both tables compare changes in fancy-loom households with changes in plain-loom households.

[15]"Rapport Adressé à Mr. Delcourt, Commissaire spécial," September 9, 1868, AML, 12 - 47 (A), Situation de l'industrie lyonnaise: ....rapports sur la soierie et les ouvriers en soie ... (1819 à 1870, No. 309.

Table 28

Distribution of Households by Loom Type, Kin Type and Percentage of Household Members Aged 14-20 (Adolescents). Croix-Rousse Sample (1851, 1866)

| | Fancy-Loom Households (1866)* | | | | | | | Plain-Loom Households (1866)* | | | | |
Percentage of Total Members of Household in Adolescent Age Group	Rel 1851	Nonrel 1866	Rel = Nonrel 1851	Nonrel 1866	Nonrel 1851	Rel 1866	Rel 1851	Nonrel 1866	Nonrel 1866	Rel = Nonrel 1851	Nonrel 1851	Rel 1866
a) Percentage of Total Households												
0 % - 49 %	70.6	72.7	42.9	40.0	62.9	50.0	70.6	85.3	75.0	42.9	62.9	87.5
50 %	9.5	4.5	42.9	60.0	11.4	0	9.5	8.8	25.0	42.9	11.4	0
51% - 100%	20.0	22.7	14.3	0	25.7	50.0	20.0	5.8	0	14.3	25.7	12.5

b) Percentile Change from 1851 (% 1866 − % 1851)

	Fancy-Loom			Plain-Loom		
0 % - 49 %	+ 2.1	- 2.9	-12.9	+14.7	+32.1	+24.6
50 %	- 5.0	+17.1	-11.4	- .7	-17.9	-11.4
51% - 100%	+ 2.7	-14.3	+24.3	-14.2	-14.3	-13.2

c) Number of Households in Sample

	Fancy-Loom							Plain-Loom				
	95	22	7	5	35	4	95	34	4	7	35	8

*Loom type of household refers only to 1866 sample. .

Sources: Sample, Dénombrement, 1851, Croix-Rousse
Sample, Dénombrement, 1866, Lyon, 4ème Canton

Table 29

Distribution of Households by Loom Type, Sex Balance and Percentage of Household Members Aged 14-20 (Adolescents). Croix-Rousse Sample (1851, 1866)

a) Percentage of Total Households

Percentage of Total Members of Household in Adolescent Age Group	Fancy-Loom Households (1866)*						Plain-Loom Households (1866)*					
	Females		Males		Females=Males		Females		Males		Females=Males	
	1851	1866	1851	1866	1851	1866	1851	1866	1851	1866	1851	1866
0 % - 49 %	72.1	56.2	66.1	75.0	52.9	66.7	72.1	91.3	66.1	87.4	52.9	57.1
50 %	9.8	12.5	5.1	8.3	41.2	33.3	9.8	4.3	5.1	0	41.2	42.9
51% - 100%	18.0	31.2	29.8	16.7	5.9	0	18.0	4.3	29.8	12.4	5.9	0

b) Percentile Change from 1851 (% 1866 - % 1851)

Percentage of Total Members of Household in Adolescent Age Group	Fancy-Loom			Plain-Loom		
	Females	Males	Females=Males	Females	Males	Females=Males
0 % - 49 %	-15.9	+ 8.9	+13.8	+19.2	+21.3	+ 4.2
50 %	+ 2.7	+ 3.2	- 7.9	- 5.5	- 5.1	+ 1.7
51% - 100%	+13.2	-12.1	- 5.9	-13.7	-16.4	- 5.9

c) Number of Households in Sample

	Fancy-Loom			Plain-Loom		
	Females	Males	Females=Males	Females	Males	Females=Males
1851	61	59	17	61	59	17
1866	16	3	17	23	7	16

*Loom type of household refers only to 1866 sample.

Source: Ibid.

Table 28 indicates a slightly stronger tendency to 'accumulate'
adolescents among fancy-loom households in which the number of non-
relatives was greater than the number of relatives (Nonrel > Rel). This
is evident in the large increase between 1851 and 1866 in the percentage
of predominantly non-relative fancy-loom households with more than half
of its members (51% - 100%) aged 14 - 20 (+ 24.3 percentiles), as compared with other kin groups and loom groups in the same predominantly-
adolescent age class. This tendency was stronger than in the predominantly-
familial fancy-loom households (Rel > Nonrel) and stronger than in both
kin-types of plain-loom households -- familial (Rel > Nonrel) and non-familial
(Nonrel > Rel). The percentage of households of the former class (familial
fancy-loom households) with more than one-half of their members in the
adolescent age group increased only 2.7 percentiles from 1851 to 1866,
while the percentage of households of the latter two classes (familial
and non-familial plain-loom households) with more than 50% of their
members aged 14 - 20 decreased between these two years.

Table 29 suggests a strong association between feminization and
retention of adolescents in fancy-loom households. The increase in the
proportion of adolescents in these households tended to be stronger in
more feminized households than in those with one-half or more than half
males. In fact, masculinization seems to have been more strongly associated
with a reduction in the proportion of adolescents in fancy-loom households
than with an increase in this proportion. The proportion of fancy-loom
households with more females than males, above the aggregate proportion
of households in this sex category in 1851, increased 13.2 percentiles.
The proportion of such households with an equal number of males and
females decreased 5.9 percentiles, and those with more males than females

decreased 12.1 percentiles.

Table 29 shows, moreover, that feminization influenced the age
balance of the household, in favor of adolescents, only in fancy-loom
households. Among predominantly female plain-loom households, for
example, the percentage of households with more than half of their
members in the adolescent age group decreased between 1851 and 1866.
Finally, feminization was not associated as strongly with the tendency
of fancy-loom households to 'accumulate' adult members as it was with
preserving or increasing the proportion of adolescents. As Table 30
(below) demonstrates, the proportion of adults in such households increased more with the addition of males relative to females than the other
way around. When males were as numerous as females or more numerous than
females, the proportion of predominantly-adult fancy-loom households increased dramatically. The feminization of the fancy-loom households in
general thus consisted largely of the feminization of the adolescent
age group.

Table 30

Distribution of Fancy-Loom Households by Sex Balance and Percentage of Household Members Aged 21 and Above (Adults). Croix-Rousse Sample (1851, 1866)

Percentage of Total Members of Household in Adult Age Group	Females > Males		Females = Males		Males > Females	
	1851	1866	1851	1866	1851	1866
a) Percentage of Total Households						
0 % - 49 %	62.3	62.5	64.7	33.3	84.7	58.3
50 %	6.6	12.5	29.4	0	6.8	0
51 % - 100 %	31.2	25.0	5.9	66.7	8.5	41.7
b) Percentile Change from 1851 (% 1866 - % 1851)						
0 % - 49 %	+ .2		-31.4		-26.4	
50 %	+ 5.9		-29.4		- 6.8	
51 % - 100 %	- 6.2		+60.8		+33.3	
c) Number of Households in Sample						
	61	16	17	3	59	12

Source: Ibid.

In summary, then, the feminization of the fancy-loom households during
the 1860's resulted in part from the departure of males from fancy-cloth
weaving, leaving behind only the daughters and female kin of the master
to perform the work in smaller, more familial households, and in part
from the addition of female non-relatives, especially apprentices and
young journeywomen, to perform work abandoned by the males or work for
which male labor was simply scarce. The males who abandoned the household
to the females were probably both children of the master and journeymen
weavers who found more lucrative and stable employment in other industries.
In March 1868, the police reported that "if a worker is able to do other
work and manages to find work for himself in this occupation, he will
leave the loom without regret."[16] Even skilled journeymen and children
of the master seem to have abandoned the weaving profession at an amazing
rate. In March 1869, "all those who manage to work at a more or less
regular job, no matter what kind of job, earning 2 francs or 2 francs
50 per day, abandon weaving rather than resign themselves to making one,
two or three pieces and then finding themselves with nothing to do after
that ... master-weavers are even having their children learn other trades."[17]
Some of these journeymen and masters' children began working as employees
of the merchant-manufacturers, as the latter increased their house staffs
to service more widely diffused production in the countryside. In the early
1870's the fabricants Faye and Thevenin reported that there existed "in
many establishments, employees on fixed salaries who are former workers

---

[16]"Rapport à Monsieur Delcourt, Commissaire spécial, sur la situation de
la fabrique des étoffes de soies," March 8, 1868, AML, 12 - 47(B), No. 310.

[17]"Rapport à Monsieur Delcourt, Commissaire spécial, sur la situation
de la fabrique," March 6, 1869, AML, 12 - 47(B), No. 312.

and sons of workers."[18] Feminization and youth were intimately related, in other words, in those households where both tendencies were most notable -- those with more fancy-cloth looms than plain-cloth looms.

The second cause of feminization of fancy-loom households -- the addition of young female non-relatives -- illustrated the intimate relationship between feminization and youth during this period. This relationship received widespread attention by contemporary publicists and politicians who concerned themselves with the position of women and children in industry. Their comments suggested a strong tendency towards feminization of apprenticeship in silk-weavers' households and, along with such feminiation, a levelling of the status of apprentice weavers to that of auxiliary workers, especially to that of dévideuses. One of the contemporary observers, the republican deputy Jules Simon, noted a strong association between feminization and apprenticeship in the mid-1860's, in an article entitled "Apprenticeship." The article was first published in the Revue des deux mondes and shortly thereafter in the radical republican daily of Lyons, Le Progrès.[19] In a reply to Simon's article, César Maire, a master weaver of silk cloths, suggested that the status of female apprentice weavers had been reduced to that of the apprentice dévideuse.[20] Both Simon and Maire probably referred primarily to conditions in the fancy-loom households, since these were the ones in which female apprentices were most likely to be present during this period.

---

[18]"[Réponses de] Mrs. Faye et Thevenin F[abric]ants de soieries à Lyon (Rhône)," Enquête Parlementaire, Troisième Questionnaire C, IX, AN, C 3021.

[19]Jules Simon, "L'Apprentissage," Le Progrès (Lyon), February 13, 1865.

[20]Letter from César Maire to Le Progrès, February 25, 1865, "A Propos d'apprentissage," Le Progrès, February 26, 1865.

In his article on apprenticeship, Simon claimed that "the female
weavers especially have the pivotal role in the industry of Lyons,
because they earn as much as the men and spend less, and also because
their position contrasts with that of the moulineuses and dévideuses."[21]
He then contrasted the position of dévideuse apprentices and weaver
apprentices, demonstrating the advantages of the latter over the former.
Simon's almost exclusive attention to female apprenticeship suggested
that most of the apprentices whom he observed, and whom he regarded as
typical of the 'state,' were females. Simon claimed, moreover, that such
apprentices were exploited beyond the norms of justice. "It is indeed
time to establish a just proportion between the advantages of the trade
and the sacrifices demanded of the apprentice," namely, four years of
'free' labor, longer than was actually necessary to learn the trade.
But for weavers these conditions were not nearly so bad as for the
dévideuses:

> They [the dévideuses] work long hard days for this
> modest sum, and are assigned nearly always, besides
> their work, all the heavy tasks of the household. . .
> Yet it is necessary to complete a four-year apprenticeship
> to become a dévideuse, and during these four years these
> unfortunate souls, fed and lodged, earn only a meager
> income of 20 or 30 francs [per month] to support themselves.[22]

In his reply to Simon published February 26, 1865, in Le Progrès,
the master-weaver César Maire objected that the conditions of the
apprentice weavers were not at all harsh or unfair, nor was the three-
to four year contract unnecessarily long as Simon had claimed. The

[21]Simon, Le Progrès, February 13, 1865

[22]Ibid.

position of the dévideuse, added Maire, was also not as terrible as Simon

had described. Yet Maire did not deny that it was a hard lot. The

dévideuse à gage, according to this master-weaver, earned only 100 to

160 francs per year, rather than the 200 to 300 francs indicated by

Simon. Maire even claimed that "their conditions of existence contrast

less with those of the female weavers than M. Jules Simon would like to

say."

> The dévideuse is fed, lodged and provided laundering at
> the expense of the master-weaver; her tasks bear much relation
> to those of a real servant, but with this difference, that
> she is considered almost a member of the family, and her
> moral position has nothing which might offend the most
> delicate sensibility.
>
> . . . .although [the female weaver] seems at first glance
> to earn more, once she has satisfied all her obligations,
> all the tasks weighing so heavily on her, once she [must]
> endure the unemployment at the end of the season, the
> apparent advantage she has over the dévideuse soon
> disappears, and her condition, apparently so different,
> is found in the end to be exactly the same.[23]

Although intended to elevate, in the eyes of the public, the

condition of the dévideuse relative to that of the female weaver,

Maire's letter was testimony rather to the lowering of the condition

of the female weaver to that of the dévideuse, a mere servant. In

short, the superior status of apprentice weavers for fancy silks

especially, as compared with the inferior status of auxiliary workers,

depended largely on the predominance of males in that state. As

---

[23]Letter from César Maire, Le Progrès, February 26, 1865.

apprenticeship became feminized in the 1860's, its status fell, and such a fall left more 'social space' for exploitation by master-weavers. Apprentices became little more than workers, even in fancy-cloth weaving, as they became more female. In 1861, Jules Simon remarked that working-class families of Lyons preferred apprenticing their daughters as seamstresses or as milliners, despite the inferior pay in these trades, because of the terrible conditions of the apprentice weaver. Even peasants from the surrounding countryside -- the normal area of recruitment of new apprentices -- began to "form scruples" about sending their daughters into the silk-weaving workshops of Lyons. Instead, they apprenticed their daughters to benevolent, paternalistic merchant-manufacturers, such as C.J. Bonnet, who set up factory-dormitories for female weavers in the countryside.[24]

From the point of view of the master-weaver, females, especially young females, were preferred to males in this period, not only because of their docility but especially because of the much lower wage they could be made to accept. "The situation of the men can still hold up despite the decline of wages," wrote the police observer in September 1868, "but that of the women is intolerable because their average wage hardly goes above 1.20 [francs] per day in some privileged categories and certainly does not exceed .75 [francs] for the largest number of those employed for ordinary tasks."[25] The supply of female labor for such impoverished work was, moreover, apparently not scarce. Most of

---

[24]Jules Simon, L'ouvrière (Paris: L. Hachette, 1861), p. 52.

[25]"Rapport à Mr. Delcourt," September 9, 1868, AML, 12 - 47(A), No. 309.

the new jobs in public works, machine and chemical industries employed
men. The wives of those who were married were thus available for work
in the fabrique. But the largest percentage of females seems to have
emigrated independently from surrounding rural areas to which the
manufacture of silk cloths was itself migrating. Between 1871 and 1876,
for example, 9 of 34 weavers (26%) born in the rural village of Avenières
(Terres Froides, Isère) and having died in that period were females who
died in Lyons. Between 1852 and 1857, by contrast, no native of the
village having died in that period was in Lyons at the time of death.[26]
The migration of silk weaving from Lyons tended to induce a high rate
of natural increase of population in the rural areas like Avenières where
weaving provided the most important industrial activity. In order to
relieve the growing population pressure in these areas, especially during
periods of inactivity in the silk industry, unmarried females were forced
to seek work in the towns. They left their parents and brothers behind
in the villages to continue working the loom on available orders -- work
in which they engaged now as a primary activity and not, as in the past,
as a mere auxiliary employment to farming. As these females became permanent
employees of the fabrique lyonnaise, as subordinate workers in the
master-weavers' households, they enabled the latter to become more
malleable economically, because of the greater facility with which women
could be exploited -- that is, forced to accept lower standards of living --
than their male predecessors.

Ease of exploitation and greater malleability of the household
economy were not, however, the only consequences of feminization.

---

[26]ADI, Q - Tables des mutations après décès, Bureau de Morestel,
1852 à 1857, 1871 à 1876.

Besides substituting for males within the weavers' households, females
working outside the household on specialized tasks replaced work once
done in the household with independent enterprise outside. In the
dévidage of silk thread especially, female mistresses directed such
enterprise in their own household shops and employed dévideuses to work
in these shops instead of in the master-weavers' households. The
dévideuse à gage, residing and working in the latter, as a 'transitional-
state' subordinate, therefore became less common than she had been in
the past. The major evidence for this is the strong familialization of
the weavers' households. Such familialization suggests that most
dévideuses who worked in the households did not reside there. But
there is also evidence that such day-laboring dévideuses working in the
weavers' households had become fewer, even exceptional, by the mid-1860's.
Instead, the specialized dévidage shops, owned by mistress dévideuses,
prepared most of the thread. These female chefs d'ateliers of dévidage
employed female workers to prepare the threads of several master-weavers
at once. Some of the mistress's workers were lodged and fed at her
expense -- taken on à gage, in other words. Just like the dévideuses
à gage and apprentices in the master-weavers' households, these dévideuses
living and working in specialized shops "were more especially at the
disposal of their mistress for all kinds of work of her household..."[27]

Contemporary critics of conditions of child and female labor
especially deplored the situation of these female laborers, cited as
typical of that of dévideuses in general. For example, E. Pariset,

---

[27]'Dévideuses,' "Rapport à Monsieur Delcourt, Commissaire spécial,
Sur la situation de la fabrique des étoffes de soies au 4e Trimestre Xbre
1866," December 8, 1866, AML, 12 - 47(A), No. 301.

reporting to the Chamber of Commerce of Lyons on the conditions of the dévideuse,described them as the worst in the trade. He referred primarily to the
dévideuses in specialized shops of dévidage, who represented presumably
the large majority of females in this occupation.

> . . . there is a category of shops where frequently all
> abuses can be found, and for which we must, Gentlemen, secure
> a prompt and strict surveillance, such are the shops of dévidage.
> One might estimate their number to be nine hundred, if one
> grants that there are thirty thousand looms in Lyons, and
> that a dévidoir serves eight looms, since each shop, on the
> average, has four dévidoirs.[28]

The important fact was the exploitation of such young females by female
mistresses rather than by male masters alone. Women were no longer only
the exploited ones, but some were also the exploiters, once they had
acquired property and the direction of their own shops.

In the report on the situation of the fabrique in the third
trimester of 1869, the police observer suggested that an important part
of the dévidage of these shops depended on orders directly from the
fabricant. "The dévideuse, who usually earns much less than the weaver,
is especially hurt by the use of these bad silk threads because the
négociant does not pay more for the dévidage than if the threads were
good. For the weavers as for the dévideuses, it is a take or leave
[proposition]."[29] Thus, not only had dévidage become a more specialized

---

[28]E. Pariset, Report to Chamber of Commerce of Lyons concerning
children in industry, June 15, 1867, annexed to deliberations of Chamber
of Commerce of June 20, 1867, Compte-rendu des travaux de la Chambre de
Commerce de Lyon, années 1865, 1866, 1867, 1868, p. 148. (BCCL)

[29]"Rapport à Monsieur Delcourt, Commissaire spécial, sur la situation
de la fabrique," September 7, 1869, AML, I2 - 47(A), No. 314.

task, separated from the household of the master-weaver, but the mistress
dévideuse was herself coming under more direct control of the merchant-
manufacturer, just like the master-weaver. The fabricant paid her a
piece-rate, as he paid the master-weaver, for dévidage of his silk
thread consigned to her. The putting-out of weaving orders to the countryside by the same merchant-manufacturers of Lyons favored this specialization
of dévidage and the enforcement of direct contact between dévideuse and
merchant. Dévideuses of Lyons prepared the silk thread put out to the
rural areas, and their work increased with the spread of rural weaving.
In September 1867 the police thus remarked that "the number of these
latter [workers] is considerable in spite of the fact that few young
workers have been trained for several years."[30]

D. The Artisanal Household: Decline in Entrepreneurship Among
    Master Silk Weavers

The separation of dévidage from the household of the master-weaver,
the strong familialization of household residents and the decrease in the
number of looms and persons in the household all suggest that the extent of
'entrepreneurship' among master-weavers in managing the internal order of
their households fell very noticeably in the 1860's. Instead of shops including several different types of workers, specialized by task and hired
for a wage, supervised by the master and working alongside him, his family,
apprentices and dévideuses, weavers' households seem to have become exclusive
family units fostering little daily contact with non-relatives and with

[30]"Rapport à Monsieur Delcourt, Commissaire spécial, sur la situation
de la fabrique des étoffes de soies," September 9, 1867, AML, I 2 - 47(A),
No. 305.

outsiders in work relations. These households apparently became more 'artisanal,' in short, concentrating the (largely auxiliary) labor of the family around that of the master's own weaving labor, rather than dispersing family auxiliary labor and the master's own supervision over additional looms worked by non-relative residents or by non-residents, as 'entrepreneurial' masters were wont to do.

In order to test the statistical validity of this impression of a decline in 'entrepreneurship' and to determine more precisely its nature and causes, an 'entrepreneurial index' (Ie) was constructed to measure, as best as possible, the level of entrepreneurship in each household. The index measures entrepreneurship by comparing the number of occupied looms in the household with the total number of persons of weaving age (14 and over in 1866, 10 and over in 1847[31]) or otherwise indicated as weavers, such as apprentices and journeyworkers in 1847. This total includes the head of the household and spouse, if any. Ie takes a value ranging from - 1, indicating total possible dependence of the household on co-resident kin labor for all the weaving in the household, to + 1, indicating total necessary dependence on wage labor living outside the household. Each household has only one value of Ie associated with it, indicating its position on this spectrum of entrepreneurship. When Ie = - 1, there is no co-resident non-relative labor aged 14 or over and no outside labor in the household. Kin labor alone is present and suffices to occupy

---

[31]The proper age group for weaving was 14 and over for both years. Because the census for 1847 distinguishes only between children under 10 and children 10 and over, the age group '10 and over' must be used for this year. The 'improper' addition of the ages 10 - 13 to the weaving group for this year ('improper' because weaving was generally not done by those under 14) concerns only children of the master weaver, however, since non-relative weavers were classified separately as 'apprentices' or as 'journeyworkers' in the 1847 census. The following sources were used to determine the 14 year

all looms -- assuming one person per loom. The value Ie increases, first,
as the proportion of non-relative co-resident labor of weaving age increases and second, as the proportion of labor living outside the household
(Livout) increases. The minimum presence of outside labor is given by a
positive difference between the number of occupied looms and the number
of household residents of weaving age. Above the value of - 1, the index
arbitrarily applies labor in the order 1.) resident labor -- a.) non-
relative co-resident labor and b.) relative co-resident labor -- and
2.) non-resident labor. Thus Ie takes a value between -1 and 0 when no
outside labor is present, increases in this range with the ratio of non-
relative co-resident labor to the number of occupied looms, and reaches
0 when the number of non-relative residents exactly equals the number of
occupied looms. Then Ie takes a value between 0 and 1 to indicate the
presence of outside labor in the household and increases with the ratio
of outside labor to the number of occupied looms. A value of Ie greater
than zero thus indicates the necessary presence of outside labor to occupy
the active looms. A value of Ie less than zero, however, indicates only
that such labor was not absolutely necessary for weaving, even though the
master weaver might in fact have hired outside labor in order to allocate
inside and outside labor more efficiently among weaving and auxiliary tasks.
(Appendix VI discusses in greater detail the construction of Ie, the meaning
of each category of values, and the validity of this index for the study of
entrepreneurship.)

Table 31 summarizes the distribution of silk-weavers' households in

minimum weaving age: Maurice Garden, Lyon et les lyonnais au XVIIIe
siècle (Paris: les Belles lettres, 1970), pp. 47-51, 57-61; A. Beauquis,
Histoire économique de la soie (Grenoble: Grands établissements de
l'Imprimerie générale, 1910), p. 360; Simon, L'ouvrière, p. 47.

the census samples of 1847 and 1866 over these various levels of
entrepreneurship (values of Ie). Besides summarizing the distribution
for all households in the sample considered together, the table considers
plain-loom households separately from fancy-loom households, in order to
trace the differences, if any, in changing entrepreneurship between these
two types of household.

Table 31

Distribution of Weavers' Households,
by Loom Type and Degree
of Sufficient Non-Relative
and Necessary Non-Resident Labor Used for
Weaving, Croix-Rousse Samples (1847, 1866)

Value of Ie	Meaning*	All HH's 1847	All HH's 1866	Plains HH's 1847	Plains HH's 1866	Fancies HH's 1847	Fancies HH's 1866
		a. Number of Households					
Ie = -1	Rel labor only	72	80	38	54	31	22
-1<Ie<0	Rel and Nonrel labor	59	21	9	11	45	7
Ie = 0	Nonrel labor sufficient	31	12	4	8	23	2
-1≤Ie≤0	Livin labor only	162	113	51	73	99	31
0<Ie<.5	Livin > Livout	4	3	1	1	2	1
Ie = .5	Livin = Livout	1	2	-	1	1	1
.5<Ie<1	Livin < Livout	-	2	-	-	-	2
0<Ie<1	Livout labor present	5	7	1	2	3	4
	Total Households	167	120	52	75	102	35
		b. Percentage of Total Households					
Ie = -1	Rel labor only	43.1	66.7	73.1	72.0	30.4	62.9
-1<Ie<0	Rel and Nonrel labor	35.4	17.5	17.3	14.6	44.1	20.0
Ie = 0	Nonrel labor sufficient	18.6	10.0	7.7	10.7	22.5	5.7
-1≤Ie≤0	Livin labor only	97.1	94.2	98.1	97.3	97.0	88.6
0<Ie<.5	Livin > Livout	2.4	2.5	1.9	1.3	2.0	2.9
Ie = .5	Livin = Livout	.6	1.7	-	1.3	1.0	2.9
.5<Ie<1	Livin < Livout	-	1.7	-	-	-	5.7
0<Ie<1	Livout labor present	3.0	5.9	1.9	2.6	3.0	11.5
	Total	100.1	99.9	100.0	99.9	100.0	100.1

Value of Ie	Meaning*	All HH 1847	All HH 1866	Plains HH 1847	Plains HH 1866	Fancies HH 1847	Fancies HH 1866
		c. Percentile Change From 1847 to 1866					
Ie = -1	Rel labor only	+ 23.6		- 1.1		+ 32.5	
-1<Ie<0	Rel and Nonrel labor	- 17.9		- 2.7		- 24.1	
Ie = 0	Nonrel labor sufficient	- 8.6		+ 3.0		- 16.8	
-1≤Ie≤0	Livin labor only	- 2.9		- .8		- 8.4	
0<Ie<.5	Livin > Livout	+ .1		- .6		+ .9	
Ie = .5	Livin = Livout	+ 1.1		+ 1.3		+ 1.9	
.5<Ie<1	Livin < Livout	+ 1.7		0.		+ 5.7	
0<Ie<1	Livout labor present	+ 2.9		+ .7		+ 8.5	

Sources: Ibid..

*See Appendix VI for explanation of each category.

As section c. of the table makes especially clear, the most significant changes in entrepreneurship between 1847 and 1866 for all households was the increase in fully artisanal households (Ie = -1) and the decrease in partly entrepreneurial households with resident non-relatives and family members in sufficient numbers to work all occupied looms. Such a result is consistent with the earlier impression of familialization of the household between the two years, eliminating or reducing the proportion of non-relatives among the household residents. The adequacy of residents for weaving in some households -- in a larger proportion of total households, in fact, in 1866 than in 1847 -- was not evident, however, from the study of familialization. This latter conclusion is demonstrated by the increase in the proportion of households in all categories of entrepreneurship which indicate the necessary presence of some non-residents to work some of the occupied looms (that is, those levels of entrepreneurship where Ie is greater than 0). Such increase (by +2.9 percentiles) in percentage of households with outside labor present (Livout), in fact compensates exactly the net decline (by -2.9 percentiles) in percentage of households able to rely entirely on their resident labor (Livin) for working its active looms. The two most important changes in entrepreneurship between 1847 and 1866, therefore, were a strong familialization of sufficient weaving labor in general and a mild increase in the proportion of house- hold weaving undertaken necessarily by hired non-residents.

Separating movements in entrepreneurship in plain-loom households from movements in fancy-loom households enables us to locate the sources of these changes more precisely. The changes were clearly concentrated in fancy-loom households rather than in plain-loom households. In the cases of both familialization of sufficient weaving labor and increase in the extent of necessary non-resident labor, the positive tendencies were stronger in fancy-loom households than in all households considered together and especially stronger than in plain-loom households. The latter, which were traditionally (i.e. in 1847) more familial, did not, on the average, familialize their weaving labor (in the manner defined by the index Ie) much more in 1866 than in 1847. These households in fact increased slightly both their tendency to accept non-relative labor as resident workers and, less strongly, their tendency to employ outside labor. Fancy-loom households, traditionally less familial, tended to rely, in much greater proportions than in 1847, on the exclusive labor of the master-weaver's children and kin, just like the majority of plain-loom households. A few more in 1847 also employed non-residents to weave on their looms. In other words, while plain-loom households remained strongly familial, with a mild tendency to accept non-relatives into the home and

shop, fancy-loom households either closed in upon the family group more
exclusively than in the past or tended to employ labor whose relation
with the master had no other basis than the wage contract. In either
case, affective solidarity was confined to kin within the household
rather than extended to non-relatives. For the latter, the household
was no longer a home but merely a shop.

The reasons for this combined familialization and contractualization
of work relations derived largely from the economic conditions of fancy-
cloth weaving during the 1860's. Among these were the frequent variation
of fancy-cloth styles, the substitution of simpler fancy cloths for the
more elegant fabrics, the reduction in the scale of household enterprise,
and frequent and severe unemployment. The first three conditions explained
the familialization of most household weaving of fancy cloths, while the
fourth condition explained the tendency of some fancy-loom households to
employ more non-resident labor than in the past. Short 'style-lives'
for orders of faҫonnés during the 1860's, forcing frequent changes of
design on the loom, created the strongest incentive for substitution of
family labor for hired labor in weaving. From an economic point of view,
such substitution was most profitable in fancy-loom households, because
of high skill rents for weaving fancy cloths and because of the high
risks of loss due to frequent mountings which hired labor did not share.[32]
This explained the masters' demand for familial labor. The shift of
product demand in favor of simpler fancy cloths and the reduction of
the scale of household enterprise as a result of chronic unemployment
made untrained family labor at least as efficient as skilled hired labor

---

[32]Chapter I, section I - B - 1, p. 65.

in weaving and mounting fancy silks and therefore made family labor
more 'available' for these tasks without loss of efficiency. The
simpler fancy dress ornaments and nouveautés favored by the market in
this period required less skill to mount and to weave, so that less-
trained or relatively unspecialized family members could perform these
tasks as well as specialized workers. The smaller number of looms, in
comparision with the past, permitted the application of more family
labor to these for auxiliary tasks with little loss of efficiency.[33]
In these ways, the 'supply' of labor suitable for weaving and auxiliary
tasks of the household could be increased by the addition of family
labor to the general pool of familial and non-familial workers. In the
choice between the former and the latter, family labor was usually
preferred, especially in extremely variable conditions of product demand.
However, for the few occasional orders for highly-wrought fancy silks,
requiring special weaving or mounting skills, masters employed journeyworkers who were not members of the family. They did not receive these
journeyworkers as household residents, as much as they had done in the
past, because of the short duration of these orders, discouraging any
commitment to provide bed and board for these subordinate workers over
a long period of time. Consequently, the proportion of statistically-
observable outsiders hired to execute individual orders increased somewhat,
even while the proportion of non-relatives residing in the households
decreased.

These reasons for changing entrepreneurship in fancy-loom households
are based largely on the general theory of the household economy developed

---

[33] Ibid., pp. 66-67.

in Chapter I and applied to the specific economic conditions of the
1860's.[34] The census data permit us to take this explanation of
changing entrepreneurship one step further for silk-weavers' households
in general, to the association between entrepreneurship, as measured by
the index Ie, and other economic and social characteristics discussed
in the present chapter -- loom type, kinship, sex and age balance of household residents other than the head and spouse -- and one additional
characteristic -- the age of the head of the household. Measuring such
association by means of multivariate regression analysis permits a
rather precise determination of the nature and extent of the relationship
between entrepreneurship and these other characteristics. Careful
examination of this relationship will also suggest (though not prove)
some of the effects of these characteristics on entrepreneurship.

In order to determine the relative strength of association between
the different characteristics and the index Ie, six economic and social
'type' variables were constructed and regressed separately and together,
in various combinations, against the entrepreneurial index Ie. Five of
these variables refer to characteristics discussed previously -- loom-
type, plain or fancy (PrOU for 1847; PrTU for 1866); kinship relations
of residents other than the spouse to the head of the household (PrREL);
sex balance of these household residents other than head and spouse (PrSXF);
and their age balance between the apprentice-adolescent age group (PrAPP
for 1847; PrTAG14 for 1866) and the journeyworker-adult age group (PrOUV
for 1847; PrTAG21 for 1866). One variable is new -- that of the age of the head
of the household (AGE), a proxy for 'life-stage' (the time factor in
a function of savings, or accumulation of wealth). Table 32 summarizes

---

[34] Ibid., pp. 62-71.

415

the results of the general regression (that is, the regression for all

households considered together) for the 1847 and 1866 census samples

of the Croix-Rousse, and the table and its key provide an exact definition

and description of each of the variables entering the regression equation.

Table 32

Regression Study of Type-Variable Determinants of Entrepreurial Index Ie. Croix-Rousse (1847, 1866)

1847

Dependent Variable Ie Regressed With

Independent Variable Standardized Coefficients and F Values

Name	Description	R^2	F	d-f	Critical F	PrOU	PrREL	PrSXF	PrAPP	PrOUV	AGE
1. PrOU	OU/OTOTUF	.11	15.29	128/1	3.92	-.33 (15.29)					
2. PrREL	REL/HH	.35	68.85	128/1	3.92		-.59 (68.85)				
3. PrSXF	SXF/HH	0	.36	128/1	3.92			.05 (.36)			
4. PrAPP	APP/WOR	.04	4.74	104/1	3.94				.21 (4.74)		
5. PrOUV	OUV/WOR	.34	53.50	104/1	3.94					.58 (53.50)	
6. AGE	AGE	0	.05	128/1	3.92						.02 (.05)
1,2,3,6		.42	22.49	125/4	2.45	-.24 (11.19)	-.56 (64.53)	.10 (2.09)			.12 (2.96)
1,2,3,4,6		.53	22.29	100/5	2.32	-.19 (7.06)	-.74 (93.93)	.12 (3.02)	-.11 (2.00)		.15 (4.27)
1,2,3,5,6		.57	26.07	100/5	2.32	-.19 (7.41)	-.53 (38.93)	.13 (3.95)		.28 (11.10)	.14 (4.28)
1,2,3,4,5,6		.58	22.87	99/6	2.20	-.17 (6.41)	-.32 (5.09)	.11 (2.66)	.22 (3.55)	.48 (12.70)	.13 (3.74)

1866

Dependent Variable Ie
Regressed With

Independent Variable Standardized
Coefficients and F Values

Name	Description	R^2	F	d-f	Critical F	PrTU	PrREL	PrSXF	PrTAG14	PrTAG21	AGE
1.PrTU	TU/TOTIF	0	.36	1/80	3.97	-.07 (.36)					
2.PrREL	REL/HH	.43	61.40	1/80	3.97		-.66 (61.40)				
3.PrSXF	SXF/HH	.02	1.60	1/80	3.97			.14 (1.60)			
4.PrTAG14	TAG14/HH	0	.02	1/80	3.97				-.02 (.02)		
5.PrTAG21	TAG21/HH	.07	5.94	1/80	3.97					.26 (5.94)	
6.AGE	AGE	0	.01	1/80	3.97						-.01 (.01)
1,2,3,6		.46	16.50	4/77	2.51	-.07 (.65)	-.66 (62.39)	.15 (3.29)			-.03 (.14)
1,2,3,4,6		.47	13.75	5/76	2.35	-.10 (1.24)	-.68 (64.99)	.14 (2.94)	-.12 (1.93)		-.03 (.17)
1,2,3,5,6		.47	13.33	5/76	2.35	-.08 (.85)	-.63 (51.29)	.14 (2.50)		.09 (.81)	-.07 (.57)
1,2,3,4,5,6		.47	11.31	6/75	2.23	-.10 (1.23)	-.67 (42.23)	.14 (2.73)	-.12 (1.10)	.01 (0)	-.04 (.14)

Key to Symbols

Ie: Entrepreueurial index

PrOU: Proportion of occupied plain looms (unis) to total occupied
plain (unis) and fancy (façonné) looms
    OU: Number of occupied unis looms
    OTOTUF: Total number of occupied unis and façonnés looms

PrREL: Proportion of relatives of the head of household living in the
household (other than spouse) to total number of persons living
in the household (other than head and spouse)
    REL: Number of relatives of the head of household, by blood
or by marriage, living in the household (other than
spouse of head)
    HH: Total number of persons living in the household other
than head and spouse

PrSXF: Proportion of females living in the household (other than head
and spouse) to total number of persons living in the household
(other than head and spouse)
    SXF: Number of females living in the household, other than
head and spouse
    HH: Total number of persons living in the household other
than head and spouse

PrAPP: Proportion of apprentices living in the household to total
number of silk workers living in the household other than
head and spouse (apprentices + journeyworkers + children
of head aged 10 or above)
    APP: Number of apprentices living in the household
    WOR: Number of apprentices + journeyworkers (OUV) + children
of head aged 10 or above (i.e. weaving age group,
including children of weaving age)

PrOUV: Proportion of journeyworkers living in the household to total
number of silk workers living in the household other than
head and spouse
    OUV: Number of journeyworkers living in the household
    WOR: Number of apprentices + journeyworkers (OUV) + children
of head aged 10 or above

AGE: Age of head of the household

PrTU: Proportion of total (occupied and unoccupied) plain looms (unis)
to total (occupied and unoccupied) plain (unis) and fancy
(façonné) looms
    TU: Total occupied and unoccupied plain looms
    TOTUF: Total occupied and unoccupied plain and fancy looms

PrTAG14: Proportion of persons living in the household, other than
head and spouse, aged 14 - 20,to total number of persons
living in the household, other than head and spouse
TAG14: Number of persons living in the household, other
than head and spouse, aged 14 - 20
HH: Total number of persons living in the household
other than head and spouse

PrTAG21: Proportion of persons living in the household, other than
head and spouse, aged 21 and above, to total number of
persons living in the household, other than head and spouse
TAG21: Number of persons living in the household, other than
head and spouse, aged 21 and above
HH: Total number of persons living in the household other
than head and spouse

R^2: Correlation coefficient (the proportion of the variation in
Ie explained by the variables against which it is regressed
to the total variation in Ie)

F: The computed F-statistic for the entire regression equation
$= (R^2/k)/((1-R^2)/(N-k-1))$. The statistic measures the ratio
of the proportional 'explained' variation of Ie (R^2), to
the proportional unexplained variation of Ie ($1-R^2$), correcting
for sample size (N) and number of independent variables in the
regression equation (k).

d-f: Degrees of freedom in the regression equation. The top figure
gives the degrees of freedom in the numerator of the F-
statistic (=k) and the bottom figure gives the degrees of
freedom in the denominator of F (=N-k)

Critical F: The F-statistic computed for a normally distributed random
sample of size N in a regression against k independent
variables, at 95% level of confidence

F-Value for Each Independent
Variable (in parentheses below
each standardized coefficient
for that variable):

The computed F-statistic for the partial correlation of that
independent variable with the dependent variable Ie, controlling for variation in the other independent variables.
This F-statistic measures the ratio of the proportional
explained variation of Ie for this partial regression ($r_{ki}{}^2$)
to the proportional unexplained variation of Ie for the
entire regression ($1-R^2$), correcting for sample size (N)
and number of independent variables (k)

420

The statistical test using the F-statistic consists of rejecting
the null hypothesis that R^2 (or r_{ki}^2) is zero only when the
computed F-statistic is equal to or larger than the critical
F-statistic for the given degrees of freedom. In this case,
the variation in Ie explained by the independent variable (s)
in the regression equation is due to actual correlation, between
Ie and the variable (s), rather than to mere random error, in 95
out of 100 cases (95% level of confidence).

The symbol β is used in the text to indicate a standardized
coefficient of an independent variable.

The one major similarity between the relationship of Ie to the
type variables in 1847 and their relationship in 1866 was the inverse
variation of level of entrepreneurship (Ie) with the familialization
of household residents (PrREL). Entrepreneurship was stronger in less
familial households, weaker in more familial households. This negative
association was indeed the one constant in both periods, remaining unchanged
even when other type variables were controlled, as in the numbered
regression sets with four or more independent variables in Table 32.
From a simple statistical point of view, this is hardly surprising.
The value of Ie changed in the same direction as the proportion of
resident nonrelatives to the number of occupied looms, hence in the
opposite direction to the remaining proportion of relatives, for values
of Ie between −1 and 0. The negative correlation between Ie and PrREL
simply confirms the conclusion that the proportion of insufficient
resident nonrelative labor and unnecessary non-resident labor moved
in the same direction as the extent of familialization of household
residents.

The main difference in the type-variable 'determinants' of
entrepreneurship between the two years was the reduction in the number
of significant type-variables in 1866, as compared with 1847, when these are
combined in a 'structural' relation of association with entrepreneurship.
By 'structural relation' I mean the combination of type variables explaining the largest percentage of variation in the entrepreneurial
index Ie for the least loss (i.e. reduction to statistical insignificance)
of type variables in a multivariate ordinary least-squares regression
equation. Table 32 suggests the relevant structural relations for each
of the two years in regression set (1,2,3,4,5,6). These relations

combine respectively all six variables in 1847 and only two variables
(PrREL and PrSXF) in 1866. I tested several other alternative combinations
and found these two 'structures' the best (highest R^2) for each year
respectively. Diagram 1 below summaries the two structures in their
'pure' form; that is, according to regressions including only the
statistically significant type variables. Correlation coefficients,
representing the strength and direction of association with Ie, are
indicated beside the arrow for each type variable, and the proportion
of variation in Ie explained by the combination of type variables (R^2)
is indicated below each structural diagram.

Diagram 1

Structures of Determination of
Entrepreneurship (Ie) by
Type Variables of Weavers'
Households, Croix-Rousse
Samples (1847, 1866)

1847   1866

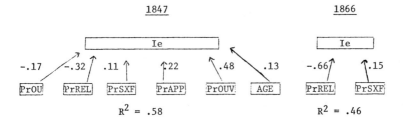

$R^2 = .58$ $R^2 = .46$

As the diagram makes clear, the major changes in the structure of
determination of entrepreneurship between 1847 and 1866 were the elimination
of loom type and the addition of feminization as significant 'determinants'
of Ie. Appendix VII analyzes in detail the specific nature of these
changes and the reasons for them, noting differences between plain-loom
households and fancy-loom households. For the present, a summary of some

of the most salient conclusions of this analysis, especially those
concerning the relationship of feminization to entrepreneurship, will
suffice. Feminization was associated positively with entrepreneurship
in both years, but it had an especially strong effect on entrepreneurship in fancy-loom households, for a given degree of familialization
of those households. Since familialization varied inversely with
entrepreneurship, the latter was strongest in the least familial, most
feminized fancy-loom households in 1866. In 1847, on the contrary, it
was highest in the least-familial fancy-loom households, regardless of
the sex balance of the members of these households.

The two years differed also in the relationship of entrepreneurship
to apprenticeship-adolescence. In 1847, those households with apprentices,
especially female apprentices, tended to have more entrepreneurial masters.
In 1866, however, apprenticeship -- more precisely, adolescence -- had
little effect on entrepreneurship, largely because of the decline of
apprenticeship in most weavers' households. In fancy-loom households,
where apprenticeship was preserved more strongly, adolescence had a
positive effect in the same regression equation. Contrary to expectations
based on earlier analysis of the distribution tables, the preservation or
increase of female apprenticeship in 1866 as compared with 1847 - 1851
was therefore not, on the average, associated with high levels of
entrepreneurship in fancy-loom households. Instead, entrepreneurship
rose in such households with feminization in general, regardless of the
age group (adolescent or adult) of female residents and regardless of
their kin relation (relative or non-relative) to the head of the household.

The proportion of resident journeymen in 1847 and of resident adults

in 1866, had a positive influence on degree of entrepreneurship in both
years. In the first year, this influence was strong both in plain-loom
households and in fancy-loom households. In the second year, it was
strong only in plain-loom households. These households tended to be
more feminine,less familial and headed by older master-weavers than the
average. Very likely these 'entrepreneurial' plain-loom households were
those employing large numbers of plain-weaving compagnonnes whom Audiganne
and Reybaud observed in the 1850's, along with older daughters and other
female kin of the master-weaver. In the early 1870's, the Chambre
Syndicale des Soieries of Lyons claimed that the group of journeyworkers
was two-thirds "women and girls," most of whom necessarily worked in the
plain-cloth sector, which largely dominated the work of the fabrique
by that time.[35] Thus, in plain-loom households as in fancy-loom
households, the use of female labor was a rather strong indication of
a highly entrepreneurial attitude towards the household economy by the
master-weaver.

The foundation of entrepreneurship on more docile resident female
labor, along with the familialization of labor in most weavers' households,
strongly influenced the economic behavior of the master-weaver in this
period of secular unemployment aggravated by reductions in piece-rates.
Anticipated profits on additional looms which the master might occupy
with family and non-family labor were low, because of the low piece-rate,
and uncertain, because of unstable employment. To prevent further decline
of his economic position, the master-weaver therefore had to focus on
reduction of costs of maintaining his household rather than on increase

[35]"Réponses de la Chambre Syndicale des Soieries," Enquête
Parlementaire, Premier Questionnaire A, Observations, AN, C 3021.

of earnings.[36] Familialization and feminization of household labor
offered one means of reducing household costs; namely, reduction in the
standards of living which consumed earnings. Familialization and feminization both placed at the disposal of the master a labor force more amenable
to this control. This was partly the result of a heightened paternal
authority between master and members of the household and partly the
effect of a relative scarcity of alternative work for the daughters of
master-weavers and for the female migrants from the surrounding rural
areas. As the prospect of reviving employment in the silk industry dimmed
with each passing semester, the master thus focused increasingly on reducing the consumption of his household, or at least the expense of that
consumption. The sudden rise of food prices in 1867, combined with another
decline in export sales of silk fabrics in that same year[37] fixed his
attention on consumption even more intensively. This increasing concern
with the consuming household economy was a major reason for the appeal
of consumers' cooperation in the neighborhoods of the silk weavers.

E. The Household Order in Movements of Association: Old Ideals
   and New Realities

Besides addressing these needs of household consumption, consumers'
cooperative movements appealed also to the master-weavers' concern with
declining entrepreneurship. At the same time, the movement recognized the
enlarged role of women in the silk industry. For these reasons, consumers'
cooperation was especially 'meaningful' to the master silk weavers, for it
reflected the new realities in their household order and provided a means
of responding opportunely to these new realities. Consumers' cooperation

---

[36]Chapter I, section I - B - 1, pp. 69-71.

[37]Graph 5, Chapter III, p. 230.

was therefore the most successful form of voluntary association among
the silk weavers of Lyons and the most popular form as well, in
practice if not always in theory, throughout most of the 1860's.
Moreover, the organization of consumers' cooperatives was almost
exclusively the work of master silk weavers -- those weavers among
whom the concern with household consumption and with declining entrepreneurship was strongest, and those most 'interested' in the position of
women in their trade.

Consumers' cooperation appealed to the master weavers both as a
means of restoring traditional roles and values and as a means of adapting
to present conditions in their household economies in a new way. Its
main appeal to tradition was its revival of the entrepreneurial role
of the master. Consumers' cooperation sought to restore to the masters
an entrepreneurial role in directing the affairs of cooperative groceries
in their neighborhoods, as a substitute for their declining entrepreneurial
role in household silk weaving. Cooperative entrepreneurship differed, of
course, from the traditional entrepreneurship of the household by its
collective character and by its application to a neighborhood retail
enterprise, rather than to a household manufacturing enterprise. The
focus on retail trade, to serve the needs of consumption, rather than on
manufacturing, to serve those of production, was, of course, coincident
with the master-weavers' greater attention to expenditures for consumption
than to revenues from production in their own households.

The main evidence for this entrepreneurial appeal of consumers'
cooperation is circumstantial. This was the excessive concern with
small-group autonomy, focused around the neighborhood organization,
among the cooperative groceries in Lyons. These groceries defended
this autonomy even when the benefits of sacrificing some of it for
wholesale purchase of food, for example, were very large. As a result,

consumers' cooperation remained a highly de-centralized movement, unlike producers' cooperation, which was highly centralized from the start. The few attempts made to organize the cooperative groceries into larger associations quickly failed. In 1865 a few prominent cooperative leaders tried to organize a centralized wholesale enterprise to lower food-purchasing costs for member societies and individuals and to help new consumers' societies form in neighborhoods without them.[38] This Vie à Bon Marché intended no interference with the internal affairs of its member organizations, but it failed to rally enough support even to register its statutes. Another attempt by several independent consumers' societies to form a similar "central commercial store" later in the same year also lost the interest of mosts of its initiators very quickly. Although the proposal stressed that the "central store must be created by the associations themselves, in order not to become for them a threat" and that these associations "must not however unite themselves so much to it, that they become no more than its branches and subsidiaries,"[39] only six of about twenty societies in Lyons agreed to make a few grocery purchases in common, in April 1867.[40] Most consumer cooperatives in Lyons were in fact so jealous of their autonomy that they prohibited their members from belonging to any other society with similar purpose.[41] One plausible explanation for this strong attachment to neighborhood

---

[38]La Vie à Bon Marché, Appel aux souscripteurs, Statuts (Lyon: Pinier, 1865), AML, I2 - 45, Sociétés coopératives de production et de consommation (1849 à 1870), No. 257.

[39]'Project de l'établissement d'un magasin central de commerce' in Eugène Flotard, "Bulletin Coopératif," Le Progrès, December 18, 1865.

[40]Flotard, "Bulletin Coopératif," Le Progrès, April 15, 1867.

[41]See, for example, Article 4-1 of Espérance Ouvrière, Statuts, 1866, ADR, 9U - Sociétés: Constitutions et modifications, August 23, 1866.

autonomy was the desire of the leaders and members of the individual
cooperative societies to preserve the latter as instruments for their
entrepreneurial ambitions.

These ambitions were originally limited to directing an enterprise
for the purpose of reducing costs of food and other primary necessities
consumed in the household. As indicated earlier, such an ambition addressed
the present needs of the individual households with a collective solution
to the problem of reducing household expenditures. Consumers' cooperation
also provided members of the societies an instrument for extending their
entrepreneurial ambitions even further, to the increase of earnings and
not only to the reduction of costs. Their ambitions moved in this direction,
however, only by sacrificing service to the community to individual profit-
making. Such a sacrifice was a high moral price to pay in terms of the
social ideology of cooperation, which theoretically substituted the promotion of social welfare for the pursuit of private profit. The attitude
of cooperative groceries in Lyons towards profit-making was therefore
fraught with ambiguity. Not all societies abandoned the original purpose
of providing their members and their neighborhoods good food at relatively
low prices, and not all of those which adopted profit-making policies
followed the capitalist model entirely. But some cooperatives did become
small capitalist enterprises and even justified their profit-making
policies in their statutes as a means of "improving the position of the
Members by having them participate directly in the profits [of grocery
commerce].[42] Among these was the Société Alimentaire du Quartier des

---

[42]Article 1, Société commerciale alimentaire du Quartier des Tapis,
Statuts, 1864, ADR, 4M - Police administrative - Associations, coops 9,
Société alimentaire du Quartier des Tapis.

Tapis, from the statutes of which this quotation was taken. This society
sold to outsiders but distributed profits from such sales only among its
members. A few societies even went beyond profit-making to investment
in government bonds, even foreign government bonds. In 1876, for example,
the consumers' cooperative La Ruche of the First Arrondissement of Lyons
had an investment portfolio valued at 35,900 francs, or 239% of the share
capital of the enterprise.[43] Not only had the weavers in these societies
re-discovered a field for their entrepreneurial ambitions, but this field
was also apparently more lucrative, or its possibilities more grandiose,
than its traditional field of entrepreneurship in silk weaving ever had
been for any but the very fortunate few.

Consumers' cooperation thus revived traditional entrepreneurial
aspirations in managing the entire budget of an economy, revenues as
well as costs. While appealing to tradition in this manner, however,
it also recognized present realities and provided a means of adapting to
the latter in a new way. As noted earlier, the movement itself was
originally a new kind of response to the present conditions of the
consumption-oriented economy of the household. Another important
response to present conditions concerned the sex balance of the household,
favoring females over males in weaving and in other tasks. The response
of consumers' cooperation to the enlarged feminization of the silk industry was the admission of females as member shareholders into the
societies. Such female admissions were very rare in small workers'
associations in Lyons before the 1860's. Women were almost never received
as members in the small mutual aid societies and only rarely admitted into

---

[43]La Ruche, "Situation," June 25, 1876, ADR, ibid., coops 10, la
Ruche.

other voluntary associations. In 1850, the Chamber of Commerce of Lyons
organized the large, city-wide Silk Workers' Society for Mutual Aid in
part to make mutual benefits available to females in the fabrique. In
contrast to the exclusively male traditions of most of the smaller
associations, many consumers' cooperatives of the 1860's had female
members, including both females in subordinate positions in the silk-
weaving households, such as compagnonnes, and females directing their
own household-shops, such as mistress dévideuses. Some female coopérateurs
were among the wealthiest shareholders of the consumers' societies, at
least according to the initial deposits on their shares. At least 6 of
103 shareholders of the Francs Coopérateurs in 1866 were female, and
among these six, two were weavers and two were mistress dévideuses.[44]
Four of the 152 shareholders of the Prévoyante in 1865 were weavers, and
two of these deposited the exceptional sums of 334 francs and 298 francs
respectively on their shares at the time of incorporation of the society.[45]
Although the number of females in these associations was not large, neither
absolutely nor relatively, the mere acceptance of females as member stock-
holders was a significant change from past practice in weavers' voluntary
associations.

Other movements of association also reflected the feminization of
the silk industry, especially the resistance movement. Women were involved
actively with men in the organization of resistance societies in 1869 - 1870.
Announcements of meetings for approving piece-rates and for deciding
negotiating tactics often explicitly addressed male and female workers.

---

[44]Francs Coopérateurs, Statutes and list of shareholders, 1866,
registered at the Tribunal du Commerce de Lyon, ADR, 9U - Sociétés:
Constitutions et modifications, September 29, 1865.

[45]La Prévoyante, Statutes and list of shareholders, 1865, registered
at the Tribunal du Commerce de Lyon, ibid., September 29, 1865.

On November 26, 1869, for example, a note inserted in the local republican newspaper of Lyons, Le Progrès, called for a meeting of "male and female weaver workers" of plain cloths.[46] One meeting of journey fancy weavers during the strike of July included 100 women among 700-800 persons attending.[47] Strike associations in some of the trades auxiliary to weaving even elected women as officers. The male and female lissage workers, for example, elected a female president in June 1870.[48] Some auxiliary trades composed exclusively of females, such as the remetteuses, tried to form their own resistance organizations even in defiance of their employers, who were master-weavers for the most part.[49] Such full participation of women in industrial resistance and strike activity was clearly a departure from tradition. This acceptance of female activism was perhaps inherited from the cooperative movement, to which women, as we saw earlier, were admitted as independent shareholders. Such acceptance was also a recognition of the daily contribution and predominant role of female labor in nearly all the activities of the fabrique, from the least skilled task work to the most proficient and prestigious weaving.

In these ways, the movements of association among the silk weavers during the 1860's, especially consumers' cooperation, manifested the double character of change in their household economy and society. This change

---

[46]"Chronique locale," Le Progrès, November 26, 1869.

[47]Police report concerning meeting of weavers of armures - façonnés at the Rotunde, July 10, 1870, AML, 12 - 47(B), Corporations: Ouvriers en Soie ... (1819 à 1870).

[48]Maurice Moissonnier, La première internationale et la commune à Lyon (Paris: Editions sociales, 1972), p. 184.

[49]Police reports 1086, 1089 and 1089bis concerning meetings of remetteuses and tordeuses in April 1870, especially meeting of April 10, 1879, AML, I2 - 47(B).

reduced the revenue-making function of the household economy and reduced
or eliminated the entrepreneurial role of the master weaver in the weaving
of silk cloths. At the same time, the home and shop of the master weaver
became more familial and feminine, and this change provided the masters
a means of preserving some household autonomy in the manufacture of silk
cloths by facilitating its reduction of expenditures. Consumers'
cooperation began as a means of achieving the latter more efficiently
and more 'humanely' than mere exploitation of family and female labor
achieved. Very quickly, however, some consumers' societies became
exploitative in another way -- of those in their communities using their
stores but not belonging to their societies. They became such as they
extended the entrepreneurial ambitions aroused by cooperative grocery
commerce from merely reducing costs of household consumption to increasing
earnings of cooperative shareholders by making profits in a 'capitalist'
fashion. From the perspective of the more egalitarian ideals of cooperative
ideology, the only consolation to this revival of entrepreneurship by making
profits was the societies' recognition that women too could make profits
along with men through voluntary association. Resistance societies and
consumers' societies which remained 'cooperative' (as opposed to 'capitalist') in their profit-sharing policies, also recognized a more egalitarian
place for women in their movements, and thus acknowledged women's importance
in the weaving of silk cloths and in the direction of dévidage in their
industry.

II. Moral Effects of the Changing Household

The emergence of a new kind of household order during the 1860's
that was both more familial and more feminine than in the past did not

eliminate the concern about 'demoralization' expressed during the 1850's, when the old order of the household was dissolving. In particular, the 'demoralization' associated with the new household order, in the minds of the master-weavers, was as 'personal' and 'individual' as that associated with the disordered household of the 1850's. The former differed from the latter not so much in its nature as in its source. During the 1850's, personal 'demoralization,' especially that of the subordinate workers, was presumed to derive from sources external to the household itself. Such were the bad habits of journeymen and child workers acquired outside the household, in the inns and on the streets, and the external economic forces eroding the traditional authority of the master and the traditional sense of responsibility for work among subordinates. The household itself, and its head, the master weaver, in particular, were considered to have morally propitious influence on the members of the household. Because of this presumed good influence, one of the major aims of voluntary association during the 1850's, especially of mutual aid societies, was the preservation of the household order and of the master's presence at home even during illness, to 'moralize' the other members of the household.

During the 1860's, however, the household became itself a source of 'demoralization,' and the master weaver, not his subordinates, became the agent of moral disorder. 'Demoralization' seemed to derive as much from the exploitation of dependent and resident labor by the master-weaver as from the master's failure to protect his subordinates from the dissipation of the streets. This larger view of 'moralization' was evident in the attention given the conditions of female and child labor by publicists, political and business leaders and private benefactors. In 1852, Audiganne

had complained of the demoralization of subordinate female workers for
whom the master showed no paternal concern. "The master-weavers act
most of the time as if they were freed of all responsibility" of
protecting these females from abuse as they passed from shop to
shop.[50] In 1861, Jules Simon was more impressed by the master-
weavers' exploitation of the labor of dependent female apprentices
and journeyworkers within the household.

> When one walks in the evening through the tortuous
> streets of the Croix-Rousse, and sees on the upper floor
> these illuminated windows behind which resounds the
> hollow noise of the barre, one's heart is grieved by the
> thought of these poor girls who have been there since
> six in the morning, poorly clothed, hardly fed, throwing
> and re-throwing the shuttle without rest or inter-
> mission. . . .[51]

In his article in the Revue des deux mondes in 1865, Simon described
the sad lot of the dévideuses in similar terms. In June 1867, Ernest
Pariset of the Chamber of Commerce of Lyons elaborated on the conditions of dévideuses living and working in the specialized shops of
the mistress dévideuse:

> It is of public notoriety that, in a large number of
> dévidage shops lodging is unsanitary. The female workers
> are squeezed into alcoves or lofts where air does not
> circulate and remains constantly sour; they usually
> sleep two in the same bed, on a straw mattress; they
> receive no attention for personal cleanliness and even
> lack the possibility of satisfying basic hygienic
> needs. . .
>
> The inadequacy of their food is attested by the numerous
> complaints brought each year before the Conseil des
> Prud'hommes. . . Sometimes poverty, sometimes a sordid
> greed makes the mistress dévideuse provide deplorable food. . .

---

[50] A. Audiganne, "Du mouvement intellectual parmi les populations
ouvrières -- Les ouvriers de Lyon en 1852," Revue des deux mondes,
22ème année -- nouvelle période, XV (August 1, 1852), 513.

[51] Simon, L'ouvrière, p. 51.

Badly lodged, hardly fed, mistreated, our little girl
ends by wearing out her health with excessive work.
Whatever her age, she works regularly from five in the
morning until nine o'clock at night, and this fourteen-
hour day of work is followed, when there are many
orders, by night work lasting until eleven o'clock and
midnight.[52]

The female ovalistes in the silk throwing shops of the city lived in

similar conditions.[53]

The result of such conditions and poor treatment within the household-

shop was physical and moral dissipation. In 1875, the Chamber of Commerce

claimed that "the excess work imposed on young girls placed in apprentice-

ship . . . produced numerous consumptives in Lyons,"[54] In the same year,

the merchant-manufacturers Faye and Thevenin declared that the "conditions

of child labor in apprenticeship are not bad in principle;" but "if the

child suffers physically and morally it is rather because of bad treatment

and immorality," presumably on the part of the master or mistress of the

household shop.[55] In response to a question concerning "measures to

protect the morality of women and young girls," the same fabricants

observed that "if there are several (workers) of the two sexes, they

are always under the eyes of the master or mistress of the shop who

works alongside them; all depends on the morality of the masters."[56]

---

[52]Pariset, Compte-rendu des travaux de la Chambre de Commerce de
Lyon..., 1868, pp. 148-49.

[53]Moissonnier, La première internationale à Lyon, pp. 80-82.

[54]"Réponses de la Chambre de Commerce de Lyon," Enquête Parlementaire (Rhône, 1872 - 1875), Premiere Questionnaire A, I, AN, C 3021.

[55][Réponses de] Mrs. Faye et Thevenin F[abric]ants de soieries à
Lyon (Rhône)," ibid., Troisième Questionnaire C XXVIII.

[56]Ibid., XXII

The major moralizing or demoralizing influence, in short, was the master

or mistress chef d'atelier.

One prominent example of this influence was the case of a master

weaver of Lyons accused of murdering the mother of his female apprentice

with whom he had had an affair. The trial of this master received complete

coverage in the daily paper "very much read" by the master weavers, Le

Progrès,[57] and "was followed with growing curiosity by an audience ... in

which the Croix-Rousse [the most concentrated silk-weavers' district in

the city] provided the largest contingent."[58] The case dramatized to

all masters immorality within the household associated with the feminization

of weaving labor and with the exploitation of females and apprentices.

On March 12, 1865, between eight and ten in the evening, Claude,

a "laborious, thrifty master-weaver" of the Saint-Georges quarter pushed

over the banks of the river Rhône Marie, the concierge of his apartment

building, with whom he had had "adulterous relations" for the past three

years. The motive for murder was the pregnancy of her sixteen-year-old

daughter Peronne. Marie had placed Peronne in apprenticeship with Claude

in April 1864. "A few months later, the young female worker, seduced by

her master, became pregnant. Her mother did not fail to notice her

pregnancy shortly thereafter and to discover the author. Her anger brust

forth against [Claude]." After a few unsuccessful attempts to abort the

child, Peronne was sent away to Grenoble or Chambery to give birth, but

---

[57]Jean Gaumont, Le mouvement ouvrier d'association et de coopération
à Lyon (Lyon: Avenir régional, n.d.), pp. 39-44. During the resistance
movement of 1869 - 1870, Le Progrès announced meetings of societies as a
forum for the 'airing of views' by resistance organizers in these societies.
This is the best evidence of the importance of this newspaper among the
silk-weavers.

[58]Le Progrès, May 30, 1865.

tension and anxiety reigned strong among Claude, the master-weaver,

Peronne, the young apprentice weaving each day at his loom, and Marie

her mother, the concierge of the building.

Peronne's pregnancy

> created a situation full of trouble and violence for her
> mother and for their common lover. Passionate, jealous,
> the woman [Marie] pursued [Claude] with her outbursts and
> threats; she told him that she would reveal everything to
> his wife. Yet more sensitive perhaps to the loss of her
> lover than to the dishonor of her daughter, who had now
> become her rival, she nagged her incessantly, announced to
> her that she would get her revenge and seemed always ready
> to take a drastic step.
>
> The fear of a revelation to his wife upset [Claude]
> terribly, the scenes made in front of the young Peronne,
> the tears he saw her shed agitated him even more. Several
> times he had made the woman [Marie] understand that if she
> did not calm down, he would kill her or poison her.
> On Thursday, March 9, 1865, on the occasion of the
> arrival home of one of the children [of the concierge],
> there was a family dinner in the house. Suddenly, at the
> sight of Peronne, the mother threw herself into a tumult of
> jealous fury, wept and tried to hurl herself onto her
> daughter, who was forced to leave. [Claude] appeared in
> the evening, had a discussion with the woman [Marie]. A
> rendez-vous was planned. Seeing the tears of Peronne, he
> told her: "Don't cry, it will end, I will put a stop to her
> for good."

It did end, indeed, in the murder in the Brotteaux. The case was tried

by the Cours d'Assizes of the department of the Rhône on May 27. The

jury found Claude guilty of murder but not   of pre-meditation.

The judge sentenced him to perpetual forced labor.[59]

Recognizing the possibility of the moral degeneration of the

household, as in the case of Claude, and recognizing the importance of

the personal behavior of the master in determining its moral climate,

weavers' voluntary associations during the 1860's continued to stress

---

[59] Ibid.

moralization, in the personal sense, as one of their aims. They
focused in particular on the 'moralizaton' of the master in order to
restore to the household its salutory moral influence. The theme of
'moralization' remained ever strong in the mutual aid societies, which
continued to demand (at least officially) guarantees of good behavior
for new members and to exclude present members for scandalous conduct.[60]
One of the most active small mutual aid societies of weavers, Society
Number 114 of "Old Friends," recalled the moralizing intention of the
organization in terms directed especially at behavior within the
household, on its membership list for 1868:

> The aim of our organization is to preserve ourselves
> from poverty, by joining our savings.
>
> To achieve this end, we must correct ourselves of all
> vice, be industrious, good masters, good fathers and good
> husbands, keep peace within the household, remember that
> if we have children, we must offer them and also those who
> are entrusted to our care, examples of morality.[61]

Cooperation also stressed moralization, in this personal,
individual sense, as one of its goals. In 1867, Eugène Flotard wrote
that "the cooperative society is founded especially on personal
qualities: they are, in a way, one might say, mutual schools of moral
perfection; their credit rests on moral value, on the good conduct, of

---

[60] See, for example, articles 4 and 39, Statuts, 8e Société de
secours mutuels dite des Maîtres Tisseurs de la ville de Lyon (1866),
ADR, 5X - 1954 - Sociétés de secours mutuels, No. 1 à 10, No. 8.

[61] Société des Vieux Amis (Tableau), 1868, ACCL, Petites sociétés
de secours mutuels Carton 4 - Subventions accordées, Demandes de
subventions, Allocations au 3e, 20e, 86e, 114e, 133e (1869).

the members who compose them."[62] In 1864, Flotard, Beauvoir and Stephan

Maynard, bookkeeper for several cooperative societies in Lyons, had

made the distinction between the 'good' worker for whom cooperation

was intended, and the 'bad' worker excluded from it, even sharper:

> association is, for the good workers, the entry into a
> new era of contentment, of independence and of dignity.
> For the good worker, we say, because without perseverance,
> without respect for the rights of others and without a
> spirit of fraternity, there is no association which
> can endure. The lazy, the querulous and the drunkard are
> slaves of their vices. Liberty is not made for them, they
> are not worthy of it, they are incapable of it. However
> long their life may be, never will they enter the new
> world, for the city of the future belongs only to the just.[63]

Several consumers' societies manifested the same attitude by eliminating

from consideration for membership any person who "does not enjoy a good

reputation of morality."[64]

The cooperative movement extended this aim of 'moralization,'

concerned with private life and household affairs, to 'moralization'

concerned with social life and communal matters. Besides promoting

private virtue, cooperation fostered social virtue as well, by advocating

self-control, self-reliance, self-confidence and a sense of purpose.

All of these were qualities necessary to organize effectively and to

'hold one's own' in the marketplace. All were required to enable the

---

[62]Testimony of Eugène Flotard, "Enquête sur les Sociétés de Coopération," January 12, 1866, in Eugène Flotard, Le mouvement coopératif à Lyon et dans le Midi de la France (Lyon, 1867), pp. 394-395.

[63]E. Flotard, Beauvoir, Maynard,"Le Credit au Travail,"Le Progrès, December 13, 1864.

[64]Article 4-1, Espérance Ouvrière, Statuts, 1866.

weavers to confront another radical change in their world of work
deriving from the economic 'crisis' of the 1860's -- the change in their
relations of class. Through its own interpretation of the older aim
of 'moralization,' therefore, cooperative ideology united the masters'
concerns for the transformed internal order of their households to
their concern about the changing external order of their relations
with the merchant-manufacturer. So different was this latter change
from the experience of class in the past that it may be said to have
caused a 'crisis' of class relations. The nature and origins of this
'crisis' form the subject of the next chapter.

CHAPTER VI

The Crisis in Relations of Class

In 1863, 1864 and 1865, almost half of the cases heard by the
Conseil des Prud'hommes of Lyons were conflicts between master-weavers
and merchant-manufacturers. Not since the coup d'état of December 1851
had this proportion been so high. In 1853 only 29% of the cases concerned masters and fabricants.[1] Apparently tension between the two
classes had increased. Another sign of tension appeared in mid-October
1866. Rumors circulated around the city concerning a large demonstration by the weavers of the Croix-Rousse in front of the prefecture.
"I receive contradictory reports" about the demonstration, telegraphed
the Prefect of the Rhône, on October 15, to his superior in Paris, "but
what is certain, is the irritation against the fabricants. It is
against them that I fear demonstrations."[2] The prominent silk merchant
Arlès-Dufour, writing the Opinion nationale a few days later, did not see
"any feeling of hatred ... stirring up the workers against the fabricants,
as was unfortunately the case in 1831 and 1834."[3] But even if the weavers

_____

[1]Jules Bonnet, Compte-rendu des Travaux du Conseil des Prud'hommes
pendant la dernière période triennale (Lyon: Imprimerie Typographique
et Lithographique de C. Bonnaviat, 1866) and Felix Bertrand, Report of
President of Conseil des Prud'Hommes de Lyon to Prefect of Rhône, June 29,
1854, ADR, U - Prud'hommes de Lyon, Correspondance relative aux élections
(1806 à 1870).

[2]Dépêche télégraphique, Prefect of Rhône to Minister of Interior,
October 15, 1866, 1:30 A.M., AN, Fic III Rhône 10, Correspondance et
Divers (1816-1870), dossier 'Ouvriers de Lyon', October 1866.

[3]Arlès-Dufour to Charles Sauvestre, Opinion nationale, October 18,
1866, as quoted in Le Progrès (Lyon), October 22, 1866.

had not reached the point of hatred and insurrection, their resentment against their employers was increasing.

This resentment had many sources, among them the remains of a perennial antagonism noted by nearly all contemporary observers. The economic conditions of their industry in the 1860's explained largely why such resentment became especially acute by 1866. These conditions, and the reactions of fabricants to them, made individual master-weavers more dependent economically on individual fabricants precisely at a time when the latter were encouraged to exploit this dependence by semi-legal trade practices or forced to abandon the interests of urban weaving to those of rural weaving. Such dependence and exploitation made the weavers 'conscious' of their traditionally subordinate class position in their industry and of their often hostile relationship with the fabricants--the 'other' class. The weavers' resentment against their employers was confused, however, by the competition between large fabricants and small fabricants in their struggle for survival or control in rapidly changing, very uncertain product and raw materials markets. The weavers had different objections against each type of fabricant and experienced their dependence upon each in a different way. Because of these differences, their conception of the 'other' class, against which the weavers defined their own class solidarity, was divided between their traditional notion, presuming subordination to the fabricants and confrontation with them, and a newer conception, presuming abandonment by the fabricants and the dissolution of any regular relationship between the two classes. The nature of class relations, and the weavers' consciousness of the identity of the 'other' class, were therefore transformed.

This transformation offered the weavers new opportunities and new reasons to organize voluntary associations, especially cooperative societies of production.

The weavers of Lyons became more dependent in the sense defined in Chapter I. They relied more intensively, or in greater proportions, on the orders of one or two fabricants at a time and thus became less like contractors, allocating their looms among several merchant--manufacturers, and more like laborers, employed by one or two alone. The statistical reason for this increasing dependence was the substitution of plain-cloth weaving for fancy-cloth weaving in the households of weavers. As we saw earlier, the number of plain-cloth looms per household tended to be smaller than the number of fancy-cloth looms, leaving fewer looms to allocate among several fabricants. The number of looms in fancy-cloth households also declined because of the large degree of unemployment in this category.

The actual extent of dependence in 1866 was in fact more severe than our data in Table 24, Chapter V suggest. Although plain-loom households had an average 2.27 looms per household and fancy-loom households had an average 3.00 looms per household, not all of the looms in most households were occupied at one time during the 'unemployment decade' of the 1860's. The number of occupied looms per household, indicating the actual degree of independence (or possible independence) of one fabricant, was therefore less than the total loom data suggest. This was especially true in fancy-loom households, on which the incidence of unemployment was strongest. As Table 33 below demonstrates, the proportion of fancy-loom households with only one occupied loom, exclusively at the service

Table 33:

Distribution of Silk Weavers' Households,
by Loom Type   and by Number of Occupied
Looms, Croix-Rousse Samples (1847, 1866)

Number of Occupied Looms per Household	All HH		Plains HH		Fancies HH	
	1847	1866	1847	1866	1847	1866
a. Number of Households						
1	48	45	26	32	18	9
2	71	57	18	33	48	20
3	34	12	7	7	26	5
4	12	5	1	2	10	1
5	2	1	–	1	–	–
Total HH's	167	120	52	75	102	35
b. Percentage of Total Households						
1	28.7	37.5	50.0	42.7	17.6	25.7
2	42.5	47.5	34.6	44.0	47.1	57.1
3	20.4	10.0	13.5	9.3	25.5	14.3
4	7.2	4.2	1.9	2.7	9.8	2.9
5	1.2	.8	0.0	1.3	0.0	0.0
	100.0	100.0	100.0	100.0	100.0	100.0
1 or 2	71.2	85.0	84.6	86.7	64.7	82.8
3,4 or 5	28.8	15.0	15.4	13.3	35.3	17.2
c. Average Number of Occupied Looms per Household						
	2.10	1.83	1.67	1.76	2.27	1.94

Sources: Sample, Recensement, Croix-Rousse, 1847, AML.
Sample, Dénombrement, 1866, Lyon, 4ème Canton, ADR, 6M-
Dénombrement

of one _fabricant_, rose from 18% in 1847 to 26% in 1866. The proportion
of fancies households with only two occupied looms, in the service of two
fabricants at most but probably only one in most cases, also rose between
the two dates, from 47% to 57%. But the proportion of households with
three or more occupied looms--those most likely, or most capable, of
diversifying their orders among several different _fabricants_--declined
from 35% to 17%. In sum, 83% of the fancy-loom households in the 1866
sample of the Croix-Rousse were relatively dependent on the orders of one
or two _fabricants_ at once, as compared with 65% in 1847.

Change in the extent of probable dependence on one or two _fabri-
cants_ was less evident in plain-loom households of the samples of the
Croix-Rousse. In fact, the proportion of these households with only one
occupied loom (dependent on one _fabricant_ at a time) decreased from 50%
in 1847 to 43% in 1866. This decrease was compensated, however, by an
increase in the proportion of households with two occupied looms (35% to
44%). Households with three or more occupied looms represented about
the same share of the sample for each year (15% in 1847, 13% in 1866).
Thus the share of relatively dependent households with one or two occupied looms changed very little (84.6% in 1847, 86.7% in 1866). The
major differences, for the sample of all households between the two
dates, were the greater percentage of highly dependent plain-loom households and the equalization of proportional 'rates of dependence' between
the traditionally different plain-loom households and fancy-loom households. Although the proportion of fancy-loom households with only one
occupied loom (26%) remained less than the proportion of plain-loom
households (43%), this difference was much weaker in 1866 (-17 percen-

tiles) than in 1847 (-32 percentiles). The proportion of relatively
dependent fancy-loom households with only one or two occupied looms
(83%), moreover, was hardly different from the proportion of plain-loom
households in this group in 1866 (87%), whereas the difference between
the two was clearly marked in 1847 (65% for fancies households, 85% for
plains households). As fancy weavers' households had become more similar to plains weavers' households in their internal order of managing
subordinate workers, so the two approached the same 'household type' in
their external order of dependence on one or two merchant-manufacturers.
Together, master-weavers of plain cloths and masters of fancy cloths
became more like laborers in their actual relations with merchant-manufacturers and less like independent contractors.

This dependence on employment by one or two fabricants at the same
time did not mean, however, that weavers relied on the same merchant-
manufacturer for successive orders. Direct and indirect evidence suggests that many changed fabricants frequently. In their response to the
Parliamentary Enquiry on the Conditions of Labor in France, in the early
1870's, the fabricants Faye and Thevenin explained the instability of
the weavers in the 'houses' of each merchant-manufacturer as a regular
condition of the industry of Lyons, related to different states of demand
for the various types of silk cloth:

> Our industry is subject to many phases, which do
> not permit us to have workers attached to our
> houses. It often happens that one kind of cloth
> sells, while another stops, and inversely, hence
> workers leave one employer, who has no work, to
> attach themselves to another who gives them work.

> We do not know, when we give employment to a worker,
> how much time we can keep him.[4]

In answering another query in the same questionnaire, the Chamber of
Commerce spoke of the "instability of workers who constantly change employers ..."[5] In February 1866 there were 450 merchant-manufacturers in
Lyons,[6] nearly all of whom put out at least some of their orders among
urban weavers. With this large number of employers and with the unstable
conditions of employment, varying among the different categories and
specialties of silk, such changes of fabricant must have been at least
as great, if not greater, in 1866 as in the early 1870's, when the
enquête was made. Such changes were probably not much less frequent among
fancy-cloth weavers than among plain-cloth weavers. As noted in Chapter I,
the advantages of remaining with a single fabricant, both for the master
and for the merchant-manufacturer, derived largely from the skills, the
knowledge and the investment required for weaving quality fancy fabrics.[7]
Most of the fancies orders during the 1860's, however, were of the inferior sort--ornaments and nouveautés--demanding less skill and investment
than the abandoned fancy dress cloths. Much of the demand for fancy
fabrics, moreover, was for samples, most of which did not have a long

---

[4]"[Reponses de] M[onsieu]rs Faye et Thevenin F[abric]ants de soieries
à Lyon (Rhône)," Enquête Parlementaire Sur Les Conditions du Travail en
France (Rhône, 1872-1875), Premier Questionnaire A, X, AN, C 3021, Enquête
sur les Conditions du Travail en France (1872 à 1875), Région du Sud-Est
(Rhône).

[5]"Réponses de la Chambre de Commerce de Lyon," Enquête Parlementaire,
Premier Questionnaire A, XX, ibid..

[6]"Soieries (Fabricants et M[archan]ds de)," February 15, 1866, AML I2-
47(B), Corporations: ouvriers en soie (1819 à 1870), No. 148.

[7]Chapter I, section I - C, pp. 90-91, 101.

'style life' and therefore did not attract subsequent orders. There was consequently less reason for master and _fabricant_ to remain together than in those cases, more frequent in the past, when several orders of a particular style followed its mounting.

Even though most weavers were not 'attached' to particular _fabricants_ and probably changed _fabricants_ often, their immediate contact was not equally frequent with all of the merchant-manufacturers for whom they wove. According to a survey of 125 _fabricants_ in February 1866,[8] a few very large-scale _fabricants_ dominated an inordinately large part of the market for weaving labor in Lyons at that time. The rest of the market was divided among a large number of smaller establishments, or rather establishments with a smaller number of occupied looms in the city. Because of the exceptionally strong presence of the few _grands fabricants_, weavers were likely to weave more often for one of them than for any single _petit fabricant_, even when they changed employers frequently. The relatively privileged access of the former to silk merchants probably also enabled them to offer more regular work than the _petits fabricants_. The only exceptions to this were the small-scale fancy-cloth and furniture-church-cloth establishments and those _fabricants_ occupying few looms in Lyons but many in the countryside in 1866. Neither of these was deprived necessarily of easy sources of raw silk. The first offered little employment because of low demand for fancy silks. The second were probably not numerous. Putting out in the countryside usually required a large initial capital, as well as an established position in Lyons.

---

[8]"Soieries (Fabricants et Mds de)," February 15, 1866, AML, 12-47 (B), No. 148.

Except in the plain-velvets category, the progress of rural weaving had
not yet gone so far as to eclipse urban weaving entirely. The result,
in any case, was the strengthening of chances of regular, hence more
frequent, employment among the merchant-manufacturers with a larger
number of occupied looms in the city. Tables 34 and 35 present evidence
for this skewed distribution of the urban labor market between grands
fabricants and petits fabricants in 1866. Table 34 shows more than half
of the 125 fabricants surveyed (out of a total of 450 fabricants in the
city) in the petit category, occupying thirty or fewer looms in the city
(or an estimated fifteen or fewer workers). More than a fourth of the
fabricants occupied fewer than twenty urban looms each (fewer than ten
workers each). No more than an eighth had 200 looms or more (100 or
more workers), but the average scale of this group was high; namely, 687
looms (345 workers). Three fabricants in the sample had 1000 looms or
more each (500 or more workers). A large majority of fabricants therefore seems to have put out on a very small scale in Lyons, but the few
fabricants who occupied many looms operated at a very large scale indeed.

Table 35 analyzes the extent of the labor market in the sample
employed by fabricants in different scales of manufacture. Nearly a
third of all sample weavers and looms worked for the three exceptionally
large-scale establishments employing an estimated 550 to 800 workers
each. That is to say, 2.4% of the 125 fabricants occupied 32.8% of all
workers and looms in the sample. About 42% worked for large establishments employing 250 or more master-weavers each, and a majority (61%)
worked for large and medium-sized establishments--those with 100 workers
or more. Although the remaining 30% of weavers of small-scale establish-

Table 34:

Distribution of Sample of Fabricants According to the
Number of Looms Occupied by Each, February 15, 1866

Estimated Number of Workers per Fabricant[9]	Actual Number of Looms per Fabricant (from source below)	Number of Fabricants	% of Total Fabricants in Sample	
100 or more	200 or more	14	11.2	
20 - 75	40 - 150	44	35.2	
10 - 15	20 - 30	32	25.6	} 53.6
1 - 9	1 - 19	35	28.0	

Total Fabricants	125
Mean Number of Looms	102.4
Median Number of Looms	30

Source: "Soieries (Fabricants et M[archan]ds de)," February 15, 1866, AML,
I2-47, No. 148.

---

[9]The numbers of workers were estimated from the number of looms by using
the distribution of looms per household occupied by the maison Bellon in 1860
as a standard. According to this distribution the following percentages of
looms were represented for each number of looms occupied per household:

(a) Number of looms per HH occupied by Bellon	(b) Number of looms in this category	(c) % of total looms occupied by Bellon
1	71	18.8
2	152	40.2
3	87	23.0
4	48	12.7
5	20	5.3
Total looms occupied by Bellon	378	

Source: Bellon Frères et Conty, Response of fabricants to request for accounts of balances with chefs d'ateliers c. 1860, ACCL, Soieries
Carton 41-I Législation-Usages (an 8 à 1936), 13. - Pétition remise
à l'Empereur, à son passage à Lyon, par les ouvriers en soie.

Each limiting value in each size category of the 1866 distribution of fabricants was multiplied by the five Bellon percentages of looms (column c)
to compute the estimated number of looms in each household category (1 loom,
2 looms, etc.) for that limiting value. Dividing each of these five estimated numbers by the corresponding household size value (1,2,3,4 or 5)
gave the estimated number of workers per household category. The sum of
these estimated workers over all five categories provided a fair estimate
of the total number of workers associated with each limiting value.

In general, the number of workers was computed to be one-half the number of
looms, that is, an average of two looms per household of each worker was occupied by each fabricant. To simplify the computations, I used this value
of one-half to estimate size categories for workers, in Tables 34 and 35.

Table 35:

Distribution of Looms and Workers in Sample
of 125 Fabricants of Lyons in February 1866,
According to Size of Establishment

Size of Establishment	Estimated Number of Workers per Fabricant	Actual Number of Looms per Fabricant	Number of Fabricants	Estimated Total Number of Workers per Size Category	Total Number of Looms per Size Category	% of Total Looms in Sample = % of Total Workers in Sample	
large	550 – 800	1100 – 1600	3	2100	4200	32.8	42.2
	250 – 350	500 – 700	2	600	1200	9.4	
medium	100 – 190	200 – 360	9	1185	2370	18.5	18.5
small	20 – 75	40 – 150	44	1917	3835	30.0	39.3
	10 – 15	20 – 30	32	407	814	6.4	
	1 – 9	1 – 19	35	188	377	2.9	
		Totals	125	6397	12,796	100.0	

Source: "Soieries (Fabricants et M[archan]ds de)," February 15, 1866, AML, I2-47, No. 148.

ments is not a negligible percentage, this percentage presumes the arbitrary definition of a small establishment as one with 150 looms or less. If 'small' is defined instead as equal to or smaller than the median-size establishment in the sample, that is, 30 looms or less, only 9% of all workers and looms were in this category. They were employed by more than half of the fabricants in the sample. The larger establishments clearly dominated the urban labor market.

This domination by large-scale manufacture combined with frequent changes of employers suggests that weavers on the whole had a highly-developed 'class consciousness' in 1866, but of a very special kind. Since the most frequent, or most repeated, contacts were those with a single grand fabricant or with a few grands fabricants, their consciousness was not unlike that of peasants of a manor confronting the lord of the domain. They regarded their employer as a distant yet individual personality upon whom their livelihood depended, rather than as a mere agent of another class. They regarded themselves as a large mass collectively dependent on this single fabricant and therefore sharing a common class identity. This personalization of the fabricant and collectivization of themselves in relation to him increased to the extent that the weavers became attached to the house of the grand fabricant, weaving for it more or less regularly.

As we have just seen, however, such attachment to a single house was broken more or less frequently during the 1860's by employment by one of the many other fabricants, especially by the petits fabricants. Except in the fancy-cloth category and in the furniture-church-cloth category, their contacts with each individual petit fabricant were rare

and ephemeral. Another kind of class consciousness, that of the _fabri-_
cants as a collective group merely represented by individual employers,
emerged out of these contacts with _petits fabricants._ Their awareness
of the _fabricants_ as a class increased by such encounters because of
the greater ability to discriminate among individuals fostered by frequent changes of employers. Such changes made the weavers' awareness of
their own class character more complex, however, than their awareness
fostered by relations with the _grands fabricants._ They encountered fewer
weavers like themselves in the _cages_ of the _petits fabricants,_ but these
fewer weavers had, like themselves, a wider range of experience of different _fabricants_ than the weavers attached to a single large enterprise.
In these cases, therefore, awareness of the mass character of the
weavers' dependence emerged indirectly, through the sharing of personal
experience, rather than directly, through immediate contact with a mass
enterprise.

The complex character of class relations between weavers and
fabricants in the 1860's was thus the result of the dual image of the
fabricant--as an authoritarian individual personality (embodied in the
grand fabricant) and as a mere agent of another class (embodied in the
petit fabricant). This complexity was also the result of the dual notion
of the weavers' own class character--as a mass laborer absorbed in a
common work force (based on experience of one or few large-scale enterprises) and as an independent artisan facing conditions of employment
similar to those of other independent artisans (based on frequent changes
of enterprise, whether large or small). These dualities persisted
throughout the decade as the uncertainties concerning product demand,

raw silk prices and regularity of employment and wage levels discouraged
the grands fabricants and their weavers from establishing permanent relations and encouraged the petits fabricants to avail themselves of
short-term opportunities opened by the general uncertainty of the economy.

These dualities were most acute in the manufacture of plain silks.
Plain-cloth weaving provided the livelihood of the great majority of
weavers in the 1860's. Even more important, the differences in scale of
manufacture in this category were generally more severe than in other
categories, as we saw in Chapter I. The largest establishment in the
sample of 125 fabricants was the maison Bellon (1600 looms), a specialist
in plain silks, and yet the median size of the fifteen plain-cloth
establishments in the sample was among the smallest of all categories;
namely, 30 looms.[10] The highly competitive product market for plain
silks in the 1860's favored large-scale manufacture, primarily because
of economies of scale and privileged access in obtaining raw silk. But
such competition also made large-scale manufacture difficult to emulate
by smaller manufacturers, because of low profit margins on each unit of
cloth put out. Survival for small producers was therefore especially
rude in the economic environment of the decade, as they competed among
themselves and against the large producers for a share of old markets
or for a portion of new ones. Because of these harsh conditions, they
were not likely to heed to sentiment or even to justice in their relations with the master-weavers. Their employment of each individual weaver
was ephemeral and not likely to be repeated in the near future. So there

---

[10]Ibid.; Table 1, Chapter 1, p. 96.

was no ostensible reason, beyond a praiseworthy moral scrupulosity, to
feel any responsibility towards them. For these _fabricants_ especially
the weaver was primarily labor cost, which it was in their interest not
only for gain but also for economic survival to reduce as much as possible.

One way to reduce this cost, at a time when the piece-rate for common
plain silks was already near the level of subsistence, was by measuring
the woven cloth in such a way as to 'discount' a portion of the wage
owed for finished work. The use of sliding canes of arbitrary length—
baffling measures to the (now) metric-minded weavers—and the refusal by
some houses to admit the weaver to the measuring room facilitated such
fraudulent 'snatching' for a few francs or centimes of justly-earned
wage. A less fraudulent custom of 'forgetting' the last few centimeters
of a newly-woven cloth, when these were less than 25 centimeters, was no
less, in the view of the weavers, "an illegal means of competiton used
habitually to the detriment of those who are unaware of it ..."[11]

The _métrage_ issue was not new, but rarely did it cause so much antagonism, individual and collective, between master-weavers and _fabricants_
as in the 1860's. Between 1863 and 1865, it was the single most important
cause of conflict brought before the _Conseil des Prud'hommes_.[12] In 1860,
1862 and 1865, different groups of master-weavers petitioned in turn the
Emperor, the Minister of Agriculture and Commerce and the Prefect of the
Rhône respectively to impose the meter as the exclusive unit for measuring
silk cloths and to force _fabricants_ to allow their weavers to observe the

[11]Response of master-weaver _prud'hommes_ to report on _métrage_ issue
by Jules Bonnet, president of the Conseil des Prud'hommes, _Le Progrès_,
April 30, 1866.

[12]Bonnet, _Compte-rendu des Travaux_, p. 6.

measurement of their cloths.[13] In 1866, the newly-elected weaver

prud'hommes took their case to the public, rebutting arguments of the

president of the Council, the fabricant Jules Bonnet, in favor of the

old measures. Apparently the fraudulent practices associated with

métrage had become more frequent since 1860, as less secure or less con-

scientious fabricants tried to compensate their reductions in profits

from lower fabric prices or from dearer raw silk, with reductions of the

weavers' piece-rate 'on the sly.' The impoverished wage of the weavers,

in the common articles where such practices probably occurred more fre-

quently, made them more sensitive to even the smallest 'picking' at their

wage.

But there was another reason for the acute preoccupation with the

issue at this time. Changing fabricants frequently and finding them-

selves totally, or almost totally, dependent on each one during the period

of their employment, the weavers were more vexed than in the past by the

arbitrary employment and wage policies of each merchant-manufacturer.

Every time the worker was employed by a new house, he was faced with a

new method of measurement, for example, against which he could not pro-

test. And if he demanded to have his fabric measured in his presence, as

the law allowed, he was threatened with dismissal.

---

[13]Petition of Tray, Desparros et al. to Emperor Napoleon III,
August 1860, ACCL, Soieries Carton 41-I-Législation-Usages (an 8 à 1936),
13.- Pétition remise à l'Empereur, à son passage à Lyon par les ouvriers
en soie; Petition of sixty-two master weavers to Minister of Agriculture,
Commerce and Public Works, April 16, 1862, and petition of "chefs d'
ateliers et ouvriers tisseurs de la ville de Lyon" to Prefect of Rhône,
1865, ACCL, Soieries Carton 22-II-Mesurage des soieries (an 13 à 1899),
1. - 2.

> The exercise of this right becomes abnormal for
> those who frequent the service, and it is notor-
> ious that, out of fear of setting a precedent,
> they quickly settle accounts with a defiant worker
> by taking away his work, since he had the nerve to
> try to create an anomaly by going beyond the order
> established in the house.[14]

The main demand of the weavers was therefore the standardization of such

policies among all the houses of the fabrique, so that unscrupulous

fabricants could not obscure their theft behind arbitrarily-defined

house policies, unfamiliar to the new worker.

> In sum, we believe that exactness consists in the
> observance of the unit determined by the law.
> That this unit should be for all uniform, invari-
> able and controlled.

> Uniform, so that the worker employed by several
> fabricants no longer be forced to return to 100,
> 115 and 120 centimes at once, as happens.

> Invariable and controlled, to prevent fraud or
> possible error which the sliding system facilitates.[15]

The standard towards which such house policies should conform did

not emerge from merely abstract reflection. It was, in all probability,

formed by the policies currently adopted in some of the more respected

and established merchant-manufacturing houses of Lyons, especially those

of the few grands fabricants with whom the plain-cloth weavers had more

repeated contact than with any individual petits fabricants. In their

response to the president of the Chamber of Commerce on the métrage ques-

tion, in 1866, the weaver prud'hommes made it clear that not all fabri-

---

[14]Response of master-weaver prud'hommes, Le Progrès, April 30, 1866.

[15]Ibid..

cants used fraudulent measuring to cheat the weaver of his wage. For
example, they demanded measuring in the presence of the master-weaver,
"as practiced in several houses."[16] Three years later a police agent
reported weavers' hopes for the end of "the petit fabricant who merely
speculates on low piece-rates." And the report continued: "they cite
many strong ones who have made colossal fortunes in the last 15 years
by reducing the piece-rates."[17] The small fabricant, in short, was a
'speculator' by trade and should "die."[18] Many large fabricants were
not exempt from the same reproach, but this was an individual blight,
not that of the group as a whole. These grands fabricants were in fact
preferred to the group of petits fabricants. Some, if not all, of the
'honorable' houses in 1866, which admitted weavers to measuring, were
probably those of grands fabricants. In the minds of the weavers, they
were preferred largely because of the frequent and regular employment
they could offer a large number of weavers of Lyons, and also because
of their relatively favorable wages and employment policies which their
superior position in labor, product and raw materials markets enabled
them to extend.

Although the weavers may have preferred the few grands fabricants
whom they knew to the many petits fabricants with whom their relations

---

[16]Ibid..

[17]"Rapport à Monsieur Delcourt, Commissaire spécial, sur la situation de la fabrique de soieries," December 7, 1869, AML, I2-47(A), Situation de l'industrie lyonnaise: ... rapports sur la soierie et les
ouvriers en soie ... (1819 à 1870), No. 315.

[18]Ibid..

were ephemeral, they were not without grievance against the former. The
weavers resented the large profits made by "many strong ones" during the
decade of unemployment and low wages for themselves. They resented the
cheapening of thread by loading it with foreign matter in black dyes.
Francois Gillet, the blacks dyer supported by C.-J. Bonnet, _fabricant_ of
silk cloths, developed some black dyes for Bonnet's Jujurieux products
which did not require loading, but he hardly abandoned loading after
this discovery.[19] Such practices made the weavers' own work more difficult and time-consuming and, according to the weavers themselves, ruined
the high reputation of the _fabrique_ of Lyons.[20] The weavers also regarded
the increasing involvement of _fabricants_ in other activities--dyeing,
throwing, spinning and commerce in silk thread--as 'speculation' harmful
to the smooth operation of the industry and therefore to the livelihood
of the workers. "What is killing the _fabrique_," said the weavers in 1866,
"is the loading of the thread during dyeing and speculation, since raw
silk does not reach the state of manufacture before having passed through
the hands of five or six speculators. The _fabricant_ becomes more and
more a merchant while ceasing to be a _fabricant_." The weavers cited the
fabricant Croizat of Lyons, for example, who "earned 150,000 francs last
year by speculating on raw silk."[21] In 1869, such 'speculation' by

[19]Michel Laferrère, Lyon: ville industrielle (Paris: Presses
universitaires de France, 1960), pp. 147-152.

[20]"Rapport à Monsieur Delcourt, Commissaire spécial, Sur la situation de la fabrique des étoffes de soies au 4e Trimestre Xbre 1866,"
December 8, 1866; "Rapport à Monsieur Delcourt, Commissaire spécial, sur
la situation de la fabrique des étoffes de soie," June 8, 1867, AML, I2-
47(A), Nos. 301, 304.

[21]"Rapport à Monsieur Delcourt," December 8, 1866, AML, I2-47(A),
No. 301.

<u>fabricants</u> delayed the return of prosperity following a large harvest
of raw silk.

> The harvest of raw silks being good this year,
> very good even, there is lots of silk, the likes
> of it have not been seen since 1849. As a result
> the silks fell in price by 25, 30 and 35 francs
> per kilo but then rose again by 10 to 15 francs
> shortly thereafter. It is the result of specula-
> tion. It causes a kind of torpor in the <u>fabrique</u>
> which hurts manufacture as it is prolonged.[22]

The weavers regarded as 'speculative' even certain practices of inventory
management to minimize losses due to reductions in the market price of
woven cloth. They considered such practices dependent on the reduction
of their piece-rates, thus saving the <u>fabricants</u> a loss at their expense.
In December 1866, they accused the very reputable <u>maison</u> Bellon of en-
gaging in these practices and thus becoming a 'speculator':

> Two years ago, Mr. Belon sold 10 to 15,000 francs
> of fabric at 5 francs per meter. At this price
> he lost 25 centimes per meter, but he was able to
> have as much woven at 25 centimes less per meter,
> and he replaced his merchandise that was getting
> old in his storerooms and that could have caused
> him a considerable loss in a short time. Such are
> real evidence that the <u>fabricant</u> is becoming more
> and more a speculator.[23]

Becoming a 'speculator' was no tribute. In fact, it was unworthy of the
status and renown of the merchant-manufacturer of Lyons, compromising his
honor in the world of industry and commerce, but especially in the eyes
of his many weavers. "Because of this speculation on raw silks," wrote

[22]"Rapport à Monsieur Delcourt, Commissaire spécial, sur la situation de la fabrique," September 7, 1869, AML, I2-47(A), No. 314.

[23]"Rapport à Monsieur Delcourt," December 8, 1866, AML, I2-47(A),
No. 301.

the police agent during the period of 'delayed prosperity' in 1869 and
echoing the sentiments of the weavers he observed, "many _fabricants_ are
losing their old renown of _fabricant_ to become _commerçants_."[24]

The strongest grievance against the large _fabricants_, however, was
putting out silks in the countryside. Many weavers regarded this as the
worst example of their new 'speculative' attitude. Not only were they
ruining agriculture for their own personal profit, but they were also
killing industry in the city, thus threatening to reduce the city itself
to insignificance.

> It has often been repeated that Lyons was the
> second city of the Empire, by its commerce and
> its population, but if the _fabrique_ of silk cloths
> had disappeared in large proportions, Lyons would
> have become insignificant. That is what the ex-
> perts say; and they added, when the _fabrique_ began
> to migrate to the countryside: All the better.
> Louis Philippe said that the weavers were revolu-
> tionaries.[25]

The weavers knew, moreover, that their own wages for common plain and
velvet cloths would not be so low nor their employment so uncertain, in
a period of high demand for plain silks, were rural labor not competing
against their own on more advantageous terms both for the rural weaver
and for the _fabricant_ of Lyons. In 1869 they complained that "these
people of the countryside have an easy lot, paying less for rent and food
and nearly all possessing a small piece of land. It is said that luxury
is taking over among them and this is to their advantage and to that of

[24]"Rapport à Monsieur Delcourt," September 7, 1869, AML, 12-47(A),
No. 314.

[25]"Rapport à Monsieur Delcourt," December 8, 1866, AML, 12-47(A),
No. 301.

the _fabricants_ and to the detriment of the weavers of Lyons."[26] The

weavers of Lyons felt their position of disadvantage most acutely in

periods of unemployment.

> In moments of unemployment the worker of the city
> is completely inactive and cannot live except by his
> savings, while in the countryside he can work in the
> fields... It is these considerations and the cheaper
> life outside the city which explain the progressive
> decline of workers in Lyons and, on the contrary, a
> very large increase in the countryside.[27]

What made countryside weaving especially painful to the weavers,

and what directed so much of the weavers' resentment against the _grands_

fabricants themselves, was the apparent lack of concern on the part of

the latter for the plight of the urban weavers. These _fabricants_ gave

greater attention to the rural sector and left the urban weavers to their

own resources. The latter were employed when conditions of demand per-

mitted, to increase profits at the margin, but immediately released when

the market threatened to turn around, so that rural weaving could continue

without interruption. Before 1850 the countryside was a mere adjunct to

the city. By 1860 these roles were reversed, the latter becoming the

vassal of the former. Not even the most 'honorable' _fabricants,_ so it

seemed, felt as responsible for the welfare of the urban weavers, or of

the economy of the city, as they had once been. They directed most of

their attention to their rural weavers. The weavers of Lyons, in short,

felt increasingly abandoned.

----

[26]"Rapport à Monsieur Delcourt, Commissaire spécial, sur la situation de la fabrique," June 7, 1869, AML, 12-47(A), No. 313.

[27]"Réponses de la Chambre Syndicale des Soieries de Lyon," _Enquête
Parlementaire,_ Premier Questionnaire A, Observations, AN, C 3021.

Two 'innovations' in the organization of silk weaving in the countryside re-enforced this sense of abandonment, especially in times of crisis. These were the counter and the factory. The Chambre Syndicale des Soieries explained the counter in its response to the enquête of the early 1870's:

> The fabricant has in a small city or village a counter for the service of workers whom he employs in the surrounding area. He furnishes the worker with the loom and all the implements needed for weaving, he gives him the warp and weft silk all ready to be woven, unlike what takes place in Lyons... These advantages offered the worker of the countryside allow the fabricant to pay a lower piece-rate, all the accessory costs being at the expense of the fabricant; the worker, when he has finished his piece, brings it to this counter, which sends it immediately to the house in Lyons.[28]

In the city, on the contrary, the "master-weaver must furnish at his expense rent, heat, lighting, depreciation of the loom and gears, dévidage and cannetage of the weft; in sum, all the expense of preparatory work necessary for weaving."[29] Thus the fabricant had much less personal investment in fixed capital and preparatory operations in the city than in the country. As a result, he had much less interest in keeping the master-weaver active. The weaving factory represented an even larger investment of the fabricant's own resources, an investment which increased with the mechanization of weaving in many such factories of the Lyons region after 1870. To these factories, nearly all of which were in the countryside as well, the fabricant gave priority in allocating production among the three sectors--urban domestic, rural domestic, and rural factory.

---

[28] Ibid..

[29] Ibid..

The fabricants of the Chambre Syndicale des Soieries made no secret of
the low priority they accorded the first sector in periods of economic
crisis:

> When these moments of unemployment arrive, they
> strike the workers of the city more directly.
> Since the fabricant has no commitment to them,
> he begins to make them wait for work several
> weeks before interrupting what he has manufactured
> in factories or on looms installed in the surround-
> ing departments, because he has every interest in
> maintaining these organizations of work.[30]

The personal interest of the fabricants of Lyons in their rural
weaving enterprises was best illustrated, however, by the paternalism
towards factory weavers on the part of some of the most renowned merchant-
manufacturers. This paternalism was unlike any ever known in the city.
The fabricants C.-J. Bonnet at Jujurieux (Ain), J.-B. Martin at Tarare
(Rhône), Montessuy-Chomer at Renage (Isère) and the Durand brothers at
Vizille (Isère), for example, all set up factory dormitories offering not
only long-term employment but also food, health care, recreation, education, religious training and savings facilities to their female workers.
The Bonnet factory at Jujurieux provided the most striking example of
this kind of paternalism. It included, along with its shops for cocoon
spinning, for silk throwing and for cloth weaving, dormitories and refectories, reading and recreation rooms, a garden and a chapel. Bonnet
accepted only single women as workers, either young girls or widows without children.[31] Girls aged 13-15 years contracted for three years as
apprentices, and older women were employed for an eighteen-month period.

[30]Ibid., Deuxième Questionnaire B, IX.

[31]Louis Reybaud, Etudes sur le régime des manufactures. Condition
des ouvriers en soie (Paris, 1859), p. 200.

They lived a strictly regulated life under the watchful eye of nuns, who never let their charges out of their sight. Their daily schedule included time for prayer and recreation besides work at the loom or elsewhere in the shops. Sundays were devoted entirely to religious services, catechism lessons and organized leisure-time activities. The latter included promenades with the nuns when weather permitted, or group readings inside when weather was bad. Reading and writing exercises also formed part of these activities.[32]

The young apprentices were kept in strict isolation from the outside world during most of their three years, even from the small-town world of Jujurieux. They could leave to visit home only every six months, and outsiders could attend services in the chapel only on special occasions, such as marriages. Other employees of the establishment, especially males with whom the apprentices had contact, were chosen "with great care." Life in the Bonnet factory was, in short, the life of a convent rather than that of a simple shop, and the religious and moral fervor of the apprentices was carefully nurtured and protected from distracting outside influence. The products of this regime were known to be ideal wives for "cultivators and men of crafts living nearby." Besides the dowry accumulated in annual stipends and occasional premiums for good work, "there is an assurance of aptitude and virtue... which is for their domestic tranquility a guarantee rarely deceived."[33] The marriage of one of the Bonnet workers was an occasion of great celebration for the entire factory

---

[32] Jules Simon, L'ouvrière (Paris: L. Hachette, 1861), pp. 52-55.

[33] Reybaud, Etudes ... Condition des ouvriers en soie, p. 203.

community. No "other festival moves their hearts so deeply." Bonnet

himself attended the ceremony, sometimes presiding over the taking of

vows beside the priest, and was even known to seek out a suitable mar-

riage partner for a worker in his establishment.[34] The person of Bonnet

hovered over this community as its paternal benefactor. The "name of

this good man is on all tongues," wrote Reybaud.[35]

Other fabricants set up similar 'moralizing' factories in the

countryside. J.-B. Martin of Tarare, manufacturer of peluches, provided

the 400-800 apprentices whom he employed in his shops with meals, organ-

ized recreation, and even lessons in reading, writing and arithmetic.[36]

The Durand brothers of Vizille and the Montessuy-Chomer firm of Renage,

both in Isère, built dormitories and refectories for their female workers,

provided medical facilities, including the services of doctor and pharma-

cist, provided a school for young girls and set up pension funds, loan

facilities and even interest-bearing savings accounts.[37] The Durand

brothers also built lodgings for married workers.[38] Both establishments

employed nuns to staff the dormitories, medical facilities and girls'

schools, and chapel and chaplain were central to these institutions. The

---

[34]Ibid., p. 204.

[35]Ibid., pp. 201-202.

[36]Ibid., p. 204.

[37]ADI, 162. M. Organisation du Travail, 3. Correspondance générale, statistique; travail des adultes, livrets d'ouvriers, divers. 1853-1855; "Réponses de Montessuy-Chomer," Enquête Parlementaire Sur les Conditions du Travail en France (Isère), Premier Questionnaire A, Observations, AN, C 3021, Enquête sur les Conditions du Travail en France (1872 à 1875), Région du Sud-Est (Isère).

[38]ADI, ibid..

Durand brothers and the Perrigaux firm in Bourgoin (Isère) set up food, bread and clothing shops where workers could make purchases at low prices.[39] Such factory-dormitories thus combined the practical economic advantages of savings banks, mutual aid societies and consumers' cooperative societies, for which the weavers of Lyons depended exclusively on their own initiative and efforts.

This *fabricant* paternalism sometimes originated in strong religious devotion, both Catholic (Bonnet) and Protestant (Perrigaux), and in a sense of moral responsibility to the workers employed in these factories. But the desire to insure a docile, stable labor force for high-risk factory weaving of silk fabrics, as well as the need to allay fears of local populations about the moral effects of this new factory regime, were not absent from the calculations of even the most genuinely devout merchant-manufacturers. The Bonnet establishment, for example, recruited its workers carefully from the mountains of Auvergne and Forez rather than from the plains of Bresse because the "worker of the mountain is in general more resigned, more docile, less demanding than the worker of the plain."[40] The Martin enterprise at Tarare had to belie the fears provoked by local artisans and peasants who tried to discourage mountain families from sending their daughters into the factory as apprentices.[41] Whatever their motives, these *fabricants* took great pride in their enter-

[39] Ibid.; "Réponses de Montessuy-Chomer" and "Réponses de Perrigaux (Bourgoin)," Enquête Parlementaire (Isère), Premier Questionnaire A, Observations, AN, C 3021.

[40] Reybaud, Etudes ... Condition des ouvriers en soie, p. 202.

[41] Ibid., pp. 207-208.

prises and objected strongly to any criticism of them, especially criti--
cism from within the city of Lyons. Their acute sensitivity on this
matter in fact embraced the rural sector in general, which they considered
their private domain, to be shielded against interference from the city.

This sensitivity was apparent in the reaction of several fabricants
of Lyons putting out silks in the countryside to an article by an anonymous 'Y' published in the April 15, 1870 issue of Le Progrès de Lyon.
The article listed several abuses by such fabricants in their relations
with rural weavers, both domestic and factory weavers, and cited the
demands of the latter for reform of these abuses presented in recent
strikes in Isère. The article referred especially to the strike of the
workers of the Lyons fabricant Gourd in Faverge, many of whom were
female employees of his factory there. The anonymous author accused
fabricants like Gourd of exploiting and deceiving their weavers:

> Facing the rapacity of the fabricants, the weavers
> of the countryside saw that it was necessary either
> to obtain guarantees and an increase of wages or
> return to the fields. Such is what they did, while
> waiting for the fabricants to decide to renounce
> their facility of exploiting them and deceiving
> them.[42]

Several weeks later, a notice appeared in the same Lyons daily that
"nineteen fabricants considering themselves defamed" had sued the paper
for 10,000 francs. Among these fabricants were Gourd, Croizat fils and
Dubost, Bonnet and Piot, and Alexandre Giraud, all of whom had factories
in the countryside. The court awarded the plaintiffs 1000 francs for
damages and decreed publication of its decision in Le Progrès plus nine

---

[42]Le Progrès, April 15, 1870.

other newspapers.[43] This reaction to criticism was much stronger than
that to similar accusations in the past concerning the policies of _fabri-
cants_ within the city of Lyons. The _fabricants_ involved regarded such
criticism as an affront to their honor. "We believe ourselves known
well enough," replied Gourd, "to several thousand master-weavers whom we
have employed successively in Lyons and who know that we are incapable
of deceiving them to have to discuss such allegations."[44]

The _fabricants_ were especially resentful of the interference by
people of the city in their activities in the countryside. In an article
of the _Salut public_, a Lyons daily favorable to the _fabricants_, an anonymous writer 'Z' expressed the hostility of many _fabricants_ to such interference. "In any situation, no one has the right to intervene between
the worker and the employer who are in agreement and satisfied with one
another, and worthy of blame is every pressure, every attempt to create
misunderstanding between them."[45] The main motive for putting out in the
countryside, claimed this writer, was the desire for freedom from such
interference--from agitation by striking workers, in other words.

> If the countryside is today competing against the
> city, it is precisely because of previous strikes
> and because of the enrichment of the city. The
> _fabricant_ who could produce or sell no longer, had
> to seek more reliable workers and cheaper labor...
> Industry needs tranquility. Not having it in the
> city any more, it goes seeking it in the calm of
> the fields or in the discipline of factories; and

---

[43]_Ibid._, July 8, 1870.

[44]Response of Gourd _et al._ to article by 'Y', _ibid._, April 17, 1870.

[45]"Z", "Les Grèves ... Les Interdits," _Le Salut Publique_ (Lyon),
March 22, 1870.

> if it cannot find these essential elements, it
> emigrates or disappears entirely.[46]

The _fabricants_ thus abandoned the weavers of Lyons in part because
they were 'unruly.' Rural labor was more compliant, besides being less
costly. The weavers' own attitude towards this abandonment was complex.
It deprived them of their livelihood, especially in times of economic
crisis, and this alone made them hostile. They resented the material benefits extended rural weavers while they languished without work or were
forced to beg from public and private charities for their next meal. But
they wanted no part of the controlled regime of the factory nor even the
various services of the counter, despite their often repeated complaints
about their own professional expenses. For the weavers of Lyons, the
master-weavers especially, were too independent-minded and wanted, above
all, control over their own means of livelihood. "Defiance vis-à-vis the
Industrialist who employs them, such is the rule of conduct of the
workers; they want to remain independent."[47] The _grand fabricant_ C.-J.
Bonnet extended the policy of distributing premiums for good work from
his Jujurieux factory to his domestic weavers in Lyons. By the early
1870's, he was not "encouraged to continue this practice in Lyons, re-
ceiving no recognition from the workers and not even succeeding to instill
in them the desire for greater production."[48] The ambivalent reaction of
the urban weavers to their abandonment by the _fabricants_ reflected the

---

[46]_Ibid._, April 4, 1870.

[47]"Réponses de la Chambre de Commerce," _Enquête Parlementaire,_ Premier
Questionnaire A, XX, AN C 3021.

[48]_Ibid._, Deuxième Questionnaire B, III.

contrast between their objective dependence on the merchant-manufacturer
and their self-image of the independent artisan.

It was this contrast which aroused their enthusiasm for the cooperative movement, especially for producers' cooperation promising to restore
the urban craft to their own proprietorship. The central message of
cooperation was self-help. This message 'made sense' to weavers who felt
increasingly abandoned by the fabricants to their own resources and who
wished to free themselves from dependence on the latter for their livelihood and welfare. The leaders of the cooperative societies of Lyons
advocated self-help by proclaiming their intention of "achieving emancipation" by having "recourse only to themselves, to their own resources,
acting on their own responsibility."[49] Such self-achieved "emancipation"
meant in particular the attainment of autonomy for their class in the
pursuit of their work. The priority given to producers' cooperation, at
least in theory, demonstrated this concern for autonomy. Charles Beauvoir,
for example, a cooperative activist in the Croix-Rousse weaving neighborhood, expressed the primacy of cooperative production in his assertion that
"the association of production is the foundation of all others."[50] The
silk weavers manifested the same priority by the special attention they
initially gave to their producers' cooperative, the Association of
Weavers. The commitment of the weavers to their Association was evident in

---

[49]'Mémoire adressé par les associations coopératives de la ville de
Lyon, à MM. les membres de la Chambre de Commerce,' in Eugène Flotard,
"Bulletin Coopératif," Le Progrès (Lyon), December 25-26, 1865.

[50]Beauvoir, "Les divers modes et les moyens les plus directs
d'arriver à la consommation," Le Progrès, September 5, 1864.

their reproach of their own elected prud'hommes in 1865 for not having
taken active part in its formation and the subsequent election of the
list of masters most strongly committed to it, including some of its
administrators.[51]

The 'moral' ideology of cooperation—its advocacy of what has been
called 'moralization'—also stressed the virtue of self-sufficiency at
this time when such emphasis was especially 'relevant' to the weavers'
actual class situation. Cooperative morality referred not only to the
private virtues associated with home life and personal relations, nurtured by the mutual aid movement, but also to the 'public' virtues of
self-reliance and self-discipline associated with effective organization
and with success in business. In 1865, representatives of the cooperative societies of Lyons spoke of the day when "thousands of workers, all
probe, laborious, thrifty, perseverant, will have succeeded, by dint of
their hardship and privation, to amass a capital and to create a society
on the success, the conservation of which will depend their future and
that of their family."[52] Cooperative leaders sought to instill such
virtues in the workers by organizing educational programs for their intellectual advancement. Jean Monet, organizer and director of the
parent society of the Association of Weavers, was a leading member of
the Professional Society for Education of the Rhône, the aim of which

[51]Report of police commissioner to Monsieur le Sénateur (Prefect
of Rhône) and to Monsieur le Procureur Impérial concerning elections
to Conseil des Prud'hommes of Lyons, December 6 and 10, 1865, AML, F-
Prud'hommes - Elections (1806 à 1871).

[52]'Mémoire adressé par les associations coopératives,' Le Progrès,
December 25-26, 1865.

was the diffusion of instruction among workers.[53] Cooperative militants
in Lyons also organized clubs for educational as well as recreational
activities for workers during their leisure hours. Some of these, like
the Beehive Club (Cercle la Ruche) were attached to established cooperative grocery stores--in this case to the Beehive store (la Ruche).
Nearly all clubs set up a library and reading room with newspapers,
journals and books on subjects ranging from classical literature to contemporary economics. Most clubs organized lectures, readings and discussions, and sometimes classes in basic arithmetic and grammer, in addition
to their lighter singing and poetry gatherings.[54] At least one of these
clubs, the Workers' Club of the Brotteaux, included training in administrative responsibilities in their program of activities, in order to prepare
their members for the work of labor organization as well. The Workers'
Club gave each of its members the opportunity to serve as an administrator
on one of its several specialized committees such as the finance, instruction or library committee.[55] In this way it prepared the members for
leadership positions in the cooperative movement and in the resistance
movement later in the decade.

The revival of industrial resistance ironically presumed a different
kind of class relationship between the weavers and the merchant-manufac-

---

[53]"La Société professionnelle d'enseignement," Le Progrès, November
29 and 30, 1864.

[54]See the separate dossiers of les Cercles (la Ruche, Travailleurs
des Brotteaux, Chefs d'atelier de Lyon, Solidarité coopérative) in AML,
I2-45, Sociétes coopératives de production et de consommation (1849 à
1870) and Flotard, "Bulletin Cooperatif," Le Progrès, February 3, March
23, 1868.

[55]Flotard, "Bulletin Coopératif," Le Progrès, February 3, 1868.

facturers than that which explained the appeal of cooperation and its
moral ideology. This was the 'older' relationship based upon the need
of each class for the other in the work of producing silk cloths and
implying class confrontation aroused by the recognition of such mutual
need. Instead of forcing the weavers to rely upon themselves for their
work and livelihood and thus encouraging autonomy in the pursuit of their
trade, this 'older' class relationship maintained the subordinate place
of the weavers in the process of production, while recognizing that place
as essential to the production process. The revival of traditional class
relations was a sign, in short, of the end of abandonment of urban
weaving to rural weaving, or at least of the weavers' sense of such abandonment, following the revival of prosperity in the silk industry in
1869. The weavers organized resistance societies to capture a greater
share of the fruits of such prosperity within the traditional class structure of their industry. Trade unionism thus persuaded them to accept
class dependence within their industry, rather than class autonomy in
cooperative industry, by promising them a 'fair' share in the earnings
of silk manufacture. Such persuasion was possible only when the economic
crisis of the 1860's seemed to have passed.

The appeal of both movements to class solidarity—of cooperation to
the solidarity of a class more dependent and more abandoned than in the
past, and of resistance to the solidarity of a class restored to its
traditional position of importance in the structure of industrial rela-
tions--implicitly presumed the unity of experience of dependence, abandonment, or importance among all the silk weavers of the urban fabrique.
Because of this presumption of common experience, the 'class' ideology of

both movements ignored the divisions among the weavers in their practice
of cooperation and in their organization of resistance. Some of these
divisions, as we saw in Chapter IV, derived from differences in experience
of social and economic change among the different categories and specialties of the silk-weaving craft. Other divisions were rooted in differences of neighborhood experience, creating conflicts among different silk-
weavers' neighborhoods that rended their unity of class in the city as a
whole. Such conflicts intensified as the social movements of voluntary
association, which dominated the collective life of the silk weavers
throughout most of the Second Empire, receded in favor of the political
movement at the end of the Empire and during the first years of the Third
Republic. The story of this penetration of unified class solidarity by
divisive neighborhood solidarity, and of the social and economic sources
of the latter, is pursued in the next chapter.

CHAPTER VII

The Change in Neighborhoods of Silk Weaving

Change in the neighborhoods of silk weaving was the result of
industrial expansion, population growth and urban renewal. This
change separated these neighborhoods from one another by their different experience of each of these three trends. As a result of this
separation, neighborhood solidarity no longer re-enforced class
solidarity, as it had done in the early 1830's, but instead caused
division within the class of silk weavers.

Neighborhood change occurred most rapidly under the Second
Empire. This was a time of rapid growth for the city of Lyons, because of the mutually enforcing character of expanding industry,
population and urban space. In industry, the newer chemical and machine manufactures increased their output and employment, even while
silk weaving declined in favor of rural industry. Auxiliary sectors
of silk manufacture, such as dyeing, silk throwing and finishing,
grew as well, as the industry of Lyons concentrated on the preparation
of thread put out for weaving in the rural households and factories.
This industrial expansion encouraged a rapid growth in urban population, largely by stimulating immigration from the surrounding rural
villages and towns. The demand for semi-skilled and unskilled
labor in the newer manufactures and in the auxiliary trades of the
silk industry, along with the demand for artisanal labor to service

-476-

urban growth, attracted labor from the countryside for permanent
settlement and employment.

Growth of industry and population stimulated in turn the demand
for urban renewal and also helped provide the supply of economic
resources to undertake such renewal. The demand for renewal derived
from the pressure of growing industry and population on the physical
capacities of urban housing, factory and warehouse space and on
traffic capacity. The supply of resources for renewal resulted from
the capital attracted to the city by industrialization and from the
expanding tax and municipal credit base provided by new industry
and by a rising income-earning population, to finance the transformation of urban equipment. The public works program of the Second
Empire undertook such transformation on a large scale and further
stimulated migration of labor from the Lyons region into the city
in search of regular employment. The annexation of three suburban
towns during the same period -- the Croix-Rousse, the Guillotière
and Vaise -- into the administrative orbit of the city underscored
this transformation of urban space and extended its effects into
some of the most concentrated silk-weaving neighborhoods.

The differential impact of industrial expansion, population
growth and urban renewal on the various silk-weaving neighborhoods
in the city became apparent in the different ideological preferences
of their voluntary associations and in the differing susceptibility
of movements of association in each silk-weaving neighborhood to
political influence. Neighborhood thus influenced the aims and
activities of voluntary association as a source of division rather
than unity within the weaver s' social movements in the city.

This division usually reflected the different social meanings of
association to weavers with varying degrees of contact with workers
in other trades or in other conditions of employment than their own,
with whom they shared, most immediately, residential space.

I. The Sources of Changing Neighborhood Environment

   A. Industrialization

Industrial expansion was the primary source of expansion and
transformation of Lyons under the Second Empire. Some of the
industries which grew at that time had been established earlier.
Among the first of these was the locomotive construction industry.
In 1829, Marc Séguin, one of the founders of the Compagnie du
Chemin de Fer de Saint-Etienne à Lyon and builder of the first railroad line in France, set up the first plant for locomotive manufacture. Financial difficulties forced Séguin's company to abandon
locomotives in the 1840's, and it sold its engine manufacture and
repair facilities to two local machine-builders, Jean Claude
Verpilleux and Alphonse Clément-Desormes. In 1844, Clément-Desormes
founded the Ateliers de Construction et Forges d'Oullins. The
Ateliers d'Oullins rapidly became one of the largest railroad locomotive and car maintenance shops in France.

Another industry established in Lyons before 1852 was boat
construction. Along the Saône and Rhône rivers which meet in Lyons,
carpenter-mechanics, forgers, boiler-makers and engine makers made
various parts for boats in their small artisanal shops. Navigation
companies, such as the Compagnie de navigation à vapeur sur la Saône,
founded in 1827, organized the assemblage of these parts along the

same rivers, using labor hired specially for this purpose, in hulls imported from abroad. Boat construction thus provided work for several specialized artisan trades in the city as well as for assemblers working on the docks.

The chemical industry was a third major manufacturing activity which had received an early start in Lyons. The firms of Perret-Olivier and Coignet first took the initiative in the discovery and production of industrial chemicals. In 1836, Perret and Olivier together discovered the industrial application of the principle of extracting sulfuric acid from pyrites. In the acid-manufacturing plant of Claude Perret, they applied the new process on a large scale. In 1840, Perret purchased the rich pyrite mine at Saint-Bel, giving him exclusive control over the raw material for the manufacture of vitriol (concentrated sulfuric acid). The Perret-Olivier firm rapidly became the most important acid manufacturer in southern France. Coignet was another early leader in applying recent chemical discoveries to industrial processes. In 1818, Alphonse Dupasquier, an early partner of Coignet, used hydrochloric acid instead of boiling to extract gelatin from animal bones. This gelatin was especially use-full for the finishing of cloths such as silks. In 1821 and 1822, Dupasquier and Coignet found another method of extracting gelatins for strong glues by means of vapor pressure. The Coignet-Dupasquier firm soon became a national leader in the manufacture of finishing gelatins and glues. Later the firm extended its range of products to black dyes, ammonia salts, Prussiate potassium and phosphoric acid -- the last a derivative of degelinated bones.

The expansion of these industries into new markets, new products and services and larger scales and concentrations of manufacture during the Second Empire was primarily the result of demand derived from the new railroad network penetrating Lyons and the rest of France in this period and from the expansion of the auxiliary sector of the silk industry. The same demand encouraged the formation of new industries as well. The railroad demand for locomotives and tooling-repair services stimulated the development of steam-engine manufacture. The latter in turn provided the basis for a new boat construction industry using the engines and the labor skills developed in engine manufacture as inputs for the manufacture of steamboats. The expansion of auxiliary silk trades, especially dyeing and finishing, benefited from the economic and technical improvements in the chemical industry and provided this industry with a large and regular local market for its products. Exchange of knowledge and expertise between the dyeing and chemical sectors helped make Lyons a major center of research in the field of industrial chemicals. The demand for labor in the newly-expanding industries of Lyons thus derived largely from two sources of industrial growth 'dominating' the economic environment of the city during the Second Empire -- the railroad and auxiliary silk trades. The mutually reenforcing character of the product demand and of the supply of skills and techniques derived from each sector enhanced the growth stimulated by each. Immigration of labor and capital and the rebuilding of the city promoted by these sectors and by the public works sector together enhanced even more the aggregate economic growth of the city.

The impact of the railroad on industrial growth in the city
was most immediately evident. The construction of the major north-
south trunk line, the Paris-Lyons-Mediterranean, and the building
of the southeastern arteries connecting this trunk with the surrounding
region, created more business for the engine re-tooling and maintenance shop of the Ateliers d' Oullins and created the market for the
newly-established railroad car construction firm of the Chantiers de
la Buire, founded in 1847 by J. Frossard de Saugy, one of the promoters
of ·the Paris-Lyons-Mediterranean company. In 1854, the Compagnie du
Chemin de Fer Grand Central de France purchased the Oullins shops from
Clément-Desormes and undertook "the complete overhaul of the three
first railroads of France."[1] The Paris-Lyons-Mediterranean company
acquired these shops in 1861 and installed powerful hydraulic presses
and equipment for casting iron and bronze locomotive parts. In
January 1866, these shops together employed more than a thousand
workers.[2] The Ateliers de la Buire also benefited from the railroad
expansion of the Second Empire, concentrating on the manufacture of
cars. Between 1857 and 1867, the Ateliers produced 700 cars per year.[3]
In late 1866, during the peak of the unemployment crisis in the urban
silk industry, these shops were so busy that they hired 130 new workers.
On December 15, the single firm of La Buire had 950 workers in its shops.[4]

[1]Michel Laferrère, Lyon: ville industrielle (Paris: Presses
universitaires de France, 1960), p. 277.

[2]'Construction de machines à vapeur,' "Situation de l'industrie
à Lyon au 15 Décembre 1866," AML, I2 - 47(A), Situation de l'industrie
lyonnaise: ... rapports sur la soierie et les ouvriers en soie ...
(1819 à 1870), No. 193.

[3]Laferrère, Lyon: ville industrielle, p. 278.

[4]'Ateliers de la Buire,' "Situation de l'industrie au 15 Décembre
1866," AML, 12 - 47(A), No. 193.

In March 1869, two smaller shops, one on the Perrache peninsula and
one at La Mouche near the former town of La Guillotière, hired an
additional 500 workers to service the P-L-M trunk line trains.[5]
Railroad construction and service clearly had a strong favorable
effect on the demand for labor in the city.

The railroad also favored the development of a new machinery
manufacture in Lyons, that of steam engines. This was partly the
result of the demand for steam locomotives and for engines to operate
the heavy mechanical equipment of the railroad shops. The encourage-
ment to steam-engine manufacture was also indirect, for the railroad
also 'released' a supply of skilled labor suitable for employment in
the high-quality steam-engine sector which developed. By building
its major trunk line to the North along the Saône River, the P-L-M
competed stiffly with water carriage there and weakened critically
the boat construction trade on the docks of the Saône. Many of the
nearby artisans employed fully or largely by this trade quickly lost
their main source of employment. These artisans abandoned the quais
of the Saône for Vaïse farther north or for Guillotière and the
Brotteaux, on the left bank of the Rhône, to seek work in the rapidly
growing industries in these areas. These carpenters, boiler-makers
and mechanics joined the forgers, founders and casters already settled
in the Brotteaux-Guillotière region to form a pool of skilled labor
admirably suited for the small-scale, high-quality steam-engine
industry developing in the same region. After 1860, on the basis of

---

[5]'Ateliers des chemins de fer, à Perrache et à la Mouche,'
"Situation industrielle au Mars 1869," AML, 12 - 47(A), No. 207.

this steam-engine manufacture, a more sophisticated construction of
river vehicles and equipment developed in turn -- steamboats, barges,
river-dredging machines and canal construction boats, used in the
piercing of the Suez Canal, for example.[6]

The steam-engine shops combined the talents of metallurgical
workers, who produced top-grade steel and iron parts for small-engine
precision and durability, and the skills of mechanics, boiler-makers
and carpenters, who designed and assembled these parts into the
finished product. Although smaller in scale than the railroad equipment and service shops and using artisanal labor for the most part,
the steam-engine industry employed as many as four hundred workers in
March 1869.[7] The industry prospered throughout most of the 1860's,
and in late 1866 even offered employment to some of the workers recently
laid off at the railroad shop of Oullins.[8]

The chemical industry of Lyons benefited from the expansion of
the auxiliary trades in the silk industry, notably dyeing and finishing.
These latter required large quantities of acids, gelatins and
artificial coloring material and thus provided a growing market for
the product of the local chemical industry. The chemical firm of
Perret-Olivier, for example, probably supplied acids for many dyers of
silk thread. The search for new colors in dyes after 1850 especially
encouraged the development and production of artificial, chemically-
based dyes. Prosper Monnet and Duruy, for example, produced the

[6]Laferrère, Lyon: ville industrielle, pp. 290-291.

[7]'Constructeurs de machines à vapeur,' "Situation industrielle
au Mars 1869," AML, 12 - 47(A), No. 207

[8]'Construction de machines à vapeur, "Situation de l'industrie
au 15 Décembre 1866," AML, I2 - 47(A), No. 193.

newly-discovered violet dye <u>harmaline</u> in great quantities after 1858
for the dyers of Lyons.[9]

Perhaps the most immediately fruitful interchange between the
chemical and dyeing industries of Lyons was in the area of research. The
best example of such interchange involved the discovery and exploitation
of the prolific red <u>fuchsine</u> dye, generator of a wide range of other colors
as well. Emmanuel Verguin, inventor of the <u>fuchsine</u>, was a student of
Alphonse Dupasquier, inventor of the hydrochloric acid process of extracting
gelatin from bones and partner in the reputable gelatin-manufacturing firm
Coignet-Dupasquier. Claude Perret, the manufacturer of acids and probably
a major supplier of the Coignet-Dupasquier firm, had introduced Verguin to
Dupasquier. Verguin's discovery yielded another interchange with chemical
manufacture equally fruitful. The <u>fuchsine</u> firm employed Prosper Monnet
as its chief chemist. Monnet had been involved in the manufacture of the
violet dye <u>harmaline</u> and after three years with the <u>fuchsine</u> firm set up
his own colored-dye manufactory in 1868. After several transformations in
the following decades, the Monnet enterprise developed into the inter-
nationally reputable chemical firm Rhône-Poulenc.[10]

B. <u>Urban Renewal</u>

The growth of the railroad and railroad works, of machinery manufacture, and of chemical and dyeing industries created a large demand for
skilled and unskilled labor. A vast public works program undertaken simultaneously with the growth of these industries augmented even more this
demand for labor, especially for unskilled labor. The program was the

[9]Laferrère, <u>Lyon: ville industrielle</u>, p. 155.

[10]<u>Ibid.</u>, p. 160.

special contribution on the Prefect Vaïsse, the 'Haussmann of Lyons,' to

the unprecedented expansion of the city during his joint tenure as mayor

of Lyons and prefect of the department of the Rhône. In 1852, Vaïsse

commissioned the Poncet building company to construct the Rue Impériale

(present-day Rue de la République) through the center of downtown Lyons.

Just before the completion of this main artery, in 1858, he contracted

with another company to construct the parellel Rue Impératrice (present-day

Rue du President Edouard Herriot). Vaïsse added several smaller streets

nearby as well, such as the Rues Grenette, Buisson, de la Bourse, and Childe-

bert. Such street building required the demolition of old structures as well

as the construction of new buildings and thus involved a wide-ranging pro-

gram of urban renewal. Such renewal included in addition the re-modeling

of city hall, the construction and beautification of public squares and

gardens in the downtown presqu'île district, and the construction of the

Palais du Commerce, the largest architectural monument of Vaisse's program.

Vaïsse also engaged the Compagnie Générale des Eaux to construct a large

water and sewerage system on the presqu'île. Renewal was not limited to the

downtown district. Vaïsse built several new quays along the Saône and the

Rhône, the two rivers meeting in Lyons, and raised the height of existing

quays to protect against floods. After the devastating flood of the Rhône

in 1856, he had re-enforcing dikes built there to prevent such calamities in

the future. Finally, he begun the construction of the magnificent Parc de la

Tête d'Or on the left bank of the Rhône, the best testimonial to taste in

public building in Second-Empire Lyons. Nearly all of these projects were

begun during the first decade of the Empire, and work continued on some of

them throughout the 1860's as well.[11]

---

[11]For a thorough description of the various public works in Lyons,

C. Population Growth

The large numbers of laborers required for industrial expansion and urban renewal came primarily from the countryside and surrounding departments. The city of Lyons was long accustomed to immigration from these areas to provide the extra labor needs of the silk industry. Until the 1860's at least, the silk industry continued to attract rural migrants during its periods of prosperity. Yet the immigration induced by silk manufacture remained largely seasonal and did not encourage permanent settlement in the city. The new labor demand associated with industrial and urban development, however, promoted more permanent residence in the city than the silk industry had done in its recent past at least. Not only was the demand ever-increasing but it was seasonally stable. Occasional slowdowns in one industry were nearly always compensated by additional labor needs in other industries; and in the worst situations of industry, the public works easily absorbed labor temporarily unemployed by a more general slowdown. Industrial growth and urban renewal thus created the basis for a permanent increase in the population of the city, and not merely temporary increases associated with the 'floating populations' of the past.

Table 36 summarizes this increase in population during the Second Empire as compared with periods immediately preceding and immediately following. The increase was most notable in the first decade of the Second Empire. Between 1851 and 1861, the population rose by nearly double the increase of the previous decade. The rise was concentrated in the years 1856-1861. During these years, all the major public works of

including the history of their construction and of methods of financing this construction, see Charlene-Marie Leonard, Lyon Transformed: Public Works of the Second Empire (Berkeley: University of California Press, 1961).

Table 36:

Population of Lyons, 1841-1876
(for Lyons intra muros, as
defined in 1852)

Year	Total, Lyons	Quinquennial Change		Decennial Change	
		Numbers	%	Numbers	%
1841	200,459 *				
1846	231,763 *	+ 31,304	+ 15.6		
1851	234,531	+ 2,768	+ 1.2	+ 34,072	+ 17.0
1856	255,960	+ 21,429	+ 9.1		
1861	297,251	+ 41,291	+ 16.1	+ 62,720	+ 26.7
1866	300,761	+ 3,510	+ 1.2		
1872	301,307	+ 546	+ .2	+ 4,056	+ 1.3
1876	321,596	+ 20,289	+ 6.7		

Sources: Yves Lequin, "Le monde ouvrier de la région
lyonnaise dans la deuxième moitié du XIXème
siècle, 1848 à 1914" (unpublished thesis for
the Doctorat d'Etat, Université Lyon II, 1975),
IV, La Progression de la Population Lyonnaise (1851-1906). Tableaux 1-7 for 1851, 1856,
1861, 1866, 1872, 1876.
Statistique de la France, Population, 2ème Série,
tome XIII, I. Résultats Généraux du Dénombrement de 1861 comparé aux Cinq Dénombrements
Anteriers,. Tableau No. 3, for 1841, 1846.

*Population of Lyons, Croix-Rousse and Guillotière

Vaïsse's renewal program were under construction, the central railroad

station of Perrache was built (1856) and the P-L-M line merged into a

single network (1857), steam-engine manufacture and river-boat construc-

tion began on the left bank of the Rhône, and the fuchsine firm was

established (1857). These activities together required an enormous supply

of labor. The silk industry required its largest work force during

these same years as well, as the demand for silk cloths of all kinds

reached its highest levels ever in 1859.

This extra labor came primarily from immigration, for, as Joseph Arminjon has demonstrated, the rate of natural increase in population actually declined during these years as a result of a fall in the birth rate, larger than the decline in mortality from improved hygiene in the city. Between 1831-1835 and 1861-1865, for example, the average annual number of births per 10,000 inhabitants in the department of the Rhône fell by 20%, from 332 to 265. The average number of deaths fell by 16% during the same period, from 274 to 231. As a result, the excess of births over deaths per 10,000 inhabitants fell from 58 in 1831-1835 to 34 in 1861-1865. During the same period, the average size of the population per 10,000 inhabitants increased by 46%, or 212 persons.[12] The population of the department thus expanded largely by means of immigration from other departments and from abroad. The role of immigration was probably even more important in supporting the rapid population growth of Lyons, the major city of the department, because of migration from the Rhône countryside as well.

Many of these migrants swelled the artisanal sectors of the urban economy, so that even after the influx of étrangers a large proportion of the working population remained artisanal. These new arrivals worked not only in the older building, textile and machine-goods industries or in the newer steam-engine construction, dyeing and locomotive maintenance industries as skilled or semi-skilled crafts-people, but also in the domestic food and clothing industries and commerce serving the needs of the rest of the laboring population.

---

[12] Joseph Arminjon, La population du department du Rhône: Son évolution depuis le début du XIXe siècle (Lyon, 1940), pp. 119, 133.

The census of 1866, analyzed in detail by Yves Lequin in his recent
thèse d'état, demonstrated this preponderance of artisanal labor among
the working class of Lyons.[13] In the industrial sector of the city's
economy, 17,787 establishments employed 131,573 persons (42% of the
total population) and furnished the livelihood of an additional
69,423 persons (23% of the population) dependent on the first. This
represented only 7.40 persons per establishment. In food and clothing
commerce, the average size of the establishment was much smaller --
1.97 persons. The number of persons depending on food and clothing
commerce for their livelihood (workers and their families) was
23,725, or 8% of the total population. In other words, nearly three-
fourths of the total population in Lyons in 1866 depended for their
income on industrial and commercial enterprise employing, on the
average, no more than eight persons per shop. Despite the impressive
growth of large-scale enterprise in the city during the Second Empire,
the labor which settled in the city remained predominantly artisanal.[14]

Yves Lequin's study of socio-professional mobility of workers
in the Lyons region between 1851 and 1901-11 suggests some reasons
for this maintenance of artisanal labor in a large urban population
growing primarily through immigration. Lequin found that the proportion
of migrants from rural areas who married in Lyons was mediocre in

---

The population figure used for each five year period is the average
of the figures of the first and last years of each period (that is,
the figures of the two quinquennial censuses associated with each)
and is therefore called an average. (Ibid., p. 117.)

[13]Yves Lequin, "Le monde ouvrier de la région lyonnaise dans la
deuxième moitié du XIXème siècle, 1848 a 1914" (unpublished thesis for
the Doctorat d'Etat, Université Lyon II, 1975), I, 345-371.

[14]"1866: Dénombrement de la population de la ville de Lyon,
1er à 5e Arr.," ADR, 5M.

comparison with the proportion from towns and small cities in the Lyons region.[15] He also found a decline in the tendency of urban workers native to the city of Lyons to follow the same craft as their fathers and a rise in the tendency of these same workers to take on spouses employed in different occupations than their own, when these spouses were also native to the city. Workers not native to the city of Lyons, however, tended to remain in the craft of their fathers, and women not born in Lyons tended to marry within their own craft as well.[16] Migrants married in Lyons thus tended to migrate in order to preserve the craft of their fathers, and they came primarily from towns and small cities rather than from the farms. They were artisans in short, moving into the city in order to remain in that state. They strengthened not only the artisanal character of the city but also the traditional attachment to a single craft. Natives of Lyons, on the contrary, weakened such attachment by pursuing other crafts than those of their fathers and by marrying outside of their own craft. Natives rather than migrants contributed most to the formation of an artisanal 'class' transcending the frontiers of a single trade by their socio-professional mobility from one trade to another, or by that of their wives.

Lequin's data do not, of course, take account of the large numbers of migrant labor which did not marry in the city and therefore is biased in favor of the settled workers. In all probability, the other migrants came more largely from the farms to work as day laborers in the construction of streets, parks, quays and buildings

---

[15] Lequin, "Le monde ouvrier de la région lyonnaise," II, 77-80.

[16] Ibid., II, 85.

and in the unskilled occupations in the dyeing, chemical, metal and textile industries. Some even worked as journeyworkers or as auxiliaries in the small artisanal shops. These alone were genuinely 'proletarian' in their conditions of work as well as in their relations to their employers, but they constituted a minority of the working 'class' of Lyons in this period of rapid industrialization and extended urbanization.

II The Differential Impact of Environmental Change

    A. The Impact on Neighborhoods in General

The growth of industry and population in the city did not affect all sections of Lyons in the same way. The growth was concentrated in the 'new' areas of the Brotteaux, the Guillotière, and Villeurbanne rather than in the 'old' areas of the presqu'île, the Croix-Rousse and the right bank of the Saône. (See map of Lyons on page 493) The population of the latter in fact stagnated somewhat between 1856 and 1876. During this twenty-year period, the population of 'New Lyons' (Brotteaux, Guillotière and Villeurbanne) increased from 83,000 to 143,000 (+ 72.3%), while that of 'Old Lyons' (arrondissements 1, 2, 4, 5) decreased from 221,000 to 218,000 (- 1.4%).[17] Although 'Old Lyons' remained the most populated section of the city, it contributed little to the growth of population over this period. Table 37 demonstrates this more precisely for the two major silk-weaving districts in these two sections of the city -- the Croix-Rousse in 'Old Lyons' and the Brotteaux-Guillotière in 'New Lyons'.

---

[17]Arminjon, La population du département du Rhône, pp. 71-72.

Table 37

a. Population of the Croix-Rousse (in 'Old Lyons'), 1829 - 1872

Year	Population	Quinquennial Change		Decennial Change	
		Numbers	%	Numbers	%
1829	12,000				
1836	17,934	+ 5,934	+ 49.4		
1841	18,790	+ 856	+ 4.8	+ 6,790	+ 56.6
1846	19,587	+ 797	+ 4.2		
1851	28,711	+ 9,124	+ 46.6	+ 9,921	+ 52.8
1856	33,000	+ 4,289	+ 14.9		
1861					
1866	33,670			+ 4,959*	+ 17.3*
1872	33,222	- 448	- 1.3		

b. Population of the Brotteaux-Guillotière (in 'New Lyons'), 1831 - 1872

Year	Population	Quinquennial Change		Decennial Change	
1831	18,000				
1836	22,890	+ 4,890	+ 27.2		
1841	25,730	+ 2,840	+ 12.4	+ 7,730	+ 42.9
1846	35,500	+ 9,770	+ 38.0		
1851	41,528	+ 6,028	+ 17.0	+ 15,798	+ 61.4
1856					
1861					
1866	109,105			+ 67,577*	+162.7*
1872	112,598	+ 3,493	+ 3.2		

Sources: 1829 (31), 1836, 1841, 1846, 1851, 1856 (Croix-Rousse): Joseph Arminjon, La population du département du Rhône, son évolution depuis le début du XIXe siècle (Lyon, 1940), pp. 35, 72.

1866: "1866: Dénombrement de la Population
de la Ville de Lyon, ler à 5e arrondissements," ADR, 5M.
1872: Statistique de la France, Résultats
Généraux du Dénombrement de 1872 (Paris,
1873), p. 249.

* Change and percentage change in population from 1851 to 1866.

Before 1850 population grew rapidly in both sections of the city.
The Croix-Rousse developed more rapidly than the Brotteaux-Guillotière
between 1829 and 1836 and between 1846 and 1851, but the latter compensated for this relative sluggishness by a more intensive growth
between 1836 and 1846. Over the whole period from 1829-31 to 1851,
the rate of population growth was not very different in the Croix-
Rousse than in the Brotteaux-Guillotière. After 1850, however, the
rate of increase in the Croix-Rousse declined while that of the Brotteaux-Guillotière spurted ahead. Between 1851 and 1872, population in
the Croix-Rousse increased only 16%, while population in the Brotteaux-
Guillotière grew by 171%. Population in the Croix-Rousse stagnated so
much in the 1860's that it even lost some of its inhabitants between
1866 and 1872.

Besides differences in population growth during the Second
Empire, these two sections of the city differed also in territorial
size, population density and especially industrial character.
Population density measured by the average number of persons per
building was higher in the smaller territorial area of the Croix-
Rousse (23.9 persons per building) than in the larger territorial
area of the Brotteaux-Guillotière (16.1 persons per building).[18]

---

[18]"1866: Dénombrement de la population de Lyon," ADR, 5M.

Map of Lyons

1869

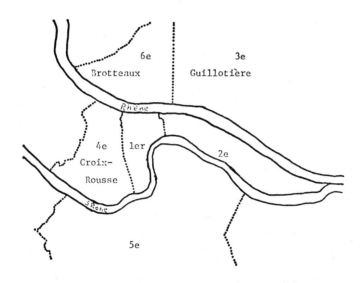

6e
Brotteaux

3e
Guillotière

Rhône

4e
Croix-
Rousse

1er

2e

Saône

5e

Source: Pierre Léon, Géographie de la fortune
           et structure sociale à Lyon au XIXe
           siècle (1815 - 1914) (Lyon: Université
           Lyon II, Centre d'histoire économique
           et sociale de la région lyonnaise, 1974),
           p. 226, Carte No. 3.

The working population of the Croix-Rousse, moreover, consisted
predominantly of silk workers, while that of the Brotteaux-Guillotière
included many more workers in other industries besides, notably in
chemicals, dyeing, machine-goods and locomotive repair and construction
industries. The Brotteaux-Guillotière was, in short, the region of
industrial as well as population growth in the city. The attraction
of this area for new industries had begun well before the time of
the Second Empire. Between 1810 and 1827, for example, about twenty
dyeing shops were set up here, most of them in the Brotteaux. Low
rents, the availability of soft, temperate waters in underground
wells, and the scarcity of space in the traditional dyeing districts
of St. Clair and the quai Sérin all motivated this choice of location.
The attraction of the area for dyeing enterprise remained strong until
1880, when a fourth of all dyeing establishments in the city were
located there.[19] Dyeing favored the development of chemical industries
in the same region. The first sulfur-manufacturing shop of Claude
Perret, for example, was situated in the Brotteaux.[20] Dyeing and
chemical firms, both large and small, were especially evident in the
industrial landscape of the Brotteaux-Guillotière after 1850, when
both industries experienced their most rapid growth.

Another industry which developed rapidly in the Brotteaux-
Guillotière after 1850 was steam-engine manufacture. As noted
earlier, the steam-engine industry developed from the merging of

[19]Laferrère, Lyon: ville industrielle, p. 28.

[20]Ibid., p. 29, note 30.

skilled assemblage and mechanic labor formerly employed on boat

construction on the Saône with artisanal metallurgical labor

indigenous to the Brotteaux-Guillotière -- "founder-forgers, metal

turners, very often of Dauphinois orgin."[21] After 1860 this steam-

engine industry "revived the Lyons docks for river construction,"

only now on the banks of the Rhône.[22] Steam engines made in the

Brotteaux-Guillotière were also used in some of the nearby railroad

car construction and locomotive repair shops. The shops of the

Buire for car construction, for example, were located in the eastern

section of the Guillotière. Farther south, the shops of La Mouche

for locomotive maintenance added another large establishment to the

industrial profile of the area. Along with the large chemical

factories in the same area, these shops gave the Brotteaux-Guillotière

industry a more factory-like 'air' than any other region of the city.

Although artisan manufacture remained predominant there as elsewhere

in Lyons, the newer form of industrial enterprise was making rapid

headway in the two decades of the Second Empire.

Silk weaving and public works construction on the quays and

dikes of the Rhône and on the Parc de la Tête d'Or also employed

an increasing share of the population of the Brotteaux-Guillotière

during the same period. Yet silk weaving was only one among several

industrial pursuits in this area and not the predominant employer

of the working population as it was in the Croix-Rousse, in the First

or Fifth Arrondissement of the city. Table 38 shows the extent of

this industrial diversity of the areas of 'New Lyons' (Third

---

[21]Ibid., p. 288.

[22]Ibid..

Table 38

Distribution of Population
of Lyons by Selected In-
dustrial and Commercial
Occupations, 1866

	Old Lyons			New Lyons	
	1st Arr.	4th Arr.	5th Arr.	3rd Arr.	3rd Banlieu
Industry					
Textile	24,779	23,008	17,367	10,559	1,028
Metal	440	201	532	2,779	59
Leather, Wood Furniture	922	527	1,440	2,661	244
Chemical	63	15	474	2,436	1,690
Building	2,187	834	3,219	11,933	1,321
Clothing	9,586	2,253	6,323	8,621	594
Food	2,632	1,094	3,052	6,117	596
Transport	320	320	2,273	5,554	671
Other	1,515	160	1,396	4,926	1,122
TOTAL INDUSTRY	42,444	28,412	36,076	55,586	7,325
Commerce					
Clothing	2,182	292	985	3,251	145
Food	1,870	1,249	2,714	4,495	440
Other	1,181	368	1,625	3,473	261
TOTAL COMMERCE	5,233	1,909	5,324	11,219	846
TOTAL, ALL TRADES	57,796	33,670	53,414	95,802	13,303

Source: "1866: Dénombrement de la
Population de la Ville de Lyon,
ler à 5e arrondissements,"
ADR, 5M

Old Lyons

Industry	1st Arr. % Ind.	1st Arr. % All Trades	4th Arr. % Ind.	4th Arr. % All Trades	5th Arr. % Ind.	5th Arr. % All Trades
Textile	58.4	42.9	81.0	68.3	48.1	32.5
Metal	1.0	.8	.7	.6	1.5	1.0
Leather, Wood Furniture	2.2	1.6	1.8	1.6	4.0	2.7
Chemical	.1	.1	0.	0.	1.3	.9
Building	5.1	3.8	2.9	2.5	8.9	6.0
Clothing	22.6	16.6	7.9	6.7	17.5	11.8
Food	6.2	4.5	3.8	3.2	8.5	5.7
Transport	.7	.5	1.1	.9	6.3	4.2
Other	3.6	2.6	.6	.5	3.9	2.6
TOTAL INDUSTRY		73.4		84.4		67.5

Commerce	% Com.		% Com.		% Com.	
Clothing	41.7	3.8	15.3	.9	18.5	1.8
Food	35.7	3.2	65.4	3.7	51.0	5.1
Other	22.6	2.0	19.3	1.1	30.5	3.0
TOTAL COMMERCE		9.0		5.7		10.0

New Lyons

Industry	3rd Arr. % Ind.	3rd Arr. % All Trades	3rd Banlieu % Ind.	3rd Banlieu % All Trades
Textile	19.0	11.0	14.0	7.7
Metal	5.0	2.9	.8	.4
Leather, Wood Furniture	4.8	2.8	3.3	1.8
Chemical	4.4	2.5	23.1	12.7
Building	21.5	12.4	18.0	9.9
Clothing	15.5	9.0	8.1	4.5
Food	11.0	6.4	8.1	4.5
Transport	10.0	5.8	9.2	5.0
Other	8.9	5.1	15.3	8.4
TOTAL INDUSTRY		58.0		55.1

Commerce	% Com.		% Com.	
Clothing	29.0	3.4	17.1	1.1
Food	40.1	4.7	52.0	3.3
Other	31.0	3.6	30.8	2.0
TOTAL COMMERCE		11.7		6.4

Arrondissement and Suburban Third) as compared with the traditional

silk-weaving districts of 'Old Lyons' (First, Fourth and Fifth

Arrondissements) in 1866. In the arrondissements of 'Old Lyons,'

nearly half or more than half of the population employed in industry

worked in textile manufacture, the largest single source of employ-

ment. The second largest employer in all three arrondissements

was the clothing trade, including tailoring, dressmaking and shoe-

making. Textiles and clothing together occupied 81% of the

industrial population of the First Arrondissement, 89% in the

Fourth Arrondissement (Croix-Rousse), and 66% in the Fifth

Arrondissement. On the left bank of the Rhône, in the heart of 'New

Lyons,' textiles occupied no more than a fifth of all persons engaged

in industry, and were only the second or third most important employer

in this area. In the Third Arrondissement (Brotteaux-Guillotière),

building was a larger employer, and in the Suburban Third (Villeur-

banne) the chemical industry and building each employed more persons

than textile manufacture.

In neither section of 'New Lyons,' however, did any single

or couple of activities dominate the labor force in the overwhelming

manner of textiles or of textiles and clothing as in 'Old Lyons.'

The two largest sectors in each section (building and textiles in

the Third Arrondissement, chemicals and building in the Suburban

Third) did not employ even half of all workers in industry, and the

three largest sectors, including textiles, employed only 56% in the

Third and 55% in the Suburban Third. The remaining 44% of the

industrial population was distributed more or less evenly among a

wide range of other activities -- food, transport, metal work, wood work, and chemical manufacture (in that order), in the Third

Arrondissement, and transport, food, clothing, wood work and metal

work in the Suburban Third. Food and clothing commerce, moreover,

absorbed a handsome share of the work force employed in all occupations

in 'New Lyons.' In the Third Arrondissement, each commercial sector

employed more than the metal-working, wood work or chemical industries,

and in the Suburban Third, food commerce was a more significant em-

ployer than metal or wood work.

The number of persons employed in trades other than textiles

and clothing was not small in the arrondissements of 'Old Lyons'

but was far less on the whole, both absolutely and proportionately,

than in 'New Lyons.' Food industries and food commerce together

employed about 7% or more of the working population in the First and

Fourth Arrondissements, and building occupied 4% of the workers in

the First Arrondissement and 2.5% in the Fourth Arrondissement.

Both food and building trades serviced the local populations, most

of whom were silk workers, and thus were mere adjuncts to the dominant

industry of their sections of the city. An additional 2% of the

working populations of these areas provided the wood-working services

for construction and repair of the weavers' looms.

The First Arrondissement, on the right bank of the Saône,

had the most diversified employment structure of all the sections

of 'Old Lyons.' Food industry, food commerce and building each

employed more than 5% of the total working population, 4% of the same

population was engaged in transport (primarily railroad work at the

new station of Vaise), and 3% worked on wood. Nevertheless, even

here textile manufacture, especially silk weaving, was a much more

important industrial activity than in the newer, growing areas on
the left bank of the Rhône. Here as in the rest of 'Old Lyons,'
most other industries served the needs of silk workers and only
rarely worked for more distant, independent, extra-urban markets as
did the chemical workers and machine-builders in 'New Lyons.'

Although industry was more diversified on the left bank of the
Rhône, it did not engage as large a percentage of the population as
it did in the older areas of the city. Only 58% of the residents of
the Third Arrondissement and only 55% of those of the Suburban Third
worked in industry in 1866, while 84% of the inhabitants of the Fourth
Arrondissement and 73% of those of the First were industrial workers.
Commerce, agriculture and rents from properties, bonds and other
investments supported a larger proportion of the population in the
newly developing areas than in the older weaving districts on the
central peninsula. About 37% of the residents of the Third Arrondissement and 41% of the residents of the Suburban Third were merchants,
farmers, property-owners or rentiers in 1866. Only 13% of the
residents of the Croix-Rousse (Fourth Arrondissement) and 19% of
the inhabitants of the First Arrondissement were in these occupational
categories. In the Fifth Arrondissement. the population was less
industrial (67%) and more commercial, agricultural or proprietary
(23%) than in the other sections of 'Old Lyons,' but more industrial
than the population of 'New Lyons.'

The arrondissements in 'New Lyons' were, in short, areas of
sharp contrasts -- both social and occupational -- as well as areas
of expanding population and industrial growth. Some of the wealthiest
and most exclusive members of the old Lyonnais notables, both

aristocratic and bourgeois, resided in the chic quarters of the
Brotteaux. Not very far from these quarters ugly shops and slovenly
habitats huddled against the inundated dirt roads, sheltering their
impoverished residents and recently uprooted arrivals from farms and
nearby villages. In 1852, A. Audiganne described the populations of
the Guillotière as "nomadic," "ill-reputed," and "vagrant," requiring
constant police surveillance. "Don't look in this confused and floating
medley for the workers of Lyons, the workers of the fabrique," noted
the sociologist.[23] Crime was most frequent in these areas and yet,
as we saw earlier, many of the workers living here were 'solid'
skilled artisans who migrated from their native towns to preserve
their craft. The effect of this mixture of different types of workers
was great instability combined with a dynamic exchange of life-styles
and traditions:

> Here social fear rests largely on the unknown and on
> the disarray of a workers' environment not known be-
> fore in Lyons, concentrated very rapidly and especially
> throwing workers with local traditions -- canuts,
> masons, tailors, etc. -- together with those of an
> entirely different sort, working in the new industries.
> On the one hand, it is the presence of a proletariat
> of the factory, on the other hand an extreme diversity
> which constitute the true originality of the Guillotière.[24]

The main feature of this originality was "the coexistence of an artisanal organization [of labor] and an industrial proletariat."[25]
Such coexistence contrasted most sharply with the self-enclosed
community of the Croix-Rousse where nearly all of the resident

---

[23]A. Audiganne, "Du mouvement intellectuel parmi les populations
ouvrières -- Les ouvriers de Lyon en 1852," Revue des deux mondes,
22ème année -- nouvelle période, XV(August 1, 1852), 510.

[24]Lequin, "Le monde ouvrier de la région lyonnaise," I, 365-366.

[25]Ibid., I, 369.

population worked in a single domestic industry:

> The working class of the Guillotière had no single
> appearance, and it was not mere chance that all
> observers of the period contrasted it with the
> Croix-Rousse ... The Third Arrondissement was a
> meltingpot where a multitude of people came into
> contact (with one another), from different occupational
> specialties and from different social ranks but were
> confounded in the same working condition, and where
> an industrial proletariat was undoubtedly formed.[26]

B. The Impact On The Neighborhoods Of Silk Weaving

The cleavage between the stagnating, mono-industrial Croix-
Rousse and the growing, poly-industrial Brotteaux-Guillotière was
especially significant in differentiating the 'neighborhood environments' of silk weavers. After 1850, urban weaving tended to concentrate increasingly in these two areas. Instead of strengthening the
craft solidarity of weavers in the city, however, this concentration
had the opposite effect. Because of the radically different social
and economic character of their respective neighborhoods, weavers
in the Croix-Rousse had a more limited, less frequent contact with
workers of other crafts and conditions of employment than weavers
in the Brotteaux-Guillotière. This division of social experience
between weavers in the two sections contrasted strongly with the
neighborhood solidarity of urban weavers in the early 1830's.
In his recent study of the Lyons uprising of 1834, Robert Bezucha
cited the formation of "distinctively working class neighborhoods --
entire quarters devoted only to weaving" between 1820 and 1834 as a
major ingredient in the development of craft and class solidarity

---

[26]Ibid..

among the silk weavers.[27] In 1834, the First and Fifth <u>Arrondissements</u> within the city and the Croix-Rousse outside formed these major weaving quarters.[28] After 1834, this "social and economic polarization" of urban weaving[29] became even more intense, as the Croix-Rousse alone absorbed an ever increasing proportion of looms in the city. The new element was the slow but certain development of weaving in the Brotteaux-Guillotière. Along with the Croix-Rousse, this new area absorbed a growing share of urban weaving at the expense of the First and Fifth <u>Arrondissements</u>. But in the Brotteaux-Guillotière, a wide range of other-industries emerged and developed besides silk weaving and gave this area its more diversified character of industrial activity. The Croix-Rousse remained a predominantly silk-weaving neighborhood and seems to have become even more exclusively devoted to this single industry than in the past.[30] Thus,as the weavers of the Brotteaux-Guillotière became integrated geographically into a more varied working environment, those of the Croix-Rousse became even more isolated from the laboring experience of the rest of the city.

---

[27] Robert Bezucha, <u>The Lyon Uprising of 1834: Social and Political Conflict in the Early July Monarchy</u> (Cambridge: Harvard University Press, 1974), pp. 27-31.

[28] <u>Ibid</u>., pp. 30-31.

[29] <u>Ibid</u>., p. 27.

[30] In 1833, silk workers constituted 61% of the population of the Croix-Rousse, according to the census taken in that year (<u>Ibid</u>., p. 32, Table 5.). In 1866, textile workers (nearly all of whom were silk workers) formed 68% of the population of the same area.(See Tables 37 and 38 of this chapter.) Even allowing for a mild 'inflation' of the latter percentage as a result of workers employed in other textiles than silk in 1866 and not included in the percentage for 1833, silk workers (especially weavers) were a component of the population of the Croix-Rousse at least as important in 1866 as in 1833, and probably more important in the later year   than in the earlier.

Table 39 traces this growing 'polarization' of urban weaving
between the Croix-Rousse (Fourth Arrondissement) and the Brotteaux-
Guillotière (Third Arrondissement) between 1829 and 1874. The table
compares the geographical distribution of looms in the city by
arrondissement (based on the 1866 definition of arrondissements)
for 1829-1833 (1829 for arrondissements 1, 2, 5 and 1833 for
arrondissements 3 and 4), for 1846 and for 1866 and the distribution
of silk workers belonging to the 11,139-member Société civile de
prévoyance et de renseignements des tisseurs de Lyon (weavers'
resistance society) in 1874. The latter is not entirely comparable
to the loom data because of the voluntary character of the resistance association and because the number of looms probably exceeded
the number of active weavers belonging to the organization. Nevertheless, the geographical representation of weavers in the Société
civile most likely reflects accurately enough the geographical distribution of weaving in the city, since most urban weavers joined
this society and no section of the city seems to have 'joined'
more intensively than any other. (See Appendix III.)

Table 39

Geographical Distribution of Silk Looms and Weavers
in the City of Lyons, by Arrondissement
as Defined in 1866

Year		1829-33		1844-46	
Arrondissement		Total Looms	% All	Total Looms	% All
1		5,623 (a)	22.1	8,787 (a)	29.5
2		5,068 (a)	19.9	2,658 (a)	8.9
3	(Brott-Guill)	2,300 (b)	9.0	2,600*(b)	8.7
4	(Croix-Rousse)	6,259 (b)	24.6	9,714 (c)	32.6
5		6,241 (a)	24.5	6,066 (a)	20.3
	All (Lyons)	25,491	100.1	29,825	100.0

Year		1866		1874	
		Total Looms	% All	Total Persons	% All
1		8,015	24.2	2,129	20.1
2		643	1.9	94	.9
3	(Brott-Guill)	3,958	11.9	1,939	18.3
4	(Croix-Rousse)	14,053	42.4	5,344	50.5
5		6,474	19.5	1,073	10.1
	All (Lyons)	33,143	99.9	10,579	99.9

Sources: 1829-33: a. "Population de 1829
Pour 1830," AML, F2 - Fabrique de
Soieries - Inventeurs - Statistiques
(1811 a 1854)
b. "Recensement de Gasparin,
Préfet du Rhône, 1833," reported in
Arlès-Dufour, Un mot sur les fabriques etrangeres des soieries, 1834,
pp. 106 ff., 129 ff., in ACCL,
Soieries - Carton 21 - Tissage de
Soieries (Statistiques), Recensement
des metiers à differentes époques
(1600 à 1844)

1844-46: a. AML, Recensement de Lyon,
1846
b. Same as 1829-33 (b)
c. AML, Recensement, Croix-
Rousse, 1844-45
1866: . M. Robin, "Situation de
Fabrique," June 1, 1866, presented
to Chamber of Commerce of Lyons in
June 1870, Compte-rendu des travaux
de la Chambre de Commerce de Lyon,
années 1869, 1870, 1871, p. 101.
1874: Membership List of Société Civile
de Prevoyance et de Renseignements
des Tisseurs de la Ville de Lyon,
1874, in ADR, 10 M 2 (2) Associations
des Tisseurs

*Estimated

The data indicate the steady progression of weaving in the
Fourth Arrondissement (Croix-Rousse), in absolute and relative terms,
the growth of weaving in the Brotteaux-Guillotière, the slow decline
in the First and Fifth Arrondissements (relatively in the Fifth),
and the near total disappearance of the industry in the Second

Arrondissement of the central peninsula. In 1829-33, the First,
Fourth and Fifth Arrondissements shared the urban looms almost
equally, and the Second Arrondissement was not far behind these in
number of looms. The Third Arrondissement (Brotteaux-Guillotière)
was relatively unimportant. By 1874, the Fourth Arrondissement
(Croix-Rousse) was by far the most important weaving quarter in the
city, with half of the weavers and almost half the looms (according
to indications in 1866). It shared this position with no other
quarter. The First and Fifth Arrondissements still had sizable
numbers of weavers, but their relative importance was much smaller
than in the early 1830's. The Brotteaux-Guillotière, on the other
hand, had grown from an insignificant weaving area to one rivalling
the Fifth Arrondissement and threatening to outdistance even the
First as a major silk-weaving neighborhood.

     The weavers who settled in this newer area were largely
plain-cloth weavers. Plain-cloth manufacture was in fact more common
in the Brotteaux-Guillotière than in the older quarters of the
Croix-Rousse or the First Arrondissement. In 1874, 91% of the
weavers of the Société civile residing in the Brotteaux-Guillotière
belonged to the plain-cloth category. Plain-cloth weavers accounted
for no more than 72% of those members inhabiting the First Arrondissement and no more than 67% in the Fourth Arrondissement. (See Table
40.) In this respect the weaving population of the Brotteaux-Guillotière was similar to that of the Fifth Arrondissement. Of the silk
workers residing in this arrondissement and contributing to the
treasury of the Société civile, 95% belonged to the plain-cloth
category in 1874. The Fifth Arrondissement and Third Arrondissement

(Brotteaux-Guillotière) thus formed a 'periphery' of less skilled
craft activity along the frontiers of the city, enclosing the more
highly skilled 'core' neighborhoods of silk weaving in the Croix-
Rousse and on the adjacent slopes of the First Arrondissement, where
the more elegant products of the industry were woven. The Brotteaux-
Guillotière in particular, bordering the plains of Dauphiné, thus
served as a 'buffer zone' between the skilled craft of the central
districts of the city and the ever more competitive unskilled craft
of rural weaving in the villages of Dauphiné.

The similarity between Fifth and Third Arrondissements in
types of cloth woven did not extend, however, to levels of wealth.
Robert Bezucha described the Fifth Arrondissement in 1834 as the
most poverty-stricken area of the city. "By 1834, the quarters on
the right bank of the Saône housed the poorest canuts ... Villermé
described the living conditions in this neighborhood as among the
worst in all of Europe."[31] In 1866 this area was little better and
perhaps even worse. Such was not the state of weavers' quarters on
the left bank of the Rhône, especially not of those in the Brotteaux,
(the northern portion of the Third Arrondissement). In a recent
study of the geographical and social stratification of wealth in Lyons
during the nineteenth century, Pierre Léon found that 84% of the
real property value owned by artisans and workers in the silk industry
for whom death inventories were registered in 1869 was situated in
the Croix-Rousse and the Brotteaux; 36% was located in the Brotteaux
alone, even though the proportion of wealth inventories registered in
that section was only 13% of all inventories registered for silk

---

[31]Bezucha, The Lyon Uprising of 1834, p. 31.

Table 40

Distribution of Silk Looms
and Weavers by Kind of
Cloth Woven in Each of
the Five Arrondissements[*]
of Lyons in 1829-33,
1844-46, 1873

Arron-dissement Cloth Type	First	Second	Third	Fourth	Fifth	All Lyons [a]
			Number of Occupied Looms			
1829-33						
Plains	3,006	2,596	?	2,254	5,380	10,982
Fancies	1,166	808		3,416	635	2,609
Velvets	354	334		534	582	1,270
Total (L)	4,526	3,738		6,204	6,597	14,861
1844-46						
Plains	4,822	2,016	?	2,819	4,403	11,241
Fancies	2,400	222		4,453	487	3,109
Velvets	373	73		916	467	913
Total (L)	7,595	2,311		8,188	5,357	15,263
			Number of Persons in SCPR			
1873						
Plains [b]	1,454	92	1,668	3,405	1,015	7,634
Fancies [c]	462	2	101	1,505	11	2,081
Velvets [d]	114	--	57	228	46	445
Total (P)	2,030	94	1,826	5,138	1,072	10,160
			Percentage of Total Looms (L)			
1829-33						
Plains	66.4	69.4		36.3	81.5	73.9
Fancies	25.8	21.6		55.1	9.6	17.6
Velvets	7.8	9.0		8.6	8.9	8.5
1844-46						
Plains	63.5	87.2		34.4	82.2	73.6
Fancies	31.6	9.6		54.4	9.1	20.2
Velvets	4.9	3.2		11.2	8.7	6.2
			Percentage of Total Persons (P)			
1873						
Plains	71.6	97.9	91.3	66.3	94.7	75.1
Fancies	22.8	2.1	5.5	29.3	1.0	20.5
Velvets	5.6	0.	3.2	4.4	4.3	4.4

[*]As Defined in 1866

Sources: 1829–30: Arr. 1,2,5: "Population de
1829 Pour 1830," AML, F2 –
Fabrique de Soieries – Inventeurs – Statistiques
(1811 à 1854)
Arr. 4: AML, Recensement,
Croix-Rousse, 1833
1844–46: Arr. 1,2,5: AML, Recensement
de Lyon, 1846
Arr. 4: AML, Recensement,
Croix-Rousse, 1844–45
1874: Société Civile des tisseurs,
List of Members, July 5, 1873,
in ADR, 10M-2, Associations
d'ouvriers tisseurs (1870-93)

1. Total arrondissements 1, 2, 5 only (city of Lyons intra muros
1829) for 1829–33 and 1844–46.

2. Categories 1, 5, 7 of Société Civile (SCPR): taffetas, satins,
foulards

3. Categories 2, 3 of SCPR: façonnés, ornements de meubles

4. Categories 4, 9, 10 of SCPR: gilets et velours façonnes,
velours frisés, velours à deux pièces

workers in 1869. The number of inventories for silk workers in the

Fifth Arrondissement in that year was about the same (14%), but the

value of immobile property held in this arrondissement was a mere 1.5%

of the total value for all silk workers registered in 1869. Moreover,

only in the Brotteaux and the Croix-Rousse did the proportion of pro-

perty value owned by silk workers exceed the proportion of death

inventories registered in the same sections of the city. In all other

arrondissements this second proportion was significantly larger than

the first.[32] (See Table 41 below.)

Table 41:

Distribution of Death Inventories by
Arrondissement of Registration, and
of Values of Real Property at
Death by Arrondissement of Holding,
for Silk Artisans and Workers of
Lyons, 1869.

Arrondissement		Death Inventories		Value of Real Property Owned at Death	
		Number	% of Total	Amount (francs)	% of Total
1		64	32.2	33,400	13.0
2		9	4.5	---	0.0
3	(Guillotière)*	12	6.1	3,786	1.5
4	(Croix-Rousse)	60	30.3	123,254	47.8
5		27	13.6	4,000	1.5
6	(Brotteaux)*	26	13.1	93,112	36.1
	Total	198	99.9	257,552	99.9

Sources: Death Inventories: "Tableau No. 87: Distribution des groupes socio-professionnelles
entre les divers arrondissements de Lyon –
Communautés, 1869," in Pierre Léon, Géographie
de la fortune et structures sociales à Lyon
au XIXe siècle (1815 - 1914) (Lyon, 1974), p. 220.

---

[32] Pierre Léon, Géographie de la fortune et structures sociales
à Lyon au XIXe siècle (1815 - 1914) (Lyon: Université Lyon II, Centre
d'histoire économique et social de la région lyonnaise, 1974), pp. 220,
223-225.

Property Values: "Tableau No. 89: Répartition
des biens immobiliers par arrondissement -
Communautés, 1869," ibid., pp. 224-225

*By 1869 the Brotteaux-Guillotière (Third Arrondissement in 1866)
had been divided into the Sixth Arrondissement (Brotteaux) and the
Third Arrondissement (Guillotière).

Since most silk workers would have been unlikely to own property
within the city outside of their arrondissement of residence, the two
sets of data strongly suggest a relative affluence of the Brotteaux
and Croix-Rousse weavers in comparison with weavers in other sections
of the city.

Since one of the main reasons for settling on the left bank of the
Rhône was lower housing costs,the apparently stronger tendency of
Brotteaux weavers to own property is less surprising than at first glance.
The importance of this tendency concerned less its cause than its effect.
It demonstrated that, on the average, weavers of the Brotteaux were not
necessarily poorer than weavers of the Croix-Rousse despite their heavier
concentration of plain-cloth weaving. The relative affluence of the predominantly plain-cloth weavers of the Brotteaux in comparison with weavers
in other plain-cloth sections of the city (such as the Fifth Arrondissement) suggests,moreover, that many of those who settled in the Brotteaux
were relatively affluent to begin with or, alternatively, were more
'insulated'economically than geographically from the competition of unskilled rural weaving. In the case of the former, fortunes were made in the
Croix-Rousse or in the First Arrondissement, in fancy-cloth weaving
during the 1840's and 1850's, or fortunes were made in nearby rural towns
and villages where weavers learned their craft from their fathers. These
weavers settled in the Brotteaux during the Second Empire to improve
opportunities for employment or to reduce costs of housing. In the

latter case, fortunes were made or maintained in the Brotteaux by
weaving the higher-paid plain cloths rather than the inferior plain
cloths put out to the least skilled workers in the fabrique. Lack of
precision in loom and worker data therefore would conceal a higher
level of skill and cloth quality in the weaving industry on the left
bank of the Rhône than our previous conclusions suggest. In this
case, the Brotteaux would have been a 'buffer zone' between the
relatively unskilled rural periphery and the relatively skilled
core neighborhoods of the Croix-Rousse only geographically, absorbing
recent migrant weavers (both skilled and unskilled) into the urban
economy, but not economically and socially, by earning and owning less
than the weavers of the Croix-Rousse. In terms of wealth and income,
denizens of the Brotteaux had no less opportunity than residents of
the Croix-Rousse of achieving or at least of maintaining a relative
artisanal affluence.

The Brotteaux weavers were like those of the First Arrondissement
-- including the second largest concentration of weavers in the city
(on the slopes of the Croix-Rousse) -- in another respect. Both had
more neighborhood contact with auxiliary workers of the fabrique and
with the few weavers of 'odd' specialties, such as tulles and passe-
menteries, than the weavers of the Croix-Rousse or any other area.
For some auxiliary trades and some silk-weaving crafts, this meant
more contact with workers in the silk industry accustomed to a shop
system of organization larger than that of the household-shop of most
silk weavers, and therefore to a system of employer-worker relations
less domestic and more factory-like, if not entirely proletarian.
For most of the auxiliary trades, this meant, moreover, contact with

'lumpenproletarian' female labor, the largest constituent of the work

force in most auxiliary industries.

Table 42 traces the progression of auxiliary labor in the Lyons

silk industry relative to weaving labor from 1833 to 1856 to 1866.

These rough estimates suggest a clear movement in favor of auxiliary

Table 42:

Auxiliary Labor Relative to
Weaving Labor in the Silk
Industry of Lyons, 1833,
1856, 1866.

	1833	1856	1866
Auxiliares (A)	4,350	12,252	14,560
Weavers (W)	36,300	50,900	40,000
A/W	.12	.24	.36

Sources: 1833: Robert Bezucha, The Lyon Uprising
of 1834, p. 33, Table 6
1856: "Tableau industriel -- Fabrique
Lyonnaise," October 31, 1856,
AML, I2-47(A), no. 165
1866: Statistique de la France.
deuxième série, tome XIX,
industrie. Résultats Généraux
de l'Enquête Effectuée dans les
années 1861 - 1865. pp. xxij,
xxiij.

trades in employing urban workers of the fabrique between 1833 and 1866.

By the latter date, the ratio of auxiliary labor to weaving labor tripled.

Both the relative decline of urban weaving in favor of rural weaving and

the increasing demand for auxiliary services to throw and dye the thread

put out to the countryside or to finish the cloth woven there for the

fabricants of Lyons, explain this increase in the proportion of workers

employed in the auxiliary trades.

Most of these trades were concentrated in the Brotteaux-Guillotière and in the First Arrondissement. As we saw earlier, some of the
largest dyeing establishments, factories with 230 or 290 workers in
1866, for example,[33] were located in the Brotteaux. The Brotteaux-Guillotière also quartered some of the major silk-throwing shops in the
city and at least one large cloth-finishing shop -- that of Monsieur
Baboin on the rue Ste-Elizabeth in the Brotteaux.[34] The First
Arrondissement had an even more diversified auxiliary sector. In a
sample of 445 heads of households of the First Arrondissement in 1866,
72 worked in the auxiliary trades. The number of different auxiliary
occupations in the sample was no less than seventeen: 41 dévideuses,
7 apprêteurs, 5 liseuses, 2 each enlaceurs de cartons, marchands de
métiers, peigniers, plieurs et mouliniers, and 1 each brodeuse, cartonnier,
dessinateur, navetier, guimpier, remetteuse, roseuse de velours,
teinturier, and tordeuse.[35] The difference in concentration of such
auxiliary trades between the First Arrondissement and the neighboring
Croix-Rousse -- as represented by a sample of 296 heads of households --
was quite marked. In the First Arrondissement sample, 16% of the

[33]'Teinturerie,' "Situation de l'Industrie au 15 7bre 1866"
(September 15, 1866), AML, I2 - 47(A), No. 192.

[34]'Tulles,' "Situation industrielle au Mars 1869," AML, I2 - 47(A),
No. 207.

[35]Dénombrement, 1866, Lyon, 3ème and 4ème Canton, ADR, 6M-Dé-
nombrement, X-XI. The sample is stratified and systematic, just like the
samples of the Croix-Rousse (Fourth Arrondissement)used in Chapter V
and described in Appendix V. Like these latter samples, that of the
First Arrondissement is stratified according to the geographical distribution of residences of members and leaders of the silk-weavers' associations discussed in this study.

household heads worked in auxiliary trades and 46% were weavers. In
the Croix-Rousse sample, only 6% worked in the auxiliary crafts, but
64% wove at the loom.[36] Clearly the Croix-Rousse was much more intensively a weaving neighborhood, and much less diversified by auxiliary
workers, than either the First Arrondissement or the Brotteaux. A
strike of the female ovalistes (silk throwers) in June-July 1869 demonstrated this 'social' solidarity between the First Arrondissement
and the Brotteaux. The strike began in the throwing shops of the latter
section but spread quickly beyond the Rhône. Several bands of female
strikers and their male companions crossed the river into the First
Arrondissement and forced the throwing shops on the Côte des Carmelites
to shut down as well.[37] Thus a community of protest emerged between
the two sections --the Brotteaux and the First Arrondissement --
despite the geographical barrier of the Rhône river, while the Croix-
Rousse plateau, adjacent to the First, remained isolated from the strike.

Besides auxiliary industries, most of the larger tulle-weaving
shops were also located in the Brotteaux. Tulles --delicate lace-like
fabric usually made of silk --were woven on special looms in shops
employing usually ten or more workers. Table 43 lists seven such
tulle shops and indicates their locations and the number of active and
inactive looms in each shop in March 1869. The table demonstrates
the rather large size of these shops, as compared with the household-
shops of other weavers in the city. The smallest tulle-weaving shop
had five looms, more than the average household shop of plain or fancy
weavers. The average tulle shop had about twenty looms.

---

[36]Ibid.; Dénombrement, 1866, Lyon, 4ème Canton, ADR, 6M-Dénombre-
ment, XVI-XVII.

[37]Police reports concerning strike of ovalistes in June-July

Table 43:

Seven Major Tulle-Weaving
Shops in Lyons, March 1869

Owner	Location	Number of Tulle Looms		
		Active	Inactive	Total
Vignon	Brotteaux	12	1	13
Peju	Brotteaux	26	0	26
Revol	Charpennes*	16	6	22
Richard, Julien Boyer, Bret and Annequin	Charpennes*	20	8	28
Dognin	Croix-Rousse	45	0	45
Morel	First Arr.	9	0	9
Baboin	Brotteaux	5	0	5

Source: 'Tulles,' "Situation industrielle au
Mars 1869," AML, I2-47(A), no. 207

*Adjacent the Brotteaux

The tulle shops were in fact more like small factories than artisanal
craft enterprises. Between masters and workers in these shops the
relation was more akin to that of manager or employer to laborer than
to that of master to journeyman. The seven master tullists were no
mere 'household heads' but small capitalist entrepreneurs. They hired
tullist workers as employees and regulated their work activity with a
system of rules, fines and personal oversight very much like that of
the early factory owners in English cotton spinning during the eighteenth
century.[38] Not surprisingly, these tullist workers expressed their
grievances against their employers by means of strikes and other forms

1869, especially reports of June 25-26, 1869, AML, I2 - 47(B), Corporations: ouvriers en soie ... (1819 à 1870), dossier Moulineuses -
Ovalistes.

[38]Paul Mantoux, The Industrial Revolution in the Eighteenth Century:
An Outline of the Beginnings of the Modern Factory System in England
(New York: Harper and Row, Harper Torchbook, 1961), pp. 375-376;
Sidney Pollard, The Genesis of Modern Management (Cambridge: Harvard
University Press, 1965), pp. 181-192.

of collective action. Weavers residing in the Brotteaux were thus
more exposed to these factory-like workers, and to their methods of
protest, than weavers in the Croix-Rousse, for the tullists working in
such conditions were more exceptional in the latter district than
in the former.

III. Neighborhood and Association

Silk weavers' associations in each of these neighborhoods reflected
their distinctive economic and social character as described above.
The extent to which such associations, or the movements of which they
were a part, were 'expansive' or 'restrictive,' egalitarian or elitist,
for example, was strongly related to the areas of the city in which
these associations and movements emerged, and thus to the specific
neighborhood experiences of the weavers involved. The tendency of
socially or economically oriented associations to become politi-
cized, and the specific political preferences of most of their members,
were also highly correlated with their areas of residence within the
city of Lyons. Leadership and initiative in forming new types of
association -- and leadership in collective protest in times of political
crisis -- also belonged to those urban quarters in which certain kinds
of experience of economic and social change prevailed. The neighborhood
environment was thus an important ingredient, along with craft, household and class, in fashioning a 'collective consciousness' among the
weavers of Lyons, expressed by them in their movements of voluntary
association.

The different social and economic experiences of weavers in the
Croix-Rousse and of weavers of the Brotteaux-Guillotière were evident in

the cooperative movement, for example. Egalitarianism and open member-

ship were stronger, to some extent at least, among the weavers of the

Brotteaux-Guillotière than among those of the Croix-Rousse. The large

consumers' society of the Croix-Rousse, the Provident, distributed

profits to its members according to the number of shares owned by each

and thus re-enforced   economic inequality among its members and

the tendency to stress individual profit-making over service either

to its own members or to its community.[39] By remaining a société à

responsibilité limitée until 1875 (rather than changing to a société

anonyme under the more liberal legislation of 1867), the Provident

impeded the expansion of its membership beyond the statutory maximum

of 400 and thus closed its doors around these 400 members.[40] The

Workers' Union, however -- the large grocery cooperative of the

Brotteaux-Guillotière -- distributed its profits according to the amount

of purchases made by each member.[41] By choosing the commercial form

of the nom collectif moreover, the Union facilitated the entry of new

members even beyond the exceptionally large number of 714 cooperators

in 1867 -- the largest in the city of Lyons at that time.[42] Thus

the Workers' Union served its members irrespective of their wealth

[39]Article 23, La Prévoyante, Statuts, 1865, ADR, 9U - Sociétés:
Constitutions et modifications, July 29, 1865.

[40]Ibid.; police report on meeting of La Prévoyante, March 7, 1875,
ADR,   4M- Police administrative - associations, coops 9, La Prévoyante.

[41]Article 44, Union ouvrière, Statuts, 1867, ADR, ibid., coops 13,
Union ouvrière.

[42]Ibid,; statistical report on cooperative societies of production
and consumption in Lyons, c. May 1867, AML, I2 - 45, Sociétés coopératives
de production et de consommation (1849 à 1870), No. 23.

and ownership of the organization and sought to increase the number of

such members to that of the neighborhood as a whole. Its aims, in

short, were communitarian and service-centered, rather than exclusivist-

elitist and profit-oriented, as those of the Provident seem to have

been.

Other consumer cooperatives, more egalitarian than the Provident

-- like the Workers' Grocery, which distributed profits equally among

members[43] -- and more communitarian, service-oriented than the 'elitist'

society -- such as the Workers' Hope, which divided profits even among

non-member clients of the store[44] -- also were organized in the Croix-

Rousse. These demonstrated that neighborhood experience alone did not

determine or influence ideologies of association. They did not prove

that such experience was insignificant, however. In the city-wide

producers' cooperative movement, wherein debate on the purpose and

means of association (notably profit-sharing policies) acquired an

intensity and a clarity often lacking in the smaller consumer's coopera-

tives, the division of opinion between the two large silk-weaving

neighborhoods (the Croix-Rousse and the Brotteaux) could not have been

more evident. The Brotteaux cells (séries) of the Association of

Weavers (producers' cooperative) objected, in the name of social

equality, to the profit-sharing policy proposed by the dominant

group within the organization from the Croix-Rousse -- the distri-

bution of profits according to number of shares owned by each member.

Several Brotteaux weavers felt so strongly about this issue

[43]Epicerie ouvrière, Statuts, 1868, ATCL, Actes des sociétés, September 20, 1868.

[44]Espérance ouvrière, Statuts, 1866, ADR, 9U - Sociétés: Constitutions et modifications, August 23, 1866.

that they seceded from the parent organization in 1867 after the
alternative statutes proposed by them had been rejected by the general
assembly of the Association.[45]

Weavers' associations in the Brotteaux-Guillotière also became
involved in political activity more readily than associations in the
Croix-Rousse. In 1873 the prefect of the Rhône dissolved the Workers'
Club of the Brotteaux, composed largely of silk weavers, for holding
"very frequent clandestine meetings" of a political nature, contrary
to its statutory prohibition of political discussion.[46] Prominent
Radical deputies often spoke there in favor of secular education --
a 'hot' political issue in this period of menancing monarchist restoration.[47] Under the Second Empire, the club was known to the police
as a meeting place for several locally prominent members of the
"militant [anti-imperial] democracy,"[48] and subsequently "the members
of the Brotteaux Club took an active part in all the revolutionary
movements of Lyons."[49] The Master-Weavers' Club of the Croix-Rousse,

---

[45]Police report to Prefect of Rhône, November 10, 1866, AML,
I2 - 45, No. 120; "L'Assemblée générale des tisseurs," Le Progrès
(Lyon), November 15, 1866; letter from Dugélay et al., Le Progrès,
November 18, 1866; "Une nouvelle société des tisseurs," Le Progrès,
December 30, 1866.

[46]Prefect of Rhône, Decree of dissolution of Cercle des travailleurs
des Brotteaux, October 11, 1873; report by Central Police Commissioner on
Cercle des travailleurs des Brotteaux,   n.d., ADR, 4M - Police administrative - Associations, cercles ouvriers et politiques (démocratiques)
gr 13, Cercle des travailleurs des Brotteaux.

[47]Report by Central Police Commissioner, n.d.; report from
"Brigadier commandant la brigade" to Commandant Gendarmerie, 8e Legion,
Compagnie du Rhône, Arrondissement de Lyon, September 6, 1872, ADR, ibid..

[48]Police report to Prefect of Rhône, June 6, 1868, AML, I2 - 45,
Cercle des travailleurs des Brotteaux.

[49]Report by Central Police Commissioner, n.d., ADR, 4M - Police
administrative - Associations, cercles ouvriers ... gr 13.

the analogous organization in this section of the city, limited its
discussion and activities to 'industrial' matters, such as weaving
technique, employment, piece-rates and cooperation. The political
preferences of the members of this club were republican but of the
moderate sort -- "democratic" ideas expressed "with moderation and
rather not to deny the past than to destroy the present order of
things."[50] Even the large consumers' society in the Brotteaux,
the Workers' Union, was not immune to 'politicization', as suggested
by a police report on the meeting of the association in May 1874,[51]
whereas the Provident, its analogue on the Croix-Rousse plateau, remained exclusively 'industrial' in its activities and concerns.

The Brotteaux weavers were distinguished from their semblables
of the Croix-Rousse not only by their receptiveness to political ideas
but also by their ambition and creativity in the practice of association.
The Workers' Union of the Brotteaux, for example, was by far the most
ambitious effort of consumers' cooperation in the city. It housed
a vast range of retail facilities and offered numerous 'alimentary'
services to its members. Its stores sold groceries, wines and
liquors, and linen and woolen cloth. It had its own breadbaking
ovens and made its own sausage and other cold cuts. In other consumers' cooperatives in the city, only one or two of these services
were provided, but in the Union ouvrière all were combined in a single
large enterprise. This enterprise served its members in three separate grocery stores plus one boulangerie dispersed throughout the

---

[50]Police report on Cercle des chefs d'ateliers de Lyon, May 31,
1867, AML, I2 - 45, Cercle des chefs d'ateliers de Lyon.

[51]Police report to Prefect of Rhône concerning meeting of Union
ouvrière, May 31, 1874, ADR, 4M - Police administrative - Associations,

Brotteaux-Guillotière.[52] Club activity among the weavers of the

Brotteaux was also ambitious and innovative. The Workers' Club of

the Brotteaux, inspired originally by the Master-Weavers' Club of

the Croix-Rousse, rapidly surpassed its model in the scope of its

activities. While the club of the Croix-Rousse limited these to

discussion of craft, leisure-time conservation, drinks and reading,

the Brotteaux club set up a program of weekly lectures, poetry and

song gatherings, classes in reading and writing (including special

classes for women and girls), and training in administration of

workers' organizations. The club became a forum for exchange and

advocacy of new ideas concerning education of workers and women,

and Jean Macé singled it out as an example of the kind of intellec-

tual and moral self-help effort he sought to inculcate among all

workers of France.[53]

In the Brotteaux rather than in the Croix-Rousse, the Inter-

national Workingmen's Association was most influential, during the

last years of the Second Empire, and in the former area as well the

movement for an anarchist-socialist Commune began in earnest after

the fall of the Empire on September 4, 1870. The International was

a new form of workers' association -- inter-professional, international,

anti-capitalist, sometimes revolutionary -- to which most of the

weavers of the Croix-Rousse remained hostile or non-committal. The

anarchist-socialist uprising of September 28, 1870, led by Michael

Bakunin and his local partisans in the International, failed when the

---

coops 13, Union ouvrière.

[52]Eugène Flotard, "Bulletin Coopératif," Le Progrès, January 14, 1867.

[53]Ibid., November 19, December 30, 1867; February 3, March 23, June 22, 1868.

national guardsmen of the Croix-Rousse came to the aid of the Radical

provisional government. The revolt of the Guillotière in April 1871

against the bourgeois government of city hall also collapsed in less

than a day without any echo of protest from the Croix-Rousse.[54]

The Croix-Rousse had in fact a very different political and social

temper in 1870 than it had had during the 'heroic' period of the early

1830's. During this latter period, the Croix-Rousse initiated and

directed collective protest in the city and did not merely follow the

lead of other neighborhoods, or retreat entirely from militancy, as it

was inclined to do in 1870-71. The insurrection of November 1831 began

on the Croix-Rousse plateau and descended thence into the central business

and administrative districts below. The other workers' quarters in the

Fifth, First and Second Arrondissements and in the Brotteaux-Guillotière

followed the lead of the weavers from the Croix-Rousse. Instead of

fighting in their own neighborhoods, most of these came to the aid of the

insurgents of the Croix-Rousse, and thus the Croix-Rousse and its slope

(the First Arrondissement) remained the center of the conflict.[55]

The April uprising of 1834 also commenced in the weavers' neighbor-

hoods in the Croix-Rousse and in the First, Second and Fifth Arron-

dissements and spread to the Guillotière, the Brotteaux and else-

where only on the second day.[56] Although fighting was fierce on the

---

[54]Faure, "Association Internationale des Travailleurs," February
1870, AML, Papiers de l'Albert Richard: Pièces relatives à l'Association
Internationale des Travailleurs, No. 27,; Maurice Moissonnier, La première internationale et la commune à Lyon (Paris: Editions sociales,
1972), pp. 264, 378-381.

[55]Fernand Rude, L'insurrection lyonnaise de novembre 1831: le
mouvement ouvrier à Lyon de 1827 - 1832 (Paris: Editions Anthropos,
1969), pp. 357-428, 436-437.

[56]Bezucha, The Lyon Uprising of 1834, pp. 150-152.

left bank of the Rhône (Brotteaux-Guillotière), it was more quickly repressed and less generalized than in the other neighborhoods of the city and suburbs. It was hardly as concentrated and as resilient as that on the First <u>Arrondissement</u> slopes leading to the Croix-Rousse, where the royal investigators presumed to see a greater degree of organization than in the other quarters.[57] The center of revolt in the 1830's, in short, coincided largely with the 'core' neighborhoods of silk weaving. By 1870, the same neighborhoods, including the Croix-Rousse, receded to the periphery of uprising, the center of gravity of which had shifted eastward to the left bank of the Rhône. This shift of 'insurrectionary geography' also coincided with a change in the aims, or dominant concerns, of the rebels -- from social and economic in 1831 and 1834, to political in 1871. The radicalization of the Brotteaux-Guillotière was eminently political, or at least it interpreted social questions in political terms. The radicalization of the Croix-Rousse, in its days of insurrectionary leadership, was little moved by political goals and moulded rather by grievances concerning craft, class and social position. By 1871 the nature of these grievances and the expectations concerning their satisfaction had changed to a form incommensurate with political longings and irrelevant to the militant socialism of the social anarchists, Internationalists and rebels of the Brotteaux-Guillotière.

The expansiveness and ambition of workers' associations in the Brotteaux-Guillotière, apparently more general there than in the Croix-Rousse, and the stronger tendency of workers in the first area to engage in militant politics and to take the lead in inter-professional

---

[57] <u>Ibid.</u>, pp. 163-165.

workers' organization as well as in political insurrection, suggest

the importance of neighborhood experience in fashioning scope and kind

of collective consciousness of weavers in the two areas of the city.

The present state of research and the available evidence limit the

definitive conclusions one can make regarding the exact kind of

importance of such neighborhood experience, but some tentative con-

clusions can be advanced on the basis of evidence presented in this

chapter. As we have seen, the major differences in neighborhood

conditions confronting weavers in the Brotteaux-Guillotière, as com-

pared with weavers in the Croix-Rousse, were two: first, more immediate

and more frequent contact with workers in other trades and in other

conditions of employment, and second, more direct experience of the

social and economic transformation of the city of Lyons during the

Second Empire -- of growing population, expanding industry, urban

renewal and their visible effects: poverty, crime, social mobility,

vagrancy, and traffic.

The effect of the first was the erosion, or the threat of

erosion, of the identification of neighborhood with craft and, with

such erosion, of the singularity or superiority of one craft (silk-

weaving) above all others. Such erosion was more likely to occur among

weavers whose craft identity had not been associated previously

with that of a particular neighborhood, or with neighborhood identity

in general. Since the Brotteaux-Guillotière absorbed not only weavers

from other areas of the city seeking lower rents but also recent migrants

from surrounding towns and rural villages, the weavers there fit this

pattern better than weavers in other sections of the city. They were

more susceptible than weavers elsewhere in the city to losing their

'craft-consciousness' or their sense of craft superiority. Besides,
relatively more weavers of the Brotteaux-Guillotière wove plain
cloths than weavers of the Croix-Rousse, and their claim to craft
superiority on the basis of skill was weaker than such a claim by
fancy-cloth weavers of the Croix-Rousse.

Weavers of the Brotteaux were therefore more willing to form
inter-craft associations (such as the International), and were less
inclined to differentiate themselves from other workers in their
neighborhood on the basis of status, function, wealth or skill within
their craft -- which explains the stronger communitarian, egalitarian
tendencies in their practice and purpose of cooperative association.
Because of this weak sense of difference from other workers, the
Brotteaux weavers were also more inclined to share perceptions of
social interest and even political opinions with workers whose
conditions of employment and whose standards of living were different
from their own. In the Croix-Rousse, on the contrary, contact with
workers in other trades or conditions of work was infrequent and
cursory, and thus neighborhood identity re-enforced craft identity
rather than eroded it. Differences of status, skill, function and
wealth traditionally associated with the craft of silk weaving were
more likely to be maintained, and even strengthened, in the movements
of association and in the social and political attitudes manifested
in these movements. Association, in short, was more likely to be restrictive, elitist and fractionalized than egalitarian and community-
oriented.

The second difference between the two neighborhood environments --
the greater intensity of social and economic change in the Brotteaux

as compared with the Croix-Rousse -- was, sociologically at least,
very much like the difference described by Charles Tilly between the
two areas of southern Anjou in the Vendée -- the Mauges and the Val-
Saumurois -- on the eve of the French Revolution. Such was the
difference between a rapidly <u>urbanizing</u> and a already <u>urbanized</u> region.[58]
The Brotteaux-Guillotière in the 1850's and 1860's was in a state that
we might call 'industrializing,' leading to more intensified urbanization, whereas the Croix-Rousse was already industrialized (or industrial) and fully urbanized as well. Moreover, the urban-industrial
'saturation' of the Croix-Rousse was based on a traditional domestic
industry, whereas the growing industry and intensified urbanization
of the left bank of the Rhône was the product of artisanal industry
combined with newly mechanized factory industry. The difference
between the two regions was therefore not simply one of change versus
lack of change, but also that of striking contrasts, imbalances and
instability among the various individuals and groups within the changing
region, as against the integration, equilibrium and stability -- if
not homogeneity of social condition -- among the various strata and
groups within the fully changed region. The former generated conflict among the various groups, notably conflict of choices in times
of political and social crisis. The latter eased the imposition or
emergence of a consensus of opinion, or at least of a stable coexistence of differing opinions on political matters during such times.

To carry Tilly's argument one step further (or aside), in the
case of the weavers of Lyons, the conflicts emerging from rapid social

---

[58]Charles Tilly, The Vendée (Cambridge: Harvard University Press,
1976).

and economic change in the Brotteaux-Guillotière during the Second

Empire, when political activity itself was repressed or discouraged,

especially among workers, fostered the <u>politicization</u> of social and

economic issues more rapidly and more intensely there, and not only

a conflict of the political opinions which did emerge. In the more

integrated, balanced, unchanging urban-industrial environment of the

Croix-Rousse, however, such politicization of social conflict and

of social concerns was much less likely. This did not mean that the

weavers of the Croix-Rousse were apolitical. Their active role in

local politics during the last years of the Empire and during the

early months of the Republic gives the lie to any such argument.

But their politics had little social content, for it was kept

distinct ideologically from their social vision and organizationally

from their industrial action.[59] Thus they were not encouraged to

take political action in the name of a social ideal or program, but

only in the name of a political aim -- democracy, the republic,

separation of church and state, or reduction of military expenditures.

Their cooperative associations, clubs and resistance (i.e., early trade-

union) societies accordingly abstained from politics, while analogous

associations on the left bank of the Rhône slipped into political

discussion and activity at the least instigation. For the same reasons,

the weavers of the Croix-Rousse refused to support revolutionary

insurrection in the name of anarchist socialism or social republicanism.

They left to the workers of the Brotteaux-Guillotière both the

[59]Moissonnier, <u>La première internationale à Lyon</u>, chapters VII-VIII, X.

initiative and the execution of plots and uprisings designed to
realize such socio-political ideals.

As differences between the neighborhood conditions of the
Croix-Rousse and the Brotteaux-Guillotière were mirrored in different
patterns of collective ideology and activity in these two areas,
similarities of social and economic condition between the Brotteaux-
Guillotière and the First _Arrondissement_ were also reflected in their
respective patterns of association. The working population of the
First _Arrondissement_ included proportionately more plain-cloth
weavers and more workers in auxiliary trades of the _fabrique_ than
the population of the Croix-Rousse. There were also more weavers
in specialties of the _fabrique_ distinguished by their small shop or
manufactory (rather than household) mode of production -- especially
weavers of _tulles_ and _passementeries_ -- and more auxiliary workers
in similar factory-like production units (dyers and twisters especially) than in the Croix-Rousse. In all these ways, the silk-working
environment of the First _Arrondissement_ was very much like that of
the Brotteaux-Guillotière.

Not very surprisingly, the First _Arrondissement_ was the only
one in central Lyons where the International had some popularity, and
notably among silk workers in these factory-like conditions of
employment.[60] Moreover, one of the best examples of imaginative,

---

[60]In a report on the leaders of the International in 1870, for
example, the police commissioner Faure listed three weavers on the
nineteen-member directing committee of the Association. Two of these
lived in the Sixth _Arrondissement_ (the Brotteaux) and the third
resided in the First _Arrondissment_. Of the remaining sixteen, five
were _tullistes_ or _passementiers_,and two more worked in the auxiliary
trades (_apprêtage_ and _lisage_). Three of these seven resided in or
nearby the Brotteaux-Guillotière, and three in the First _Arrondissement_.

community-service consumers' cooperation in 'Old Lyons' was located in the First Arrondissement -- the Frank Cooperators.[61] In both respects, the First Arrondissement resembled the Brotteaux-Guillotière in its patterns of association. The resemblance did not go much further than this, however, and so it would be futile to seek any 'environmental determinism' in explaining collective attitudes and political behavior among the silk workers of Lyons. Nevertheless, affinities of neighborhood experience of social and economic conditions probably explained some similarities in the aims and practice of association within the city, as well as occasional alliances between workers of different city districts sharing similar conditions of life and work, just as the differences between the Croix-Rousse and the Brotteaux-Guillotière seem to have explained much of the variation in patterns and aims of association and political activity between these two areas.

These two were also similar in one important respect, however. The average levels of wealth of their silk weavers, as indicated by Léon's study of death inventories, were far above those of weavers in other arrondissements of the city in 1869, but similar to one another. Such exceptionally high concentration of wealthier silk weavers probably explained the exceptionally high concentration of associations among weavers in these two areas of the city as compared

---

Only one, a passementier, inhabited the Croix-Rousse. (Faure, "Association Internationale des Travailleurs," AML, I2 - 55, No. 27.)

[61]The Francs Coopérateurs distributed profits to all clients, for example. See George Sheridan, "Idéologies et structures sociales dans les associations ouvrières à Lyon, de 1848," Bulletin du Centre d'Histoire économique et sociale de la Région lyonnaise, 1976, No. 2, 30-32.

with other areas. The only exception was the First Arrondissement,
a very active foyer of association despite its relatively low concentration of wealth as compared with the Croix-Rousse and the
Brotteaux-Guillotière. Since this arrondissement was located on
the slopes of the Croix-Rousse, and its association activity might
be considered, quite reasonably, as an extension of the movement of
the Croix-Rousse, this exception does not weaken the rule very much.

In his well-known article comparing patterns of strike activity
in France among different groups of workers under the July Monarchy,
Peter Stearns argued that labor organization and strike planning
were more likely to be "vigorous" among artisans whose wealth and
income were above the norm of workers in general.[62] If Stearns'
argument is correct, we should not be surprised to find the most
active movements of association among those artisans in Lyons who
were relatively affluent in their trade or in their neighborhood,
or at least in those trades or quarters of the city where such artisans
assumed the leadership. Were we to draw a map of the extent and
intensity of voluntary association in Lyons in the 1860's, the
Croix-Rousse, the Croix-Rousse slopes (First Arrondissement) and
the Brotteaux would emerge readily as the foyers of association par
excellence. These areas would rate high not only by the proportion
of their working populations engaged in voluntary associations, but
also by the variety of forms of association organized in the same
areas, which included all of the four discussed in this study --

---

[62]Peter N. Stearns, "Patterns of Industrial Strike Activity
in France During the July Monarchy," American Historical Review, Vol.
LXX, No. 2 (January 1965), 387-388.

mutual aid, cooperation, educational - recreational - professional
clubs, and industrial resistance.

In the Fifth Arrondissement, on the right bank of the Saône,
by contrast, there were no clubs, except in the isolated district
of Saint-Just on the slopes of Fourvières, away from the central
quarters of the arrondissement. There were also few resistance
societies and no strikes in 1869-70, and, as best as I can determine,
no major meetings of the producers' cooperative, Association of
Weavers, were ever held in the Fifth as they were on the Croix-Rousse
or in the Brotteaux. Except for a few small consumers' cooperatives
and mutual aid societies, the Fifth Arrondissement merely followed
the lead of the Croix-Rousse, participating in programs of association
initiated there or in the Brotteaux-Guillotière. Weavers of the
Fifth thus had relatively little life of association of their own.

The Fifth Arrondissement, we will remember, was probably the
poorest district of the city. Although it had more silk weavers,
absolutely and proportionally, than the Brotteaux-Guillotière, their
relative poverty inhibited them, or at least failed to encourage
them, from organizing associations as intensely or as variously as
the weavers of 'New Lyons,' or as actively as the weavers in the
central districts of 'Old Lyons.' In the political life of the city,
this poverty of the Fifth was translated even more acutely into
impotence and apathy. If the Croix-Rousse and the First were politically silent after September 1870, by contrast with the political
'noise' of the Brotteaux-Guillotière, the Fifth was politically
absent, non-existent even. In the 1780's and in the 1830's, social
and political radicals were formed in the Fifth Arrondissement,

insurrections and strikes raged as strongly as in the Croix-Rousse.
It was a quarter that evoked fear in the minds of the police and
political authorities.[63] In April 1871, the police feared a revolt
in the Croix-Rousse in response to the abortive uprising of the
Guillotière, but they hardly inquired of the mood of workers on the
right bank of the Saône, so much had this district fallen to the
periphery of revolt.

In summary, then, the relative affluence of the weavers of the
Croix-Rousse and the Brotteaux favored a concentration of association
in these sections, but the different social and economic conditions
of these three areas oriented the nature, scope and aims of association in different directions in each section. In the 'Old Lyons'
quarters of the Croix-Rousse, stagnant and dominated by a single
trade, the weavers directed the movements of association largely
in the interests of their craft alone and especially in the name of
the independent artisanship identified pre-eminently with their craft.
Theirs was association to preserve a dying order of household
manufacture and a city perceived as the national and international
capital of that manufacture. In the 'New Lyons' quarters of the
Brotteaux-Guillotière, growing rapidly with an influx of workers
of various trades, the silk weavers were only one among several

---

[63]Denis Monnet, suspected of plotting the riot of 1786 and leader
of the movement for the tarif in the 1780's, resided in the Fifth
Arrondissement. ("Interrogatoire de Denis Monnet,"November 22, 1786,
ADR, Série B, Sénéchaussée/Criminel; Maurice Garden, Lyon et les
lyonnais au XVIIIe siècle (Paris: Les belles lettres, 1970), pp.
590-592.) During the insurrection of 1831, the Fifth Arrondissement
rebelled along with the other quarters of the city. Among the residents
of this section at that time were Pierre Charnier, founder of the
first mutuelliste society, and Lacombe, leader of the paramilitary

groups of associators. Their interests and aims in associating
were less craft-centered and more 'class-conscious '(in the broadest
sense of this term),with an extension, though highly vulnerable,
to the intention of preserving the artisan ideal. The city, town
or village lives of their youth were too diverse, too distant
in space if not in time, and too susceptible to corrosion to survive
as an attachment to a particular urban image in the alien, ever-
changing industrial quarters of the Brotteaux-Guillotière, let alone
to re-enforce an identification with a single trade. Change rather
than order was the norm of their social existence, and association
gave them the means -- so they hoped -- to reap the best advantage,
to suffer the least adversity, or at least to forge a meaningful
collective identity in a new environment of industry and social
intercourse.

This difference of social experience between the two leading
silk-weaving sections of the city explained why neighborhood
solidarity became a source of division rather than unity within
the class of master-weavers, in their movements of voluntary
association after 1860. The divisiveness of neighborhood was even
stronger than that of craft category, associated with the different
economic conditions of plains and fancies weavers during the crisis
of the 1860's, and reflected in the attachment to category autonomy in the resistance movement late in the decade. Such category

Volontaires du Rhône, which played a major role in the military
events of November 1831. (Rude, L'insurrection lyonnaise de
novembre 1831, pp. 386-387, 275).

differences did not prevent the organization of a unified resistance
federation, the Société civile, out of the autonomous category societies,
whereas different neighborhood experiences were at least partly
responsible for the different political behavior of the Croix-Rousse
and the Brotteaux-Guillotière in the events of 1870 - 1871.
Neighborhood solidarity during the 1860's therefore competed with
other collective solidarities in forging a social identity among the
weavers, instead of complementing or re-enforcing these.

Three of these other solidarities -- craft (in its unifying
aspects as described in Chapter IV), household and class -- united
the master-weavers of Lyons on the basis of common experience of
economic and social change, or on that of the equalization of economic
and social situation as a result of such change. One additional
solidarity, that of the polis, united the weavers on the basis of
a common idea --that of the expected role of government in their
economic life. As the economic crisis of the 1860's modified the
nature of the solidarities of craft, household and class, forging a
common material basis for a unified social identity among the weavers,
so the political evolution of the imperial regime after 1860 changed
their conception of the solidarity of the polis, providing a common
ideological foundation for their social unity. This change introduced
economic freedom as a positive notion into the vocabulary and mentality
of the silk weavers without eliminating their traditional attachment
to government intervention in their economic affairs. The solidarity
of the polis, like the solidarities of craft, household, class and
neighborhood, therefore also fostered ideological ambivalence rather
than clarity during this decade of transition in the weaver's world
of work.

CHAPTER VIII

The Liberal Transformation of 'Political' Solidarity

The silk weavers of Lyons traditionally regarded free enterprise

as the worst plague of their industry. Unlimited free trade, argued

the master silk weaver 'J.A.B.' in 1832, delivered the working class

into the "murderous" hands "of insatiable ambition."[1] In 1850, the

master weaver Weichmann blamed the "unrestrained freedom of trade" for

the "impious struggle in which workers are pressured, demoralized by

frequent reductions of wage ..."[2] Competition, both foreign and local,

in product markets and in labor markets (but especially in the latter),

was condemned as harmful to the weavers' welfare and to the prosperity

of the industry. Such competition had to be contained, to prevent it

from destroying the industry and impoverishing the weaver. In the

traditional opinion of the weavers, only the government and the law

could achieve such containment. The solidarity of the polis therefore

presumed regulation of industry by both. The "prosperity of the fabrique,"

declared another master weaver in 1849, "has depended above all on

regulation."[3] This 'regulatory mentality' was evident in the weavers'

---

[1] J.A.B., chef d'atelier, De la nécessité d'une augmentation des prix de fabrication des étoffes, comme moyen d'assurer la prosperité du commerce (Lyon: Imprimerie de Charvin, 1832), p. 10. (BMTL, C. 1559).

[2] Weichmann, 'Causes de la décadence de l'industrie,' "Mémoires recueillis par le citoyen Weichmann, chef d'atelier, rue du sentier, no. 8 à la Croix-Rousse," April 2, 1850, AN, F-12-2203 (2): Machines à tisser (1844 à 1866).

[3] Vernay, chef d'atelier, La vérité au sujet du malaise de la fabrique des étoffes de soie à Lyon. Moyens d'y remédier. Mémoire pour servir à l'enquête (Lyon: J.-M. Bajot, 1849), p. 3. (BMTL, C. 1559).

demand for a <u>tarif</u> -- a schedule of minimum piece-rates -- in 1831,[4]

in their proposals for special commissions to regulate wages, apprentice-

ship, rural industry and mechanization during the Second Republic and the

early Second Empire (1848 - 1853),[5] and in their demand in 1860 for an

'industrial code' to correct abuses in cloth measuring, in allotment of

thread wasted during weaving, and in mounting of designs for silk fabric.[6]

"The law alone can restore life to this industry," concluded the petition

of 1860 making this demand.[7]

By the mid-1860's, the weavers' attitude towards free trade -- or

the attitude of the most prominent master weavers at least -- had begun

to change. Freedom of trade -- meaning freedom from government regula-

tion of industry -- was no longer considered a social evil or a plague,

but rather part of a more general political and social liberty that

---

[4]See Fernand Rude, L'insurrection lyonnaise de novembre 1831: le mouvement ouvrier à Lyon de 1827 - 1832 (Paris: Editions Anthropos, 1969), Chapter V.

[5]Weichmann, 'Création d'une commission spéciale,' "Mémoires recueillis ...," April 2, 1850; Vernay, La vérité au sujet du malaise ..., pp. 14-15; Citoyen Xavier Pailley, Système de réforme industrielle ou projet d'association entre tous les citoyens qui concourent au commerce et à la fabrication des articles de soieries (Lyon: Chanoine, 1848), pp. 6-8 (BMTL, C.1558); Philippe Thierrat, Du malaise de la classe ouvrière et de l'institution des prud'hommes appliquée à l'augmenta-tion du travail dans la fabrique lyonnaise (Lyon: J. Nigon, 1848), pp. 32-33 (BMTL, C.1559); report from Special Police Commissioner to Prefect of Rhône, "Rapport sur la Pétition des Chefs d'atelier," s.d. (Response to letter from prefect to police commissioner, April 1, 1853), AML, F2 - Fabrique de Soies - Règlement - Tarif - Affaires diverses (1810 à 1874).

[6]Petition of Tray et al. to Emperor Napoleon III, August 1860, ACCL, Soieries Carton 41-I - Législation - Usages (an 8 à 1936), 13. - Pétition remise à l'Empereur, à son passage à Lyon par les ouvriers en soie.

[7]Ibid.

was beneficial and desirable. The principles of liberty, declared the
Proudhonian silk weaver J.-M. Gauthier, were "without question the true
generators of every society."[8] Weavers like Gauthier were more willing
to accept free enterprise than they had been in the past, because of
their confidence in the cooperative movement, organized on the principle
of self-help, to achieve for them a position of strength and prosperity
in a competitive economic environment. "Free trade forces us to progress
or to die of hunger," declared the representatives of twenty-one
cooperative societies of Lyons, many of them silk weavers, in a statement of their aims in 1865.[9] "[A]ll our means of action, all our force
must be combined to place us in a position to advance as equals with
our competitors..."[10] Their movement would thus enable them to prosper
in a free-trade world, and they too would reap the advantages of
economic freedom. The belief that free trade could be beneficial was
not exceptional even for the weavers who suffered most from reduced
wages and unemployment. The journeymen weavers planning to demonstrate
in 1866, for example, against the freedom of merchant manufacturers to
put out silk cloths in the countryside acknowledged in their declara-
tion of protest that "freedom is very good ..."[11] After 1860, in

---

[8] Eugène Tartaret, ed., Exposition universelle de 1867. Commission
ouvrière de 1867. Procès-verbaux, tome II, p. 257. (BCCL, L1-284).

[9] 'Mémoire adressé par les associations coopératives de la ville de
Lyon, à MM. les membres de la Chambre de Commerce,' in Eugène Flotard,
"Bulletin Coopératif," Le Progrès (Lyon), December 25-26, 1865.

[10] Ibid.

[11] "Réunion Général [sic] des Tisseurs à la préfecture, Le 15 Octobre
[1866]," AML, 12-47 (B), Corporations: ouvriers en soie (1819 à
1870), No. 887.

other words, the weavers' conception of the solidarity of the <u>polis</u>
no longer remained associated exclusively with paternal, interventionist
government but merged with more liberal notions of economic and social
order emphasizing self-determination.

The acceptance of free trade, or at least of some degree of
commercial freedom, by several weavers in the 1860's was encouraged by
social policy and political opinion representing to them more advantages
of free enterprise than they had been accustomed to observe in the past.
The <u>laissez-faire</u> social and economic policies of the 'liberalizing'
Empire of the 1860's, for example, differed very much in this sense from
the 'free-trade' policy of the July Monarchy. The latter was used most
frequently to justify government support for employers in their conflicts
with workers, by proscription and suppression of strikes and by control
of the size and aims of workers' voluntary associations.[12] The liberal
program of Napoleon III included, by contrast, the legalization of
strikes from 1864 and the freedom of non-political meetings and tolera-
tion of strike organizations from 1868. Moreover, <u>laissez-faire</u> in
product markets under the Second Empire, promoted, for example, by the
Cobden-Chevalier low-tariff treaty of 1860 between England and France,
proved advantageous rather than ruinous to the prosperity of the
<u>fabrique</u> of Lyons. At a time when the important American market was
cut off by the war between the states, the British market, 'liberated'

---

[12]See Robert Bezucha, <u>The Lyon Uprising of 1834: Social and Political
Conflict in the Early July Monarchy</u> (Cambridge: Harvard University
Press, 1974), p. 136 and Peter N. Stearns, "Patterns of Industrial
Strike Activity in France During the July Monarchy," <u>American Histori-
cal Review</u>, vol. LXX, no. 2 (January 1965), pp. 382-383.

by the treaty to the advance of French silks, compensated somewhat

for the loss and gave work (although on an inferior-quality cloth)

to many weavers who would have been otherwise unemployed.[13] Finally,

liberal economists and republican deputies of the 'opposition,' elected

with the workers' votes in the major French cities, praised and promoted

the weavers' cooperative associations -- designed to improve the welfare

of their class by their own efforts -- by stressing the affinity of

cooperation with the basic principles of economic liberalism. Eugène

Flotard, a local cooperative promoter of Lyons and a prominent republi-

can lawyer, claimed that cooperation had "liberty, individual initiative"

as its basis and "privilege and authoritarian tutelage" as its "anti-

thesis."[14] The real demon in the organization of economic life was

therefore not free trade or free competition, but rather monopoly and

government control. "Competition is synonymous with freedom," declared

the liberal Swiss economist Dameth lecturing the workers of Lyons on the

advantages of free trade in 1866. "Without liberty, there is no competi-

tion, [but then] all kinds of freedom must be abandoned. Then monopoly

or privilege will rule, and then an inevitable decline, the despotism

of past ages [will set in.]"[15]

The strongest advocate of free trade among the workers was the

imperial government of Napoleon III, especially after 1864. The

---

[13]See Chapter II.

[14]Eugène Flotard, Le mouvement coopératif à Lyon et dans le Midi de la France (Lyon, 1867), p. iii.

[15]Dameth, Lecture at the Palais Saint-Pierre, Lyons, on November 24, 1806, from notes taken by Jn. Abel, AML, I2-46 (A), Sociétés et clubs, cercles et conférences; Franc-Maconnerie (1788 à 1870), No. 321.

strength of the government's message was its affirmation in action,

not only in word. In particular, it adhered closely to a laissez-

faire position in conflicts between weavers and their employers, with

an impartiality that often favored the weavers. On May 24, 1864, the

Corps législatif modified articles 414, 415 and 416 of the Penal Code

to permit strikes not resulting from a "concerted plan" and not

accompanied by "violence, assaults, threats or fraudulent schemes...".[16]

Nearly two years later, when sixty satin-stitch weavers of the firm

Avril-Cottin of Tarare stopped working to demand a wage increase, the

government demonstrated its intention of following the modified Code.

On March 10, 1866, the sub-prefect of Villefranche reported to the pre-

fect of the Rhône his plan to visit Tarare personally in a few days, if

the situation failed to improve, "in order to offer some official

admonishments to the Employers and to the Workers."[17] Such a gesture

by a higher authority was not an uncommon method of resolving local

disputes in such rural towns, and the prefect welcomed the plan.[18] But

the Minister of the Interior did not agree. "The Government of the

Emperor," wrote the minister to the prefect on March 13,

> desires that the largest latitude be left to
> employers as well as to workers for the discussion

[16]Bulletin des lois, Law of May 24, 1864: Modification of articles
414, 415 and 416 of the Penal Code, reprinted in J.B. Duvergier, ed.,
Collection complète des lois, décrets, ordonnances, règlements et
avis du Conseil d'état ... année 1864 (Paris: Charles Noblet, 1864),
Tome 64, 188-189, 194-195.

[17]Letter from Sub-Prefect of Villefranche to Prefect of Rhône,
March 10, 1866, AML, I2-48, Délits de coalition ouvrière et grèves.
Grèves hors Lyon (1803 à 1870).

[18]Letter from Prefect of Rhône to Sub-Prefect of Villefranche,
March 10, 1866, AML, I2-48, No. 450.

> of their interests, and the administration should
> intervene only to keep order if it is troubled, and
> to protect those who might be the object of threats or
> violence. The presence of M. the Sub-Prefect of Ville-
> franche at Tarare, his effort of conciliation could be
> seen badly and give way to misleading interpretations
> by suggesting that the authorities are taking sides
> either for the employers or for the workers.[19]

The government, in short, wished to leave the resolution of industrial

conflicts to the parties involved.

A month later, the prefect wrote the same sub-prefect, again on

the orders of the Minister of the Interior, to allow collections for

strikes taken up in the workshops, "given the liberal intentions ex-

pressed by the Empire, given especially the difficulty of preventing

secret collections."[20] Again two months later, the prefect instructed

the sub-prefect to allow several satin-stitch weavers of Valsonne, near

Tarare, to form an "Industrial Society" to discuss their common

interests, including those related to their current strike.[21] The

prefect based his instruction on the Emperor's recent announcement "in

his speech on opening the legislative session, that the authorization

to meet should be granted to all those who, outside of politics, wish

to deliberate on their industrial or commercial interests."[22] Thus,

---

[19] Letter from Minister of Interior to Prefect of Rhône, March 14,
1866, AML, I2-48.

[20] Letter from Prefect of Rhône to Minister of Interior, April 16,
1866; letter from Prefect of Rhône to Sub-Prefect of Villefranche,
April 16, 1866, AML, I2-48.

[21] Letter from Mayor of Valsonne to Sub-Prefect of Villefranche, June
8, 1866; letter from Prefect of Rhône to Sub-Prefect of Villefranche,
June 16, 1866, AML, I2-48.

[22] Letter from Prefect of Rhône to Sub-Prefect of Villefranche, June
16, 1866, AML, I2-48.

under the rubric of a 'public meeting,' workers were permitted to 'concert' in preparation for a strike -- a rather liberal interpretation of the Penal Code, hardly unfavorable to the workers.

The government demonstrated the same tolerance in several strikes by tulliste weavers between 1864 and 1868. In May 1865, for example, the police investigated complaints by the master-tullists Baboin and Péju concerning threats against their workers to force them to strike. The police found no evidence of threats but only polite, friendly efforts by strikers to persuade their comrades to join their action. "The attitude of the strikers is beyond reproach," reported the gendarme on May 5.[23] One fabricant stopped by the police even complained that the authorities were obstructing the "men of order" while allowing large gatherings of workers in the streets.[24] In a strike of tullist weavers nearly a decade earlier (Fall 1856), the police had not been so tolerant to the workers. In September 1856 they arrested several of the strikers and thus put a quick end to their action.[25] Times had indeed changed since then, much to the advantage of the weavers.

This official impartiality in labor disputes, often favorable to the weavers, eroded their traditional dependence on the government to mediate between them and the merchant-manufacturers in industrial matters. Their strong 'regulatory mentality,' evident as recently as

---

[23]Reports of police agent to police commissioner concerning strike of tullist weavers, May 4-5, 1865, AML, I2-47 (B).

[24]Report of Special Police Commissioner to Prefect of Rhône concerning strike of tullist weavers, May 20, 1865, AML, I2-47 (B).

[25]Police reports concerning strike of tullist weavers, September 4-5-6, 1856, AML, I2-47 (B).

1860, was already sufficiently weakened by 1865 to persuade the leaders of the weaving communities to seek improvement of their conditions of work by their own efforts. This was especially apparent in their enthusiasm for producers' and consumers' cooperation, the programs of which explicitly rejected state aid. In 1865, a list of weaver candidates to the Conseil des Prud'hommes (industrial court) easily defeated the weaver incumbents on the Conseil in the elections of that year in part because the latter had "not participated in the formation of the ... Grande Société industrielle [the producers' cooperative of silk weavers]."[26] These victorious weaver prud'hommes had been "sought out preferably among those who have given proof of their advanced liberalism."[27]

Such abandonment of a regulatory attitude was not always shared, or not shared to the same degree, by all silk weavers. In early October 1866, journeymen weavers planned to descend the slopes of the Croix-Rousse to demonstrate in front of the prefecture against the emigration of silk-weaving from Lyons into the countryside. These weavers wanted the authorities to restrict the freedom of the merchant-manufacturers to put out thread and cloth orders in the rural areas. As a handwritten poster found on the Place de la Croix-Rousse declared, these weavers were not questioning the advantages of free trade in general. But when free enterprise deprived the people of work, it had to be limited:

---

[26] Report of police commissioner to Monsieur le Sénateur (Prefect of Rhône) and to Monsieur le Procureur Impérial concerning elections to Conseil des Prud'hommes of Lyons, December 6 and 10, 1865, AML, F - Prud'hommes - Elections (1806 à 1871).

[27] Ibid.

> Messieurs Les négociants ... tell us that they have,
> freedom to trade. Freedom [sic] is very good but
> it must have a limit to prevent the export of the
> earned bread of the people, who suffer from want.[28]

Economic liberalism was thus received with mixed favor among the

silk weavers of Lyons. For many it represented freedom to strike, to

form strike associations, and to organize cooperative societies to

liberate the weavers from their tutelage to the merchant-manufacturers.

For others it merely gave to the latter license to undermine the tradi-

tional fabrique of the city for the advantage of the countryside,

which was more amenable to weaving at a lower piece-rate. The authori-

ties tried to convince themselves that the difference of opinion repre-

sented a difference of economic position and status within the class of

weavers, between the prominent master-weavers -- the leaders of the

weaving communities -- and the 'masses' -- journeyworkers and 'small'

masters with few looms. The prefect of the Rhône believed "that the

principal master-weavers [would] not take part" in the demonstration

planned in October 1866,[29] that it was rather an affaire of ouvriers

tisseurs. This belief had some plausibility, in fact, for the 'masses'

of the urban fabrique wove the inferior-quality plain silks which were

most exposed to the competition of rural labor and of foreign silk

industries. The 'prominent' master weavers of fancy silks and of

medium or better-quality plain silks, on the other hand, were more in-

sulated from such competition, because of the necessary skills and

---

[28]"Réunion Général [sic] des Tisseurs à la préfecture, Le 15
Octobre (1866)," AML, I2-47 (B), No. 877.

[29]Dépêche télégraphique from Prefect of Rhône to Minister of
Interior, October 15, 1866, AN, Fic III Rhône 10, Correspondance et
Divers (1816 à 1870), dossier "Ouvriers de Lyon."

surveillance by the _fabricant_, for the provision of which urban
weaving commanded a relative advantage. Or their industrial problems
had sources other than rural competition -- the American Civil War and
Parisian fashion design -- over which the government had little or no
power. These 'elite' weavers could thus accept the arguments in favor
of free competition with much less hesitation, for they were not
directly subject to its rigors.

But such an easy division between 'free-trade-minded' elite artisan weavers and 'regulation-minded' silk-working masses was probably
much farther from reality than the authorities claimed or hoped it was.
When the prefect called upon the 'masses', in October 1866, to abandon
their project for a demonstration and to send him representatives to
present their grievances, the weavers commissioned their traditional
leaders -- prominent master weavers, weaver _prud'hommes_ and cooperative
leaders -- to state their case along with a smaller number of journeymen.[30] More likely, ambiguity concerning free trade thus characterized
the opinions of all weavers, not only those of weavers most threatened
by rural industry. The government itself, moreover, cultivated such
ambiguity by continuing its traditional displays of paternal 'benevolence' during periods of duress in the silk industry, while preaching,
by word or by deed, the virtues of economic liberalism. In 1865, for
example, during the unemployment crisis following the American Civil
War, the prefect of the Rhône, Henri Chevreau, organized a "Commission
of Charity" to collect funds for those without work. The Emperor added

---

[30]"Les Réclamations des Tisseurs," _Le Progrès_, October 20, 1866.

another 100,000 francs to assist the poor.[31] Then in 1867, at another

trough in the trade cycle of the industry, the army purchased 66,200

meters of silk gauze for its rifles, even though the fabriques of

Zurich and Paris could have made these more cheaply.[32] Unlike the

similar paternal acts of government during the 1850's, however, which

associated the solidarity of the polis with imperial authoritarianism,

these gestures of official benevolence demonstrated the compatibility

of liberalism with paternalism under the imperial regime of Napoleon III.

The most spectacular gesture of Imperial benevolence -- one that

commanded national attention -- was provoked by the same threatened

demonstration of silk weavers in October 1866 which revealed their

ambiguities towards free trade. In response to the five demands of the

weavers' delegates to the prefect -- one of which called for restrictions

against countryside weaving and another of which sought liberalization

of the commercial law to facilitate the organization of cooperative

societies -- the Emperor invited the weavers to submit the statutes of

their faltering producers' cooperative for approval as a société anonyme

(with assurances of acceptance by the Conseil d'Etat), thus relieving

the embryonic association of legal impediments to its growth and poten-

tial success. The Emperor and Empress agreed to lend the new society

300,000 francs from the Société Prince Impérial to enable it to establish

itself immediately, and then promised to order from it silk fabric for

---

[31] Le Sénateur, Préfect du Rhône, Letter of invitation, April 17,
1865, AN, Fic III Rhône 10.

[32] Letter from Prefect of Rhône to Minister of Interior, March 15,
1867; letter from Minister of War to Minister of Interior, March 25,
1867, AN, Fic III Rhône 10.

the Imperial Court valued at 300,000 francs. The government would
provide an additional 300,000 francs to the weavers of Lyons to assist
them in the formation of other cooperative societies.[33]

The offer was, strictly speaking, a breach in the government's
official policy of 'impartiality,' or non-intervention in the affairs
of the marketplace. And acceptance of the offer by the silk weavers --
with enthusiasm and, ironically (from a free-trade point of view), at
the sacrifice of any restriction against putting-out in the countryside --
violated the so-called 'liberal' ideology of cooperation, which rejected
state aid for cooperative societies. But such breach and violation of
free trade on the part of government and weavers was in fact quite consistent with the 'liberal' opinion of both. This opinion might be
described best as 'tempered liberalism.' Tempered liberalism was
essentially ambivalent towards economic freedom, for it allowed government intervention in the marketplace to restore the balance among actual
or potential competitors, to prevent any one from absorbing or destroying
the others by means of its 'natural' economic advantage. Such liberalism
invoked the argument of preserving competition along with social welfare,
like anti-trust ideology in the United States. Unlike the latter, however, tempered liberalism used this argument to justify positive intervention by the government to support the weaker competitor or class --
the weavers, for example -- against the stronger, not merely negative
intervention to break up monopoly. "The Government," argued the prefect
of the Rhône in November 1866, in defense of the Emperor's gesture, "by

----

[33]Letter from Minister of Interior to Prefect of Rhône, Biarritz,
October 17, 1866, AN, Fic III Rhône 10, dossier "Ouvriers de Lyon";
"Lettre de M. de la Valette (Minister of Interior to Prefect of Rhône)
sur le chômage lyonnais," Le Progrès, October 28, 1866.

extending the freedom of workers' associations did not want to accord
[the workers] only an illusory favor, ... from which the lack of
capital would have prevented them from taking advantage."[34] Economic
liberalism -- at least that of the Second Empire -- thus did not exclude government activism to aid the 'naturally' disadvantaged party to
compete on equal or nearly equal terms. Such a notion of commercial
freedom was at least compatible, if not entirely coincident, with the
notion advanced in posters and flyers by spokesmen for the weaving
'masses' threatening to demonstrate in October 1866:

> The laws should be for one as for the other, there
> must be a balance in everything. To re-establish the
> balance there must be a dike against free trade.[35]

Such convergence of opinion concerning free trade between government and weavers encouraged the authorities to use the cooperative movement to wean the weavers away from their current political allegiance
to the republican opposition. The Minister of the Interior and the prefect hoped that the cooperative society aided by the Emperor in 1866
"would occupy their minds" and abate any tendency to disorder[36] that
would profit only the enemies of the regime. For a while at least,
the hopes of the government were not disappointed. On November 8, 1866,

[34]Report from Prefect of Rhône to Minister of Interior, November
8, 1866, AN, Fic III Rhône 5, Comptes-Rendus administratifs (An III à
1870).

[35]Untitled statement of principles in demands of ouvriers tisseurs,
October 1866, AML, I2-47 (B), No. 878.

[36]Letter from Minister of Interior to Prefect of Rhône, Biarritz,
October 18, 1866, AN, Fic III Rhône 10, dossier "Ouvriers de Lyon"; re-
port from Prefect of Rhône to Minister of Interior, November 8, 1866, AN,
Fic III Rhône 5.

the prefect was able to report to his superior in Paris:

> minds are calm, hope has replaced despondency and
> irritation. The cooperative movement is naturally
> very active; each day I see a large number of
> master weavers and I note with pleasure that they
> abandon political theories almost entirely, as
> being powerless to improve the condition of the
> class of workers. [37]

In December the police agent observing the conditions of the silk industry
claimed that "Napoleon III will not have better supporters than the
weavers if the good action which he has lavished on them could one day
make people say that he stopped the decline of the fabrique lyonnaise ..."
"[T]oday," he continued, "the Emperor is loved by the working population
of Lyons."[38] Two years later the prefect could report the same happy
news: "The cooperative movement is the main preoccupation of the working
class..."[39]

But such optimism did not last for long. The liberalization of
press and meeting laws in 1868 unleashed a new torrent of political
propaganda and organization. This torrent rekindled a dormant passion
for democratic republicanism and labor militancy among the workers of
Lyons. Without abandoning entirely the 'pragmatic program' of cooperation, the Lyonnais workers directed their most intense energies elsewhere. They formed political and educational clubs, some of which

---

[37]Report from Prefect of Rhône to Minister of Interior, November
8, 1866, ibid..

[38]"Rapport à Monsieur Delcourt, Commissaire spécial, sur la
situation de la fabrique des étoffes de soies au 4e Trimestre Xbre
1866," December 8, 1866, AML, I2-47 (A), No. 301.

[39]Report from Prefect of Rhône to Minister of Interior, November
18, 1868, AN, Fic III Rhône 5.

became regular forums for discussion of the political and social

programs of the radical democrats. Beginning in 1869, with the return

of industrial prosperity in the silk industry, they formed 'societies

of resistance,' embryonic trade unions, to negotiate and enforce wage in-

creases with their employers. And in 1867, and again in 1869-1870,

workers in several different trades in the city organized the Lyons

Section (later Lyons Federation) of the International Workingmen's

Association to unite all workers and workers' societies, especially

societies of resistance, into a single, inter-professional, semi-revolu-

tionary organization. As the police commissioner of Lyons remarked with

some disappointment in December 1869:

> The cooperative movement of production and
> consumption does not advance rapidly ... The
> ideas of the workers concerning this matter have
> changed much in the last two years and especially
> since political liberties have been enlarged. The
> social theories have regained much ground over the
> practical ideas encouraged by the Government.[40]

Common to these newer forms of workers' organization was strict

independence from the government, if not outright hostility to it. Un-

like the cooperative movement, supported morally and -- in the case of

the weavers' producers' cooperative -- materially by the government, the

new organizations neither received government favor nor accepted funds

from the authorities. They belonged to movements that the government

could tolerate at most, but could not control or direct in its own

interest. The Lyons branch of the International was especially immune

to such government interference. Albert Richard, leader of the Lyons

---

'Observations générales,' "Situation industrielle au Décembre
1869," AML, I2-47 (A), No. 212.

Federation in 1870, made it clear to his followers that internationalism
meant "war against capital, against the bourgeoisie and against
authority under whatever form it takes, political, social or religious."[41]

The silk weavers participated actively in all of these new associations, except for the International (which attracted only a few weaver
activists). Despite the preferential favor bestowed upon them by
Imperial 'benevolence,' they too stepped out beyond the protective
umbrella of official paternalism and pinned their hopes for a liberal
society to the banner of republicanism -- especially to the banner of
radical republicanism. When Napoleon III fell at Sedan on September 4,
1870, the silk weavers of the Croix-Rousse and elsewhere joined other
republicans in Lyons to celebrate the end of the Empire. No tears were
shed for the Emperor once "loved by the working population of Lyons."[42]

Yet to presume from this that the weavers had also abandoned their
old expectations of government intervention in their industrial affairs
would surely be an exaggeration. Only weeks before the weavers of the
Croix-Rousse cheered the advent of the Republic, the police overheard
murmurs among them, suggesting that the imperial prefect had taken their
side in the current strike against merchant-manufacturers of fancy cloths
and expressing hope for his intervention to force the fabricants to
concede their demands. The strike of fancy-cloth weavers had broken
out in early June to force two 'offending' merchant-manufacturers to

[41]Report to Minister of Interior on meeting of the International
in Lyons, March 14, 1870, AML, I2-55, Papiers d'Albert Richard: Pièces
relatives à l'Association Internationale des Travailleurs ...

[42]"Rapport à Monsieur Delcourt ...," December 8, 1866, AML, I2-
47 (A), No. 301.

accept a schedule of minimum piece-rates agreed upon by their colleagues

and the weavers. The newly-formed weavers' resistance society, the

Société civile de prévoyance, was financing the strike. Early in the

strike, the weavers believed that the prefect was resisting pressure from

the fabricants to force them to return to work. According to one woman,

> The heads of the four largest establishments of Lyons
> have gone to see Monsieur le Préfet to ask from him
> authorization to close their counters temporarily, in
> order to bring the workers to terms and to force them
> to accept work at rates lower than the tarif accepted
> and signed by the fabricants. Monsieur le Préfet
> refused this authorization and answered in these terms:
> 'You support the consequences of what you want to do
> and that will just be too bad for you.'[43]

Later in the strike, the weavers imagined the prefect threatening to

use force if the fabricants did not settle with the strikers. On July 3,

police agents overheard groups of workers on the Croix-Rousse saying

that "Monsieur le Sénateur Chevreau [the prefect] attended the meeting

[between representatives of weavers and fabricants] and said that, if

the fabricants had not accepted the new tarif within 15 days, he would

have their counters closed."[44] On July 14, a "female worker, mother of

a family" was heard saying:

> Monsieur le Préfet is getting involved in this
> business: he has heard all that has happened and has
> sent agents to Ravier and Piotet [the fabricants
> against whom the strike was initially called] to find out
> what they planned to do. We are certain that Monsieur
> le Préfet will take care of things.[45]

---

[43]Report of Special Police Commissioner to Prefect of Rhône concerning strike of fancy-cloth weavers, June 25, 1870, AML, I2-47 (B).

[44]Report of Special Police Commissioner to Prefect of Rhône, July 3, 1870, AML, I2-47 (B).

[45]Report of Special Police Commissioner to Prefect of Rhône, July 14, 1870, AML, I2-47 (B).

Whether or not these popular beliefs were true (probably they were not), they indicated the persistence of a 'sense of dependence' on government authorities in social and economic matters, and the identification of solidarity of the _polis_ with interventionist government, at least among the 'masses' of silk weavers in the city. Even while radical politicians and revolutionary militants were leading these 'masses' into the folds of the enemies of the Empire, this expectation of government intervention to 'right the balance' between themselves, the weaker class, and their employers endured. It was not a question of loyalty to a regime, but rather of loyalty to an idea -- the idea that the _fabrique_ of Lyons flourished, that its trades people prospered, only under the protective shield or with the positive support of a 'benevolent,' concerned authority. The solidarity of the _polis_ remained dependent upon the vigilant eye and the occasional helping hand of concerned government in industrial life. The acceptance of economic liberalism by the silk weavers of Lyons in the 1860's implied no rejection of this fundamental notion, sanctioned by a long tradition of intervening government.

CONCLUSION

Solidarity and Association

Sreten Maritch, the first historian of the Second Empire
workers' movement in Lyons, described the course of that movement as
a progression from an elite movement of master artisans to a mass
movement of proletarian workers. The elite movement produced mutual
aid societies dependent on the government and cooperative societies
of consumption, production and credit, most of which began 'autono-
mously' but some of which eventually accepted government aid as well.
The mass movement generated strikes, militant trade unionism --
called 'industrial resistance' -- and revolutionary socialist political
organization. The mass movement alone appealed to the common
proletarian interests of journeymen and factory workers and therefore
achieved true class consciousness. The elite movement represented
instead the retrograde, petty-bourgeois interests of master craftsmen,
especially those of the master silk weavers of the fabrique lyonnaise,
and therefore failed to produce a genuine workers' movement.[1]

Maritch's interpretation of the 'social movement' (as he called
it) of Second Empire Lyons has been criticized in some of its details,

---

[1]
Sreten Maritch, Histoire du mouvement social sous le Second
Empire à Lyon (Paris: Rousseau, 1930), especially chapters I, IV,
V, VII, IX, X.

notably by Jacques Rougerie in his work on the International Workingmen's Association.[2] Yves Lequin will offer a more thorough revision
of Maritch in his forthcoming book on the workers' world in the Lyons
region, by situating the Second Empire movement of Lyons in the context
of the eight-department région lyonnaise, for the period 1848 to 1914,
with greater breadth of sociological research and understanding, than
Maritch's thesis permitted.[3] But at least before Lequin's doctoral
thesis (which will form the substance of his book), Maritch's interpretation was generally accepted by social historians of Lyons. In The
Lyons Uprising of 1834, for example, Robert Bezucha relied upon this
interpretation to distinguish the strength and militancy of the
silk-workers' movement of 1831-1834 from the weakness and social
conservatism of silk workers in the 'social movement' of the Second
Empire. The former was "predicated on the protoindustrial solidarity
between master-weavers and their journeymen," while the latter depended
exclusively on masters, whose "mentality was increasingly that of
petit-bourgeois craftsmen who believed themselves superior to the
factory worker employed in the new chemical and metallurgical industries."[4] In La première internationale et la commune à Lyon, Maurice

2
  Jacques Rougerie, "La première Internationale à Lyon (1865 - 1870),"
Problèmes d'histoire du mouvement ouvrier français. (Annali dell'Insti-
tuto Giangiacomo Feltrinelli, 1961), pp. 126-193.

3 Yves Lequin, Les ouvriers de la région lyonnaise dans la
seconde moitié du XIXe siècle (1848 - 1914) (Lyon: Presses universitaires de Lyon, 1977).

4 Robert J. Bezucha, The Lyon Uprising of 1834: Social and
Political Conflict in the Early July Monarchy (Cambridge: Harvard
University Press, 1974), pp. 194-195.

Moissonnier also stressed the conservatism of weavers' social and
political movements under the late Empire, early Republic. Moissonnier
explained this conservatism by the prominence of master weavers in
these movements, who "found hard-nosed social theories repugnant and
who refused to question private property of the means of production."[5]
Both Bezucha and Moissonnier traced the social origins of this conservatism to the paucity of journeymen weavers — "true workers possessing
only the force of their labor"[6] -- in the fabrique of Lyons under the
Second Empire.[7]

In developing his interpretation of the workers'movement, especially
that among the weavers of the fabrique, Maritch relied upon many of the
same documents from which the present study has been fashioned. The
present work adds some new sources, especially quantitative data on
social and economic conditions, but offers, above all, a different
method for understanding the same social movements. This method has
consisted of the 'decomposition' of social and economic change, and of
voluntary association reflecting such change, into five collective
solidarities, prior to the 'reconstruction' of the movements of voluntary
association as a whole. The task of decomposition by collective solidarities is now complete. The task of reconstruction remains. The
question naturally arises, whether this reconstruction will modify the

---

[5]Maurice Moissonnier, La première internationale et la commune
à Lyon (Paris: Editions sociales, 1972), p. 24.

[6]Ibid.

[7]Ibid.; Bezucha, The Lyon Uprising of 1834, p. 194.

'standard' interpretation made by Maritch nearly fifty years ago
in any essential way. Without attempting this reconstruction here --
this concluding chapter will suggest some of its major probable directions
and some of the major modifications of Maritch's interpretation which
these directions may require.

This reconstruction would describe and interpret the course of
the weavers' movement as a passage from a movement deeply rooted in
the traditional solidarity of the polis to a movement deeply rooted in
the new solidarity of the neighborhood. 'Depth' in both cases would
refer to the extent of ideological appeal by these movements to the
'structures' of social solidarity in the weavers' world of work --
to old, unchanging structures, in the case of 'traditional' appeal, or
to new or changing structures, in the case of 'novel' appeal. The
first movement, based on the solidarity of the polis, would be described
as reflecting a unity of craft and class solidarities in the weavers'
social identity. The second movement would be described as manifest-
ing a dissociation of craft from class and a new ideological division
in the notion of class solidarity. The agent of such dissociation and
division would be the new solidarity dominating the weavers' social
identity in the later period -- the solidarity of the neighborhood.

Following this interpretation, the first movement would be described
as generating mutual aid societies appealing largely to tradition for
their ideological and organizational élan. These societies dominated
collective action among the weavers of Lyons throughout the 1850's.
The organization of the Silk Workers' Society for Mutual Aid in 1850,

initiating the movement of the 1850's, best demonstrated the traditional alliance of craft, class and 'political' solidarities explaining
the appeal of mutual aid. As indicated in Chapter III, the organization
of the Society effectively recognized the importance of the weavers of
Lyons in their city -- the polis of most immediate attention -- and
in their trade, especially in its 'horizontal' dimension of craft solidarity.[8] The establishment of the Society also recognized, at least
implicitly, the traditional identity and social and political significance of the silk weavers as a class. It was formed, probably
mainly, out of fear of the political power and class militancy of
the weavers, demonstrated most recently by the Voraces -- a paramilitary association of republican weavers -- during the first five
months of the Second Republic in Lyons.[9] The Society reproduced in
its administrative council, moreover, the traditional pattern of class
representation of the Conseil des Prud'hommes, affirming, in effect,
the specific class identity of the weavers, although in their traditionally subordinate position of power vis-à-vis the fabricants.[10]

---

[8]Chapter III, section II-B-1, pp. 266-269.

[9]Francois Dutacq, Histoire politique de Lyon pendant la révolution
de 1848 (Paris: Edouard Cornely, 1910), pp. 170-186, 382-385.

[10]On the administrative council of the Silk Workers' Society,
silk-worker 'participating members' were represented equally with
'honorary members,' most of whom were merchant-manufacturers of the
fabrique. The president of the council, however, was ex officio
the president of the Chamber of Commerce of Lyons, 'weighting'
the balance of the council in favor of the mercantile - bourgeois
members by one member. On the Conseil des Prud'hommes, the balance
was also 'weighted' in favor of the fabricants by one member.

By recognizing the integrity and significance of polis, craft and
class together in this fashion, the Silk Workers' Society anchored
its ideological appeal in a structure of social solidarity familiar to
the weavers, while the economy of the silk industry still kept that
structure intact. Napoleon III's promotion of the smaller mutual
aid societies appealed more strongly to the traditional solidarity of
the polis than to the solidarities of craft and class, and interpreted
the polis in an imperial rather than urban sense. But even this
promotion presumed and sought to preserve a social order based on
traditional class hierarchy and did not question the traditional
foundations of craft solidarity.

The second, later social movement generated political militancy
and organization under the late Second Empire and early Third Republic
(1870 - 1871) and appealed to new sources of social identity with new
ideologies of social reform. The movement followed a period of
active voluntary association, adding cooperative societies, clubs and
resistance organizations to the established mutual aid societies. It
also followed a period of fundamental economic and social change in the
silk industry and in the city of Lyons. Between the revival of mutual
aid during the 1850's and the emergence of the political movement in
1869-1870, the fabrique lyonnaise traversed one of the longest and
deepest economic crises of the century; and intensified industrialization,
urban renewal and population growth transformed the 'neighborhood'
environment of the city of Lyons. The crisis of the fabrique
weakened 'structurally' (that is, in a deep, fundamental way) the

traditional solidarities of craft and class and replaced these, to

some extent, with new craft and class solidarities. The transformation

of Lyons created new and deep social and economic divisions by neighbor-

hood.[11] In some neighborhoods, such as the Brotteaux-Guillotière,

this transformation dissociated craft solidarity from class solidarity,

by exposing silk weavers to workers in other trades and conditions of

employment. Such exposure encouraged weavers in these neighborhoods

to reform their notion of class, from the traditional notion associated

for the most part with a single trade, to a new conception of class

solidarity extending beyond the frontiers of individual trades. In

other neighborhoods, such as the Croix-Rousse, isolation from the

forces of urban transformation 'spared' the denizens this exposure to

new elements and preserved their traditional identification of class

with craft. In these ways, neighborhood solidarity profited from the

weakening of traditional craft and class solidarities by asserting its

own priority in determining the weavers' social identity.

This assertion of neighborhood over other solidarities explained

much of the political conflict between the Croix-Rousse and the

Brotteaux-Guillotière concerning the form of the Republic after the

---

[11]Here, as throughout the previous chapters, the word 'neighborhood' has been used somewhat loosely to characterize certain sections of the city, such as the Croix-Rousse or the Brotteaux-Guillotière, each of which consisted of several quarters. The word 'neighborhood' is applied to the entire section, not only to each quarter, because of its primary reference to a form of social solidarity which most quarters in each section shared in common. Thus, the residents of the Croix-Rousse, regardless of their quarter within this section, experienced a certain 'Croix-Rousse'identity -- here called a particular 'neighborhood' identity.

fall of the Empire on September 4, 1870. The Croix-Rousse defended
the Radical Republic and even 'permitted' this Republic to become
moderately conservative. The Brotteaux-Guillotière -- or rather, the
Lyons Federation of the International Workingmen's Association, with
its base of support in the Brotteaux-Guillotière -- fought for a
socialist Commune. This political conflict was really a conflict between neighborhoods, each of which 'carried' a different class
ideology, but not a radically different class character in one trade
at least -- that of silk weaving. The political movement manifested,
in effect, the 'triumph' of neighborhood over craft and class in
determining the collective consciousness of the silk weavers of Lyons.

The differences between this interpretation of the history of
the social movement in Lyons and that of Maritch and his followers do
not appear very significant at this point. Maritch described the
mutual aid movement as a deliberate, although unsuccessful, attempt
on the part of the Emperor "to turn workers away from politics"[12]
by "canalizing" workers' organization, that is, "by placing it under
his patronage."[13] Mutual aid was, moreover, an instrument for preserving the established social order, "for turning [the workers] away
from hazardous enterprises," in particular, "an obstacle rather
than an instrument for strike[s]."[14] Like the present study, Maritch
described mutual aid as an attempt to defend a traditional order of

---

[12]Maritch, Histoire du mouvement social à Lyon, p. 34.

[13]Ibid., p. 31.

[14]Ibid., p. 39.

'political' solidarity, here identified with a particular regime, and
a traditional hierarchy of class. The interpretation of the present
study claims a bit more 'success' for the movement, by stressing the
'depth,' or rootedness, of mutual aid ideology in socially-meaningful
solidarities still grounded in current economic conditions. Moreover,
with more sociological precision, the present interpretation locates
the source of this 'depth' in the weavers' social and economic experience.
The main orientations of the two interpretations -- that of Maritch
and that of this study -- are nevertheless the same.

Moissonnier's adaptation of Maritch to the political events
of the late Empire and early Republic also produced an interpretation
of these events generally similar to that of the present study. Like
the present study, Moissonnier stressed the different political loyalties and class ideologies of different neighborhoods in the city and
explained these as the result of the different social character
of the neighborhoods. The Croix-Rousse, dominated by master-weavers
of the fabrique, was socially conservative and therefore supported
the Radical party. The Guillotière, dominated by workers in the
newer industries of the city, was socially progressive and rallied
behind the International.[15] Moissonnier's interpretation of those
tendencies, like Maritch's interpretation of mutual aid, was
sociologically less precise than the present interpretation.

---

[15]Moissonnier, La première internationale à Lyon, pp. 24,
26-27 ff.

Moissonnier did not specify, for example, whether the socialist class
ideology of workers in the Guillotière was simply the consequence of
their common proletarian class situation, or whether it was also, as
the present study argues , the consequence of greater contact of master
artisans with proletarian workers, eroding the traditional unity of class
and craft solidarities among these masters and promoting among them a
sense of class solidarity similar to that of the true proletarians in
the area. Despite this lack of precision, Moissonnier's general argument and the present interpretation appear similar in their most
salient features.

Such apparent similarities between Maritch and his followers, on
one hand, and the present study, on the other hand, become less
significant when compared with the different interpretations of the
cooperative and resistance movements by the two. Both of these
movements were 'transitional' from one form of workers' voluntary
association, mutual aid, to another form, including both socialist
political organization, such as the International or the (Guesdist)
Parti ouvrier, and syndicalist unionism. The first form was dependent
upon the state for support and promoted class collaboration; the
second rejected state aid or intervention and was ouvrieriste or
anti-capitalist in orientation. Among the silk weavers of Second-
Empire Lyons, the cooperative and resistance transitions between
these two forms reflected the long and severe economic crisis in the
silk industry during the 1860's. Maritch's interpretation of these
transitional movements stressed the defensive, reactionary character
of the cooperative movement, exacerbated by economic crises revealing

the threat of modern industry to the master silk weaver, and the
offensive, progressive character of the resistance movement, fruit of
the return of economic prosperity and generator of class solidarity,
class consciousness, and socialist organization. The present interpretation, by contrast, emphasizes the 'expansive,' progressive nature of
cooperation, based on a recognition and acceptance of new solidarities
created by the changing economy, and the 'restrictive', reactive
character of industrial resistance, reviving and consolidating traditional notions of class relations favored by the return of prosperity.

The cooperative movement coincided with the worst years of
economic depression and reflected the crisis of the 1860's both in its
disruptive aspects, destroying or weakening old collective solidarities,
and in its reformative effects, laying the foundations of new
solidarities. Cooperation appealed to traditional concerns over the
destruction or weakening of old solidarities by evoking traditional
perceptions, aspirations and ambitions in its statement of aims, in its
program of activities and in its mobilization of membership, leadership
and support. Cooperation directed its strongest appeal, however, to
the new solidarities created by social and economic change during the
1860's. Its aims and methods were new and especially responsive to
the new conditions of the weavers' world of work, and it was eminently
open and receptive to the incorporation of new aims, new forms of
organization and new groups of workers into the movement. In 1865, the
leaders of twenty-one cooperative societies of Lyons stressed this
novel character of cooperation by declaring: "The cooperative associa-

tions are a <u>new economic force</u>."[16] Because of the open, receptive
character of cooperation, it accepted old ideals along with new
aims and methods, building social reform on the foundations of traditional values. This joint appeal to novelty and tradition in fact
constituted the special genius of the cooperative movement during
this period of economic and social transition. Such appeal was the
special source of the ideological strength of cooperation among the
silk weavers of Lyons.

In contrast to this openness of cooperation, the resistance
movement was ideologically restrictive in its appeal to social solidarity. Instead of encouraging new ideas and new forms of voluntary organization, the resistance movement consolidated and concentrated the
weavers' organizational energies around a single collective solidarity --
that of class -- and in its traditional hierarchical form. Although
the movement appealed somewhat to a broader notion of class, in the
sense of 'mass', by integrating rural weavers, journeymen and women
into the movement, it accepted the 'traditional' notion of the 'other'
class -- the merchant-manufacturers to whom the weavers were subordinate
in the process of production -- and the hierarchy of classes upon which
such notion was founded. Resistance appealed to this traditional
hierarchical notion by stressing the need of classes for one another
in the manufacture of silks and by promising the weavers, the subordinate
class, a 'fair share' in the gains of manufacture -- insured, so to
speak, by this need -- without upsetting the traditional class

16,'Mémoire adressé par les associations coopératives de la ville
de Lyon, à MM. les membres de la Chambre de Commerce,' in Eugène
Flotard, "Bulletin Coopératif," <u>Le Progrès</u> (Lyon), December 25-26, 1865.

hierarchy. In this sense, resistance was not only a movement more
ideologically closed than cooperation but also a movement more traditional,
or 'regressive,' in the sources of its ideological appeal.

The progressive character of the cooperative movement was apparent
in its appeal to new forms of collective solidarity in defining
its aims among the weavers, and in the novelty of its organizational
program and method. Its appeal to new or changing collective solidarities -- in particular, to solidarities of class, household and polis
-- was 'deep'; that is, it addressed explicitly and precisely the
economic and social 'questions' posed by changes in these solidarities
and proposed responses to these 'questions' that were both 'efficient'
-- profiting from new opportunities emerging from the same changes --
and 'radical' -- demanding the constitution of new forms of organization of work and/or community and not merely the marginal correction
or redressing of old forms. Since the changes in solidarities thus
addressed by cooperation were themselves 'structural' in many respects,
cooperative ideology reached into some of the deepest social and economic roots of the urban fabrique.

Cooperative production, for example, accepted the new class
situation of the urban master-weavers and fostered the continued
transformation of traditional class relations by its pursuit of
autonomy in the work process through self-help. The new cooperative
silk-weaving enterprise, for example -- the Association of Weavers --
would enable the weavers to "emancipate" themselves from their onerous
dependence on the orders of a single fabricant, many of whom,
especially the petits fabricants, had no concern for their welfare

and no scruples about cheating them of their low piece-rates by
fraudulent mesurage of woven fabric. Cooperation would enable them
to achieve such "emancipation" by their own efforts -- in particular,
without the assistance or cooperation of the once paternal grands
fabricants, who were abandoning the urban weavers to their rural
fábriques and who were thereby losing concrete class relationship with
the weavers of the city. Cooperative consumption enabled the weavers
to respond more 'efficiently' to the new economic and social situation
of their households. The procurement of household necessities at
wholesale cost through the organization of cooperative groceries
reduced expenditures on these items at a time when the individual
master-weaver's attention was focused on expenditures rather than on
revenues of the household budget. This attention to expenditures was
in part the result of the impossibility of increasing revenues, because
of low piece-rates and high unemployment, and in part the result of
the familialization and feminization of the household, facilitating
the reduction of household expenditures by reducing living standards
of household members. Consumers' cooperation provided an institutional
mechanism for accommodating this reorientation of household budget
management, even permanently(hence the structural 'depth' of its appeal),
and also 'humanized' this accommodation by relieving the more easily
exploitable family and female household members from some of the
burden of re-adjustment. The cooperative movement as a whole, finally,
presumed a new kind of 'political' solidarity -- in particular, one
receptive to liberalism -- and fostered the acceptance of this new
solidarity among weavers who traditionally regarded liberalism with

hostility. The gradual 'liberalization' of the Empire after 1859 gave

the workers more freedom to organize cooperative societies and even

encouraged such organization by the commercial laws of 1864 and 1867.

Even more importantly, the cooperative movement of the 1860's weaned

the weavers away from their 'traditional' attachment to state-sponsored

voluntary association--whether 'utopian' cooperative association of

the Second Republic or subsidized mutual aid of the early Empire--

and encouraged their acceptance of a 'tempered liberalism' in other

areas of their social and economic life as well. Cooperation thus

served as an agent of the transformation of their ideal of the <u>polis</u>

and of their solidarity with the government founded on that ideal.

Besides appealing 'deeply' in these ways to new or changing soli-

darities of class, household and <u>polis</u>, cooperation also appealed to new

solidarities of household, craft and class in a more superficial manner.

Cooperative societies reflected, for example, the feminization of the

household by admitting a few female shareholders, but members of these

societies never elected women into positions of leadership. The coopera-

tive movement also reflected the new 'vertical' solidarity of craft

among master weavers, based on equality of earnings, by concentrating

on the reform of the distributive mechanism of the economy--its more

'superficial' (or 'superstructural') dimension--to increase the earnings

of weavers, rather than on the transformation of productive organization and

technique, to 'revolutionize' the work process as such.[17] This
greater concern with distribution also fostered a semblance of class
unity among the masters, by appealing to an interest shared equally
by all -- in greater earnings. The weakness of this foundation for
class solidarity was revealed by the ease with which the small-group
autonomy of consumers' cooperation, and the ideological divisions
within producers' cooperation, rapidly eroded class unity within the
movement after 1866.

Cooperation combined such appeals to new or changing solidarities
with appeals to tradition. Like the former, the latter included both
'deep' and 'superficial' responses to changing economic and social
conditions, but unlike the latter, these responses were reactive,
intending to restore old, threatened solidarities or at least to
preserve habits and ambitions traditionally 'founded' on these old
solidarities, in new conditions of economic and social life. Such
appeals to tradition responded in this manner to changes in weavers'
households, in a 'deep' way, and to changes in their craft solidarity,
in more 'superficial' ways. Cooperation addressed the former by
promoting entrepreneurship in the small consumers' societies. Consumers'
cooperation replaced the household with the small retail business as
a field of entrepreneurial endeavor. This replacement permitted the
master to extend his traditional entrepreneurial ambitions over a much
wider range and scale of activities than he had ever been able to do

---

[17]
    The producers cooperative of silk weavers, the Association of
Weavers, sought, for example, to preserve urban hand-loom weaving
and the domestic economy of silk manufacture from the competition of
mechanized factory weaving as well as from the competition of rural
domestic weaving.

in the domestic economy of silk weaving, by making available to him
two new instruments for increasing revenues -- profit-making and portfolio investment. Producers' cooperation addressed changes in the
craft solidarity of the weavers but more superficially. Two of the
most prominent changes were the emigration of the fabrique to the
countryside, undermining the traditional centrality of Lyons in the
'horizontal' solidarity of craft, and the levelling of fancy-weavers'
income to that of plain-cloth weavers, eroding the traditional preeminence
of fancy-cloth weavers in the 'vertical' solidarity of craft. Defense
of these two foundations of craft solidarity was, however, more informal
than that of entrepreneurship. Defense of the urban fabrique was a
mere hope on the part of the Association of Weavers, not a carefully-
developed program, and defense of the status of the fancy-cloth weavers
was an 'informal' (that is, unofficial) interest of the majority of the
administrators of the Society, who were fancy-cloth masters. Nevertheless, even these superficial bases of appeal added a breadth to the
depth of cooperative ideology and thereby gave the weavers more
reason to subscribe to the cooperative program.

The appeal of consumers' cooperation to traditional entrepreneurial
ambitions, once exercised in the household, and the appeal of producers'
cooperation to traditional notions of 'horizontal' and 'vertical'
solidarity of craft, would seem to justify Maritch's argument that
the cooperative movement "was no more than a defensive reaction"
against the "rationalization of production" by the mechanization of
industry and by the erosion of skill to the level of the "non-qualified"

(that is, unskilled) worker.[18] The appeal to entrepreneurial ambition,
associated traditionally with the autonomous or semi-autonomous household,
might be argued to have reflected the master-weaver's attachment to
"the life of the family" and his "petty-bourgeois" "sense of independence."[19] The appeal to traditional craft solidarity, based on distinction
of skill in an exclusively urban craft, might be said to have manifested
the master-weaver's elitist, corporative assertion of his "only remaining
defense" against the "democratization" of labor by the machine and
against the competition of rural labor -- "craft skill acquired by a
long apprenticeship."[20] Both appeals thus would justify Maritch's
claim that the cooperative vision was narrow, closed in upon family and
craft, and retrograde, seeking to revive an obsolete form of work. His
contention that the cooperative movement could never have become
"a workers' movement, that is a movement for the emancipation of the
masses, a socialist movement" would therefore also seem to be accurate.[21]

Maritch's perception of the traditional bases of appeal of cooperative ideology was in fact quite accurate, but his failure to situate
these bases with those explaining the appeal of cooperative novelty

---

[18]Maritch, Histoire du mouvement social à Lyon, p. 109.

[19]Ibid., pp. 128-130. This is, of course, stretching the similarity somewhat. Maritch's description of the 'typical' master-
weaver is closer to the 'artisal' master than to the 'entrepreneurial' master, as these were defined in Chapter I. (See Chapter I,
section I-B-I.) The similarity consists primarily of the original
attachment of Maritch's 'type' and this study's 'entrepreneurial'
master to the domestic economy of silk weaving.

[20]Ibid., pp. 110-111.

[21]Ibid., p. 129.

distorted the 'truth'value' of his perception. In other words, his recognition of a partial truth of the cooperative movement -- its appeal to traditional solidarities -- became a vehicle of false understanding when taken as the whole truth of the movement -- that is, as a claim that the movement appealed only to these solidarities. Besides appealing to the latter in household and craft, the cooperative movement also addressed changing solidarities of craft, household, class and polis. This joint appeal to novelty and tradition was at the essence of its particular kind of 'utopianism' -- one that pointed to a new society and to new social relations founded on traditional ideals and experience. By focusing only on these foundations and by ignoring the direction of the cooperative movement, Maritch failed to appreciate its progressive character.

Maritch also failed to appreciate the revolutionary potential of cooperative ideology and the democratic sources of at least some of its appeal. Cooperation did not produce a revolution, nor even a revolutionary consciousness, nor probably could it ever have done so, but it welcomed and 'disciplined' ambitions for 'deep' social reform to the point where they could be mobilized by other movements for revolutionary purposes. Cooperation persuaded the weavers to accept economic liberalism for the first time, for example, and thereby weaned them away, to some extent at least, from dependence on the government in social and economic affairs and in the organization of voluntary associations. The International capitalized on this acceptance of autonomy in industrial affairs and on the wider experience of autonomous workers' organization by appealing to autonomy in its

revolutionary aims and organizational methods. The cooperative
capacity for tapping the roots of revolutionary consciousness was
the result of its 'depth' of ideological appeal to 'deeply' changing
solidarities in the weavers' world of work. Cooperation was rooted,
in other words, in the structural transformation of the fabrique
during the 1860's, and it responded to this structural change (in
part, at least) by encouraging it or by formulating its own aims and
building its own programs on the effects of this change. Among these
effects were the erosion of certain traditional differences among
weavers in the fabrique -- such as differences of earnings, of
household size and of household dependence on single fabricants,
between plains and fancies weavers, and differences of task within the
household economy, between male and female workers. Such erosion
effectively equalized -- or "democratized" -- the economic situations
of these weavers, without transforming the techniques or organization
of their household economy as such. As indicated in Chapters IV, V,
VI,[22] cooperative ideology appealed to these newly "democratized" solidarities as well as to some of the older solidarities based on
hierarchical distinctions within the craft. It appealed, in other
words, to new egalitarian experiences of a traditional type of workers
produced by changes in their economic conditions rather than to the
experiences of new types of workers emerging out of a radical transformation in productive organization and technique. Maritch

---

[22]Chapter IV, section II-C; Chapter V, section I-E; Chapter VI.

underestimated the impact of the first kind of change on the recept-
ivity of cooperative ideology to social democracy.

The weakness of the cooperative movement was not its antipathy to
progress, revolution or social democracy but rather its inability to
promote class unity -- solidarity of class in the sense of 'mass'
-- even within a single trade, such as silk weaving. This was partly
the result of its 'open,' receptive character, stressing autonomy
and individual initiative in the organization of cooperative enterprise.
In Lyons, this attachment to autonomy was manifested in the organization
of small consumers' cooperatives, each concentrated in a particular
silk-weaving neighborhood and each jealous of its independence from
other consumers' societies.[23]   Such jealousy prevented the organization
of a unified federation of consumers' cooperatives and consequently
of a unified, class-conscious workers' movement on the basis of these
societies. The greatest weakness of the cooperative movement in its
efforts to promote class unity among the silk weavers was, however,
also the source of the ideological appeal of producers' cooperation,
considered by most observers to be the most 'class-conscious' part of
the cooperative movement. This was the diffuse, ambiguous character
of class relations to which producers' cooperation offered the most
ambitious response. Because of their abandonment by the large merchant-
manufacturers, the weavers' conception of the other class, against

---

[23]Societies demonstrated this jealousy by prohibiting their
members from belonging to any other association with a similar purpose.
See, for example, Article 4-1, Espérance ouvrière, Statuts, ADR, 9U -
Sociétés: Constitutions et modifications, August 23, 1866.

which they defined their own class solidarity, was that of one losing
concrete relationship with themselves. They were faced with a situation,
in other words, in which the notion of class as such became ever less
meaningful, because of the departure of the other class (or at least of
the grands fabricants, who represented the weavers' 'ideal' of the
other class) from the scene of traditional class confrontation. In
this situation the weavers' own class solidarity could be maintained
only in idea -- through cooperative ideology, for example -- without
the concrete support of daily class interaction. The class ideology
of the cooperative movement was therefore acutely susceptible to
division by other collective solidarities, such as neighborhood.

Such division first emerged in the form of ideological orientations
of prominent consumers' societies of one neighborhood area -- the Croix-
Rousse -- as compared with those of another neighborhood -- the
Brotteaux-Guillotière. The former tended to be elitist and exclusive
in their recruitment of members and sharing of profits, while the
latter tended to be more egalitarian and expansive. Such differences
did not cause serious conflict within the cooperative movement until
1866. Then, in October of that year, the silk weavers had to decide
whether to abandon certain cherished principles of their movement --
independence from government assistance and capitalist involvement and
equality in the sharing of business profits -- in order to secure for
their slowly budding producers' association the legal advantages of
recognition as a société anonyme and the financial benefits of a
government loan. The Emperor himself proposed such recognition and
assistance in response to a set of demands by the weavers which they
finally presented to the prefect through some of their elected

representatives, after first threatening a mass demonstration.
The majority of the weavers accepted the proposals, following the
leadership of master-weavers of the Croix-Rousse. A minority, following
the séries (organizational cells) of the Brotteaux-Guillotière, at
first lobbied for reform of the new statutes and then seceded from
the parent Association to join another producers' society whose "goal
[was] cooperation; that is, equality of conditions under the heading
of the distribution of profits."[24] This split within the producers'
movement reflected the divisions of social ideology and of social
and economic experience between the two silk-weaving neighborhoods
and rended class unity within the cooperative movement as a whole. As
Chapter VII indicated, these divisions also became apparent in club
activity after 1868 and in the extent and direction of politicization
of clubs and consumers' cooperatives after 1870.[25]

This weakness of class solidarity prevented the cooperative
movement from becoming a mass movement with a socialist ideology.
The resistance movement, by contrast, consolidated and concentrated
class solidarity and organized the working 'masses' into unified class
associations. Industrial resistance achieved such consolidation and
concentration, however, only by an ideological and psychological
'closing in,' or focussing, of 'associational' energy and purpose
around the single-minded pursuit of class unity and class organization.
Among the silk weavers at least, this 'closing in' had curious impli-
cations for a movement described by Maritch and Moissonnier as

---

[24]"Une nouvelle société des tisseurs," Le Progrès, December 30, 1866.

[25]Chapter VII, section III, pp. 520-524.

progressive; namely, a revival of traditional notions of class solidarity
and an acceptance of traditional class hierarchy. Unlike the cooperative
movement, which sought to achieve complete autonomy for the workers
from the fabricants, industrial resistance recognized, at least implicitly, both the subordination of weavers to fabricants and the need
of the fabricants for the labor of urban weavers -- the two traditional
foundations of their class relations. Resistance sought to obtain for
the weavers a 'fair share' in the earnings of industry within this
traditional class hierarchy. By reviving tradition in this manner,
resistance promoted class consciousness among the weavers by appealing
to their common experience of 'exploitation,' which at least clarified
their reasons for class unity, rather than to their experience of
abandonment, which obscured class unity and left room for the assertion
of other solidarities. The single-minded pursuit of class unity thus
made the resistance movement 'regressive' and narrow, instead of
'progressive' and open like cooperation.

In the name of class unity, the resistance movement nevertheless
extended beyond the frontiers of class as defined in the past --
especially the frontiers of urban, master and male weavers -- to a
broader view of class including rural weavers, journeymen, and women
workers in the fabrique. In this way, resistance became a 'mass'
movement in the fabrique more thoroughly than cooperation or mutual
aid had ever been. In some instances, this extension of resistance to
the silk-weaving masses undermined the original intentions of the
movement based on more traditional notions of class solidarity. The
weavers hoped, for example, that resistance would restore the old

'horizontal' primacy of the urban craft over rural weaving, but the
need for class unity in the largest sense, to preserve negotiated
increases in the piece-rate, required the organization of rural weavers
into societies of resistance as well. Such organization effectively
extended the notion of class solidarity to the region rather than con-
fining this notion to the city alone. The acceptance of journeymen
weavers as equal partners of masters in the same resistance organizations
and the acceptance of female workers in the same societies on more than
a 'token' scale, extended class solidarity to additional workers
within the urban fabrique as well. In the early 1830's, masters of
the Society of Mutual Duty had allied with journeymen of the Society
of Ferrandiniers for mutual assistance during strikes,[26] but rarely did
masters and journeymen organize for resistance in the same association,
as they did in the 'category' societies and in the Société civile de
prévoyance federating ten of these categories in 1869-1870.[27]
Cooperative societies admitted a few women during the 1860's, but
never before had women associated in large numbers with male masters
and journeymen weavers for militant strike activity, as they did in
the resistance movement of the late Second Empire.

Because of this 'depth' of appeal to a single consciousness
of class and because of the breadth of class organization in the
resistance movement, Maritch's assertion that the strike (applied
resistance) "was a great school of solidarity and discipline, organizing

[26]Bezucha, The Lyon Uprising of 1834, pp. 106, 123-125.

[27]See Chapter IV, section II-C, pp. 358-360.

the mass[es] and awakening in them the consciousness of class"
was fully justified.[28] What was not justified was his and Moissonnier's
description of the movement as uniquely progressive. As we have seen,
resistance aroused class solidarity and class consciousness by appealing
to the past -- to a traditional order of hierarchical class relations.
Because of his failure to recognize this importance of tradition,
Maritch regarded the moderation of the weavers' societies as a
deviation from the 'essence' of industrial resistance. Such deviation
was evident in the refusal of the weavers' Société civile to join
the International along with most other societies in the city.
Maritch explained this refusal by the dominance of the master weavers
in the movement, who feared inciting journeymen and other subordinate
workers to resistance against themselves.[29] When tradition is instead
regarded as the core of resistance, the same facts and events advanced
by Maritch as evidence for his argument receive a different interpretation. The examples he offers of master-journeyman hostility in
the movement, for example, become exceptions to a triumph of traditional
organizational and ideological solidarity between masters and workers,[30]
and the revolutionary program and organization of the inter-craft
International become deviations from the original and essential

---

[28] Maritch, Histoire du mouvement social à Lyon, p. 248.

[29] Ibid., p. 249.

[30] Ibid., pp. 249-251. As evidence of such master-worker hostility
among the weavers of plain cloths, Maritch cites the separate meetings
of journeymen to discuss the proposed tarif of piece-rates. He relies
heavily on this evidence to support his argument. It is doubtful that
separate meetings to discuss rates paid by fabricants and earned in
equal shares by masters and journeymen can serve so strongly as evidence
for hostility between the latter two parties. In fact, the only firm
evidence of hostility between masters and journeymen offered by Maritch

stabilizing, restorative goals of craft-centered resistance. These

goals were pursued conscientiously and scrupulously by the trade most

conscious of the sources of its strong class solidarity in the past

and most practiced in expressing its class identity independently and

confidently -- the trade of the silk weavers. The transition from

industrial resistance to the International, and from there to socialist

and anarchist politics, was therefore not a logical, linear progression,

as Maritch and Moissonnier would have one believe, but rather a step

in a different direction of social ideology and collective organization.

This step introduced, or rather re-introduced, neighborhood soli-

darity as a significant determinant of social ideology. As in the

cooperative movement, neighborhood became a source of division among

the weavers of Lyons. Only now, in the political movement, that division

focussed on two questions posed most acutely by the resistance movement

-- the notion of class solidarity and the relationship of resistance

to politics. One neighborhood, the Croix-Rousse, generally identified

class solidarity with craft solidarity, limiting class action to one

trade and scrupulously keeping resistance organization and goals

separate from those of politics. Another neighborhood, the Brotteaux-

Guillotière, regarded class solidarity as intersecting or transcending

craft solidarity and resistance as a means of promoting the aims of

social revolution. Some silk weavers and many other workers residing

in the Brotteaux-Guillotière therefore subscribed to the inter-professional,

---

was strikes in shops of tulle-weaving and passementerie. These exceptions
occurred in branches of the silk manufacture that were exceptional by their
technology, cloth texture, and organization of manufacture. They were
not, as Maritch claims, simply "the rich and prosperous specialties" of
the silk-weaving trade proper (that is, of the weaving of étoffes de soie).

revolutionary program of the International as the latter sought to federate the newly-formed resistance societies in 1869 - 1870. The same militants of the Brotteaux-Guillotière supported the Lyons Federation of the International in its struggle for an anarchist-socialist Commune after the fall of the Empire on September 4, 1870. They were opposed by the silk weavers of the Croix-Rousse, whose notions of class and of the relationship of resistance to politics were more compatible with the Radical and liberal republicanism dominating the early Third Republic in Lyons than with the socialism of the International. The 'industrial' solidarity of resistance was thus split by a 'political' conflict of neighborhoods, but only after the issues on which neighborhoods separated from one another -- the issues of class solidarity and class organization -- had been posed with clarity and intensity in the resistance movement.

This neighborhood conflict emerged most dramatically during the first months of the Republic in Lyons. On September 28, 1870, Bakunin and his fellow conspirators of the International, with headquarters in the Brotteaux-Guillotière, staged a coup against the Municipal Council of the Commune of Lyons, dominated by Radical democrats. The coup failed because of the intervention of two National Guard battalions of the Croix-Rousse. The battalions were commanded respectively by Chavant, a dyer, and by Antoine Arnaud, a master silk weaver. A few months later, the Croix-Rousse saved the 'bourgeois' Republic from socialism by refusing to follow the lead of the Guillotière in revolting against the Versailles government and its accomplices in Lyons. On April 30, 1871, some fifteen workers in the Guillotière occupied

the mairie (town hall) to prevent elections to the Municipal Council
and thus registered a protest against the dismantling of the Commune.
A crowd of some 150 persons gathered around the mairie, apparently in
support of the insurgents. Several National Guardsmen sent to eject
them from the building joined the crowd and fraternized with the rebels.
Later in the day the regular army under the command of the prefect
suppressed the revolt and liberated the mairie. The death toll,
totalling some thirty persons, was relatively light in comparison with
similar events in the past. What the government feared most was an
even more severe reaction in the Croix-Rousse to the aborted rebellion.
In fact, the Croix-Rousse did not revolt. The few insurgents plotting
in this district were unable to rally any mass support. They were
finally persuaded to dismantle the few barricades they erected. The
day passed with little incident in the neighborhood of the silk weavers.[31]

Unlike the Guillotière, the Croix-Rousse was not interested in
social revolution, especially not in revolution favoring a class
solidarity alien to the traditional experience of class in this silk-
weaving neighborhood. This experience concentrated the notion of class
around a single craft and around a single neighborhood dominated by
that craft. The continued prominence of the silk weavers in the Croix-
Rousse in 1870 confirmed this notion of class, then as during the early
1830's. The notion of class solidarity in the name of which the
International staged its coup of September 28 and for which the workers
of the Guillotière revolted on April 30 presumed, on the contrary, a
dissociation of craft from class. Such class solidarity transcended

---

[31]Moissonnier, La première internationale à Lyon, pp. 262-264,
366-381.

the frontiers of individual trades and recognized a common proletarian
identity among workers in all trades. Among the silk weavers residing
in the Brotteaux-Guillotière, such solidarity was a consequence of
their daily neighborhood contact and exchange with workers in other
trades and conditions of employment. As a result of such contact,
their recognition of their subordination to the _fabricants_ as the 'other'
class and of their own 'massive ' character within the _fabrique_ of
Lyons extended to a recognition of their subordination to capitalists
in general and of their common proletarian identity with workers in
society as a whole. The International appealed successfully to such
recognition in this neighborhood, where daily experience confirmed
this larger notion of class, but its socialist and revolutionary message
fell on deaf ears in the neighborhood of the Croix-Rousse, where craft,
class and neighborhood solidarities still converged.

Maritch and Moissonnier cited such differences of appeal, with
much reason, as evidence of the social conservatism of the Croix-Rousse
and of the social progressivism of the Brotteaux-Guillotière. They
tended to explain such differences by those of class types dominant
in each of the two areas -- of property-owning masters in the Croix-
Rousse and of laboring proletarians in the Brotteaux-Guillotière. The
present interpretation of the political movement, based on the
analysis of social solidarities, suggests that the explanation lay
elsewhere than in these fixed social and economic types -- masters or
workers -- bound by certain class situations and therefore confined
to a particular class ideology. The explanation lay instead in
changing historical circumstances -- circumstances that altered the
material conditions, the social and economic situations and the

notions of class and other solidarities of the same master artisans,
without changing their class position vis-à-vis their subordinate
workers. These changing circumstances first favored the expression
of several social solidarities at once, in both traditional and novel
forms, through cooperation; then favored class solidarity above all
others, through resistance; and finally asserted the prominence of
neighborhood solidarity in shaping social ideologies and political
loyalties, in the political movement. Differences of neighborhood
contact and of neighborhood experience, more than differences of
dominant class types as such, explained the different political and
social opinions of weavers of the Croix-Rousse as compared with
weavers and workers of the Brotteaux-Guillotière. Among the silk
weavers of the fabrique lyonnaise, such division of opinion and
party manifested the triumph of neighborhood solidarity over all
other solidarities in the weavers' world of work.

Although this strength of neighborhood solidarity was apparently
a novel feature of that world, this strength did not affect the balance
of political power in the city in a new way. In 1870-1871, that balance
was held by the silk weavers of the Croix-Rousse, as it had been held by
them in 1831 and in 1848. The Croix-Rousse asserted its influence
in the Commune by providing necessary support and some leadership
for the formation of the new Municipal Council, by successfully
preventing the overthrow of the Council by Bakunin and his conspirators
on September 28, and by refusing to intervene on the side of the
Guillotière rebels on April 30. In 1881, the Croix-Rousse had led
other quarters of the city in the insurrection of November, and

during the same insurrection, several master-weavers of the Croix-
Rousse, members of the Conseil des Seize, assumed control of the city
government until the forces of order regained power.[32]   In 1848, the
Voraces of the Croix-Rousse had controlled the city during the first
month of the Revolution of 1848, by occupying the forts of the
Bernardines, and remained an occult power in Lyons throughout the
Second Republic.[33]

In all three years--1831, 1848 and 1870--the Croix-Rousse was at
or near the center of the local political movement toppling the old
regime or threatening the present one. In 1831 and in 1870, the Croix-
Rousse defended the original revolution from more radical elements and
then complied with the shift to a more conservative settlement. Its
political strength in 1870-1871 as before was rooted in the same sociological fact; namely, in the convergence of craft, class and neighborhood solidarities among the master silk weavers residing there. The
triumph of the Croix-Rousse over the Brotteaux-Guillotière in the republican 'settlement' of 1870 - 1871 was thus a confirmation of the continuing power of tradition in the weavers' world of work, even after
the profound disruption of that world by the crisis of the 1860's.

The force of tradition in fact remained strong in that world for
many decades thereafter. When it finally 'died,' it did so

---

[32]Fernand Rude, L'insurrection lyonnaise de novembre 1831:
Le mouvement ouvrier à Lyon de 1827-1832 (Paris: Editions
Anthropos, 1969), pp. 357-428, 507-521.

[33]Dutacq, Histoire politique de Lyon pendant la révolution de
1848, pp. 170-186, 382-385.

without the fanfare of ideological onslaught and without the
brutality of catastrophic industrial revolution. Instead it died
slowly, peacefully and almost quietly, as the silk industry continued
to migrate out of Lyons, as mechanization steadily replaced artisan
labor, and as Lyons became less an industrial center and more a
center of tertiary economic activity--of trade and commerce, of
banking and finance, of administration and culture. Silks were
dethroned, and the world of the silk weavers passed away, as the
consumers and producers of the modern age turned their favors to
woolen, cotton and synthetic fashion fabrics. But this demise of
craft and tradition had a certain dignity and grace, for the change
of regime in textiles was achieved without revolution.

APPENDICES

Appendix I:

Estimation of Class Dependence

of Master Weavers

in an Illustrative Silk-Weaving Enterprise

(Maison Bellon-Conty)

Construction of Table 2, "Evaluation of Potential Class Consciousness," requires the quantitative specification of probability of dependence of master-weavers on a single merchant-manufacturer, in order to
indicate a level of discrimination of the class character of fabricants
and of weavers respectively in large-scale plain-cloth establishments.
By comparing the distribution of looms of a single large merchant-manufacturer of plain cloths, the maison Bellon-Conty in 1860, among different
households, with a sample distribution of plain-cloth households in the
Croix-Rousse in 1866, according to the number of looms per household, we
can trace a tentative pattern of 'dependence probability' among the 200
or so weavers of this establishment. Such a pattern should provide a
reasonable estimate of 'class' discrimination for the purposes of Table
2, the value and intent of which are merely illustrative.

The data for the maison Bellon-Conty are taken from a financial ac-
counting sheet listing master-weavers employed currently by the establishment along with the number of looms occupied in the household of each
by the same maison. The list was compiled in response to a petition of
masters in 1860 complaining of certain practices of compensation for wastes

of silk thread during weaving.[1] The sample data for the Croix-Rousse,
the major weaving district in the city of Lyons in 1866, was taken from
the population census of that year, which recorded number and type of
looms along with personal information for each household in the district.[2]
The method of sampling these households is described in Appendix V. Unfortunately the data for the establishment and for the sample of households are not entirely comparable. Besides their different dates, the
two distributions measure different variables. The Bellon distrubution
measures the frequencies of putting out one, two, three, four or five
looms per household without specifying whether these households were occupied entirely by the maison Bellon, that is, without specifying, for
example, how many households in the one-loom group had only one loom in
the household, and how many had additional looms besides, occupied by other
fabricants. The Croix-Rousse sample distribution, on the other hand, measures the frequency of households with a total of one, two, three, four
or five looms respectively, without indicating how many of the households
with two or more looms were occupied by more than one merchant-manufacturer. The missing 'joint probability' of an n - loom household (a household with a total of n looms) with k looms occupied by the Bellon establishment prevents any certain generalizations from the existing data. Yet
a direct impressionistic comparison of the two data sets suggests a probable trend for the different household categories towards or away from

---

[1] Bellon Frères et Conty, Response of fabricants to request for accounts of balances with chefs d'ateliers, c. 1860, ACCL, Soieries Carton
41-I-Législation-Usages (an 8 à 1936), 13. -Pétition remise à l'Empereur
à son passage à Lyon, par les ouvriers en soie.

[2] ADR, 6M-Dénombrement, 1866, Lyon, 4ème arrondissement, XVI, XVII.

exclusive dependence on the orders of this single _fabricant_. The trend
is summarized by the following tables and graphs of the relative and cumulative frequency distributions of households by looms--total looms occupied
by the _maison_ Bellon, in the case of the Bellon sample, and total looms
owned by the master-weaver, in the case of the Croix-Rousse sample:

Table 44

	A. Distribution of Households According to the Number of Looms Occupied per House- hold by the Bellon-Conty Establishment, 1860			B. Distribution of Households According to the Total Number of Looms Per Household in the Croix-Rousse Sample of House- holds with Plain-Cloth Looms Only, 1866		
Number of Looms	Number of Households	% of Total HH (relative)	% of Total HH (cumulat.)	Number of Households	% of Total HH (relative)	% of Total HH (cumulat.)
1	71	36.98	36.98	16	19.70	19.70
2	76	39.58	76.56	34	41.97	61.67
3	29	15.10	91.66	25	30.90	92.57
4	12	6.25	97.91	5	6.17	98.74
5	4	2.08	99.99	1	1.23	99.97
Totals	192			81		

Sources: A. Bellon Frères et Conty, Response of _fabricants_ to request
for accounts of balances with _chefs d'ateliers_ c. 1860,
ACCL, _Soieries_ Carton 41-I Législation-Usages (an 8 à 1936),
13.-Pétition remise à l'Empereur à son passage a Lyon, par
les ouvriers en soie.

B. ADR, 6M - _Dénombrement_, 1866, Lyon, 4ème arrondissement,
XVI, XVII.

Graph 10

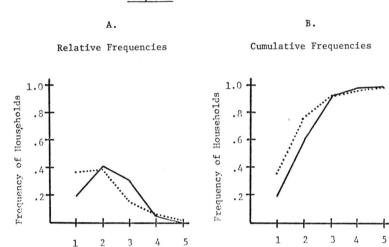

A.

Relative Frequencies

B.

Cumulative Frequencies

——— Croix-Rousse Sample 1866

····· Bellon-Conty Establishment 1866

The tables and graphs illustrate the much stronger tendency of the Bellon establishment to put out one loom of plain cloth per household (37% of all households) than of the plain-cloth households of the Croix-Rousse to possess only one loom (20% of the total). A relatively large percentage of Bellon's one-loom-occupied households very likely possessed more than one loom and therefore accepted orders from other <u>fabricants</u> at the same time. At the other extreme, Bellon's master-weavers who occupied four or five looms with his fabric probably had no obligation to any other <u>fabricants</u>, because these four or five looms were all they possessed. This is suggested by the slightly greater tendency of the Bellon households to concentrate in the four-and five-loom-occupied groups (8.33%)

in comparison with the movement of the Croix-Rousse households into these

same size groups for looms owned (7.40%).[3] The proportion of these four-

to five-loom-occupied households in the Bellon distribution was not large

in any case, at least not as compared with the two-or three-loom-occupied

households. These two latter groups represented in effect the transition

from the diffusion among several _fabricants_, or relative independence,

which seems to have been characteristic of the one-loom-occupied weavers

of the Bellon establishment, to the exclusive dependence on the _maison_

Bellon among the four-to five-loom-occupied weavers. The two-loom-occu-

pied Bellon weavers and especially the three-loom-occupied Bellon weavers

were both relatively less represented than their corresponding two-loom

households and three-loom households respectively in the Croix-Rousse

sample. Graph 10-A shows this most clearly. The two-loom group is the

'transition point' from relative abundance of Bellon households to rela-

tive dearth, in relation to the household sample of the Croix-Rousse.[4]

---

[3]Unlike the Bellon one-loom-occupied households, the Bellon four-or
five-loom-occupied households cannot be 'distributed' over the 'remainder'
of the Croix-Rousse sample included in the one-, two-, or three-loom cells,
because each household in the relevant cells must have at least four or
five looms. Hence a larger relative proportion for the Bellon sample, as
compared with the Croix-Rousse sample, suggests exclusive and total occupancy of the weavers' looms—that is, complete dependence on Bellon—in the
case of the four- and five-loom-occupied households, whereas a larger Bellon
proportion suggests diffusion of several _fabricants_ over several looms by
the weavers occupying only one loom with orders from Bellon—that is, their
relative independence of the Bellon establishment.

[4]This transition is in no way 'cushioned' or 'absorbed' by the four-
or five-loom-occupied or loom-owned household groups, if our conclusion of
'high' exclusiveness (complete dependence) is indeed correct for these.
The only 'cushion' is the non-represented household of six or more looms
which can absorb all others. The Croix-Rousse sample suggests that these
were rare.

One might say, very roughly, that the 'extra' two-or three-loom household

percentage in the Croix-Rousse sample above the percentage of households

fully occupied by the Bellon two-or three-loom-occupied groups, absorbed

the surplus percentage of Bellon one-loom-occupied households in two-or

three-loom-owned households with two or three different fabricants.

Chances were strong, in other words, that the merchant-manufacturer of

plain cloths occupying only two or three looms per household thus occupied

the entire household, but that many other households in the weaving dis-

trict owning two or three looms took only one order from that same mer-

chant-manufacturer and occupied the rest of their looms with orders from

one or two other fabricants. We might summarize these various tendencies

to exclusive occupation of looms in the weaver's household by one fabri-

cant in the following manner:

From the Perspective of the Fabricant		From the Perspective of the Weaver	
Number of Looms Occupied	Tendency to Exclusive-ness (Dependence of Weaver on this Single Fabricant)	Number of Looms Occupied	Tendency of Exclusive-ness (Dependence on One Fabricant)
1	Weak	1	Very Strong (Certain)
2,3	Strong	2,3	Weak
4,5	Very Strong	4,5	Uncertain (Probably Weak)

Returning to the same tables, we must now situate the importance of

each loom category--and of each degree of exclusive occupancy by a single

fabricant, associated with each loom category--within the entire Bellon
entreprise, on the one hand, and within the entire sample of plain-cloth
households in the Croix-Rousse, on the other. This will offer some indication of the distribution, of 'dependent' and 'independent' weaver-
fabricant relations, both from the perspective of the fabricant's enterprise, 'typified' by the Bellon establishment, and from that of the class
of master-weavers, 'typified' by the Croix-Rousse sample. Simple observation shows that within the Bellon establishment, some 40% of the weavers
occupied tended to be 'independents,' that is, were likely to weave for
other fabricants besides Bellon at the same time, and that the remaining
60% tended to depend more or less exclusively on orders from him. This
assumes that all 71 one-loom-occupied households were 'independent' (i.e.
37%), and that an additional 3% from the remaining 121 households was in
the same 'independent' category. The assumption is of course very strong
and the estimates are therefore subject to a large margin of error--for
the data is extremely inadequate--but the guess is not unreasonable.
Within the Croix-Rousse sample of plain-cloth households, about 20% of
the weavers was entirely dependent on the orders of a single fabricant,
with absolute certainty, for these weavers owned only one loom each; a
minimum 18%--the difference between the Croix-Rousse and Bellon percentages in the 2-3 loom category--was 'independent' with relatively high
certainty; and of the remaining 62%, about three-fifths (37%) was possibly
'dependent'--a figure based on the estimated proportion of 2 to 5 loom-
occupied households in the Bellon group dependent on Bellon alone (60%)--
and the remaining 25% was 'independent.' In sum, about 43% of the weavers
in the sample was 'independent' and about 57% 'dependent.' This propor-

tion is effectively the same as that of the Bellon group of households--
a not unreasonable conclusion if all plain-cloth fabricants occupied
their weavers, on the average, in the same proportion of 'independent'
and 'dependent' status, as the Bellon establishment. On the whole, therefore, dependence of the individual master-weaver on a single fabricant
seems to have been the dominant trend among plain-cloth households, at a
60:40 likelihood, although chances that such weavers might become 'independent' by occupying their several looms with the orders of several
fabricants simultaneously were not insignificant--probably 40% at least.

Appendix II:

Construction of Cost-of-Food Index

The cost-of-food index I traces the percentage change in costs of
three major food items from 1830 to 1878, relative to the base year 1830:
bread, meat and potatoes. The index I is computed from official prices
of bread (P_B), meat (P_M) and potatoes (P_p), quoted on the mercuriale of
the market of Lyons. The prices are used as proxies for expenditures
(E) on these items. According to one response of the Enquête Parlementaire of 1848 concerning conditions of industry in the city of Lyons, a
celibate worker spent at that time, on the average, about 65% of his annual budget on food. This food expenditure was shared among the different food items in the following way (daily expenditure):

bread	30 centimes	
meat	10 centimes	
wine	10 centimes	
soup	20 centimes	(1)
fruit, cheese, vegetables	20 centimes	
TOTAL	90 centimes per day[1]	

In the construction of the index, potatoes were used as a proxy
for fruit, vegetables and cheese. Fifteen centimes of the expense on
soup were divided equally among additional expenditures on bread, meat
and potatoes, since all three probably entered soup as major ingredients.
With these simplifications, food expenditures were itemized in the following manner:

---

[1] Yves Lequin, "Le monde ouvrier de la région lyonnaise dans la
deuxième moitié du XIXème siècle, 1848 à 1914" (unpublished thesis for
the Doctorat d'Etat, Université Lyon II, 1975), II, 168.

Item	Expenditure	% of Total Food Expenditure (E)	
bread (B)	35 centimes	47	
meat (M)	15 centimes	20	(2)
potatoes (P)	25 centimes	33	
total food expenditure (E)	75 centimes	100	

This total food expenditure (E) represented 83% of the actual average daily food expenditure given by the Enquête of 1848, and 54% of the average annual budget of a celibate weaver. Although this was only slightly more than half of the budget, the estimate is quite conservative. Since food was an item of first necessity, its proportion in the weaver's budget was more likely to increase at the expense of other items, especially in periods of low employment, low wages, or high food prices. Other items, such as clothing, benefited more from the income effect of low food prices, rather than the other way around, because of the relatively inelastic demand for basic food items. It is therefore not unreasonable to regard costs of food as dominating the costs of living throughout the period under study.

Since the mercuriale quoted only market prices (p) rather than quantities sold (q), some method of using prices as reasonable proxies for expenditures (pq) was needed. This method was derived by assuming that the quantity of each food item consumed remained constant for changes in their relative prices and that the quantity of all food consumed remained constant for changes in the relative prices of food and other items in the weaver's budget. These assumptions simplify the exposition and were probably not often discordant with 'reality,' since bread, meat and potatoes seem to have constituted staples of the weavers' diets (meat, in other words, was not a 'luxury good' among the weavers of Lyons), and thus were consumed in 'standard' amounts regardless of the relative price structure.

Given these assumptions, total expenditures (E) varied only with the variation in the prices of the three food items of which the index I was constructed. In symbolic terms, this may be expressed as:

$$E = P_B \bar{q}_B + P_M \bar{q}_M + P_P \bar{q}_P \tag{3}$$

where E = total food expenditure

P_B = unit price of bread $\bar{q}_B$ = quantity of bread consumed

P_M = unit price of meat $\bar{q}_M$ = quantity of meat consumed

P_P = unit price of potatoes $\bar{q}_P$ = quantity of potatoes consumed

$\bar{q}_B, \bar{q}_M, \bar{q}_P$ are all constant

The change of expenditure on food in one year relative to the total food expenditure on a previous (or common base) year may be expressed as dE/E, where dE equals the difference between the given year expenditure and the base year expenditure--the given year E minus the base year E. The value dE/E is the difference between the given year expenditure expressed as a percentage of the base year expenditure, and the base year value 100 (one hundred percent). This value dE/E is therefore labelled _i_, where _i_ signifies the increment (positive or negative) of a given year value, expressed as a percentage of the base year value, above or below the standard base value of 100. The value _i_ for each year after 1830 traces the percentile change in expenditure for that year relative to the expenditure of the base year 1830.

The problem is to compute i = dE/E using only the prices of the three food items--p_B, p_M, and p_P-- and assuming that the quantities of these items consumed remained constant throughout the period 1830-1878 ($\bar{q}_B$, $\bar{q}_M$, $\bar{q}_P$). Computation of an appropriate formula for $\underline{i}$ proceeds in the following manner: First, the total derivative of E with respect to p_B, p_M, and p_P is calcualted:

$$dE = \bar{q}_B dp_B + \bar{q}_M dp_M + \bar{q}_P dp_P \qquad (4)$$

Then $\underline{i}$ equals:

$$i = dE/E = (\bar{q}_B dp_B + \bar{q}_M dp_M + \bar{q}_P dp_P)/E \qquad (5a)$$

$$= \bar{q}_B dp_B/E + \bar{q}_M dp_M/E + \bar{q}_P dp_P/E \qquad (5b)$$

Let us now return to the table of itemized expenditures for the three food items (2). Assuming the relative proportion of each item in this table is valid and unchanged for the entire period, 1830-1878, the expenditure on each item can be expressed as a separate but constant proportion of the total expenditure E. In other words:

Expenditure on bread	=	$p_B \bar{q}_B$	= .47 E
Expenditure on meat	=	$p_M \bar{q}_M$	= .20 E
Expenditure on potatoes	=	$p_P \bar{q}_P$	= .33 E
Total food expenditure	=	E	= 1.00 E

(6)

Solving for E in each equation in (6) gives:

$$E = p_B \bar{q}_B/.47$$
$$E = p_M \bar{q}_M/.20 \qquad (7)$$
$$E = p_P \bar{q}_P/.33$$

Now substituting the values for E in the expression (5b) for $\underline{i}$ in the following manner:

$$i = dE/E = \bar{q}_B dp_B/(p_B \bar{q}_B/.47) + \bar{q}_M dp_M/(p_M \bar{q}_M/.20)$$
$$+ \bar{q}_P dp_P/(p_P \bar{q}_P/.33) \qquad (8)$$

and simplifying and cancelling terms gives:

$$i = dE/E = .47\ dp_B/p_B + .20\ dp_M/p_M + .33\ dp_P/p_P$$
$$= .47\ i_B + .20\ i_M + .33\ i_P \qquad (9)$$

where $i_B = dp_B/p_B$ = percentile increment in bread prices relative to price of bread in base year (1830)

$i_M = dp_M/p_M$ = percentile increment in meat prices relative to price of meat in base year (1830)

$i_P = dp_P/p_P$ = percentile increment in potato prices relative to price of potatoes in base year (1830)

For each year after 1830, then, the percentile increment in food expenditures i is calculated as a linear function of the percentile increments in food prices i_B, i_M, and i_P. The cost-of-food index I, charted on Graph 5, Chapter III, is simply the sum of i and the base value 100, or

$$I = 100 + i = 100 + (.47\ i_B + .20\ i_M + .33\ i_P).$$

Note on Sources

The prices of bread, meat, potatoes are calculated from the mercuriales for the department of the Rhône available in A.N. series F11*. The mercuiales were quoted twice each month (approximately every two weeks) on the major markets of the department--the market of Lyons, for the arrondissement of Lyon, and the markets of Beaujeu, Belleville and Tarare, for the arrondissement of Villefranche. The market of Lyons dominated prices in most other markets of the department, so that movements in departmental averages very nearly approximate movements for the city of Lyons. Bread prices were usually quoted per kilogram, separately for three kinds of bread--pain blanc (best quality), pain bis-blanc (medium quality) and pain bis (poorest quality). Prices for pain bis-blanc were used for the index I. Meat prices included separate quotations for beef, mutton, and pork, per kilogram. The average of the three was used for the single meat price index. Potato prices were quoted per quintal.

For the years 1830-1836 and 1860-1878, yearly averages of mercuriale quotations were used to arrive at a single annual price for each item. These yearly averages were easily calculated from the monthly averages recorded concisely in A.N. F11*-2848-2849 (for 1825-1836) and in A.N. F11*-2850 à 2857 (for 1860-1878). For the years 1837-1859, however, the mercuriales in the archives (A.N. F11-1924*, ..., 2187*) are recorded separately for each month. Limitations on consultation privileges and on research time required selection of one 'base' month for each year during this interval. This did not allow, of course, computation of the yearly average. The month of January was chosen, so that the index I for the period 1837-1859 consists only of movements of prices from one January to the next, rather than from one year's average to the next.

Appendix III:

Use of Membership List of

Société Civile des Tisseurs

As a Source for Loom Data

In Tables 11 (Chapter IV) and 40 (Chapter VII), the membership list
of the silk-weavers' resistance federation, the Société civile de prévoyance et de renseignements pour le travail des tisseurs de la fabrique
lyonnaise (abbreviated SCPR: List of Members, July 5, 1873, ADR, 10M-2,
Associations d'ouvriers tisseurs (1870-93)) was used as a proxy for a
loom census in estimating the changes in distribution of looms in the
city by cloth category and by neighborhood from 1844-46 to 1873. A proxy
was required for the latter year because of the lack of a census of looms
for the entire city with type and neighborhood specifications since 1846.
This list promised to serve well as such a proxy. The span of membership
of the SCPR covered the entire city and, with very few exceptions, only
the city. The membership promised, moreover, to reflect closely the
character of the silk-weaving population as a whole, because SCPR was a
'mass' organization. The information concerning each member, finally,
was sufficiently detailed to permit the tabulation of membership distribution by cloth category and by neighborhood of residence.

The list was submitted to the prefecture of the Rhône about one year
before the prefect dissolved the Société civile. The prefecture had
requested the list in August 1872. Apparently, the very large size of
the association (11,137 members) delayed the final completion of the list
until July 1873. (See letter from Pally, Rochet, Mathé aîné to Minister
Commerce, September (?) 1874, ADR, 10M-2, Associations d'ouvriers tisseurs
(1870-93).)

Because of this delay, it is likely that the list includes all weavers
who signed the registers of the Society at any time during the intervening years (plus members still on the registers in August 1872) and
not only members remaining in July 1873. In other words, there is
little chance that a large drop-out rate, incurred as a result of unemployment throughout the year, for example, made the list seriously unrep-
resentative of the weaving masses.

For each individual member, the list gives name, exact address
(street and house number), and cloth category—one of the ten categories
which originally constituted the SCPR. From these specifications, the
distribution of members by cloth category and by arrondissement can be
determined. The question nevertheless remains, whether this membership
data can properly serve as a reliable proxy for loom data, with which it
is compared in Tables 11 and 40. The two sets of data—loom data for
1844-46 and membership data for 1873—are comparable only if we assume:

1.) a fixed ratio of x occupied looms in 1873 per member of the SCPR,

2.) similar levels of employment of looms and members in both years, and

3.) either the representation of all occupied looms in the fabrique by
the membership of the SCPR or the randomness of the sample of looms represented by the members of the SCPR relative to the entire population of
looms in the city in 1873. The second assumption is most easily accepted,
the third probably valid and the first questionable.

As for the second assumption, both periods represented by loom and membership data respectively—1844-46 and 1872-1873—were prosperous years in
the fabrique, so that levels of employment of looms and of weavers were likely
to have been similar. Moreover, most weavers joining the SCPR were likely

to have been employed at the time of their entry into the organization, because its purpose was defense of piece-rates, not preservation of employment, and because it was financed by portions of the piece-rate paid its members for weaving silks. They had to be working to pay these dues. Even presuming some unemployment during the period in which the list was compiled, the delay in completing this compilation gave the organization more time to enroll weavers working at some time during this interval, so that the final list reflected a situation of full employment more closely than the total actual membership at any particular time. (The year 1872-1873 was not a time of exceptional unemployment.)

The third assumption is probable, at least for the purpose for which the data are used in this study. No single cloth category or section of the city had more or less reason to join the organization. For this reason, all categories and 'neighborhoods' were equally likely to join, so that for practical purposes the list can be considered statistically as good as a random sample for its use in this study.

The first assumption is more questionable. The organization served weavers alone, and so all of its members—or nearly all of them—represented at least one loom and, for reasons mentioned above, this loom was occupied sometime during the period in which the list was compiled. The number of looms represented by each member, however, is obscure. Journeymen weavers 'typically' represented only one occupied loom. (I say 'typically' because conceivably, two or more journeymen members of the SCPR could have worked at the same loom at different times of its activity during the period of compilation of the list, so that each represented 'statistically' only a fraction of a loom.) Master-weavers 'typically'

represented the number of occupied looms in their household, which might
have been one or more, depending on the number of looms they owned and
on the state of activity of their looms during the period of compilation.
This uncertainty is compounded by the fact that journeymen and masters,
considered as 'representatives' of looms, were not mutually exclusive
sets and therefore cannot simply be 'added' (even when presuming a certain loom-weight for each) to obtain the total number of looms represented in the SCPR. Surely some of the journeymen and journeywomen members of the SCPR worked on the looms belonging to the masters in the
same organization and thus reduced the effective loom-weight of the
latter. To the extent that this occurred, however, the assumption of
one member of the SCPR representing one loom becomes more probable.
(The master himself presumably worked at least one loom in all cases.)
It is unfortunately impossible to know to what extent this did occur and
therefore impossible to assign to each member a loom-representation
weight, even presuming we knew whether each was a master or a journeyman
weaver (which we do not know).

There are two consolations to these apparently insuperable difficulties concerning the first assumption. First, the number of looms per
household, hence per master, was likely to be quite low (2 or 3 at most)
in 1872-1873, after the crisis of the 1860's had reduced the number of
looms each household could support. Because of this small number of
looms per household, the difference in loom representativeness between
master and journeyman was reduced significantly. Second, this reduction
was probably greatest for the fancy-cloth category of looms and members,
since the intersection of the journeymen set and master set was likely

to be strongest in this category (that is, strongest tendency for journeymen members to weave for master members of the SCPR). Journeymen
fancy-cloth weavers were likely to have been more 'settled' in the city
than journeymen plain-cloth weavers and were thus more likely to join
the SCPR than the latter. Moreover, many journeymen, members of the
SCPR, were active during the fancy-weavers' strike in June–July–1870
--more than one would expect from the low employment in their category--
and this suggests that nearly all journeymen fancy-cloth weavers were
members of the resistance federation. Among journeymen plain-cloth
weavers, on the contrary, there were probably still many 'floating'
journeymen who did not join the SCPR, because of their 'uprooted' situation. Consequently, the statistical distribution of the membership of
the SCPR by cloth category is more likely to overestimate the proportions for the fancy-cloth category, when membership is used as a proxy
for looms and when each member of the SCPR is given the same 'loom-
weight.'

For the use of the SCPR list in Table 11 (Chapter IV), this latter
conclusion is especially welcome. The table is used to demonstrate the
relative decline in fancy-cloth weaving as compared with plain-cloth
weaving. If the proportion of fancy-weaving members was in fact an
overestimate of the proportion of fancy-cloth looms--as seems to be the
case--this relative decline in fancy-cloth weaving is more than adequately confirmed by the table. The use of the list in Table 40 (Chapter
VII) is less fraught with dangers of comparing loom proportions for an
earlier census with membership proportions for the later date. The
table compares distributions of loom types for the different arrondissements of the city synchronically. In other words, the table focusses

on one period alone (1871-1873, the period of compilation of the list) and uses the same source to invoke the comparison. The 'neighborhood' analysis in Chapter VII does not require a comparison of loom-type proportions as such, but only a comparison of the extent of 'contact' of weavers with the more elegant specialties of the fabrique among the different neighborhoods. Such concentration may have been the result of relatively more fancy-cloth looms in the Croix-Rousse as compared with the Brotteaux-Guillotière, or it may simply have been the effect of more workers 'associated' with each fancy cloth loom, on the average, in the first neighborhood than in the second. Such association may have been the result of frequent changes of weavers on each fancy-cloth loom in the Croix-Rousse, for example, because of the short duration of orders given to each. In either case, the more extensive contact of the Croix-Rousse with the 'elite' specialties of the craft would have been accurately reflected simply by the category distribution of members of the SCPR.

Appendix IV:

Use of Police Reports on the State of

Industry for Analyses of

Conditions of Employment and

of Wage Movements and Levels

1859-1870

In Chapter IV, the study of conditions of employment and of wage
movements and levels in the fabrique lyonnaise during the 1860's relied
exclusively on trimestrial reports by the local police on the state of
the silk industry in Lyons. These reports, the "Situations industrielles" in AML, I2-47 (A), Situation de l'industrie lyonnaise: . . .
rapports sur la soierie et les ouvriers en soie . . . (1819 à 1870),
were compiled by the Special Police Commissioner at the Prefecture of
the Rhône from notes of police agents, such as the "Rapports à Monsieur
Delcourt, Commissaire spécial, sur la situation de la fabrique des
étoffes de soies," in AML, ibid. The agents' notes and the Commissioner's reports both specify the exact range of wages prevailing in the
urban fabrique at the end of each trimester and, more impressionistically,
the levels, stability and 'quality' (favored specialty) of employment,
both during the trimester and at its end, in each of the six cloth categories discussed in Chapter IV and in each of several auxiliary and
other related sectors of the fabrique, such as dévidage and tissage de
tulles. Each trimestrial note and report also includes general observations on the industry as a whole--such as the nature of product demand

and the sources of current 'crises' of unemployment--and observations
on the economic conditions of the silk workers--their poverty or prosperity, apprenticeship, and female labor. Some of these miscellaneous
observations are also included occasionally in the separate reports on
each cloth category or auxiliary branch of the silk industry.

The quality of the writing of the agents' notes, especially its
grammar, spelling and puncuation, and their detail suggest that the
agents were both 'of the people' and very knowledgeable of the trade.
They were probably silk weavers, former weavers or residents of silk-
weaving neighborhoods. The information they offer is specific and
apparently accurate. Even when reporting weavers' opinions on the conditions of their trade, they are faithful to their sources. They report
unfavorable opinions along with the favorable, even when the former are
critical or damaging to the imperial regime. Perhaps partly because of
their lack of education and cultivation, the agents demonstrate little
tendency to interpret facts, events and opinions, but simply reproduce
what they see and hear. The historian of social and economic conditions
could have few sources more reliable than these agents' reports for
communicating the same information.

The agents' sources are not always evident from the documents. We
can therefore only speculate on their character and reliability. The
weavers' expressions of opinions reported by these agents had the quality
of quotation and indicate that the agents received some of their information, at least, by visiting the weavers' quarters and discussing
industrial conditions with them. Among the information they seem to
have received in this manner were wage data. Wages, specified to the

centime, were daily earnings of journeymen weavers, and their source was
either the journeymen themselves and/or master-weavers. In either case
a selected 'trustworthy' few were probably consulted for each report.
Information concerning conditions of employment, especially approxima-
tions of levels of employment, came more likely from certain fabricants,
from the Chamber of Commerce, or from the Conseil des Prud'hommes.
Their information on employment, though not comprehensive, was more
current than that of the prefecture itself, which took censuses of
active and inactive looms only occasionally, and was informed by a wider
vision than that of the master or journeymen weavers. Other information,
such as that concerning cloth specialties favored by the market or the
conditions of apprentices, was probably secured from weavers or from
fabricants according to their proximity to the matter. Or this information may have been simply gleaned from general impressions made by
both in the course of discussion. In any case, the agents' final observations do not seem to suffer from any lack of precision or accuracy
not evident from the notes themselves.

Unfortunately, the agents' notes have not been preserved for the
entire decade of the 1860's. As a result, this source could not be
used for constructing systematic wage series and for reading employment
conditions for the decade as required in Chapter IV. Instead, the
chapter relies on the summaries of the notes in the reports by the
Special Police Commissioner on the "Situations industrielles" of the
fabrique. These have not only the advantage of more complete coverage
of the decade than the original notes, but also the advantage of more
systematic and clearer presentation of wages and employment conditions

than the notes. This presentation allows the investigator to follow the same issues from one trimester to the next without 'getting lost' in too much extra data pertinent only to one trimester. The major disadvantage of the reports, however, is their slightly stronger tendency to interpret events, trends and statistics. This tendency derives partly from their systematic, summary quality and partly, perhaps, from the intellectual culture of the Special Commissioner who also was not as familiar, by training or by intimate acquaintance, with the technical and social details of the _fabrique_ as were his agents. This disadvantage nevertheless did not lessen the utility of these reports for the analytic purposes of Chapter IV.

Nature and Utility of Employment Information

Information concerning conditions of employment leaves much to be desired, especially for the purposes of quantitative analysis. In most reports, employment conditions are not specified beyond general indications, such as "recovery" or "decline," "great activity" or "little activity," "satisfactory" or "unsatisfactory," "good" or "bad." In all these pairs, the first predicate referred indiscriminately to an increase or to a regularity of number of looms active, of number of weavers working at the loom and of number of cloth orders put out. Such rising trends all suggest prosperity or at least activity, at some level of the _fabrique_. The second predicate referred to a decrease in all or some of these numbers or to a stagnation at a low level, indicating actual or oncoming depression. Because of this indiscriminate 'lumping' of three different signs of economic prosperity or depression--all of

which affected rates of employment, to be sure, but not all in the same
way or at the same time or pace--it is impossible to specify exactly
how often, how long and at what rate[1] the silk weavers were working at
their trade during any particular trimester.

Usually the police observers were more interested in whether or not
the weavers were idle than in business prosperity or economic growth as
such. Idleness, in their minds, bred agitation, created fertile soil
for political opposition to the regime and therefore needed to be recognized immediately and eliminated, preferably by useful employment in
the private sector. The comments of the police on the state of the
industry therefore presumably reflected, above all, their interpretation
of the prospects for falling or rising idleness among the weavers.
Whether such interpretation was based on actual observation of more
urban weavers working or merely on rising output or sales of silk cloth
by fabricants is not always clear from these general reports. If the
second basis was the grounds for the optimistic interpretation, this
interpretation was very weak. Rising output or sales of silks could be
achieved by putting out more orders or orders of longer duration to
weavers already employed part-time, by putting out more orders to the
countryside, or by selling accumulated inventories, none of which would
raise the number of employed workers in the city. Moreover, the extent
of employment or unemployment of workers and looms in relation to the
total number of workers employed or looms active in 'normal' times (that

---

[1]That is, the number of weavers in relation to all weavers seeking
work in their trade.

is, before 1860), on the one hand, or in relation to the total number
of weavers seeking work in their trade, or of looms present in the
weavers' households, on the other hand, is not specified either. As a
result, 'rates of employment' are also impossible to evaluate at any
particular time. In some reports, the proportion of weavers employed
or the proportion of looms active in relation to a total is indicated
as two-thirds, one-half, or three-quarters of workers or looms, for
example. But failure to specify which totals are used as standards of
comparison (for example, proportion of weavers currently seeking work
in their trade, or proportion of weavers 'normally' employed) and failure to use one or another proportion (of looms or of workers) regularly
weakens the value of these proportions for specifying rates of employment at any particular time and also weakens them for tracing changes in
these rates with any quantitative exactness.

Even these very inadequate reports on employment conditions, however, can serve as useful indicators of comparative prosperity or depression among the six cloth categories when examined over a relatively long
period of time, such as a decade. They may not indicate clearly whether
weavers are working in greater numbers, for longer hours, or at higher
rates (in relation to a total) in a particular cloth category as compared with the immediate past. But they do indicate whether weavers
would tend to remain in the trade of their training and skill, or to
return to this trade, and they also would indicate generally how strong
or weak this tendency would have been in one cloth category as compared
with another. Such tendencies are suggested, with reasonable confidence,
by the history of prosperity and depression in each category, raising or

lowering expectations of rising employment or of continuing high levels
of employment in the future. Such a history is 'constructed' from the
frequency and persistence of "satisfactory" and "unsatisfactory" observations on the state of the fabrique over two or more years. Inter-
preting employment information in this manner presumes that "satisfactory" observations eventually (that is, within one or two years) become
translated into a rising demand for labor and probably also into a rise
in the number of urban weavers at work, and that "unsatisfactory" observations have the opposite effect. Such an assumption is not unreasonable for the fabrique, even during the 1860's.

Such an interpretation of employment reports also permits differ-
entiation of employment trends by specialty as well as by cloth category.
In this way, the transformation of 'vertical' craft solidarity can be
observed not only between cloth categories but also within each category.
Chapter IV examines the evolution of employment primarily in comparative
fashion, among different cloth categories and specialties, and therefore
does not strain the sources upon which its argument is based beyond their
credibility and exactness. The discussion of conditions of employment in
section II-A of the chapter presumes, of course, the particular notions
of employment and unemployment described above; namely, tendencies based
on expectation rather than necessarily actual increases in numbers of
weavers employed or unemployed during any particular trimester.

Nature and Utility of Wage Data

Wage data present problems of interpretation similar to those of
employment information and also lend themselves to similar use. As

indicated earlier in this appendix and in the text of Chapter IV, these

data describe daily earnings of journeymen weavers in each cloth cate-

gory. They provide no direct information, however, concerning the level

of the piece-rate,[2] the length of the working day, and the productivity

of the journeymen weavers, all of which influenced the average level of

journeymen's earnings. Moreover, these data are averages of daily earn-

ings of journeymen differing perhaps in some or all of these matters,

for one or several of the following reasons: 1) they worked on cloths

put out by different fabricants and therefore may have received differ-

ent piece-rates for the same type of work; 2) they had different working

habits, or they worked for masters with different working schedules,

causing variations in the length of the working day; or 3) they had

different physical capacities or skills and thus wove more or less pro-

ductively for each hour worked. Besides these possible variations

within each average wage, the constitution of the average also remains

a mystery. It is impossible to determine whether it is a simple average

of a carefully selected sample of journeymen, an average weighted by

some criteria--such as the three elements mentioned above--or simply an

impression based on discussions with a few 'trusted' journeymen and

masters. For all of these reasons, the exact meaning of each wage value--

---

[2]The piece-rate was usually paid by the fabricant to the master-
weaver rather than to the journeyman working on the loom. The master
received a certain salaire calculated as the piece-rate (so many centimes
per unit of cloth) times the length of the cloth. The master then gave
one-half of this salaire to the journeyman working at the loom. In some
cases, the fabricant paid the salaire directly to the journeyman, who
then gave the master a portion for rental of loom, light, dévidage, and
so forth. In both instances, the fabricant determined the piece-rate.
The manner of dividing the salaire between master and journeyman thus
had no impact on its amount.

its constituents (piece-rate, length of working day, productivity) and
their relative importance in determining an average wage--are obscure.
Consequently, any effort to extrapolate from the wage back into any of
its components, such as levels of piece-rates and rates of employment,
would be a vain endeavor.

Certain characteristics of these wages and of the manner of reporting them in the "Situations industrelles" nevertheless make these data
useful for the analytic purposes of Chapter IV. Unlike most reports on
conditions of employment, wage reports are both numerically precise and
static readings at a single point in time--at the date of the trimestrial
report--rather than averages for the entire trimester. Because of this
exactitude and temporal specificity, these wages are not distorted by
averaging over time. The average wages reported, in other words,
represent only daily earnings of currently employed weavers. These
weavers may indeed have differed in the number of hours worked each day,
but this synchronic variation in daily employment was probably not very
large, especially not during the crisis decade of the 1860's, when
weavers accepted whatever work they could find and remained at work as
long as possible. It is reasonably certain, therefore, that daily
earnings of most weavers working at the end of the trimester during the
1860's were at or near the level indicated in the reports.

Another advantage of these wage reports is their specification of
several different averages for each cloth category, notably their indication of a minimum wage and of a maximum wage for each. These reports
are made in several different ways, such as "The wage _salaire_ varies
between 1.75 _francs_ and 2.25 _francs_" and "The average wage varies among

2.10 francs, 2.40 and 3.60." In all cases, I interpreted the minimum
reported wage as that of the 'common' specialty within each category,
and the maximum wage as that of the 'rich' specialty. This interpretation seemed reasonable, especially given the context in which wages
were usually reported--immediately following the report of employment
conditions in each of the separate specialties. In a few cases, the
attribution of the maximum wage to the 'rich' specialties and of the
minimum wage to the 'common' specialties was made explicit in the text
and presumed that minimum and maximum wages had the same implicit attribution even when this was not stated explicitly. This indication of
daily earnings by specialty not only provides further confirmation of
the exactness of wage reporting but also permits a comparative analysis
of wage movements and levels by specialty as well as by cloth category.

In fact, it is precisely for such comparative analysis that these
wage data are especially useful. Wages for all categories and for all
specialties were read at the same time, and all were based on the
earnings of employed journeymen. Because of this derivation of wage
data from the employed only, differences in employment conditions among
categories and specialties probably did not affect relative wages among
these very much. Moreover, differences in the length of the working day
probably also had little impact on relative wages during the 1860's,
when all employed weavers seemed to work long days. The only remaining
cause of synchronic variation in wages among categories and specialties,
besides the piece-rate, was productivity. This varied primarily as a
function of skill, and such variation was probably reflected in corresponding differences of piece-rates, the more difficult cloth categories and

specialties commanding a higher piece-rate. Relative wages, as reported
in the "Situations industrielles," therefore were probably good proxies
for relative piece-rates of the categories and specialties, even though
the importance of the piece-rate in determining the absolute size of the
wage in each category or specialty remained obscure.

Chapter IV profits from these characteristics of the reported wage
data by examining movements and levels of wages of different cloth categories and specialties comparatively, and by focusing on the effects of
relative earnings rather than on the constituents of each level of
earnings. Such an examination provides the information needed to assess
the nature and sources of changing 'vertical' solidarity of craft, for
which the analysis was primarily designed. Such assessment requires
neither knowledge of the movement of wages nor information concerning
rates of employment between wage readings. It requires only the observation of shifts of position of the daily wage of one category or specialty
relative to another, from one reading to the next. The absolute increase
or decrease of piece-rate in any single category or specialty and the
rise or fall of total annual earnings of any one are immaterial for
this analysis of 'vertical' solidarity. For this reason, wage movements
can be analyzed meaningfully, for the purposes of the chapter, without
a continuous wage series and without knowledge of the effects of reported
wage levels on total annual earnings.

In the discussion of the effects of wage movements and levels on
'vertical' craft solidarity, the chapter offers occasional explanations
of 'absolute' wage movements and traces the sources of such movements
in changing levels of the piece-rate. Such explanations are intended

to be merely intelligent guesses, not confirmed hypotheses. They
presume a strong reflection of piece-rate movements in wage movements--
a stronger reflection, perhaps, than the wage data warrant with confidence. These explanations intend, primarily, therefore, to provoke
further reflection and research. The main concern of the chapter lies
elsewhere, in any case, than in the causes of wage movements and levels.
This concern is the effects of such movements on vertical solidarity of
craft.

To facilitate presentation of the argument, the graphs in the
chapter average trimestrial wage data for the same category and specialty
on a yearly basis. Correlation analysis of the wage series, however,
uses the entire series of trimester data, without any inter-temporal
averaging. In the case of trimesters missing from some reports but not
from others, I estimated missing wages as simple averages between the
wage levels of prior and succeeding trimesters. In this way, all wage
series were given the same number of trimestrial components--twenty-nine
in all.

Appendix V:

Description of Census Data and Method of

Sampling Households From Census

The census data used in this study, especially in Chapter V, were
extracted from three separate sources: the registers of households in
the fiscal census of the town of the Croix-Rousse in 1847 (AML, Recensement, Croix-Rousse, 1847); the registers of households in the population
census of the Croix-Rousse in 1851 (ADR, 6M-Dénombrement, Croix-Rousse,
Tomes XXIII-XXIV); and the registers of households in the population
census of the Fourth Arrondissement (the Croix-Rousse as incorporated
into the city of Lyons in 1852) in 1866 (ADR, 6M-Dénombrement, 1866,
Lyon, 4éme arrondissement, Tomes XVI, XVII). The dénombrements of 1851
and 1866 are handwritten copies of the original census manuscripts--
probably second or third copies[1]--and copyists changed throughout the
registers, as indicated by changes of handwriting and sometimes by names
of copyists specified in an introductory ledger. The change was not
very frequent, however, in the district of the Croix-Rousse (Fourth
Arrondissement) from which the household samples were taken. The fiscal
census of the Croix-Rousse for 1847 seems to have been transcribed by
the same person. It is apparently, also, a copy of the manuscript censuses but closer to the original than the copies of the 1851 and 1866
censuses (that is, a first copy), as indicated by the frequent strike-
overs and generally sloppy appearance.

---

[1]Interview with Yves Lequin, Caluire, France, January 1974.

Nature of the Information Available

As indicated in Chapter V, the kind of information available for these three censuses is similar in several respects but not entirely comparable. Table 45 below summarizes, in comparative fashion, the information concerning several different economic and social characteristics available in these three sources.

Table 45:

Comparative Summary of Information Available
in Censuses of 1847, 1851 and 1866 of the
Croix-Rousse (Fourth Arrondissement)

Economic or Social Characteristic Concerning	1847	1851	1866
Head of Household			
Name	x	x	x
Address (Number & Street)	x	x	x
Occupation (a)	x	x	x
Civil Status (b)	x	x	x
Age	x	x	x
Place of Birth	x		
Family of Head			
Resident Children			
Number	x	x	x
Ages (d)	x	x (exact)	x (exact)
Sexes	x	x	x
Occupations		x	x
Children in Nursing	x		
Resident Parents	x		
Spouse			
Maiden Name		x	x
Age		x	x
Occupation (a)		x	x
Looms in Household			
Occupied (Active) Looms			
Number	x		x
Type (c)	x		x

Table 45: (Continued)

Economic or Social Characteristic Concerning	1847	1851	1866
Looms in Household			
Unoccupied (Inactive) Looms			
Number	x		x
Type (c)			x
Other Household Residents			
Number	x	x	x
Ages		x	x
Sexes	x	x	x
Occupations (a)	x (some)	x	x
Surnames		x	x
'States' (Journeyman, etc.) (e)	x		
Other Household Information			
Rents, etc. (f)	x		

Notes: a. The specificity of occupational information is extremely
varied within each census register as well as between yearly
registers. In all cases, the profession of weaver (tisseur
or ouvrier en soie) is unambiguous. Frequently, the 'state'
of the weaver is specified also--chef d'atelier (master-
weaver), ouvrier tisseur or compagnon tisseur (journeyman
weaver), or apprenti (apprentice weaver). Certain weaving
professions differing by technique and household organization are also differentiated, such as tullistes, sometimes
with 'states', such as 'ouvrier tulliste' for a journeyman
weaver of tulles. Auxiliary tasks are always distinguished
from weaving proper; that is, dévideuses, plieurs, liseurs,
and so forth are specified as such. For other trades, the
same variety of distinction prevails, but the specification
of 'state' is haphazard. Only in the 1847 census is the
'state' of subordinate workers in the household specified
systematically. Moreover, in 1847 and 1866, the 'state'
of the household head can usually be inferred from the presence or absence of looms. In these cases, masters had looms
in their households, whereas journeymen had none.

b. Civil status is specified as one of the following six types:
unmarried male, married male, widowed male; unmarried female,
married female, widowed female. Such specification thus indicates both marital state and sex.

c. Looms are distinguished according to one of the following types: uni, façonné, velours, châle, tulle, bas, passemen-terie.

d. In the 1847 fiscal census, only two categories of ages of resident children are specified--children less than 10 years, and children aged 10 or above. In the 1851 and 1866 censuses, the exact age of each resident child is given.

e. The 'states' specified in the 1847 fiscal census are: domestic, journeyman, apprentice, pensioner.

f. The other household information in the 1847 census is the fol-lowing: rents of household and shop, floor of household, number of rooms, numbers of doors and windows, number of dévidage machines distinguished by type (round or elongated).

As indicated in Chapter V, certain information available in one census can be inferred, given certain assumptions, from one or both addi-tional censuses in order to establish comparable, or nearly comparable, information. For example, kin relations of members of the household to the head (blood relations or marital relations) can be reasonably inferred, for the 1851 and 1866 censuses, by comparing surnames of members of the household with those of the head and with those of his spouse. In the 1847 census, comparable kin relations can be inferred by counting all residents classified by state--domestics, journeyworkers, and apprentices--as non-relatives, and the remainder of the household (spouses, parents, children) as relatives. Inferences in both cases (1851-1866 and 1847) are obviously liable to certain errors--in the first case, the error of missing distant relations with the surname of neither head nor spouse, or the error of counting as relatives non-kin with (coincidentally) the same surname, and in the second case, the error of ignoring relatives apprenticed to the master or working or living in his household as domestic or journeyworker. The danger, in my opinion, is greatest in the second case. Yet the lia-bility to error is probably not sufficiently great to justify invalidating

most conclusions concerning kin relations advanced in this study. These
conclusions are reasonable, albeit tentative, until further research in
more precise documents of comparable scope (if such do indeed exist) can
be undertaken.

Method of Sampling Households

The samples of households taken from the three census registers
were originally intended to provide an independent perspective on the
economic and social characteristics of silk weavers of their neighborhoods to compare with the same characteristics of members of silk-weavers'
associations residing in the same neighborhoods of the Croix-Rousse. The
selection of the samples was therefore guided primarily by the residential
patterns of a sample of household members of several weavers' associations
which could be traced in the registers, especially in the register of
1866--the year when data for individual members of associations were most
abundant.[2] Such a selection criterion would permit a more meaningful
analysis of the relationships between social and economic change and voluntary association among the silk weavers than indiscriminate sampling of
weavers' households in the city as a whole.

All members of associations residing in the Croix-Rousse and traced
in the 1866 census were distributed by street of residence. Those streets
with the largest number of traced association members were used as the
basis for selecting the 'independent' sample of Croix-Rousse households.

---

[2]The associations for which the members were traced in the censuses,
the number of successful tracings for each association and the number of
silk weavers among these tracings are tabulated in George Sheridan, "Idéologies et structures sociales dans les associations ouvrières à Lyon, de
1848 à 1877," Bulletin du Centre d'Histoire économique et sociale de la
Région lyonnaise, 1976, No. 2, 10.

In order to form a more geographically coherent sample, a few streets in the outlying regions of the Croix-Rousse were excluded. The sample therefore includes only streets in the eastern region of this district (east of the Grande Rue de Cuire), where the great majority of traced members of associations resided.

The sample size was set arbitrarily at 250 households. The distribution of these 250 households by street was the same as that of the households in the sample of association members. In other words, the proportion of households in the latter sample located on a particular street determined the proportion of the 250 households in the 'independent' sample on the same street and therefore the number of households to be selected from that street for this second sample. The households were then selected 'systematically'; that is, the total number of households on the street was divided by the number to be selected from that street, giving a quotient n and then each n-th household on that street was selected from the register, in order of listing, beginning with the first household on the street. To reduce systematic bias, the selection procedure was varied, in more or less random fashion, by starting with the second or third household on the street (as listed in the register), instead of the first, and sometimes also by sampling households at varying intervals on the same street (taking the n-th, m-th, s-th and t-th households, for example, instead of every n-th household).

Circumstances of research, including the condition of the census registers and the time and resources available for sampling, were partially responsible for this method of selecting the 'independent' sample. Such circumstances were also responsible for slight differences in sample

size for the years 1851 and 1847 as compared with 1866. Additions of
new streets between 1847 and 1866 in the sampling area also caused
such inter-temporal variations in sample size. To correct for such
variations, the 'raw' samples taken in the archives were pruned even
further, so that sample size, street representation and even distribution of households by street would be exactly comparable. The method
of random selection, with a table of random digits, was used to prune
the relatively over-sized street sample for one year down to a size
equal to that of the year with which the former was to be compared. By
means of such pruning, two sets of comparable, equally-sized samples
were constructed, including households of weavers and non-weavers in
the eastern section of the Croix-Rousse. One set compares samples for
1847 and 1866, and the other set compares samples for 1851 and 1866.
Table 46 below indicates the streets represented in each set of samples
and the number of households in each sample.

Table 46:

Distribution of Sample Households by Street

Samples for 1847 and 1866 (a)		Samples for 1851 and 1866 (a)		Total Number of Households on This Street in 1866
Name of Street	Number of Households	Name of Street	Number of Households	
Fossés – Austerlitz (b)	30	Fossés – Austerlitz (b)	30	354
Chariot d'Or	20	Chariot d'Or	20	270
Place de la Croix-Rousse	18			289
Grande Rue de la Croix-Rousse	57			937
Gloriettes	16	Gloriettes	16	195
Henry IV – Ivry (b)	30	Henry IV – Ivry (b)	30	320
Mail	50	Mail	50	413
Chapeau Rouge – Saint Vincent de Paul (b)	30	Chapeau Rouge – Saint Vincent de Paul (b)	30	301
Place de la Visitation	8	Place de la Visitation	8	107
Dumenge	9			243
Dumont d'Urville	8	Dumont d'Urville	8	107
Petite Rue des Gloriettes	5	Petite Rue des Gloriettes	5	12
Pailleron	5			217
Pavillon	5			74
Montée Rey	5	Montée Rey	5	117
		Visitation	25	259
		Sainte Rose	5	100
TOTALS	296		232	4,315

Notes: a. Two samples were taken from the 1866 census, one for comparison with the sample from the 1847 census and the other for comparison with the sample from the 1851 census.

b. Hyphenated street names indicate changes of name between the two census years. The first name is that of the earlier census year, the second name that of the later census year.

Construction of Entrepreneurial

Index Ie

The value Ie was computed for each household in the samples of
weavers' households in 1847 and 1866 for which loom data are available.
Ie takes a value from - 1 (zero entrepreneurship) to + 1 (highest entrepreneurship). As indicated in Chapter V, it is computed on the basis of
comparison of the number of occupied looms in the household with the
total number of persons residing in the household and old enough to weave;
that is, all persons aged 14 or above in 1866, including the head of the
household and spouse, and all aged 10 or above in 1847. (The difference
between the two years is the result of different types of age data
available for each of the two censuses.) Let us label the number of
occupied looms OTOT and the number of persons of weaving age in the household TAGEW. Then A = TAGEW/OTOT is the ratio of persons of weaving age
to the number of occupied looms.

If TAGEW exceeds OTOT or is equal to OTOT (TAGEW $\geq$ OTOT), or $A \geq 1$,
then the labor available in the household is sufficient to occupy all
active looms, assuming one person occupying one active loom. This
assumption is valid, of course, at the limit of economic necessity; that
is, in times of economic crisis. Presumably the weaver will then occupy
as many of his looms as he can with labor residing in the household,
which he can exploit more easily by greater control over its standard
of living, before hiring labor from the outside. If all of this resident
labor of weaving age is also familial, related to the head of the household or to his spouse, then the level of entrepreneurship, defined as

the extent of employment of non-relative and/or non-resident labor to occupy the active looms, is at its lowest value, namely, - 1. Symbolically this is expressed as: $A \geq 1$ and NORAGEW = 0 implies Ie = - 1, where NORAGEW signifies the number of non-relative residents of weaving age.

If some of the residents of weaving age are non-relatives, the index Ie should represent this fact. To achieve this in an unambiguous manner, we assume that the master-weaver occupies his active looms with resident non-relatives first and then with resident relatives. We have no proof, of course, of this pattern of occupancy of looms either generally or in the cases of the specific households in hand. In many households, some or all non-relatives probably worked on auxiliary tasks, such as dévidage, instead of weaving. Their presence in the household nevertheless demonstrated with little doubt the application of non-relative labor to some tasks. This fact is represented most conveniently (that is, quantitatively, with no ambiguity in computed results) by assuming the above order of application of non-relative labor to weaving proper. Thus the strength of presence of such non-relative labor is given as a proportion of the number of non-relative residents of weaving age to the number of occupied looms, or NORAGEW/OTOT. Since the master is more entrepreneurial to the extent that this proportion is larger, we express the effect of the presence of non-relatives on Ie as a difference from zero entrepreneurship, or total familialization of weaving labor (Ie = - 1), in the direction of higher levels of entrepreneurship (Ie > - 1). Algebraically, we achieve this by defining Ie = (NORAGEW/OTOT) - 1 for $A \geq 1$ and $0 <$ NORAGEW $<$ OTOT.

Along our scale of rising entrepreneurship, thus computed on the presumption of sufficient resident labor for occupying all active looms, we encounter the level at which the number of non-relative residents alone suffices to occupy all these looms. At this level, NORAGEW = OTOT, and, according to our formula above, Ie = (1) - 1 = 0. Suppose we move one step beyond this level to the case where NORAGEW > OTOT; that is, where, according to our assumption, all active looms are occupied by non-relative residents and where the remainder of the household, including at least one additional non-relative of weaving age, is employed at auxiliary tasks. Strictly speaking, our index Ie should represent this over-abundance of non-relative labor beyond the need for weaving labor. For such is also evidence of entrepreneurship in managing the total work of the household. Yet to do so by allowing Ie to exceed the value of 0, for example, would confuse two qualitatively different forms of entre-preneurship which the index should differentiate. One form, already discussed, involved employment of resident non-relative labor. The other form, to be discussed, involves the employment of non-resident labor. This second form, as we saw in Chapter I, minimized affective solidarity between the master and non-resident worker and approached the modern form of wage contract, or 'pure' hired labor, more closely than the resident worker. To avoid this confusion, we define Ie = 0 for all cases in which non-relative resident labor is sufficient to occupy all active looms, whether or not there is an excess of such labor beyond weaving needs. Symbolically, Ie = 0 when A ≥ 1 and NORAGEW ≥ OTOT. This manner of defining Ie minimizes, of course, the extra degree of entrepreneurship due to employing non-relatives for auxiliary tasks in addition to employ-ing them for weaving. This is indeed a weakness in the construction of Ie. The weakness is compensated, at least partially, however, by the non-ambiguity of Ie for the purpose of distinguishing between entrepre-neurship limited to relations of affective solidarity with subordinate workers and entrepreneurship including contractual relations with hired, non-resident laborers.

The reason for the possible confusion of the two forms of entrepreneurship, by allowing Ie to exceed 0 for NORAGEW > OTOT, derives from
the manner of calculating Ie when non-resident labor is required to
occupy at least some of the active looms. We want Ie to approach the
value of 1 (highest level of entrepreneurship) as the proportion of
looms occupied by non-residents, as compared with the total number of
occupied looms, increases. According to our original assumption concerning patterns of applying labor to looms, this proportion will exceed
zero only when the total number of household residents of weaving age is
less than the total number of occupied looms; that is, when TAGEW < OTOT,
or A < 1. In this case, the proportion of looms occupied by non-residents
will be the difference between OTOT and TAGEW expressed as a proportion
of OTOT, or (OTOT - TAGEW)/OTOT. Algebraically, this is the same as
1 - (TAGEW/OTOT), or 1 - A. This value, which shall be called B
(B = 1 - A) and defined as the value of Ie when A < 1 (Ie = B), will
always be greater than 0. But it may be as close as possible to 0, close
enough to coincide with the value of Ie for NORAGEW > OTOT, had we
allowed Ie to rise above 0 in this case. So in order to preserve both a
'pure' quantitative difference between the two forms of entrepreneurship
and the symmetry of arithmetical construction of Ie for each of the two
forms on each side of the threshold value 0, we allow Ie to exceed 0
only when non-residents must be hired to occupy some of the active looms.
Our index constructed in this manner also retains the 'proper' hierarchy
between the two forms of entrepreneurship -- the 'lower' form, consisting
of employment of residents alone and taking on lower values of Ie
(Ie $\leq$ 0), the 'higher' form consisting of employment of non-residents as
well and taking on higher values of Ie (Ie > 0). However, Ie never

reaches the value 1, representing the highest level of entrepreneurship, because the head of the household is <u>always</u> assumed to occupy one of the active looms and is present, of course, in every household.

The construction of Ie may be summarized in the following manner:

Given: TAGEW = Total number of persons of weaving age residing in the household (residents aged 10 or above in 1847, residents aged 14 or above in 1866)

NORAGEW = Total number of non-relatives of weaving age residing in the household (not related to head of household or spouse, as determined by difference of surname)

OTOT = Total number of occupied (active) looms in the household

A = TAGEW/OTOT

B = 1 − A

Then: Ie = − 1 <u>if</u> A ≥ 1 and NORAGEW = 0

Ie = (NORAGEW/OTOT) − 1

<u>if</u> A ≥ 1 and 0 < NORAGEW < OTOT

Ie = 0 <u>if</u> A ≥ 1 and NORAGEW ≥ OTOT

Ie = B <u>if</u> A < 1

Appendix VII:

Regression Study of Entrepreneurship

As indicated in the text of Chapter V, section I - D., regression
of the six type variables against the entrepreneurial index Ie preserved
all six variables -- PrOU, PrREL, PrSXF, PrAPP, PrOUV, AGE -- in 1847 and
eliminated all but two -- PrREL and PrSXF -- in 1866. Several features
of this reduction in significant type variables are worth noting. (See
Table 32 and Key and Diagram 1, reprinted on the following pages.) The
most striking is the elimination of the loom-type variable PrOU as a
significant determinant of entrepreneurship. In 1847, fancy-loom households tended to be more entrepreneurial than plain-loom households, as
the negative correlation between Ie and PrOU suggests. In 1866, the
degree of entrepreneurship was, on the average, indifferent to the type
of silk cloth woven. The main reason for this was the following: The
residents of fancy-loom households had become familialized over the
twenty-year interim to a level not very different from that of plain-loom
households. Moreover, the relatively low state of activity of the more
numerous fancy looms enabled fancy-cloth masters to occupy all or nearly
all looms with this resident family labor, as plain-cloth weavers had
always done in the past.

A second notable feature is the elimination of apprenticeship and
journeymanship as determinants of entrepreneurship -- or of adolescence
and adulthood, to use the type-variable names of the 1866 sample. In
1847 apprenticeship (PrAPP) and especially resident journeymanship (PrOUV)
strongly influenced the degree of entrepreneurship. Both PrAPP and PrOUV
strengthened Ie in the same sense as their own proportional representation
in the group of working household residents. In 1866, the adolescent and

-631-

Table 32

Regression Study of Type-Variable Determinants of Entrepreurial Index Ie.
Croix-Rousse (1847, 1866)

1847

Dependent Variable Ie
Regressed With

Independent Variable Standardized
Coefficients and F.Values

Name	Description	R^2	F	d-f	Critical F	ProU	PrREL	PrSXF	PrAPP	ProUV	AGE
1. ProU	OU/OTOTUF	.11	15.29	128 / 1	3.92	-.33 (15.29)					
2. PrREL	REL/HH	.35	68.85	128 / 1	3.92		-.59 (68.85)				
3. PrSXF	SXF/HH	0	.36	128 / 1	3.92			.05 (.36)			
4. PrAPP	APP/WOR	.04	4.74	104 / 1	3.94				.21 (4.74)		
5. ProUV	OUV/WOR	.34	53.50	104 / 1	3.94					.58 (53.50)	
6. AGE	AGE	0	.05	128 / 1	3.92						.02 (.05)
1,2,3,6		.42	22.49	125 / 4	2.45	-.24 (11.19)	-.56 (64.63)	.10 (2.09)			.12 (2.96)
1,2,3,4,6		.53	22.29	100 / 5	2.32	-.19 (7.06)	-.74 (93.93)	.12 (3.02)	-.11 (2.00)		.15 (4.27)
1,2,3,5,6		.57	26.07	100 / 5	2.32	-.19 (7.41)	-.53 (38.93)	.13 (3.95)		.28 (11.10)	.14 (4.28)
1,2,3,4,5,6		.58	22.87	99 / 6	2.20	-.17 (6.41)	-.32 (5.09)	.11 (2.66)	.22 (3.55)	.48 (12.70)	.13 (3.74)

1866

Dependent Variable Ie
Regressed With

Independent Variable Standardized
Coefficients and F Values

Name	Description	R^2	F	d-f	Critical F	PrTU	PrREL	PrSXF	PrTAG14	PrTAG21	AGE
1.PrTU	TU/TOTUF	0	.36	1 80	3.97	-.07 (.36)					
2.PrREL	REL/HH	.43	61.40	1 80	3.97		-.66 (61.40)				
3.PrSXF	SXF/HH	.02	1.60	1 80	3.97			.14 (1.60)			
4.PrTAG14	TAG14/HH	0	.02	1 80	3.97				-.02 (.02)		
5.PrTAG21	TAG21/HH	.07	5.94	1 80	3.97					.26 (5.94)	
6.AGE	AGE	0	.01	1 80	3.97						-.01 (.01)
1,2,3,6		.46	16.50	4 77	2.51	-.07 (.65)	-.66 (62.39)	.15 (3.29)			-.03 (.14)
1,2,3,4,6		.47	13.75	5 76	2.35	-.10 (1.24)	-.68 (64.99)	.14 (2.94)	-.12 (1.93)		-.05 (.17)
1,2,3,5,6		.47	13.33	5 76	2.35	-.08 (.85)	-.63 (51.29)	.14 (2.50)		.09 (.81)	-.07 (.57)
1,2,3,4,5,6		.47	11.31	6 75	2.23	-.10 (1.23)	-.67 (42.23)	.14 (2.73)	-.12 (1.10)	.01 (0)	-.04 (.14)

Key to Symbols

Ie: Entrepreueurial index

PrOU: Proportion of occupied plain looms (unis) to total occupied
        plain (unis) and fancy (façonné) looms
    OU: Number of occupied unis looms
    OTOTUF: Total number of occupied unis and façonnés looms

PrREL: Proportion of relatives of the head of household living in the
        household (other than spouse) to total number of persons living
        in the household (other than head and spouse)
    REL: Number of relatives of the head of household, by blood
        or by marriage, living in the household (other than
        spouse of head)
    HH: Total number of persons living in the household other
        than head and spouse

PrSXF: Proportion of females living in the household (other than head
        and spouse) to total number of persons living in the household
        (other than head and spouse)
    SXF: Number of females living in the household, other than
        head and spouse
    HH: Total number of persons living in the household other
        than head and spouse

PrAPP: Proportion of apprentices living in the household to total
        number of silk workers living in the household other than
        head and spouse (apprentices + journeyworkers + children
        of head aged 10 or above)
    APP: Number of apprentices living in the household
    WOR: Number of apprentices + journeyworkers (OUV) + children
        of head aged 10 or above (i.e. weaving age group,
        including children of weaving age)

PrOUV: Proportion of journeyworkers living in the household to total
        number of silk workers living in the household other than
        head and spouse
    OUV: Number of journeyworkers living in the household
    WOR: Number of apprentices + journeyworkers (OUV) + children
        of head aged 10 or above

AGE: Age of head of the household

PrTU: Proportion of total (occupied and unoccupied) plain looms (unis)
        to total (occupied and unoccupied) plain (unis) and fancy
        (façonné) looms
    TU: Total occupied and unoccupied plain looms
    TOTUF: Total occupied and unoccupied plain and fancy looms

PrTAG14: Proportion of persons living in the household, other than
head and spouse, aged 14 – 20, to total number of persons
living in the household, other than head and spouse
TAG14: Number of persons living in the household, other
than head and spouse, aged 14 – 20
HH: Total number of persons living in the household
other than head and spouse

PrTAG21: Proportion of persons living in the household, other than
head and spouse, aged 21 and above, to total number of
persons living in the household, other than head and spouse
TAG21: Number of persons living in the household, other than
head and spouse, aged 21 and above
HH: Total number of persons living in the household other
than head and spouse

R^2: Correlation coefficient (the proportion of the variation in
Ie explained by the variables against which it is regressed
to the total variation in Ie)

F: The computed F-statistic for the entire regression equation
$= (R^2/k)/((1-R^2)/(N-k-1))$. The statistic measures the ratio
of the proportional 'explained' variation of Ie (R^2), to
the proportional unexplained variation of Ie ($1-R^2$), correcting
for sample size (N) and number of independent variables in the
regression equation (k).

d-f: Degrees of freedom in the regression equation. The top figure
gives the degrees of freedom in the numerator of the F-
statistic (=k) and the bottom figure gives the degrees of
freedom in the denominator of F (=N-k)

Critical F: The F-statistic computed for a normally distributed random
sample of size N in a regression against k independent
variables, at 95% level of confidence

F-Value for Each Independent
Variable (in parentheses below
each standardized coefficient
for that variable):

The computed F-statistic for the partial correlation of that
independent variable with the dependent variable Ie, controlling for variation in the other independent variables.
This F-statistic measures the ratio of the proportional
explained variation of Ie for this partial regression (r_{ki}^2)
to the proportional unexplained variation of Ie for the
entire regression ($1-R^2$), correcting for sample size (N)
and number of independent variables (k)

The statistical test using the F-statistic consists of rejecting the null hypothesis that R^2 (or r_{ki}^2) is zero only when the computed F-statistic is equal to or larger than the critical F-statistic for the given degrees of freedom. In this case, the variation in Ie explained by the independent variable (s) in the regression equation is due to actual correlation, between Ie and the variable (s), rather than to mere random error, in 95 out of 100 cases (95% level of confidence).

The symbol β is used in the text to indicate a standardized coefficient of an independent variable.

adult age-group variables (PrTAG14 and PrTAG21 respectively) had no

apparent influence on entrepreneurship in the general structure of

determination, and yet the adult variable PrTAG21, regressed separately

with Ie, was significantly and positively associated with Ie. (See

Table 32: $\beta = .26$, $F = 5.94$, $R^2 = .07$.) The different behavior of the

age-group variables in the two periods was partly the result of statisti-

cal bias favoring the inclusion of PrAPP and PrOUV and the exclusion of

PrTAG14 and PrTAG21. The type variables PrAPP and PrOUV exaggerate the

actual proportion of apprentices and journeymen in the weavers' house-

holds in 1847, since these variables represent these proportions relative

to working members of household only rather than to all members of the

household. The type variables PrTAG14 and PrTAG21, however, represent

the proportions of adolescents and adults relative to all members of the

household (other than head and spouse) in 1866. Since apprentices and

journeymen in 1847 were also classed automatically as non-relatives, and

adolescents and adults in 1866 were classed as non-relatives only if

their surname indicated them as such, the bias in favor of the former,

as a determinant of Ie, was exaggerated further, for Ie measured in part

the proportion of non-relatives sufficient to occupy active looms in the

household. These biases were largely the result of census information

which was not perfectly comparable in its details.

Another reason for the exclusion of the age-group variables in 1866

was the much stronger negative association of PrREL with Ie ($R^2 = .43$,

$\beta = -.66$) than positive association of PrTAG21 with Ie ($R^2 = .07$, $\beta = .26$).

The association of the two age-group variables with Ie was concentrated,

so to speak, in PrTAG21, since Ie regressed bivariately with PrTAG14 was

insignificant, and PrTAG21 was significantly and negatively associated

with PrREL (Table 47: $R^2 = .08$, $\beta = -.28$). In regressing Ie with PrREL

Table 47

Regression Study of Determinants of State and Age-Group Variables.
Croix-Rousse Samples (1847, 1866)

1847

All Households

Dependent Variable	Regressed With	R²	F	d-f	Critical F	Independent Variable Standarized Coefficients and F Values					
						PrOU	PrREL	PrSXF	PrAPP	PrOUV	AGE
PrOUV	1. PrOU	0	.45	1-104	3.94	-.07 (.45)					
	2. PrREL	.38	63.89	1-104	3.94		-.62 (63.89)				
	3. PrSXF	.03	3.27	1-104	3.94			-.17 (3.27)			
	4. AGE	.01	.95	1-104	3.94						-.09 (.95)
	1,2,3,4	.39	16.40	4-101	2.48	.02 (.04)	-.61 (52.21)	-.12 (2.19)			.01 (0)
PrAPP	1,2,3,4	.20	6.12	4-101	2.48	-.08 (.71)	-.40 (19.81)	.21 (5.47)			.04 (.21)

1847

Plains Households

Dependent Variable	Regressed With	R2	F	d-f	Critical F	Independent Variable Standardized Coefficients and F Values					
						PrCU	PrREL	PrSXF	PrAPP	PrOUV	AGE
PrOUV	2. PrREL	.52	20.80	1-19	4.38		-.72 (20.80)				
	3. PrSXF	.02	.42	1-19	4.38			-.15 (.42)			
	4. AGE	0	.08	1-19	4.38						-.06 (.08)
	2,3,4	.58	7.89	3-17	3.20		-.75 (22.62)	-.23 (2.19)			-.07 (.22)
PrAPP	2,3,4	.31	2.50	3-17	3.20		-.41 (4.09)	.32 (2.41)			-.16 (.23)

Fancies Households

Dependent Variable	Regressed With	R2	F	d-f	Critical F	PrCU	PrREL	PrSXF	PrAPP	PrOUV	AGE
PrCUV	2. PrREL	.32	38.17	1-81	3.97		-.57 (38.17)				
	3. PrSXF	.02	1.99	1-81	3.97			-.15 (1.99)			
	4. AGE	.01	.52	1-81	3.97						-.08 (.52)
	2,3,4	.33	12.90	3-79	2.73		-.56 (35.26)	-.09 (.87)			.04 (.16)
PrAPP	2,3,4	.18	5.96	3-79	2.73		-.42 (15.95)	.19 (3.40)			.07 (.51)

1866

All Households

Dependent Variable	Regressed With	R²	F	d-f	Critical F	Independent Variable Standardized Coefficients and F Values					
						PrTU	PrRel	PrSXF	PrTAG14	PrTAG21	AGE
PrTAG21	1. PrTU	0	.09	1-80	3.97	.03 (.09)					
	2. PrREL	.08	7.07	1-80	3.97		-.28 (7.07)				
	3. PrSXF	.03	2.88	1-80	3.97			.19 (2.88)			
	4. AGE	.19	18.56	1-80	3.97						.43 (18.56)
	1,2,3,4	.31	8.84	4-77	2.51	.12 (1.58)	-.29 (9.20)	.18 (3.56)			.45 (22.05)
PrTAG14	1,2,3,4	.08	1.66	4-77	2.51	-.24 (4.52)	-.13 (1.48)	-.07 (.43)			-.02 (.04)

1866

Plains Households

Dependent Variable	Regressed With	R²	F	d-f	Critical F	Independent Variable Standardized Coefficients and F Values					
						PrTU	PrREL	PrSXF	PrTAG14	PrTAG21	AGE
PrTAG21	2.PrREL	.09	5.12	1-54	4.02		-.29 (5.12)				
	3.PrSXF	.08	4.39	1-54	4.02			.27 (4.39)			
	4.AGE	.21	14.19	1-54	4.02						.46 (14.19)
	2,3,4	.38	10.83	3-52	2.79		-.33 (9.02)	.25 (5.13)			.48 (19.48)
PrTAG14	2,3,4	.05	.86	3-52	2.79		-.17 (1.54)	-.12 (.82)			-.06 (.18)

Fancies Households

Dependent Variable	Regressed With	R²	F	d-f	Critical F	PrTU	PrREL	PrSXF	PrTAG14	PrTAG21	AGE
PrTAG21	2.PrREL	.07	1.87	1-24	4.26		-.27 (1.87)				
	3.PrSXF	0	0	1-24	4.26			.01 (0)			
	4.AGE	.19	5.75	1-24	4.26						.44 (5.75)
	2,3,4	.23	2.15	3-22	3.05		-.19 (.94)	.02 (.01)			.40 (4.31)
PrTAG14	2,3,4	.01	.07	3-22	3.05		-.07 (.11)	.02 (.01)			.05 (.06)

and PrTAG21 together, therefore, the weaker positive association of Ie
with the latter was 'absorbed' into the stronger negative association
of Ie with the former by the effect of multicollinearity between PrREL
and PrTAG21. In 1847, the independent positive association of PrOUV
with Ie (R^2 = .34, β = .58) was not very different (not stronger or
weaker) from the independent negative association of PrREL with Ie
(R^2 = .35, β =-.59). Thus, although the association between PrOUV and
PrREL was strong (Table 47: R^2 = .38, β = -.62), neither absorbed the
other entirely in the multivariate regression with Ie.

The major changes in the relationship between the age-group
variables and the entrepreneurial index Ie, from 1847 to 1866, were the
elimination of apprenticeship (or adolescence) and the elimination of
journeymanship (or adulthood) as significant determinants of entrepreneurship. These changes took place differently in plain-loom households and
in fancy-loom households. In 1847 only PrREL was significantly correlated
with PrOUV, and the correlation was strong and negative. This was true
both in plain-loom households and in fancy-loom households. (See Table
47.) In 1866, however, PrTAG21 was strongly associated with two other
type variables besides -- with the degree of feminization (PrSXF) and
with the age of the head of the household (AGE). The correlation with
AGE was positive (R^2 = .19, β = .43). The association with PrSXF was
weaker but also positive when the effects of loom type (PrTU), familialization (PrREL), and age of the head (AGE) were controlled (β = .18).
Regression of these four type variables (PrSXF, PrTU, PrREL, AGE) with
PrTAG21 separately for plain-loom households and for fancy-loom households demonstrates that the association of PrTAG21 with PrSXF (bivariately
regressed) was exclusively a characteristic of plain-loom households.
The positive association of PrTAG21 with AGE, however, was characteristic

of plain-loom households and fancy-loom households alike. Bivariate
regression of Ie with PrTAG21 separately for the two loom-types of
household demonstrates, moreover, that these were positively associated
also in plain-loom households alone. (See Table 47 for these correlations.)

As we have already seen, feminization along with familialization
together defined the structure of determination of entrepreneurship in
1866. (See Diagram 1, p. 422) As we shall see shortly, familialization alone
(PrREL) remained significantly associated with Ie in plain-loom households in 1866. The correlation of Ie with PrSXF was insignificant.
Through the positive, bivariate association of PrTAG21 with Ie in such
households, however, the 'original' association of PrSXF and PrREL with
Ie was preserved. For PrTAG21 was also significantly correlated with
these two type variables in the same direction as they were respectively
correlated with Ie in the 'original' structure (that is, undifferentiated
by loom-type of household) of determination of entrepreneurship
(negatively with PrREL, positively with PrSXF). In other words, the
degree of entrepreneurship increased in plain-loom households with their
de-familialization and with their feminization together, largely because
the degree of entrepreneurship in such households tended to increase as
the proportion of adults in them increased. The latter tended to
accumulate more frequently, in turn, in the less familial, more feminized
households of plain-cloth weavers.

A third feature of the structures of determination of entrepreneurship for both years was the entry of feminization as a significant
determinant only after the effect of other significant type variables
was controlled. Bivariate correlations of Ie with PrSXF were insignificant in both periods, but correlations of Ie with PrSXF became significant
in the more general multivariate regressions. In particular, introduction

of control for apprenticeship (PrAPP) and for journeymanship (PrOUV) in 1847, and for familialization (PrREL) in 1866, made the association of Ie with PrSXF significant. (See Table 32.) Since controlling for PrAPP and PrOUV was largely the inverse of controlling for familialization (because of the high negative association between PrREL and PrAPP, PrOUV), the control factors in both periods were not very different. They suggested that for a given level of familialization, entrepreneurship increased with feminization. Since by definition entrepreneurship increased as familialization decreased, Ie was highest in highly non-familial, highly feminized households.

This suggests that the differences between the two periods concerning the effect of feminization upon entrepreneurship were trivial. In fact they were not. This can be seen by regressing the structural equation for each of the two years separately for plain-loom households and for fancy-loom households. Table 48 summarizes the results of such a regression. For 1847 the regression produced insignificant coefficients for PrSXF in both loom-types of household. In 1866 the coefficients of PrSXF were insignificant only for plain-loom households. For fancy-loom households, the coefficient was significant (β = .28). (See Table 48, Regression Equation 15.) The apparent association between entrepreneurship and feminization in 1847, for the entire sample of households undistinguished by loom type, was largely the result of random variation, hence spurious. The association between the two variables in 1866, however, was not spurious, but this association derived exclusively from a relatively strong positive correlation between Ie and PrSXF in fancy-loom households alone. The higher proportion of plain-loom households in the 1866 sample, where feminization was not significantly correlated with entrepreneurship, reduced the overall association between Ie and

Table 48

Regression Study of Type-Variable Determinants of Entrepreneurial Index Ie Separately for Plain-Loom Households and for Fancy-Loom Households. Croix-Rousse Samples (1847, 1866)

1847

Dependent Variable Ie Regressed With

Plains Households	R^2	F	Degrees of Freedom	Critical F	Independent Variable Standardized Coefficients and F Values				
					PrREL	PrSXF	PrAPP	PrOUV	AGE
1. PrREL	.36	19.53	1-34	4.13	-.60 (19.53)				
2. PrOUV	.61	29.82	1-19	4.38				.78 (29.82)	
3. PrREL, PrSXF, PrAPP, PrOUV, AGE	.82	13.69	5-15	2.90	-.30 (.88)	.10 (.73)	.21 (.83)	.63 (4.62)	.13 (1.30)
Fancies Households									
4. PrREL	.31	40.00	1-90	3.96	-.55 (40.00)				
5. PrOUV	.27	30.37	1-81	3.97				.52 (30.37)	
6. PrREL, PrSXF, PrAPP, PrOUV, AGE	.49	14.72	5-77	2.35	-.34 (4.09)	.10 (1.49)	.21 (2.02)	.44 (7.15)	.13 (2.45)

1866

Dependent Variable Ie
Regressed With

Independent Variable Standardized
Coefficients and F Values

Plains Households	R2	F	d-f	Critical F	PrREL	PrSXF	PrTAG14	PrTAG21	AGE
7. PrREL	.42	38.79	1-54	4.02	-.65 (38.79)				
8. PrTAG21	.08	4.49	1-54	4.02				.28 (4.49)	
9. PrREL, PrSXF	.43	19.83	2-53	3.18	-.64 (38.04)	.10 (.92)			
10. PrREL,PrSXF,AGE	.44	13.70	3-52	2.79	-.63 (36.52)	.10 (.99)			-.12 (1.26)
11. PrREL, PrSXF, PrTAG21,AGE	.46	11.02	4-51	2.57	-.57 (25.80)	.06 (.27)		.19 (.27)	-.21 (2.97)
12. PrREL,PrSXF, PrTAG14,PrTAG21, AGE	.46	8.66	5-50	2.41	-.56 (20.13)	.06 (.26)	.02 (.03)	.20 (1.71)	-.21 (2.87)

1866

645

Dependent Variable Ie Regressed With

Independent Variable Standardized Coefficients and F.Values

Fancies Households	R²	F	d-f	Critical F	PrREL	PrSXF	PrTAG14	PrTAG21	AGE
13. PrREL	.48	21.88	1-24	4.26	-.69 (21.88)				
14. PrTAG21	.06	1.59	1-24	4.26				.25 (1.59)	
15. PrREL, PrSXF	.55	14.25	2-23	3.42	-.73 (27.11)	.28 (3.94)			
16. PrREL, PrSXF, AGE	.56	9.28	3-22	3.05	-.72 (23.88)	.27 (3.63)			.07 (.26)
17. PrREL, PrSXF, PrTAG21, AGE	.56	6.66	4-21	2.84	-.71 (21.57)	.27 (3.46)		.03 (.03)	.06 (.15)
18. PrREL, PrSXF, PrTAG14, PrTAG21, AGE	.65	7.50	5-20	2.71	-.82 (30.96)	.29 (4.62)	-.45 (5.35)	-.34 (2.44)	.23 (2.02)

PrSXF to a level not very different from that of the 'spurious'
association between the two variables in the 1847 sample.

The positive association of entrepreneurship with feminization in
fancy-loom households in 1866 suggests that the master-weavers of fancy
cloths who remained 'entrepreneurial' used female labor more than in
the past. Cheaper, more docile, able to weave the less elegant fancy
cloths demanded by the market, the labor of females prevented the total
familialization of the households of these masters and saved them
from returning to the purely paternal role of most of their fellow chefs
d'atelier. It is important to note, however, that such female labor
which preserved a certain entrepreneurial role for fancy-cloth masters
was not necessarily young. In particular, it was not the labor of female
adolescents (apprentices or young journeyworkers). In the regression of
Ie against five type variables -- PrREL, PrSXF, PrTAG14, PrTAG21, AGE --
in 1866, for fancy-loom households alone (see Table 48), the statistically
significant effects of feminization (PrSXF) and adolescence (PrTAG14) on
entrepreneurship (Ie) operated in opposite directions. Feminization, as
expected, was positively associated with entrepreneurship in such households, but adolescence was negatively associated with Ie. The retention
or increase of apprentices thus appeared more indicative of an 'artisanal'
attitude than of 'entrepreneurial' behavior in fancy-loom households in
1866 -- contrary to our expectations based on analysis of the distribution
tables in the text of Chapter V. Feminization in general, however,
indicated greater rather than less entrepreneurship, regardless of the
age of female residents or their relationship to the head of the household (relative or non-relative). Fancy-cloth masters who used female
labor were therefore more likely than most other masters to have preserved
an 'entrepreneurial' attitude toward their household economies.

The life-stage proxy AGE, finally, correlated with Ie in a manner quite similar to that of PrSXF. In 1847, AGE also became a significant determinant of entrepreneurship only with control for the effects of the other type variables. In particular, AGE entered the structural equation only with control for the effects of loom type (PrOU) and familialization (PrREL). PrREL and AGE were significant determinants of Ie, however, only in fancy-loom households, which formed the majority in the Croix-Rousse sample of that year. (See Table 48, Regression Equation 6.) Older masters weaving fancy cloths thus tended to use non-relative or non-resident labor more than younger masters weaving fancy cloths, but masters weaving plain cloths were more or less entrepreneurial regardless of their age. In 1866, the variable AGE appeared insignificant in all cases. Regression of Ie with PrREL, PrSXF and AGE separately for the two loom types of household confirm this result, with one exception. (See Table 48, Regression Equation 10, 16.) When the effects of the proportion of adults in the household (PrTAG21) are controlled in plain-loom households, AGE becomes significantly and negatively associated with entrepreneurship (β = -.21, F = 2.87). (See Table 48, Regression Equation 12.) In other words, younger master-weavers of plain cloths tended to be more entrepreneurial than older master-weavers of such cloths, for a given proportion of adults in the household. But adult-hood (PrTAG21) in plain-loom households was <u>positively</u> associated with entrepreneurship (Ie) (Regression Equation 8: R^2 = .08, β = .28, F = 4.49) and strongly and <u>positively</u> correlated with AGE (R^2 = .21, β = .46, F = 14.19, not indicated in Table). As a result, adulthood and AGE pulled in opposite directions in 'determining' entrepreneurship -- the former increasing Ie, the latter decreasing Ie, for each increase in proportion of adults in the household. This effect of mutual cancellation, along with the negative collinearity of PrTAG21 and PrREL, also explained why neither PrTAG21 nor AGE was a significant determinant of Ie in the overall structural relation for 1866.

BIBLIOGRAPHICAL ESSAY

This study has focused on the relationship between two topics:
economic and social change in the silk industry and in the city of Lyons,
and the social ideology of voluntary association among the Lyons silk
weavers. To date very little literature has studied the relationship
between economy and society, on the one hand, and movements of workers'
association, on the other hand, in the Lyons region. Yves Lequin's
"Monde ouvrier de la région lyonnaise dans la deuxième moitié du
XIXème siècle, 1848 à 1914" (unpublished thesis for the Doctorat d'Etat,
Université Lyon II, 1975), 4 volumes, to be published as Les ouvriers
de la région lyonnaise dans la seconde moitié du XIXe siècle (1848-1914)
(Lyon: Presses universitaires de Lyon, 1977), and Robert J. Bezucha's
Lyon Uprising of 1834: Social and Political Conflict in the Early July
Monarchy (Cambridge, Massachusetts: Harvard University Press, 1974) are
the two most prominent examples of this literature. Both of these fine
works make some effort to relate the development of workers' movements
to social and economic change. In both, this effort is truncated somewhat
by the separate treatment of each of the two topics in distinct chapters
or volumes. Lequin's grand vision of patterns and tendencies in regional
workers' movements, however, bears an affinity to the main lines of social
and economic change as he interprets these in the first two volumes. Thus
he transcends indirectly, almost subtly, this truncation. Bezucha's
effort to relate one topic to the other is less ambitious and less
grandiose than Lequin's. Bezucha nevertheless makes some valuable discoveries in his more modest enterprise, such as that of neighborhood

-649-

'polarization' explaining the strength of class solidarity and class consciousness among the silk weavers. Both of these works satisfied the present study's hunger for relevant information. Such relevancy was, to some extent, a product of the two authors' interest in the social and economic foundations of association. Both works will be discussed at greater length in sections of this essay concerning the specialized areas in which they contributed most of this information.

Most of the literature upon which this study has relied -- both primary and secondary, published and manuscript -- treats only one or the other topic (economy and society, movements of association) separately. For this reason, this essay, unlike the study itself, will review this literature in the same fashion. First, documents and works pertaining to structure and change in the economy and society of silk weaving, and to the urbanization of Lyons, will be discussed. Then sources concerning the history, ideology, organizational forms and patterns of behavior of voluntary associations -- especially associations among the weavers of Lyons -- will be examined.

This study has relied primarily on archival sources, including both manuscript and pamphlet literature, and on published 'primary' literature in libraries. Most of the archives and libraries housing these sources are located in the city of Lyons. They are listed below with corresponding abbreviations used in footnotes and bibliography. Some secondary literature was also consulted, especially for the broader questions of this study, such as the history of the silk industry, the economic development and urbanization of Lyons, and the history of political movements in Lyons. Archival sources, primary

published literature and, to a lesser extent, some secondary literature
include both quantitative and literary materials. In most cases, the
latter are also separate from one another, but in a few important instances they derive from the same source. This essay will refer to these
various distinguishing characteristics -- archival or published, primary
or secondary, quantitative or literary -- where appropriate.

The following French archives and libraries were consulted:

Archives

ACCL, Archives de la Chambre de Commerce de Lyon
ADI, Archives Departementales de l'Isère
ADR, Archives Départementales du Rhône
AML, Archives Municipales de Lyon
AMTL, Archives du Musée des Tissus de Lyon
AN, Archives Nationales
AP, Archives du Progrès (Lyon)
ATCL, Archives du Tribunal de Commerce de Lyon

Libraries

AML (Bibliothèque), Bibliothèque des Archives Municipales de Lyon
BCCL, Bibliothèque de la Chambre de Commerce de Lyon
BCHRL, Bibliothèque du Centre d'histoire économique et sociale de
       la région lyonnaise
BML, Bibliothèque Municipale de Lyon
BMTL, Bibliothèque du Musée des Tissus de Lyon
BN, Bibliothèque Nationale
BUL, Bibliothèque de l'Université Lyon II

I. Sources Concerning Economic and Social Structure and Change

Sources concerning economy and society will be discussed separately
below. The economy will be considered somewhat arbitrarily as including
only the technology of silk weaving and two (relatively) macroeconomic
spheres of activity -- the development of the silk industry and the intensified urbanization of Lyons. Most of the sources for these two topics
are published secondary works. 'Society' will include the microeconomic

sphere of the household economy, labor-related issues, such as wages and employment, and the institutional aspects of economic life, such as the Conseil des Prud'hommes. Sources for these social issues are primarily manuscript and primary pamphlet literature.

A. The Economy of the Silk Industry and of the City of Lyons

1. Technology

Understanding the economic development of the Lyons silk industry first requires a knowledge of silk technology, especially weaving technique, including the development of weaving technology during the nineteenth century. E. Pariset's Industries de la soie (Lyon: Pitrat Aîné, 1890) is the best introduction to the subject. Pariset describes the technology of all sectors of the industry, including spinning, throwing and weaving, with clarity and ample illustration. The book fails, however, to describe the history of silk technology adequately. A.Beauquis' Histoire économique de la soie (Grenoble: Grands Etablissements de l'Imprimerie Générale, 1910) undertakes this historical description more comprehensively and rather competently. Without sparing too much technical detail, Beauquis traces the various modifications in loom technology throughout the nineteenth century and discusses spinning and throwing technique besides.

Specialized aspects of silk technology are treated in several published and manuscript sources. Two imposing technical treatises, one by a Frenchman, Natalis Rondot, Les soies (Paris: Imprimerie nationale, 1885), 2 volumes, another by a German, Henri Silbermann, Die Seide: Ihre Geschichte, Gewinnung und Verarbeitung (Dresden: Gerhard Kuhtman, 1897), Vol. 2, analyze the biological aspects of sericulture and the physical

and chemical properties of silk fiber. These are among the best sources
for information concerning silkworms, their habitats, their feeding, and
the different kinds of fiber produced by each. Silk weaving technology is
best learned by consulting the texts of professors of weaving theory in
Lyons during the nineteenth century, explained and amplified, if possible,
by present-day experts of weaving technique. The most accessible collection of such texts is that of the BMTL. Most of these are in manuscript form and are amply illustrated. This study relied on one of the
few published texts of the Second Empire, F. Peyot's Cours complet de
fabrique pour les étoffes de soie (Lyon: Louis Perrin, 1866) (BMTL,
B.31) -- a standard work of the period -- and on one earlier manuscript,
F. Bert's "Theorie de la fabrication des étoffes de soie enseignée par
F. Bert de Lyon," 1842, BMTL, MSS.. Professor Jean Vial of the Ecole de
Tissage de Lyon and also curator at the BMTL generously and patiently explained elementary principles and some finer aspects of silk-weaving
technique from his wide-ranging knowledge of present-day weaving technique
and of its historical antecedents. (Discussions with Professor Jean
Vial, BMTL, April and May 1975)

2. The Silk Industry

General histories of the silk industry of nineteenth century are few,
and none is both comprehensive (covering the entire period for all aspects
of the industry) and analytically sophisticated. Michel Laferrère's
section on the industry in Lyon: ville industrielle (Paris: Presses
universitaires de France, 1960) is the best. Laferrère surveys the
economic history of the industry from 1825 to 1960. His research is
thorough, his knowledge of technical detail is refined, and his exposition

is not devoid of some useful analytical insights, although it is mostly
descriptive. He traces especially well the evolution of fabric demand
and the changes in dyes and dyeing technique in response to new product
demands from 1850 to 1875. E. Pariset's old and still authoritative
Histoire de la fabrique lyonnaise (Lyon: A. Rey, 1901) suffers from
rambling style and lack of precision, but remains a necessary introduction
to the subject, if only for the sake of its detailed information. A.
Beauquis' Histoire économique de la soie fills some of the gaps in
Pariset but unfortunately gives little attention to the economic history
of the industry. Two maîtrise theses in the BCHRL are useful for additional general information on the period: Janine Boisson's "Fabrique
lyonnaise de soierie: aperçu économique et social (1850-1873)" (unpublished mémoire de maîtrise under the direction of Pierre Léon,
Faculté des Lettres et Sciences Humaines, Université de Lyon, June 1955)
(BCHRL, Mémoire de maîtrise No. 16) and Yves Lequin's "Aspects écono-
miques des industries lyonnaisesde la soie (1870 - 1900)" (unpublished
D.E.S. under the direction of Pierre Léon, Faculté des Lettres et
Sciences Humaines, Université de Lyon, April 1958) (BCHRL, Mémoire de
maîtrise No. 31). Boisson's thesis is best for a description of commercial institutions of the silk industry of the Second Empire and includes
some useful commercial statistics. Lequin's much superior study provides
ample quantitative detail and is insightful in parts besides. Lequin
analyzes the organization and geography of silk manufacture, the evolution of demand, the business cycle in the industry and especially the
development of commerce in raw silk and silk thread. He describes the
latter very well, especially the rise and fall of Lyons as the center of

this commerce. The late Pierre Léon, professor at the University of
Paris and founder of the Centre d'histoire économique et sociale de la
région lyonnaise directed both of these theses.

More specialized treatments of the economic history of the silk
industry are Louis Gueneau's Lyon et le commerce de la soie (Lyon:
L. Bascou, 1923) and Tcheng Tse-Sio's Relations de Lyon avec la Chine
(Paris: L. Rodstein, 1937), for the history and institutions of raw-
silk and silk-thread commerce; Henriette Vanier's enjoyable and in-
formative little book, La mode et ses métiers: frivolités et luttes des
classes, 1830 - 1870 (Paris: Armand Colin, 1960), for the evolution of
silk dress and ornament styles in Parisian fashion markets; and
M. Coulesque, "La crise américain et la crise de la soierie lyonnaise
(1860 - 1864)," Cahiers d'histoire, Vol. IX, No. 3 (1964), 261-278, for
a description of the effects of the American Civil War on the Lyons
silk industry. A few contemporary publications provide additionally
useful information for specialized periods. The fabricant Léon
Permezel's Industrie lyonnaise de la soie: son état actuel, son avenir
(Lyon: Alf. Louis Perrin, 1883) includes valuable statistical tables and a
description of foreign silk industries as well as a discussion of the
industry of Lyons in the 1870's and early 1880's. Some mémoires and
pamphlets by fabricants in the late 1820's, notably Guerin-Philippon et
al., Mémoire présenté à Son Excellence le Ministre du Commerce et des
Manufactures par les Fabricans d'étoffes de soie de la ville de Lyon
(Lyon: Gabriel Rossary, 1829) (BMTL, C.1557), discuss causes for the
crisis of 1829 in the fabrique and propose remedies for it. Most of
these pamphlets are available in BMTL, series C.1557, C.1558 and C.1559,

Yves Lequin's thesis, "Le monde ouvrier de la région lyonnaise,"
Vol. I, traces the migration of the fabrique and of its auxiliary industries (especially throwing and spinning) throughout the région
lyonnaise with clarity and authority. P. Cayez will investigate the
economic development of Lyons and its region, including the fabrique,
more thoroughly in his forthcoming thèse de doctorat. Three fine
products of French university scholarship, all of them thèses de
doctorat, provide useful and carefully-researched detail
concerning the dispersion of silk weaving in particular provinces of
the région lyonnaise; Pierre Léon's Naissance de la grande industrie
en Dauphiné (Paris: Presses universitaires de France, 1954), Vol. II,
for the migration of the fabrique to the east of Lyons before 1870;
Pierre Barral's Département de l'Isère sous la Troisième République,
1870 - 1940 (Paris: Armand Colin, 1962), for the spread of silk weaving
in Isère after 1870; and Gilbert Garrier's Paysans du Beaujolais et du
Lyonnais, 1800 - 1870 (Grenoble: Presses universitaires de Grenoble,
1973), 2 volumes, for the migration of the fabrique to the west of Lyons
during the nineteenth century. Joseph Jouanny's even more specialized
Tissage de la soie dans le Bas-Dauphiné (Grenoble: Allier Père et Fils,
1931) remains a valuable complement to Léon and Barral for studying the
development of silk weaving in this sub-region, especially for statistical detail concerning this development. The ruralization of the
fabrique of Lyons is discussed more generally but with insight, with
quantitative specificity and within a French and European perspective
in Maurice Lévy-Leboyer's justly acclaimed Banques européennes et l'in-
dustrialisation internationale dans la première moitié du XIXe siècle

(Paris, 1974). Unfortunately, Lévy-Leboyer's penetrating study is confined to the period before 1850.

The rise of competition by foreign silk industries and by other textile manufactures within France is discussed in a variety of specialized literature. Henri Silberman's Die Seide, Vol. I, describes the progression and sources of rising German competition during the second half of the nineteenth century, and Raton C. Rawlley's Economics of the Silk Industry: A Study in Industrial Organization (London: P.S. King and Sons, 1919) suggests possible reasons for the decline of the British industry during the same period. Léon Permezel's Industrie lyonnaise de la soie, mentioned earlier, traces the evolution and current situation of several foreign fabriques with competence but also with apprehension, warning the scholar against possible exaggeration in some of Permezel's conclusions. Claude Fohlen's Industrie textile au temps du Second Empire (Paris: Librairie Plon, 1956) unfortunately ignores silk manufacture but discusses the evolution of French cotton and woolen manufacture and commerce during the Second Empire with erudition.

Construction of tables and graphs of exports of silk cloth, prices and quantities of silk thread inputs, and location, concentration and mechanization of silk weaving required research in a variety of published and unpublished quantitative documents. Regular statistical data concerning growth, quality (cloth type) and destination of exports of French silk fabrics -- the only available indication of growth and quality of output in the fabrique lyonnaise -- were reported annually in Ministère des travaux publics, de l'agriculture et du commerce, Statistique de la France. Commerce extérieur (Paris: Imprimerie royale, 1838), for the period 1815 - 1836,and in Administration des douanes, <u>Tableau décennal du</u>

<u>commerce de la France</u> (Paris: Imprimerie nationale), 2e Partie, for

the period 1837 - 1876 in separate volumes for each decade. Since the

<u>fabrique lyonnaise</u> relied heavily on its export sector for most of its

sales and since most silk exports (under the rubric <u>Commerce spécial</u>)

were products of Lyons, these export data are adequate indicators of

change in output for the general purposes of this study. The same pub-

lications trace the growth of imports of silk fabric from abroad and

exports of other French textiles (woolens, cottons, mixed cloths), both

of which are important for the analysis of competition by foreign

<u>fabriques</u> and by other textiles. More precise specifications of

exports (such as specifications of country of destination and not only

region) are occasionally found in the annual reports on the <u>fabrique</u>

in the <u>Compte-rendus des travaux de la Chambre de Commerce de Lyon</u>,

BCCL. These reports provide precise data on raw silk and silk thread

prices besides, as well as data concerning the number and type of looms

in the <u>fabrique</u>. The value of this source for the study of the industry

over a long period, however, is uneven. The publication of the <u>Compte-</u>

<u>rendus</u> did not begin until 1864, and earlier reports are available only

in the less accessible ACCL. The statistical reports of the <u>Compte-</u>

<u>rendus</u> are not equally detailed, moreover, and some reports are not con-

tinued from one year to the next.

A more regular data series, often used as a proxy for output in

studies of the silk industry, is that of silk thread passing through the

<u>Condition des Soies de Lyon</u> -- the drying and weighing station instituted

to prevent fraud in silk commerce. The <u>Relevés du mouvement de la</u>

Condition publique des Soies et des Laines de Lyon, available in BMTL,
include all of these data from 1805, when the Condition was established.
The Société d'agriculture, histoire naturelle et arts utiles de Lyon
published most of these Condition data after 1870 in its Bulletin. Use
of these data as indices of output of silk cloths, however, is hazardous,
primarily because of the risk of double counting. From 1842 on, not only
thrown silk (ouvré) but also raw silk (grège) passed through the Condition
de Lyon.[1] It is impossible to determine how much of this grège passed
through the Condition a second time in the form of ouvré, once it had
been thrown in Lyon. The Relevés du mouvement de la Condition nevertheless remain a good source for tracing the origins of raw and thrown silk,
since these are specified by country, and to some extent for determining
the relative proportions of warp (organsins) and weft (trame) thread
used in the fabrique besides, since these are also specified. These
proportions are useful for tracing the evolution of cloth complexity.
The Relevés, finally, have the special merit of completeness for the
entire century from 1805 and also the merit of monthly reporting for
most of the century.

Statistical data concerning the number and type of looms in the
fabrique and their geographical distribution between Lyons and the
countryside are to be found in several specialized quantitative sources
complementing the tables in Bezucha, Lequin, Lévy-Leboyer and Jouanny.

---

[1]Adrien Perret, Monographie de la Condition des Soies de Lyon
(Lyon: Pitrat Aîné, 1878), pp. 76-77.

Among these sources, the fiscal recensements in AML for Lyons (1846)

and for the Croix-Rousse (1844–1845); the Bureau de la Statistique

Générale, Statistique de la France (Deuxième Série: Tome XIX): In-

dustrie. Résultats généraux de l'enquête effectuée dans les années

1861 – 1865 (Nancy, 1873); and ACCL, Soieries Carton 21: Tissage de

soieries (statistiques) are especially useful for information con-

cerning number and type of looms in Lyons. The last two sources are

also helpful for estimating the number of looms in the countryside of

the Lyons region. ACCL, Soieries Carton 21 contains data on the geo-

graphical distribution of mechanical looms in factories of the Lyons

region. Département de l'Isère, Arrondissement de la-Tour-du-Pin,

"Situation industrielle au 31 Décembre 1857," ADI, 136M-17:

Statistiques diverses relatives aux Centres industriels du département

de l'Isère, 1855 – 1858 differentiates looms by commune and by or-

ganizational type (household or factory loom) in the arrondissement

of La-Tour-du-Pin (Isère), an important countryside weaving area.

Finally, the dossier on industrial conditions in the fabrique during

the 1860's in AML, I2 – 47(A) and (B), Situation de l'industrie

lyonnaise: ... rapports sur la soierie et les ouvriers en soie ...

(1819 à 1870) contains useful statistical summaries of looms, dis-

tinguished by cloth type in 1856 and by fabricant in 1866.

3. The City of Lyons

The transformation of the city of Lyons under the Second Empire --

its industrialization, population growth and urban renewal -- is

described clearly, concisely and accurately in F. Dutacq and A.

Latreille's De 1814 à 1940, Vol. 3 of the   Histoire de Lyon (Lyon;

Pierre Masson, 1952), edited by A. Kleinclausz. Particular aspects of
that transformation are discussed with authority in three works: Michel
Laferrère's Lyon: ville industrielle, mentioned earlier, for the industrialization of the city; Joseph Arminjon's Population du département
du Rhône: Son évolution depuis le début du XIXe siècle (Lyon: Bosc
Frères, M. et L. Riou, 1940), for population growth; and Charlene Marie
Leonard's Lyon Transformed: Public Works of the Second Empire, 1853 –
1864 (Berkeley: University of California Press, 1961), for urban renewal. Laferrère describes the transformation of the industrial geography of Lyons, the evolution of technique for silk, chemical and
machinery manufacture, and the institutional history of industrial
development in Lyons -- the history of patents, of entrepreneurs, and
of individual firms (for which he offers several illuminating case
studies) -- with erudition, clarity and occasionally penetrating insight.
His economic history nevertheless remains descriptive and narrative for
the most part, and his economic analysis is rarely very sophisticated.
Yves Lequin's discussion of the industrialization of Lyons and its region
in Vol. I of his "Monde ouvrier de la région lyonnaise" and the "Situations
industrielles "in AML, I2 - 47(A), Situation de l'industrie lyonnaise
provide additional detail to supplement Laferrère's description of industrial development in the city.

Joseph Arminjon's population study is a competent analysis of the
demographic sources of population growth in the Rhône during the nineteenth and early twentieth century. For the purposes of the present
study, Arminjon's analysis was especially useful for distinguishing
relative growth rates in 'Old Lyons' from those in 'New Lyons.' Most

of the population data is aggregated by place (department or departmental arrondissement) and by time (five-and ten-year periods). For this reason, this study is useful only as an introduction to the demographic history of the Rhône and of Lyons, and it is a very sketchy one at that. The subject needs more sophisticated treatment with methods of modern historical demography, such as family reconstitution wherever possible. For the general purposes of the present study, however, Arminjon was adequate. His conclusions can be placed best in a national perspective by comparing his growth tables with those of André Armengaud's Population française au XIXe siècle (Paris: Presses universitaires de France, 1971).

Charlene Marie Leonard's study of urban renewal is a thorough and competent description of all forms of public building in Lyons under the Second Empire. Leonard also elucidates well the sources of financing urban renewal and some of the internal conflicts between government and residents or contractors over compensation and bids. Leonard's discussion of the social and economic effects of urban renewal is meager, however. Her discussion of the politics and financing of urban renewal, moreover, is less astute than David Pinkney's discussion of similar matters in the Paris of Baron Haussmann in his Napoleon III and the Rebuilding of Paris (Princeton: Princeton University Press, 1958).

Construction of population series required reference to additional secondary works, notably Table I-7 in Vol. 4 of Lequin's "Monde ouvrier de la région lyonnaise" and population data published by the French government, such as Statistique de la France, Population, 2e Série, 1. Résultats généraux du dénombrement de 1861 comparée aux cinq dénombrements antérieurs (Strasbourg: Imprimerie administrative de Ve

Berger-Levrault, 1864(?)), Vol. XIII and Statistique de la France,

Résultats généraux du dénombrement de 1872 (Paris, 1873). The un-

published results of the census of 1866 for Lyons, "1866: Dénombrement

de la Population de la Ville de Lyon, 1er à 5e arrondissements," ADR,

5M, includes population data differentiated by arrondissement within

the city for 1866 along with occupational distribution of this popu-

lation for the same year.

B. The Society of the Silk Weavers

In the following review of literature concerning social structure

and social change are included all sources describing material conditions

of labor (such as wages, employment, costs of living); organization of

work, economy of the household and social structure of households;

distribution of wealth; industrial relations on all levels (master –

subordinates; master – fabricant; government and the rest), including

labor conflicts and their adjudication; workers' attitudes towards their

trade and towards the household economy, their notions of class and their

perceptions of the role of government in the economy; and institutions of

the fabrique, in particular the Conseil des Prud'hommes. Such are the

sources behind most of the present study, especially Chapters I, III – VI

and VIII. Most of these sources illuminate several of these questions at

once. To facilitate discussion of them and to elucidate their character

in a different manner from their use in the text, they will be discussed

by type of source rather than by problem or question for which the source

was used in this study. The following types of sources will be reviewed:

published secondary literature, published primary literature of a (primar-

ily) non-quantitative sort (first, published observations by contemporary

'outsiders' written largely as sociological reports on the fabrique, and
second, pamphlets and memoirs by 'insiders' written for polemical purposes), enquêtes and petitions, serial reports by government authorities
on industrial and labor conditions, miscellaneous reports concerning the
Conseil des Prud'hommes and strikes, and statistical sources. All except
the last type include literary and quantitative documents together;
the literary documents are most useful for the purposes of the present
study. The last source is entirely quantitative, consisting primarily of
population and loom censuses.

1. Published Secondary Sources

Secondary literature on social conditions was consulted for both
eighteenth and nineteenth centuries. Only literature concerning Lyons
will be discussed here. For the Old Regime of the fabrique lyonnaise,
Justin Godart's Ouvrier en soie. Monographie du tisseur lyonnais.
Première partie: la réglementation du travail, 1466 - 1791 (Lyon:
Bernoux et Cumin, 1899) and Maurice Garden's Lyon et les lyonnais au
XVIIIe siècle (Paris: les Belles lettres, 1970) together provide a
thorough survey and penetrating analysis. Godart focuses on the institutional structure and evolution of the Grande Fabrique under the
Old Regime, while Garden analyzes demographic change and behavior, social
structure, popular mentality and labor conflicts among the silk weavers.
Godart's work is much older, but its minute description of the corporate
institutions of the Communauté of the Fabrique, of their evolution since
the fifteenth century, of the living conditions and work relations among
masters, journeymen and apprentices and especially between masters and
merchant-manufacturers is very fine indeed. Although based almost

entirely on règlements of the Communauté and on petitions to its master-
guards, Godart's abundant documentation and careful analysis of these
sources makes this study valuable both for its clear exposition of a
difficult subject and for its citation from primary documents.

Garden's more recent study penetrates deeply and systematically into
the demography, social structure, wealth distribution and mentalities
behind institutions and formal petitions. Despite the wide scope of the
study, concentrating on all classes and all crafts in eighteenth-century
Lyons, silk weavers and fabricants are given ample attention throughout
the work. Based on the author's thèse de doctorat, Lyon et les lyonnais
uses family reconstitution, wills, tax rolls, apprenticeship contracts
and abundant literary sources to trace changes in population growth and
behavior, social structure, popular attitudes and class relations during
the eighteenth century. Garden's discussion of the social evolution and
social movements of the Grande Fabrique is perceptive, clear and concise.
It is by far the best treatment of the subject.

Two good studies of social conditions in nineteenth-century Lyons,
for the period preceding 1852, are products of American scholarship.
These are chapters 1 and 2 of Robert Bezucha's Lyon Uprising of 1834
and the first half of Mary Lynn McDougall's doctoral dissertation
"After the Insurrections: the Workers' Movement in Lyon, 1834 - 1852"
(unpublished Ph.D. dissertation, Department of History, Columbia
University, 1974). Both describe the vie intérieure of the fabrique
with illuminating detail based on careful research. Bezucha is strongest
in describing weavers' mentality and culture underlying their conception
of class relations, status and community. Some of his tables and conclusions -- especially his discovery of the formation of silk-weaving

neighborhoods as a source of class consciousness -- were especially valuable for parts of the present study. Bezucha's earlier article, "The
'Preindustrial' Worker Movement: The Canuts of Lyon," in Modern European
Social History, ed. Robert J. Bezucha (Lexington, Massachusetts: D.C.
Heath, 1972), pp. 93-123, describes vividly the class position of silk
weavers in their daily contacts with the fabricants and offers a concise
'statement' of the economic and social situation and mentality of the
pre-industrial artisan. McDougall's dissertation explores the living and
working conditions of weavers and other workers during the subsequent two
decades in many areas of social life. Her well-documented, abundant
detail are obviously the product of extensive research. Occasionally the
dissertation evinces keen insight, but its main value is descriptive
rather than analytical. Laura Sharon Strumingher's doctoral dissertation
"Les Canutes: Women Workers in the Lyonese Silk Industry, 1835 - 1848"
(unpublished Ph.D. dissertation, Department of History, University of
Rochester, 1974) illumines a specialized aspect of the social life of
the weavers during the same period -- that of female workers in the
fabrique.

For the period after 1850, there is no substitute for Yves Lequin's
"Monde ouvrier de la région lyonnaise." This work is indeed the product
of a master in the field of sociological labor history. The scope is vast
(eight departments, many industries and towns discussed individually, for
more than a half century, 1848 - 1914), the range of topics imposing
(evolution of industry in city, town and country; population growth; occupational structure and geographical distribution of the labor force; occupational and geographical mobility; standards of living; patterns of
strikes; political and social movements of voluntary association), the

research meticulous, including as sources both local and national, and
public and private archives; and the analysis is sophisticated and intense
in parts. The combination of these qualities in a single work of such
scope is truly impressive. Although covering such a wide geographical
area and workers in all industries in this area, Lequin's work gives
much attention to Lyons, its fabrique and its silk weavers. It has the
special merit of tracing changes of economy, society and association among
the weavers in the context of the 'regionalization' of the silk industry.
For the present study, Lequin's thèse served primarily as a source for
illustration and quantitative data for the development of some
specific arguments. The present study clearly needs to be situated within
the context of the larger regional and temporal vision of the workers'
movement and its sources as expressed by Lequin. Such a task awaits the
publication of Lequin's forthcoming book based upon his thesis, Les
ouvriers de la région lyonnaise dans la seconde moitié du XIXe siècle
(1848 - 1914).

A useful monograph for the study of wealth distribution during the
nineteenth century is Pierre Léon's Géographie de la fortune et structures
sociales à Lyon au XIXe siècle (1815 - 1914) (Lyon: Université Lyon II,
Centre d'histoire économique et sociale de la région lyonnaise, 1974).
Relying primarily on the inventaires après décès, Léon traces the changes
in distribution of wealth in Lyons among the different socio-professional
'classes' and in different sections of the city, as well as the changing
character of wealth (type of investment, area of investment, and so forth)
of residents of Lyons. Léon's study was especially useful in the present
work for its statistical tables. Its analysis of these tables is careful

and expert but may need more econometric refinement before its conclusions are firm. The research for Léon's study was the joint effort of the staff of the Centre d'histoire économique et sociale de la région lyonnaise. Through its quarterly Bulletin, its seminars and its collection of thèses de maîtrise, the Centre offers abundant resources for studying the history of economic and social conditions and change in Lyons and its region.

2. Published Primary Literature (Non-Quantitative)

a. Contemporary Sociological Observation

The voluminous studies of French workers by contemporary social observers during the nineteenth century, especially under the Second Empire, still form some of the most valuable sources for investigating the living and working conditions and mentalities of workers. Despite the class or party biases and 'moralizing' tone of many of these studies, they contain a wealth of reliable information derived from personal observation of workers in their daily habitats and from interviews with them, with their employers and with other individuals (such as clergy or police) close to them in their daily lives. Sometimes the perception of these observers is very keen. Georges Duveau relied heavily on this source in his monumental Vie ouvrière en France sous le Second Empire (Paris: Gallimard, 1946) to great advantage. Four such observers who examined the fabrique of Lyons first-hand during the Second Empire and earlier informed the social analyses of the present study. These were Louis-René Villermé, Tableau de l'état physique et moral des ouvriers employés dans les manufactures de coton, de laine et de soie (Paris: J. Renouard, 1840), especially Vol. 1; A. Audiganne, "Du mouvement intellectuel parmi les populations ouvrières -- Les ouvriers de Lyon en

1852," Revue des deux mondes, 22ème année -- nouvelle période, XV(August 1, 1852), pp. 508-545; Louis Reybaud, Etudes sur le régime des manufactures. Condition des ouvriers en soie (Paris, 1859); and Jules Simon, L'ouvrière (Paris: L. Hachette, 1861) and "L'apprentissage," Le Progrès (Lyon), February 13, 1865. Of these, Villermé and Reybaud produced the most extensive studies for their respective periods -- Villermé for the 1830's and Reybaud for the 1850's. Audiganne's report is shorter but exceptionally keen in perception of weavers' character and attitudes. Simon's study of female labor is more limited, somewhat general and of questionable reliability in parts. His article on apprenticeship is shorter but more illuminating, better informed and more precise.

Villerme examined primarily social and economic conditions rather than opinions. His descriptions of weavers' budgets, wealth, economic crises and standards of living are useful. Villermé is sensitive to distinctions in some of these matters between plain and fancy cloth masters and between masters and journeymen. His portrait of the household economy aided in the reconstruction of the 'internal order' of the fabrique in Chapter I. The two letters from the master-weavers Charnier and Falconnet to John Bowring, published in Bowring's testimony to the Select Committee on the Silk Trade, June 18, 1832, in Great Britain, House of Commons, Report from Select Committee on the Silk Trade With the Minutes of Evidence, an Appendix and Index, ordered by the House of Commons to be printed 2 August 1832 (London, 1832), pp. 556-557, were also enlightening for this purpose.

Villermé's investigation was remarkably 'objective' for his period. Later studies, such as those by Audiganne, Reybaud and Simon, were overtly biased or opinionated in their evaluation of situations and events and in

their propositions for reform. Audiganne and Reybaud were more interested
in weavers' attitudes than Villermé, and both evaluated such attitudes from
the 'stance' of social conservatism; that is, as defenders of the established social order and class hierarchy but paternally solicitous for
the weavers' welfare. Of these two, Audiganne was the more astute
reader of weavers' mentality. Reybaud, however, provides some revealing
examples of behavior and attitudes and some illuminating excerpts from interviews with weavers. Both Audiganne and Reybaud give ample attention to
the household relations between masters and their subordinates and to
class relations between masters and merchant-manufacturers. Both offer
useful insights into the character and behavior of journeymen weavers and
fabricants. Reybaud has scattered but helpful detail concerning wealth,
effects of economic crises and charitable institutions. He describes
vividly the factory dormitories of Bonnet at Jujurieux and of Martin at
Tarare. Neither observes economic organization or conditions very well,
however. Both ignore, for example, the important differences between
situations of plain-cloth weavers and fancy-cloth weavers in matters such
as distribution of wealth or attitudes towards work.

Jules Simon is the least satisfying of these four contemporary observers, except in his article on apprenticeship. His observations in many
instances appear 'second-hand'; he relies often, it seems, on previous
studies by Audiganne and Reybaud for most of his information and for jus-
tifying his own interpretations. His style and intent are also more polemical, although his enthusiasm for Gewerbefreiheit and the free market
is tempered somewhat by his recognition of the virtues of industrial
paternalism for saving the workers from the worst effects of mechanization
and re-organization of industry in factories. Simon's special attention

to female labor -- to its role in silk manufacture, to its conditions of
work and living, and to the behavior and attitudes of female silk workers -
nevertheless gives L'ouvrière a special utility for the period. Moreover,
Simon's occasionally scintillating style portrays the female silk worker
in a manner probably not too distant from 'reality.' His article on
apprenticeship -- more precise, concrete and detailed -- 'fleshes out'
the situation of females in the fabrique even more by focusing on
apprenties dévideuses and tisseuses.

b. Pamphlets and Memoirs

Pamphlets and memoirs written by weavers or by local publicists
familiar with their situation are another valuable source of information
concerning conditions and social attitudes in the fabrique. Most of the
pamphlets were written during periods of social or political activism
and during periods of economic crisis. Consequently, they often have a
strong polemical or argumentative tone. Despite their possible biases,
in particular their possible tendency to exaggerate grievances in order
to justify demands for change, they represent weavers' opinion, often in
their own words, and provide useful information besides on a variety of
social issues. They are, in effect, among the best expressions of
weavers' mentality.

Most of this pamphlet literature was published around the time of
the Second Republic. Pamphlets proposed solutions to the 'social question'
or to the industrial 'chaos' of the fabrique, giving reasons to justify
these remedies. They were motivated either by reformist ideology among
the weavers of this period or by the Parliamentary Enquiry Concerning
Industry and Agriculture. The latter provided a forum for the statement

of traditional grievances and of propositions to resolve these grievances.
One of these 'responses' to the Enquiry, La vérité au sujet du malaise de
la fabrique des étoffes de soie à Lyon. Moyens d'y remédier. Mémoire
pour servir à l'enquête (Lyon: J.-M. Bajot, 1849) (BMTL, C.1559) by
Vernay, master-weaver, proposes a traditional remedy to the current
'disorder' and 'demoralization' of the fabrique. Vernay calls for a
restoration of regulations in the fabrique and rejects association as
a solution to the social question. His statement reflects superbly, in
effect, the 'mind' of the traditional master-weaver. More favorable to
association but also hostile to unlimited competition are Xavier Pailley's
Système de réforme industrielle ou projet d'association entre tous les
citoyens qui concourent au commerce et à la fabrication des articles de
soieries (Lyon: Chanoine, 1848) (BMTL, C.1558) and Philippe Thierrat's
Du malaise de la classe ouvrière et de l'institution des prud'hommes
appliquée à l'augmentation du travail dans la fabrique lyonnaise (Lyon:
J. Nigon, 1848) (BMTL, C.1559). The publicist Kauffmann's De la
fabrique lyonnaise (Lyon: Midan, 1846), written a few years earlier,
is especially useful for attitudes relating household, craft pride and
competitiveness of the Lyons fabrique with foreign manufactures. Kauffmann
obviously knew the fabrique quite well, but it is difficult to tell how
much of the attitude he describes was that of the weavers themselves and
how much was simply that of sympathetic bourgeois observers like Kauffmann
himself. (My guess is that his attitude in these matters was not very
distant from the attitudes of the weavers themselves.)

One of the most valuable pamphlets for the present study was Pierre
Dronier's Essai sur la décadence actuelle de la fabrique lyonnaise (Lyon:
Nigon, 1860) (BMTL, C.1559). Dronier was a journeyman weaver, probably

a weaver of fancy silks. His description of the conditions and habits of journeymen, of the state of industry in 1860 and of the functions and status of the master-weaver   reflects attitudes of the journeyman weaver at the entry into the crisis of the 1860's. The pamphlet is especially valuable for this rare view of the mind of a journeyman. Another useful pamplet for an earlier period -- one of the hundreds that appeared then -- was written by a master weaver: J.A.B., chef d'atelier, De la nécessité d'une augmentation des prix de fabrication des étoffes, comme moyen d'assurer la prosperité du commerce (Lyon: Imprimerie de Charvin, 1832) (BMTL, C.1559).

Joseph Benoît's well-known memoir, Confessions d'un prolétaire (Lyon, 1871), ed. Maurice Moissonnier (Paris: Editions sociales, 1968), is even more replete with testimony concerning weavers' mentality -- that of the author, a master-weaver propelled into national politics in 1848, and that of the weavers he 'radicalized' and organized into clandestine   associations in Lyons. Benoît is also useful for some interesting details concerning the social conditions of the fabrique lyonnaise during the 1830's, when most of his political activity was concentrated in Lyons.

3. Enquêtes and Petitions

Two of the most important nineteenth-century inquiries (enquêtes) concerning social and economic conditions in France -- that of 1848, concerning the situation of industry and agriculture, and that of 1872, concerning conditions of labor -- 'bracketed,' so to speak, the Second Empire, the period of focus of the present study. Unfortunately, most of the returns for the 1848 inquiry for Lyons were lost. Occasionally,

however, it is possible to find valuable sous-enquêtes (my term) serving
as sources for responses to the more general questions of the national
survey. With good fortune, I discovered one such sous-enquête focusing
on the conditions of the silk weavers in Lyons. The document is located
in the AN series on technology, AN, F12 - 2203(2): Machines à tisser
(1844 à 1866), and includes several mémoires by master-weavers. The
master-weaver Weichmann assembled these "Mémoires recueillis par le
citoyen Weichmann, chef d'atelier, rue du sentier, no. 8 à la Croix-
Rousse," April 2, 1850, and summarized their major
conclusions and grievances. Despite the stilted language and bad
spelling of these mémoires, they provide accurate, detailed information
concerning all aspects of the weavers' shop management. Some of this
is quantitative data of the most illuminating sort; namely, shop accounts
of several different masters in Lyons for several years before 1850.
The document is also a fine source for weavers' mentality. It reiterates
in passionate tones the grievances of masters, in the words of one of
their number, concerning apprenticeship, free entreprise, wastes of silk
thread and class relations in their trade.

The returns from the enquête of 1872 are preserved in their entirety
for the department of the Rhône in AN, C 3021, Enquête sur les Conditions
du Travail en France (1872 à 1875), Région du Sud-Est (Rhône). For the
present study, this enquête was especially valuable for focusing on weavers'
living and working conditions, and not only on industry and agriculture
in general. The inquiry has specific questions in each of three areas --
material and economic situation (A), wages and worker-employer relations
(B), and moral and intellectual situation (C). Responses to these
questions are usually as specific as the questions themselves. Sometimes

responses for the fabrique volunteer additional information, explaining
the presumed 'peculiarities' of the silk industry of Lyons as compared
with other French industries. These additional comments abound in the
'Observations' following each set of questions A,B, and C. All responses
for the fabrique are 'bourgeois.' None (apparently) were given by
weavers themselves. This ha s obvious disadvantages for the investigator of conditions of labor at the time. But at least some of the
'bourgeois' who responded were intimately familiar with the fabrique.
Among these were two prominent fabricants (Faye and Thevenin), the
Chamber of Commerce, and the Chambre syndicale des soieries -- the
professional association of fabricants. For understanding the organization of the industry and the vie intérieure of the putting-out
enterprise -- including the relationship of fabricant with the
weavers in his enterprise -- these responses are especially useful.

Both enquêtes -- that of 1848 and that of 1872 -- have been
preserved in their entirety for the department of Isère. The ADI
contains all responses to the enquête of 1848 in ADI, 162.M. Organisation du travail, 1.-2., and some of the response to the enquête of
1872 in ADI, 162.M. Organisation du travail, 3.. The AN has none of
the former but all of the latter responses in AN, C 3021, Région du
Sud-Est (Isère). Both enquêtes are useful for tracing the economic
and social development of countryside weaving, including the establishment of factory-dormitories and the social services offered by
the latter. The enquête of 1872 is especially valuable for this
purpose, since fabricants operating such factories in Isère, such as
Montessuy-Chomer of Renage and Perrigaux of Bourgoin, responded individually to the enquête, and these individual reports are preserved

in the archives. These reports elaborate in detail the 'paternal' expenditures of _fabricants_ on their factory workers. Their perspective
is obviously 'bourgeois,' so that in these reports, as in those for
Lyons, the views of weavers themselves are under-represented.

The Second Empire was a time of much petitioning by the workers
to the Emperor and to his administrators. The latter advertised their
concern for the working classes, and the workers often 'tested' this
concern by bringing their traditional grievances to the government
for satisfaction 'from above.' In Lyons, the silk weavers hastened
to present such demands for a new industrial court, for stronger regulation of industry, for control of unruly subordinates and for a
mercuriale of piece-rates in 1852 and 1853, soon after the proclamation
of Empire. Most of these early petitions are located in manuscript
form, with responses by local police and other officials, in AML,
F2 - Fabrique de soies - Règlement - Tarif - Affaires diverses (1810
à 1874). These were largely petitions by individuals or by small
groups of master-weavers. In 1860, on the occasion of a visit by the
Emperor to Lyons, the silk weavers petitioned on a larger scale and
in more organized fashion. About 550 weavers signed the statement of
grievances, and the master-weaver prud'hommes presented the petition
to the Emperor. Unlike the petitions of 1852-1853, which focused each
on one or two grievances, that of 1860 combined several different
grievances and underlined their common origin in a lack of rules in
the _fabrique_ or in a failure to enforce existing rules. The petition
provoked an extensive, unfavorable response by a commission composed
largely of silk merchants and _fabricants_ of the Chamber of Commerce.
The petition and the response to it are preserved in ACCL, Soieries

Carton 41 - I - Législation - Usages (an 8 à 1936), 13. - Pétition
remise à l'Empereur, à son passage à Lyon, par les ouvriers en soie.
One of the major grievances concerned the measuring of silk cloth to
determine the earnings for each piece. It was the subject of continued
petitioning to the prefect of the Rhône by individuals, by small, independent groups of weavers and by weaver prud'hommes throughout
the 1860's. These and other earlier petitions concerning métrage
are available in ACCL, Soieries Carton 22 - II - Mesurage des
soieries (an 13 à 1899), along with responses to each request by the
prefect, by the Chamber of Commerce or by the Conseil des Prud'hommes.

In October 1866, the silk weavers made their most dramatic
statement of demands to the prefect by threatening to demonstrate
en masse and then agreeing to present their demands through their
delegates. A description of these demands, of the events surrounding
the petition, and the response of government and public opinion to
the demands and events are found in several sources, the most important of which are the articles in Le Progrès (Lyon), October-
November 1866, on the petition; the dossier "Ouvriers de Lyon" in
AN, Fic III Rhône 10, Correspondance et divers (1816 à 1870), especially valuable for the rationale behind the government's 'gesture
of benevolence' to the weavers' producers' cooperative, in response
to their demands; and the dossier concerning the threatened demonstration of October 1866 in AML, I2 - 47(B), Corporations: ouvriers
en soie (1819 à 1870), especially pieces 877 and 878, for the weavers'
attitudes towards government intervention in the economy, as expressed
in their demands.

4. Serial Reports Concerning Industry and Working Conditions

Of a very different nature and use than enquêtes and petitions
are the reports concerning the situation of industry and the conditions
of labor by the Prefect of the Rhône to the Minister of the Interior,
by the Special Police Commissioner to the Prefect of the Rhône, and by
police agents to the Commissioner. Each of these reports was compiled
from the one following, in succession. Two of these, the reports
of the Special Police Commissioner and the notes of the police agents
from which these notes were written, are described and 'evaluated'
in Appendix IV. They are the best sources for industrial and working
conditions for the period 1859 - 1870. Both are located in AML,
I2 - 47 (A), Situation de l'industrie lyonnaise: ... rapports sur
la soierie et les ouvriers en soie ... (1819 à 1870).

For the 1850's, the more general reports by the Prefect of the
Rhône to the Minister of the Interior are alone available in the
archives. These (usually) bi-monthly reports on the political,
economic and moral situation of the department are located in AN,
Fic III Rhône 5, Compte-rendus administratifs (An III à 1870). These
reports are especially enlightening for the role of the government
in the economy and for the political rationale motivating government
intervention. After 1860 the extant reports
are fewer and generally less useful than the police reports in AML,
I2 - 47(A) for tracing the conditions of industry. They continue to
reveal, however, the attitudes of government towards the cooperative
movement, which evolve with the realization that cooperation served
as a strong antidote for political activism among the workers. The
prefect's reports need to be supplemented with dossiers on specific

issues and events in AN, Fic III Rhône 10, <u>Correspondance et divers</u>
<u>(1816 à 1870)</u>, for elaboration of these attitudes.

5. <u>Miscellaneous Sources</u>

Certain archival sources concerning the <u>Conseil des Prud'hommes</u>
and strikes contain useful quantitative data and literary observation
on social conditions among the weavers. Most useful are the annual
reports of the president of the <u>Conseil des Prud'hommes de Lyon</u> concerning hearings of the Council and the general situation of the
<u>fabrique</u>. These reports are located in ADR, U - <u>Prud'hommes de</u>
<u>Lyon, Correspondance relative aux élections (1806 à 1870)</u>. Reports
of the years 1854, 1856, 1858, and 1866 include both quantitative
data concerning number and type of cases presented to the Council
and analyses of reasons for recurrent conflicts. These analyses
clarify the nature of relations within the household, between
master-weavers and subordinate workers, and outside, between masters
and merchant-manufacturers. In AML, F - <u>Prud'hommes - Elections</u>
<u>(1806 à 1871)</u>, there are several useful decrees, reports and posters
concerning the institution of the Council itself, including elections
to it. The <u>Usages du Conseil des Prud'hommes de la ville de Lyon pour</u>
<u>les industries de la soierie</u> (Lyon: L. A. Bonnaviat, 1872) (BMTL,
C.1558) and the "Extrait des Minutes de la Secrétaire d'Etat, au
Palais de St. Cloud le 3 juillet 1806 ... Conseil des Prud'hommes,"
AML, F2 - <u>Fabrique de soies - Règlement - Tarif - Affaires diverses</u>
<u>(1810 à 1874)</u> (brought to my attention by Monsieur Berthelon) together
provide the best information on the legal structure and precedents
governing the industrial relations in the <u>fabrique</u> and used as a

basis for adjudication by the Council during the nineteenth century.

Dossiers concerning strikes among weavers of Lyons in AML,

I2 - 47(B), Corporations: ouvriers en soie (1819 à 1870) and I2 - 48,

Délits de coalition ouvrière et grèves. Grèves hors Lyon (1803 à

1870), and among weavers of Isère in ADI, 166M - 1, Grèves (1858 à

1877), occasionally contain information on social conditions, wages,

employment, or apprenticeship. ADI, 166M - 1, for example, has useful

information on the organization of industry in the countryside -- in

particular, the distribution of manufacturing tasks between factory

and domestic labor in this area.

6. Statistical Sources

Most of the quantitative sources for analyses of social structure

of households and for distribution of looms and workers by neigh-

borhood are fiscal, population and loom censuses. The household

samples described in Appendix V were taken from censuses in register

(that is, household listing) form. These were the fiscal census of

the Croix-Rousse in 1847, in AML, Recensement, Croix-Rousse, 1847;

the population census of the Croix-Rousse in 1851, in ADR, 6M -

Dénombrement, Croix-Rousse, volumes 23 and 24; and the population

census of the Fourth Arrondissement in 1866, in ADR, 6M -

Dénombrement, 1866, Lyon, 4ème arrondissement, volumes 16 and 17.

Data used integrally, rather than sampled, were taken from census

summaries. For the Croix-Rousse in 1833, 1842, and 1844-1845,

and for Lyon in 1846, these summaries are located in the back of the

household registers of the Recensements in AML. The summary of

the census of 1866 of Lyons is located in ADR, 5M, "1866:

Dénombrement de la population de la ville de Lyon, 1er à 5e arrondissements." All of these censuses and census summaries except
the summary of 1866 provide information concerning number, type,
and activity of looms.

Other sources for information concerning workers and looms in
the fabrique are AML, F2 - Fabrique de soieries--Inventeurs -
Statistiques, 1811 - 1854; ACCL, Soieries Carton 21, Tissage de
soieries (statistiques), Statistique des métiers de tissage avant
1900 - divers; and M. Robin, "Situation de Fabrique," June 1, 1866,
presented to the Chamber of Commerce of Lyons in June 1870, in Compte-
rendu des travaux de la Chambre de Commerce de Lyon, années 1869,
1870, 1871, p. 101. The first two liasses include abundant loom and
worker data for 1820 - 1829. The data for 1825 in ACCL and for 1829
in AML are specified by quarter of the city, and the former includes
data on the few rural looms of the fabrique lyonnaise as well. Robin's
data distinguish workers and looms by neighborhood as well but, unlike
the AML and ACCL data, make no distinctions of loom type. For this
reason, the membership list of the Société civile des tisseurs,
July 5, 1873, in ADR, 10M-2, Associations   d'ouvriers tisseurs (1870-93)
had to be consulted for constructing some tables. (See Appendix III.)

A final document, needed for constructing indices of food costs
in Chapter III, was the mercuriale of bread, meat, potato and coal
prices on the market of Lyons. Monthly averages of these prices
are readily accessible in AN, F11* - 2848 à 2849, for 1825 - 1836,
and in F11* - 2850 à 2857, for 1860 - 1878. For 1837 - 1859, only
the bi-weekly reports in monthly registers are available in AN,
F11 - 1924* à 2187*. The use and limitations of this source are

discussed in Appendix II.

II. Sources Concerning Movements of Association

a. General

The general literature on movements of voluntary association in France and in Lyons in particular is sparse and of uneven quality. The older labor histories, such as Edouard Dolléans, Histoire du mouvement ouvrier (Paris: A. Colin, 1936-1939), 3 volumes, Jean Jaurès, gen. ed., Histoire socialiste (1789 - 1900) (Paris: J. Rouff, 1907), Vol. 10: Le second empire (1852 - 1870) by Albert Thomas, and E. Levasseur, Histoire des classes ouvrières et de l'industrie en France de 1789 à 1870 (Paris: A. Rousseau, 1903-1904), 2 volumes, usually discussed these movements in general terms for France as a whole. In most cases, this meant focusing on the labor movement in Paris. All except Levasseur were institutional histories written in narrative form. The few studies of movements of association in Lyons from 1830 to 1870 (or later) are fortunately based on extensive research in local archives, and some of these extend beyond institutional history to the history of social change and popular culture besides.

Fernand Rude's Insurrection lyonnaise de novembre 1831: Le mouvement ouvrier à Lyon de 1827 - 1832 (Paris: Editions Anthropos, 1969) and Robert J. Bezucha's Lyon Uprising of 1834 together offer an excellent introduction to the movement of workers' association during the early July monarchy. Both are ambitiously researched and thoroughly documented. Rude's history is older and narrative in form. It abounds in illuminating detail and extensive quotation, and therefore serves as a compendium of source material as well as a story of events

leading to and following the November insurrection of 1831. Bezucha's
discussion of the workers' movement in Lyons from November 1831 to
1834 is more analytical. Bezucha's sense of the political dynamics
of that movement is superb. He traces carefully and with interesting
anecdote the separate development of a silk-weavers' movement of
association for industrial resistance and of a Republican political
movement in Lyons. He explains how the government's misguided search
for a social policy in the interests of the industrialists provoked a
convergence of these two separate movements into common protest and
then rebellion against the law on associations. Bezucha describes
the social and economic background to the workers' movement clearly
and informatively but does not relate this background very rigorously
or 'deeply' to the movement or to its ideology. The only exception
is his perceptive identification of settlement among the masters
and of neighborhood 'polarization' among the weavers in general as
sources of class consciousness and class solidarity dominated by
the master-weavers. Bezucha also fails to give much attention to
that 'silent' source of all workers' association (the paradigm of
association among them, one might say) in this period -- the mutual
aid society. Rude is also less than adequate in this respect, but
he recognizes, at least, the importance of mutual aid as a forerunner
of _mutuellisme_ and expresses that recognition by describing some
mutual aid societies in detail.

For the period 1834 - 1852, Mary Lynn McDougall's dissertation,
"After the Insurrections: the Workers' Movement in Lyon, 1834 - 1852,"
is the best survey. McDougall discusses nearly all aspects of that
movement thoroughly and intelligently, including cooperation, strikes,

secret societies, political clubs, workers' press, and utopian

socialism. She too fails, however, to relate this movement to the

social and economic change discussed in the first half of her thesis

in any rigorous fashion. She also fails to discuss mutual aid at least

to the extent of its importance in the workers' movement of this

period.

    For the period after 1848, the best survey is Yves Lequin's

"Monde ouvrier de la région lyonnaise," Vol. 4. Lequin's discussion

of the workers' movement in a separate volume from the first two con-

cerning economic and social change might suggest the same failure

to relate the latter to the former in a rigorous fashion. To some

extent, this problem remains 'untackled' even in Lequin's work, since

the relationship is not explored systematically. But the careful reader

will discover in Lequin a vision of the whole process of the workers'

movement that corresponds to the process of economic and social change

as described in the first two volumes. This vision captures subtly and

with insight the flux of 'solidarities' underlying the workers'

movement in the Lyons region -- solidarities that shift among in-

dustrial, sub-regional or urban, and class identities. There is a

sense of striving among the workers to achieve unity on the basis of

one of these -- class -- but which always fails. This failure sug-

gests that the dissemination of industry throughout the région

lyonnaise acted as a force for decentralization in social movements

by providing local 'orbits' of class formation and class consciousness

within which relatively independent workers' movements could thrive.

Lequin's opus merits close and frequent readings to penetrate and to

elucidate such perspectives on the workers' movements. Lequin's third

volume also is a mine of information concerning all aspects and
'phases' of the workers' movement in the Lyons region, from compag-
nonnage and mutual aid to organized party politics.

In 1899 the Labor Office of the Ministry of Commerce and
Industry began publishing an extremely useful survey of workers'
associations in France during the nineteenth century. The
Republique Française, Ministère du Commerce, de l'Industrie, des
Postes et de Telegraphes, Office du Travail, Les associations professionnelles ouvrières (Paris: Imprimerie Nationale, 1899 - 1904)
discusses major forms, periods, regions and industries of workers'
association with illuminating detail. Sometimes the information is
incomplete or (less frequently) inaccurate, but much of the information is not available elsewhere and therefore useful. The
section "Tisseurs de Lyon" in Vol. 2, pp. 241-340 is replete with
valuable detail, especially for the period after 1860, and generally
reliable. The authors of this survey profited from memories of living
participants and probably also from private archives of existing
workers' associations in gathering this information -- two sources
which are lost or unknown to us today.

B. Period Movements

This study has referred to three periods of militant association
among the weavers of Lyons in its discussion of workers' ideology and
organization. These were the early 1830's (1831 - 1834), the Second
Republic and its preceding three years (1845 - 1851), and the Second
Empire (1852 - 1870), on which this study has focused. Movements of
association are treated separately for each of these periods in the

available literature. Some of this literature has been discussed, but a few additional works need to be mentioned.

For the 1830's, the books by Rude and Bezucha should be supplemented by their articles on the same period. Fernand Rude's "Insurrection ouvrière de Lyon en 1831 et le rôle de Pierre Charnier," Révolution de 1848, 35, No. 164 (March 1938) is enlightening on the personal background and beliefs of Pierre Charnier, founder of mutuellisme in Lyons. Robert J. Bezucha's "Aspects du conflit des classes à Lyon, 1831 - 1834," Le Mouvement Social, No. 76 (July – September 1971), 5-24, destroys the old conservative argument that the insurrection of 1834 was the result of a Republican plot among the weavers. Bezucha thus preserves the autonomy of the weavers' movement during this period. Rude and Bezucha both relied on three sources primarily in their articles and books, and these three are in fact the most important documents for studying weavers' ideology and association during the early 1830's. These were the Documents Gasparin in AML, the dossier Mutuellisme in AN, CC 558: Cour des Pairs: Evénements d'avril 1834, Lyon, and L'echo de la fabrique, the 'house organ' of the Society of Mutual Duty, preserved in its entirety in BML, Journaux 5707.

For the period 1845 - 1852, Mary Lynn McDougall's dissertation, already discussed, is the best survey. McDougall examines the Revolution of 1848 in Lyons quite thoroughly in this survey from the workers' perspective. A closer look at the Revolution as a whole during its first six months is Francois Dutacq's erudite Histoire politique de Lyon pendant la Révolution de 1848 (Paris: Edouard Cornely, 1910). Dutacq analyzes quite well the

role of different political forces and groups in first making and then
'undoing' the Revolution of February. Dutacq gives fair attention to
workers' clubs in this political process, especially to the Voraces
in the silk-weavers' quarters. For closer examination of workers'
associations in this period and later in the Second Republic, however,
Dutacq must be supplemented by McDougall, to be sure, and especially
by one of her sources, A. Gilardin, Procureur Général, to
M. le Garde des Sceaux, "Rapport sur les associations ayant un carac-
tère politique à Lyon. Vues législatives sur la matière," January 23,
1850, AN, BB18 - 1474(B): Clubs et associations: Cours de Lyon.
Christopher Johnson's very fine Utopian Communism in France: Cabet
and the Icarians, 1839 - 1851 (Ithaca: Cornell University Press,
1974), finally, is well-informed on the silk weavers of Lyons, among
whom Cabet won many converts during the 1840's. Johnson's book
offers keen insight into important dimensions of the 'social meaning'
of utopian association among the silk weavers during this pre-Repub-
lican period.

The 'social movement' of voluntary association under the
Second Empire in Lyons is the subject of Sreten Maritch's Histoire
du mouvement social sous le Second Empire à Lyon (Paris: Rousseau,
1930). This first survey of the (entire) workers' movement has
only recently been superseded by Yves Lequin's "Monde ouvrier de
la région lyonnaise." Lequin's treatment is by far the more satisfactory in all respects, although Maritch is still worth consulting
for details concerning workers' participation in political affairs.
Jacques Rougerie questioned Maritch's interpretation of the International Workingman's Association in Lyons and proposed an alternative

view in "La première Internationale à Lyon (1865 - 1870),"
Problèmes d'histoire du mouvement ouvrier français (Annali dell'
Instituto Giangiacomo Feltrinelli, 1961), pp. 126-193. Rougerie's
well-argued interpretation restores cooperation to the ideology of
the militants of the Lyons International and thus undermines Maritch's
effort to denigrate the cooperative movement in favor of the
International. Maurice Moissonnier took account of this re-inter-
pretation and other recent work on the late Empire in Lyons in writing
his history of the First International in Lyons, including its role
in the Commune of Lyons. Moissonnier's Première internationale et la
commune à Lyon (Paris: Editions sociales, 1972) still offers a
Marxist interpretation of political events of the late Empire, early
Republic in Lyons but one that is more refined than that of Maritch.
Moissonnier's own experience of political organization as a Communist
militant make him more aware of the complexities of interaction
between mass movements and party leadership. This awareness enables
him to understand the reasons for the failure of the Bakuninist
International in September 1870. Although his social analysis is rather
weak   (as compared with his political analysis), his book is the
best on the subject, based on careful and extensive archival research.
Louis M. Greenberg's Sisters of Liberty: Marseilles, Lyon, Paris and
the reaction to a centralized state, 1868 - 1871 (Cambridge, Massachusetts: Harvard University Press, 1971), finally, describes the political and ideological evolution of the Commune of Lyons in a national
perspective. Greenberg is a necessary supplement to Moissonnier for
understanding the political evolution of the Commune as a whole. It
is well done, and its argument that the Commune was a 'decentralist'

reaction to the centralized state as such merits consideration.

C. Movement Types

Many books, articles and archives focus on one type of workers'
movement only. These formed the most useful sources for the research
of the present study. Sources for four of these types will be
discussed here: mutual aid, cooperation and clubs, industrial resistance and the International - political movement.

1. Mutual Aid

The best published introduction to the history of mutual aid
societies in Lyons is J.-C. Paul Rougier's Associations ouvrières.
Etude sur leur passé, leur présent, leurs conditions de progrès
(Paris and Lyon, 1864). Rougier describes best the operation of
these societies under the Second Empire and the nature of the
government's policy of 'approval.' His assessment of attitudes of
silk-worker members of the Silk Workers' Society for Mutual Aid
towards this Society, as compared with attitudes of members of the
smaller societies towards their associations, is instructive and
probably accurate. Rougier describes the first as distant, formal
and 'contractual' and the second as intimate, affective and
'fraternal.' Emile Laurent's Pauperisme et les associations de
prévoyance (Paris, 1865) is a necessary supplement to Rougier for
situating the mutual aid movement in Lyons in a national perspective.

The most important sources for the history of mutual aid in
Lyons are archival. The series ADR, 5X - 1954 - Sociétés de secours
mutuels contains most of these sources. This series includes separate
liasses for individual societies, with statutes, membership lists,

financial accounts, petitions by individuals to the prefect, reports
on meetings and so forth. These liasses were the product of police surveillance before 1852 and of surveillance along with administration
of 'approved' societies after 1852. Documents for the latter period
are therefore most voluminous. Statutes for some societies which are
missing from the ADR liasses can be found in AML (Bibliothèque). Membership lists for a few societies of silk weavers, which are also not
available in ADR, can be found in ACCL, Petites sociétés de secours
mutuels, Carton 4, Subventions accordées, Demandes de subventions, for
the period 1867 - 1876. These societies submitted these lists to the
Chamber of Commerce to justify requests for subsidies on the same
basis as those granted to the Silk Workers' Society; namely, the
large proportion of silk workers in each society. Of course, the
ACCL includes many more documents on the Silk Workers' Society, which
the Chamber sponsored and funded, than on the small weavers' societies.
ACCL, Société de Secours Mutuels et Caisse de Retraites des Ouvriers en
Soie de la Ville de Lyon, Cartons 1 and 2, contain statutes of the
Society, lists of administrators, one list of members, copies of some
deliberations of the Society and of the Chamber of Commerce concerning
its establishment, and various other documents besides. Carton 7 of
this same series includes many useful statistical tables concerning
the mutual aid movement in Lyons as a whole, including the number of
'approved' societies, membership size and financial resources of each.
In AML (Bibliothèque), 702.068, there is a small collection of published annual reports of the Silk Workers' Society. These are especially useful sources of 'ideology' fostered by the leaders of the
Society. Each report publishes the president's annual address to the

members, in which 'moral' themes are especially prominent.

2. Cooperation and Educational - Recreational - Professional Clubs

Jean Gaumont's monumental Histoire générale de la coopération en France (Paris: Fédération nationale des coopératives de consommation, 1923-1924), 2 volumes, is the best introduction to the cooperative movement in Lyons. This work examines the ideologies, institutions, personalities and political tendencies of the cooperative movement in several different regions of France throughout the nineteenth century. Volume 1 includes the history of cooperation in Lyons from 1830 - 1870 and focuses on the role of the silk weavers in the movement there. Gaumont is more favorable to 'utopian' cooperation of the 1830's and 1840's in Lyons than to 'positive' cooperation of the 1860's. According to Gaumont -- a cooperative activist himself -- the latter movement betrayed the grand vision and mass appeal of Rochdale and Fourierist cooperation by accepting government aid and by giving more attention to simple material needs and profits than to the transformation of economic and social relations. Despite his reservations about the movement of the Second Empire, Gaumont is fair and thorough in his treatment. His book is valuable both for its detailed information and for its identification of cooperative movements in each period with particular ideological trends, such as Fourierism, Saint-Simonism, and liberalism. Gaumont's shorter Mouvement ouvrier d'association et de cooperation à Lyon (Lyon: Avenir régional, n.d.) summarizes the history of cooperation in Lyon without sacrificing pertinent detail. It is the best brief introduction to the subject.

One of Gaumont's sources was Eugène Flotard's <u>Mouvement coopér-</u>
<u>atif à Lyon et dans le Midi de la France</u> (Paris, 1867). Although
rather disorganized, rambling and biased towards liberalism, this
little book has some useful information concerning finances, membership and history of individual cooperative societies in the Lyons
region as well as a transcript of the inquiry concerning cooperative
societies by the Imperial government, on January 12, 1866, with testimony by some prominent cooperators of Lyons, including Jean Monet,
a master silk weaver. Flotard's own expressions of cooperative
aims and his perceptions of tendencies in the cooperative movement
are valuable statements of cooperative 'ideology' by one of the
movement's foremost advocates, very influential among the workers of
Lyons besides. <u>Le mouvement coopératif</u> is, in effect, a valuable
primary document as well as a survey of the local movement to date.

Flotard wrote his book largely from notes he wrote weekly for
<u>Le Progrès</u> (Lyon), the "Bulletins coopératifs," from 1865 to 1869.
These "Bulletins" provide, by far, the best regular reporting on the
the movement during this period. Through them and through occasional
publication of 'position papers' by cooperative activists, <u>Le Progrès</u>
served as a cooperative press. The "Bulletins" and 'position papers'
are useful not only for detailed information concerning meetings,
finances, and activities of individual societies but also for statements of cooperative aims and ambitions by the activists themselves.
Cooperative 'ideology' of this sort is also found in abundance in
the reports by the Lyons workers' delegates to the universal exposition of 1862 (London), in Commission ouvrière, <u>Rapports des</u>

délégués lyonnais envoyés à l'Exposition universelle de Londres

(Lyon: Commission ouvrière, 1862), and to the exposition of 1867

(Paris), in Eugène Tartaret, ed., Exposition universelle de 1867.

Commission ouvrière de 1867. Procès-verbaux, Vol. 2 (BCCL,L1 - 284).

For understanding the cooperative movement in any depth,

two series of archives are indispensable. These are AML, I2 - 45,

Sociétés coopératives de production et de consommation (1849 à 1870)

and ADR, 4M - Police administrative - Associations, coops. Documents

on the cooperative movement in the AML series concern only the

Second Empire; those in the ADR series focus more extensively on

the movement of the Third Republic. All of these documents are

police reports or the products of close police surveillance. They

include statutes of individual societies, membership lists, balance

sheets, minutes of meetings, reports concerning elections within the

societies and biographical data on the leaders. Classification of

documents by individual society permits a study of the move-

ment on a microscopic level. Most reports concern consumers'

cooperatives, but the AML series also has a lengthy dossier on

the Association of Weavers (producers' cooperative). The AML

series includes police reports and tabular data on the movement as

a whole in Lyons and a transcript of another inquiry concerning the

movement, this time by the Chambre de Commerce de Lyon, Commission

des Manufactures,"Enquête sur les sociétés coopératives, délibéra-

tions," December 7, 1865. Dossiers on individual clubs in Lyons,

with documents similar to those of cooperative societies, are located

in the same AML series, I2 - 45, for the Second Empire, and in ADR,

4M - Police administrative - Associations, cercles ouvriers

non-catholiques, for the period after 1870.

For the purpose of tracing leaders and members of cooperative societies in population censuses, membership lists in the AML and ADR series had to be supplemented by lists submitted to the Tribunal of Commerce of Lyons at the time of incorporation of these societies. (Such tracing was required for determining, for example, the proportion of leaders of the Association of Weavers who had fancy-cloth looms in their households.) Complete membership lists are available in the archives of the Tribunal only for sociétés à responsabilité limitée and for sociétés anonymes, but this caused no serious problems for the analytical purposes of the present study. The lists for such sociétés incorporated before July 1, 1867, are located in ADR, 9U – Sociétés: Constitutions et modifications, dissolutions, and those incorporated after this date are available in ATCL, Actes des Sociétés. Use of these lists for determining social and economic characteristics of members of·associations is described more fully in George J. Sheridan, Jr., "Idéologies et structures sociales dans les associations ouvrières à Lyon, de 1848 à 1877," Bulletin du Centre d'Histoire économique et sociale de la Région lyonnaise, 1976, No. 2, 1-47. The same article presents preliminary results of analysis of the social and economic foundations of association ideology by this method of tracing.

3. Industrial Resistance

The resistance movement of the late Second Empire is best described for the Lyons region by Yves Lequin's "Monde ouvrier de la région lyonnaise," Vol. 3. The Office du Travail, Associations professionnelles ouvrières, Vol. 2, pp. 269-285, surveys the movement

among the silk weavers of Lyons rather well. Mathé aîné's Tisseurs

en soie de Lyon (1900) (BN, 4 V 5056) does the same in more sketchy

fashion. The movement of 1869 - 1870 is best reconstructed, however,

from the police archives, especially AML, I2 - 47 (B), Corporations:

ouvriers en soie . . . (1819 à 1870), and from the "Chroniques locales"

of Le Progrès (Lyon). The AML liasse has minutes of meetings, reports

on leaders, statutes and proposed statutes for the Société civile des

tisseurs, and copies of tarifs of piece-rates proposed or accepted

in negotiations with the fabricants, for each of the cloth categories.

The articles in Le Progrès include notices of meetings, agendas and

minutes of meetings, reports concerning tarif negotiations and

responses to the fabricants. Le Progrès thus served as a press

for the resistance movement as it had served as a cooperative press

earlier in the decade.

The resistance movement after 1870 among the silk weavers is

well documented in ADR, 10M - 2, 3, Associations d'ouvriers tisseurs

(1870-93). As in the AML series for the movement of 1869 - 1870, the

ADR series includes minutes of meetings, reports on leaders, and so

forth for each of the cloth categories composing the Société civile des

tisseurs and also for the plain-velvet weavers of the Corporation

des tisseurs de velours unis, ville et campagne. ADI, 166M - 1:

Grèves (1858 - 1877) and AML, I2 - 48, Délits de coalition ouvrière

et grèves. Grèves hors Lyon (1802 - 1870) document the extension

of resistance in the silk industry to the countryside. The first

source traces the 'mission' of the weavers of Lyons to the rural

weavers of Isère, supporting the latter in their strike of April - May

1870. The second source examines the extension of resistance to other areas of the department of the Rhône and to other departments nearby, especially to Ain.

4. The International Workingmen's Association and the Political Movement

The history of the Lyons branch of the International is the subject of chapters in Sreten Maritch, Histoire du mouvement social à Lyon, of the article by Jacques Rougerie, "La première Internationale à Lyon," and especially of the book by Maurice Moissonnier, La première internationale et la commune à Lyon. All three studies have been discussed under 'Period Movements.' Among the important archives on the International in Lyons is AML, I2 - 55, Papiers d'Albert Richard: Pièces relatives à l'Association Internationale des Travailleurs. Piece No. 27, a police report entitled "Association Internationale des Travailleurs," February 1870, by Faure, was especially useful for the present study. In addition to summarizing the history of the International in Lyons from 1864 to 1870, the report identifies leaders of each 'tendency' within the Association and provides extensive biographical, occupational and political information about each leader. The overt hostility of the author of the report to the International does not lessen its reliability for occupational and residential information concerning each leader. The present study used the report only for this information.

Yves Lequin, "Le monde ouvrier de la région lyonnaise," Vol. 3, Louis Greenberg, Sisters of Liberty, and Maritch and Moissonier, mentioned above, are the best secondary studies of the political movement among workers in Lyons during the late Empire, early Republic. More thorough investigation of political affairs requires consultation of the extensive police reports on political activities in AML. The police remained active and powerful during the 1860's, despite the liberalization of imperial social policy, and they left many detailed reports to testify to their vigilance. None of these sources was consulted for the present study. They remain on the horizon for future work.

DISSERTATIONS
IN
EUROPEAN ECONOMIC HISTORY
1981

An Arno Press Collection

Bensidoun, Sylvain. **Le Dynamisme de la Vallee du Zeravšan (Uzbekistan-U.R.S.S.).** 1972

Brabander, Guido L. De. **Regional Specialization, Employment and Economic Growth in Belgium From 1846 to 1970.** 1979

Casey, Joan Droege. **Bordeaux, Colonial Port of Nineteenth Century France.** 1973.

Chandler, David L. **Health and Slavery in Colonial Colombia.** 1972

Dalgaard, Bruce R. **South Africa's Impact on Britain's Return to Gold, 1925.** 1976

Davis, John A. **Merchants, Monopolists and Contractors.** 1975

Deal, Zack J.,III **Serf and State Peasant Agriculture.** 1978

Ellis, Joyce. **A Study of the Business Fortunes of William Cotesworth c 1668-1726.** 1975

Engberg, Holger L. **Mixed Banking and Economic Growth in Germany, 1850-1931.** 1963

Hammond, Charles. **Factors Affecting Economic Growth in France: 1913-1938.** 1958

Harder, Klaus Peter. **Environmental Factors of Early Railroads.** 1968

Hausman, William John. **Public Policy and the Supply of Coal to London, 1700-1770.** 1976

Heyn, Udo. **Private Banking and Industrialization.** 1969

Hoffman, Elizabeth. **The Sources of Mortality Changes in Italy Since Unification.** 1972.

Inoki, Takenori. **Aspects of German Peasant Emigration to the United States 1815-1914.** 1974

Ishii, Osamu. **Cotton-Textile Diplomacy.** 1977

Kössler, Armin. **Aktionsfeld Osmanisches Reich.** 1978

Marker, Gordon Allan. **Internal Migration and Economic Opportunity.** 1964.

Melby, Eric D.K. **Oil and the International System.** 1978

Mendels, Franklin F. **Industrialization and Population Pressure in Eighteenth-Century Flanders.** 1969

Nipp, Luitgard. **Kapitalausstattung Im Ländlichen Kleingewerbe in der 2. Hälfte des 19. Jahrhunderts.** 1978

Ohlin, Per Goran. **The Positive and the Preventive Check.** 1955

Paas, Martha White. **Population Change, Labor Supply, and Agriculture in Augsburg, 1480-1618.** 1979

Pallanti, Giuseppe. **La Maremma Senese Nella Crisi Del Seicento.** 1977.

Papendieck, Henner. **Britische Managing Agencies im Indischen Kohlenbergbau, 1893-1918.** 1978

Pris, Claude. **Une Grande Entreprise Française Sous L'Ancien-Regime.** 1973. 2 vols.

Prochnow, Peter-Michael. **Staat Im Wachstum Versuch Einer Finanzwirtschaftlichen Analyse der Preussischen Haushaltsrechnungen, 1871-1913.** 1977. 2 vols. in 1.

Reed, Clyde George. **Price Data and European Economic History.** 1972

Rettig, Rudi. **Das Investitions-Und Finanzierungsverhalten Deutscher Grossunternehmen 1880-1911.** 1978

Rostow, Walt, W. **British Trade Fluctuations, 1868-1896.** 1940

Sheridan, George J.,Jr. **The Social and Economic Foundations of Association Among the Silk Weavers of Lyons, 1852-1870.** 1978. 2 vols.

Stigum, Marcia Lee. **The Impact of the European Economic Community on the French Cotton and Electrical Engineering Industries.** 1961

Thbaut, L[ouis]. **Le Mecanicien Anobli Pierre-Joseph Laurent 1713-1773.** 1974

Wade, William W. **Institutional Determinants of Technical Change and Agricultural Productivity Growth.** 1973

Whyman, J[ohn]. **Aspects of Holidaymaking and Resort Development Within the Isle of Thanet, with Particular Reference to Margate, Circa 1736 to Circa 1840.** 1980. 2 vols.